iPod® & iTunes®
FOR
DUMMIES®
8TH EDITION

by Tony Bove

WILEY

Wiley Publishing, Inc.

iPod® & iTunes® For Dummies®, 8th Edition

Published by
Wiley Publishing, Inc.
111 River Street
Hoboken, NJ 07030-5774

www.wiley.com

Copyright © 2011 by Wiley Publishing, Inc., Indianapolis, Indiana

Published by Wiley Publishing, Inc., Indianapolis, Indiana

Published simultaneously in Canada

For general information on our other products and services, please contact our Customer Care Department within the U.S. at 877-762-2974, outside the U.S. at 317-572-3993, or fax 317-572-4002.

For technical support, please visit www.wiley.com/techsupport.

Wiley also publishes its books in a variety of electronic formats. Some content that appears in print may not be available in electronic books.

Library of Congress Control Number: 2010937163

ISBN: 978-0-470-87871-2

Manufactured in the United States of America

10 9 8 7 6 5 4 3 2 1

WILEY

About the Author

Tony Bove has written about every iPad, iPod, and iPhone model and every update to iTunes from the very beginning, and not only provides free tips on his Web site (www.tonybove.com) but also developed an iPhone application (*Tony's Tips for iPhone Users*). Tony has written more than two dozen books on computing, desktop publishing, and multimedia, including *iPod touch For Dummies* (Wiley), *iPad Application Development For Dummies* (Wiley), *iPhone Application Development All-In-One For Dummies* (Wiley), *Just Say No to Microsoft* (No Starch Press), *The GarageBand Book* (Wiley), *The Art of Desktop Publishing* (Bantam), and a series of books about Macromedia Director, Adobe Illustrator, and PageMaker. Tony also founded *Desktop Publishing/Publish* magazine and the *Inside Report on New Media* newsletter, and he wrote the weekly Macintosh column for *Computer Currents* for a decade, as well as articles and columns for a variety of publications including *NeXTWORLD*, the *Chicago Tribune* Sunday Technology Section, *Macintosh Today*, the Prodigy online network, and *NewMedia*. Tracing the personal computer revolution back to the 1960s counterculture, Tony produced a CD-ROM interactive "rockumentary" in 1996, *Haight-Ashbury in the Sixties* (which explains his taste in music in this book's examples). He also developed the Rockument music site, www.rockument.com, with commentary and podcasts focused on rock music history. As a founding member of the Flying Other Brothers, which toured professionally for a decade and released three commercial CDs (*52-Week High, San Francisco Sounds*, and *Estimated Charges*), Tony performed with Hall of Fame rock musicians.

Dedication

This book is dedicated to my sons, nieces, nephews, their cousins, and all their children . . . the iPod generation.

Author's Acknowledgments

I want to thank John and Jimi Bove for providing technical expertise and performing valuable testing. I also want to thank Rich Tennant for his wonderful cartoons, and Dennis Cohen for technical expertise beyond the call of duty. And let me not forget my Wiley editor Beth Taylor for ongoing assistance that made my job so much easier. A book this timely places a considerable burden on a publisher's production team, and I thank the production crew at Wiley for diligence beyond the call of reason.

I owe thanks and a happy hour or three to Carole McLendon at Waterside, my agent. And finally, I have Executive Editor Bob Woerner at Wiley to thank for coming up with the idea for this book and helping me to become a professional dummy — that is, a *For Dummies* author.

Publisher's Acknowledgments

We're proud of this book; please send us your comments through our online registration form located at `http://dummies.custhelp.com`. For other comments, please contact our Customer Care Department within the U.S. at 877-762-2974, outside the U.S. at 317-572-3993, or fax 317-572-4002.

Some of the people who helped bring this book to market include the following:

Acquisitions and Editorial

Project Editor: Beth Taylor

Executive Editor: Bob Woerner

Copy Editor: Beth Taylor

Technical Editor: Dennis Cohen

Editorial Manager: Jodi Jensen

Sr. Editorial Assistant: Cherie Case

Cartoons: Rich Tennant
   (www.the5thwave.com)

Composition Services

Project Coordinator: Kristie Rees

Layout and Graphics: Joyce Haughey

Proofreaders: Rebecca Denoncour,
   Linda D. Morris

Indexer: Rebecca Salerno

Special Help
   Elizabeth Kuball

Publishing and Editorial for Technology Dummies

   Richard Swadley, Vice President and Executive Group Publisher

   Andy Cummings, Vice President and Publisher

   Mary Bednarek, Executive Acquisitions Director

   Mary C. Corder, Editorial Director

Publishing for Consumer Dummies

   Diane Graves Steele, Vice President and Publisher

Composition Services

   Debbie Stailey, Director of Composition Services

Contents at a Glance

Table of Contents

Introduction

● ●

*L*aunched on October 23, 2001, the iPod has become the icon of the decade. You don't need much imagination to see why. Imagine no longer needing to take CDs or DVDs with you when you travel — your favorite music and videos fit right in your pocket and you can leave your precious content library at home. With the iPhone and iPad, you can extend this convenience to books, magazines, documents, Web sites, e-mail, and even software applications.

How the first device came to be called "iPod" is still, to this day, a mystery, but the word not only stuck, it also spawned "iPhone" and "iPad." Some say a freelance copywriter came up with it after thinking of the phrase "Open the pod bay door, Hal!" from the movie *2001: A Space Odyssey*. According to a team member quoted by Steve Levy in *The Perfect Thing* (Simon & Schuster), back in 2001, Apple chairman Steve Jobs "just came in and went, 'iPod.' We all looked around the room, and that was it." It's certainly true that Jobs rode hard on its design and user interface, making all final decisions. When one of the designers said that obviously the device should have a power button to turn the unit on and off, Jobs simply said no. And that was it.

When I first encountered the iPod, it fulfilled my road warrior dreams — in particular, the dream of filling up a car with music as easily as filling it up with fuel. After nine years of grabbing every iPod model released, along with iPhones and the iPad, I still use older models with my home stereo, my beach boom-box speakers, and my sports outfit. And, of course, I use a fully loaded iPod classic in my car connected to a custom in-vehicle interface adapter. I've also used a cassette adapter, and even an FM radio transmitter, to make a iPod work in a rental car or boat (see Chapter 5 for many of these accessories).

There were other MP3 audio players when the iPod was introduced, but none that offered as much capacity for holding music, and none that could change the entire experience of acquiring, playing, and storing your music the way the iPod did. And that's because the iPod is not alone: it is an integral part of an ecosystem that centers on the iTunes application on your computer, and includes the iTunes Store and App Store on the Internet.

iTunes is the center of my media universe and the software that manages content on all my iPods, iPhones, iPads, and even my Apple TV. I bring all my content into iTunes — from CDs, the iTunes Store, and other sources — and then parcel it out to various devices for playback. Even though I buy content and apps directly with my iPad, iPhone, and iPod touch, and occasionally use Apple TV rather than my computer to enter the iTunes Store to rent or buy movies, everything I obtain is automatically synchronized with my iTunes library on my computer (where it can be easily backed up to preserve the files). I can even burn audio CDs and data DVDs. You can manage all these activities with iTunes.

iTunes was originally developed by Jeff Robbin and Bill Kincaid as an MP3 player called SoundJam MP, and released by Casady & Greene in 1999. It was purchased by Apple in 2000 and redesigned and released as iTunes. Since then, Apple has released numerous updates of iTunes to support new devices, fix bugs, and add new features to improve your content library and your iPad, iPod, or iPhone experience. All the important features are covered in this book. iTunes is getting better all the time, and this book gets you started.

About This Book

The publishers are wise about book matters, and they helped me design *iPod & iTunes For Dummies,* 8th Edition, as a reference. With this book, you can easily find the information you need when you need it. I wrote it so that you can read from beginning to end to find out how to use iTunes and your iPad, iPod, or iPhone from scratch. But this book is also organized so that you can dive in anywhere and begin reading the info you need to know for each task.

I didn't have enough pages to cover every detail of every function, and I intentionally left out some detail so that you won't be befuddled with tech-nospeak when it's not necessary. I wrote brief but comprehensive descrip-tions and included lots of cool tips on how to get the best results from using iTunes and your iPad, iPod, or iPhone.

At the time I wrote this book, I covered every iPad, iPod, and iPhone model available and the latest version of iTunes. Although I did my best to keep up for this print edition, Apple occasionally slips in a new model or new version of iTunes between book editions. If you've bought a new iPad, iPod, or iPhone that's not covered in the book, or if your version of iTunes looks a little differ-ent, be sure to check out the book's companion Web site for updates on the latest releases from Apple, as well as the Tips section of my Web site (www.tonybove.com) for free tips.

Conventions Used in This Book

Like any book that covers computers and information technology, this book uses certain conventions:

✔ **Choosing from a menu:** When I write "Choose iTunes⇨Preferences in iTunes," you click iTunes in the menu at the top of the display, and then click Preferences in the iTunes menu that appears.

With an iPod classic or iPod nano, when you see "Choose Settings⇨ Brightness from the iPod main menu," you scroll (rotate your finger clockwise around) the click wheel to highlight Settings on the main menu, press the Select button (the center button) to choose Settings, and then highlight and choose Brightness from the Settings menu.

With an iPad, iPod touch, or iPhone, when you see "Choose Settings⇨ Brightness from the Home screen," tap the Settings icon on the Home screen and then tap Brightness in the menu that appears.

✔ **Sliding, scrolling, and flicking on an iPad, iPod touch, or iPhone:** When you see "Slide the screen" or "Flick the screen," I mean that you need to use your finger to slide slowly or quickly (flicking) over the screen. When I write "Scroll the list on the iPod touch Settings screen," I mean that you should slide your finger over the list so that it scrolls.

✔ **Clicking and dragging:** When you see "Drag the song over the name of the playlist," I mean that you need to click the song name, hold the mouse button down, and then drag the song — while holding the mouse button down — over to the name of the playlist before lifting your finger off the mouse button.

✔ **Keyboard shortcuts:** When you see ⌘-I, press the ⌘ key on a Mac keyboard along with the *I* key. (In this case, after selecting a content item or app, ⌘-I opens the Information window in iTunes.) In Windows, the same keyboard shortcut is Ctrl-I (which means press the Ctrl key along with the *I* key). Don't worry — I always tell you what the equivalent Windows keys are.

✔ **Step lists:** When you come across steps that you need to do in iTunes or on the iPad, iPod, or iPhone, the action is in bold, and the explanatory part follows. If you know what to do, read the action and skip the explanation. But if you need a little help along the way, check out the explanation.

✔ **Pop-up menus:** I use the term *pop-up menu* for menus on the Mac that literally pop up from dialogs and windows; in Windows, the same type of menu actually drops down and is called a drop-down menu. I use the term *pop-up menu* for both.

And Just Who Are You?

You don't need to know anything about music, video, or computer technology to discover how to make the most of your iPad, iPod, iPhone, and iTunes. Although a course in music appreciation can't hurt, these devices and iTunes are designed to be useful even for rockin' grandmas who don't know the difference between downloadable music and System of a Down. You don't need any specialized knowledge to have a lot of fun while building your digital content library.

However, I do make some honest assumptions about your basic computer skills:

- ✔ **You know how to use the Mac Finder or Windows Explorer.** I assume that you already know how to locate files and folders and that you can copy files and folders from one hard drive to another on the computer of your choice: a Mac or a Windows PC.

- ✔ **You know how to select menus and applications on a Mac or a Windows PC.** I assume that you already know how to choose an option from a menu, how to find the Dock on a Mac to launch a Dock application (or use the Start menu in Windows to launch an application), and how to launch an application directly by double-clicking its icon.

For more information on these topics, see these excellent books, all published by Wiley: *Mac OS X Snow Leopard All-in-One For Dummies* (Mark L. Chambers), *Windows Vista All-in-One Desk Reference For Dummies* (Woody Leonhard), or *Windows XP Gigabook For Dummies* (Peter Weverka).

A Quick Peek Ahead

This book is organized into six parts, and each part covers a different aspect of using your iPad, iPod, or iPhone and iTunes. Here's a quick preview of what you can find in each part.

Part 1: Touching All the Basics

This part gets you started with your iPad, iPod, or iPhone: powering it up, recharging its battery, and connecting it to your computer. You install and set up iTunes on your Mac or your Windows PC and learn what you can do with it. You also find out all the techniques of an iPad, iPod, or iPhone road warrior: setting your alarm and multiple clocks for time zones, keeping time with your stopwatch, changing your display settings, setting the passcode to lock up the device so that others can't use it, and setting restrictions on content and the use of applications. I also describe how to connect an iPad, iPod touch, or iPhone wirelessly to the Internet, how to use your iPad, iPod, or iPhone on the road with car stereos and portable speakers, and what types of accessories are available.

Part II: Filling Up Your Empty Cup

This part shows you what you can do with iTunes. To acquire music, you can download it from the iTunes Store or other online services (such as Amazon), record it directly into your computer (using recording software such as GarageBand) and import it into iTunes, or rip audio CDs into iTunes. You can also download podcasts, audio books, movies, TV shows, and music videos from the iTunes Store or import them into iTunes from other sources. You find out how to download applications for the iPad, iPod touch, or iPhone from the App Store, and how to download music, podcasts, videos, and applications directly to your iPad, iPod touch, or iPhone. I also show you how to synchronize your iPad, iPod, or iPhone with your iTunes library on your computer, and with your personal contacts, e-mail accounts, Web bookmarks, and calendars.

Part III: Managing Your Library

This part shows you how to sort the content in your iTunes library by artist, album, duration, date, and other items. You find out how to add and edit iTunes content information, and even fine-tune the sound. You also discover how to arrange content into iTunes playlists that you can transfer to your iPad, iPod, or iPhone and how to burn audio CDs with playlists and complete albums. This part also contains crucial information about locating and backing up your iTunes library.

Part IV: Playing It Back on Your iPad, iPod, or iPhone

I show you how to locate and play all types of content — music, audio books, podcasts, movies, TV shows, and videos — on your iPod, and on the iPod section of your iPad and iPhone. You discover how to control playback, adjust the volume, and equalize the sound. I also describe how to synchronize photo albums with your iPad, iPod, or iPhone and display photo slide shows, as well as how to share images by e-mail and play YouTube videos with your iPad, iPod touch, or iPhone.

Part V: Touching the Online World

This part describes how to use your iPad, iPod touch, or iPhone and the Safari application to surf the Web. You also find out how to check and send e-mail, look at your stock portfolio, check the weather in your city and other cities, and display maps and driving directions. I also show how to use your iPad, iPod touch, or iPhone to locate and communicate with friends on Facebook, MySpace, Twitter, and other social networks and how to instantly chat with people. You also discover how to enter and edit calendar entries in the Calendar application, and enter and sort contacts in the Contacts application.

Part VI: The Part of Tens

In this book's Part of Tens chapters, I provide initial troubleshooting steps and details about updating and restoring your iPad, iPod, or iPhone. I also provide useful tips that can help make your iPad, iPod, iPhone, and iTunes experience a more satisfying one.

Bonus Chapters

This book includes a number of bonus chapters on its companion Web site at www.dummies.com/go/ipod8e. Scattered through those chapters you can find even more great informational nuggets. Topics include the following:

✔ Earlier iPod and iPhone models and the cables for connecting them to your computer

✔ Choosing audio encoders and quality settings for importing music

✔ Preparing photo libraries, videos, address books, and calendars for your iPad, iPod, or iPhone

✔ Managing multiple iTunes libraries and sharing iTunes libraries over a network

✔ Setting up and using Apple TV with iTunes

✔ Getting wired for playback and using iPad, iPod, and iPhone accessories

Icons Used in This Book

 The icons in this book are important visual cues for information you need.

Remember icons highlight important things you need to keep in mind.

 Technical Stuff icons highlight technical details you can skip unless you want to bring out the technical geek in you.

Tip icons highlight tips and techniques that save you time and energy — and maybe even money.

Warning icons save your butt by preventing disasters. Don't bypass a Warning without reading it. This is your only warning!

On the Web icons let you know when a topic is covered further online at www. dummies.com/go/ipod8e, this book's companion Web site. I also use it to call your attention to specific areas within Apple's site (www.apple.com), and to the free tips section of my site at www.tonybove.com.

Part I
Touching All the Basics

"Why can't you just bring your iPod like everyone else?"

In this part . . .

Part I shows you how to do all the essential tasks with your iPad, iPod, or iPhone to get you started as quickly as possible.

✓ Chapter 1 gets you started with your iPad, iPod, or iPhone. Here you find out what it can do, how to connect it to power and to your Mac or Windows PC, and how to get the most from your battery.

✓ Chapter 2 describes how to install iTunes — including the iPad, iPod, and iPhone software — on a Mac or Windows PC, and what you can do with iTunes.

✓ Chapter 3 gets you started with a quick tour of the iPad, iPod touch, and iPhone Home screens, icons, and the on-screen keyboard, and the iPod nano and iPod classic menus and buttons.

✓ Chapter 4 sets you up with the right time and date, clocks for different time zones, alarms, the timer, and the stopwatch. You discover how to set a passcode to lock your iPad, iPod, or iPhone so that no one else can use it. You also find out how to set the display's brightness, turn the sound effects on or off, and set restrictions on an iPad, iPod touch, or iPhone so that your kids can't jump onto YouTube or download explicit tunes.

✓ Chapter 5 describes the accessories you need to listen to tunes whenever you go on the road or stay at the "Heartbreak Hotel."

Chapter 1

Firing Up Your iPad, iPod, and iPhone

*T*he iPod has evolved into a range of mobile devices — from the iPod shuffle, iPod nano, and iPod touch models to the iPhone and iPad models. Along the way, Apple has not only completely changed the way people play music, audio books, and videos, but also has changed the way people shoot photos and videos, play games, check e-mail, use computer applications, and use the Internet.

But don't just take my word for it. "It's hard to remember what I did before the iPod," said Grammy Award–winner Mary J. Blige in an Apple press release. "iPod is more than just a music player; it's an extension of your personality and a great way to take your favorite music with you everywhere you go." Lance Armstrong, seven-time Tour de France champion, takes his running shoes and iPod with him everywhere. "I listen to music when I run. Having my music with me is really motivating." Pope Benedict XVI has an iPod engraved with his coat of arms. President Barack Obama gave the U.K.'s Queen Elizabeth II an iPod preloaded with rare songs by Richard Rodgers. And when Bono of U2 gave an iPod shuffle to George H. W. Bush, the former president joked, "I get the shuffle and then I shuffle the shuffle."

The iPod was first invented for playing music, but now you can download movies and TV shows and select from a library of hundreds of thousands of applications (known as *apps*) for the iPad, iPod touch, and iPhone that offer everything from soup to nuts.

This chapter introduces the iPad, iPod, and iPhone models, and how to power them up and connect them to your computer, which are essential tasks. (You may as well get used to the "iPad, iPod, and iPhone" phrase, as the devices share many features and functions.)

Introducing the iPad, iPod, and iPhone

The convenience of carrying music on an iPad, iPod, or iPhone is phenomenal. For example, the least expensive iPod model — the $49 2GB iPod shuffle — can hold 500 songs, which is plenty for getting around town. The 64GB iPod touch ($399) can hold about 14,000 songs as well as run apps, connect to the Internet, make FaceTime video calls, and play video on a slick screen, whereas the $249 160GB iPod classic, which is designed more for playing music, can hold around 40,000 songs — that's more than eight weeks of non-stop music played around the clock. (Prices may vary as Apple introduces new models.)

A common misconception is that your iPad, iPod, or iPhone becomes your library of music, video, and apps. Even though you can download content items directly to your iPad, iPod touch, or iPhone, storage on an iPad, iPod, or iPhone should be considered temporary — in the process of troubleshooting problems or upgrading your device's software, you may have to erase everything during a restore operation (as I describe in Chapter 21). That's why you must always sync your iPad, iPod touch, or iPhone to your computer's iTunes library after downloading content, as I describe in Chapter 8. That way, your content is safely tucked away on your computer and managed by iTunes. Your library files on your computer should then be backed up to another hard drive or other medium, as I describe in Chapter 14. If you practice safe backups, you'll never have to buy the content and apps again.

iTunes (for Mac or Windows) lets you synchronize content with your iPad, iPod, and iPhone, and also the Apple TV player for your home TV and stereo. iTunes on your computer is also a portal to the online iTunes Store, where you can get free or priced content, and the App Store, where you get free or priced apps. You also use iTunes to organize your content and apps, make copies, burn CDs, and play disc jockey without discs. I introduce iTunes in Chapter 2.

The iPad, iPod touch, and iPhone all work in some respects like personal computers that let you enter data, access the Internet, and run apps as well as play content. The fourth-generation iPod touch can shoot videos and still pictures, just like the iPhone 3GS and iPhone 4 (whereas the iPhone and iPhone 3G can shoot only still pictures). You can keep track of your calendar and contacts with any model iPad, iPod, or iPhone, but with an iPad, iPod touch, or iPhone, you can enter and edit calendar and contact entries, check and send e-mail, visit your favorite Web sites, get maps, obtain driving directions, check the current weather, and even check your stock portfolio, to name just a few things.

Comparing iPod Models

Introduced way back in the Stone Age of digital music (2001), each model of the iPod family has grown by several generations (see Figure 1-1), now including the fourth-generation iPod touch, the eighth-generation iPod classic, the wearable sixth-generation iPod nano, and the tiny fourth-generation iPod shuffle.

Figure 1-1: The iPod family includes (left to right) the iPod shuffle, iPod nano, and iPod touch (iPod classic not shown).

Here's a rundown on today's iPod models:

✔ **The iPod touch:** The iPod touch shares the design characteristics and many of the features of its more famous cousin, the iPhone, including the multi-touch-sensitive screen, motion detection (detecting motions such as rotation and shaking), location detection (not as accurately as an iPhone but close), and the ability to download apps and content directly, as well as surf the Web and check e-mail, by connecting through Wi-Fi. (Wi-Fi, which is short for *wi*reless *fi*delity, is a popular connection method for local area networks that I describe in detail in Chapter 4.)

✔ **The iPod classic:** Following the original iPod design, this model offers the highest capacity for content (160GB).

✔ **The iPod nano:** The current iPod nano is small enough to clip you're your clothes, comes in a variety of colors, and responds to touch gestures — and you can shake it to shuffle your songs!

✔ **The iPod shuffle:** You can clip the tiniest iPod to your sleeve, and its voice tells you the song title and artist.

To find out more about previous generations of iPods, including detailed information about cables and connections, visit this book's companion Web site (see the Introduction for details). For a nifty chart that shows the differences among iPod models, see the Identifying Different iPod Models page on the Apple iPod Web site (`http://support.apple.com/kb/HT1353`).

Fingering the iPod touch

The iPod touch is much more than a media player. Less than a third of an inch thick and weighing less than four ounces, the iPod touch is really a pocket computer — it uses a flash memory drive and an operating system that can run applications. Just like the iPhone, it offers a touch-sensitive screen with icons for launching apps, an on-screen keyboard for entering information, a Home button on the front, and built-in speaker and volume controls.

Apple offers the following sizes of iPod touch models as of this writing, and they all use the same battery that offers up to 40 hours of music playback, or 7 hours of video playback:

✔ **The 8GB model** holds about 1,750 songs, 10,000 photos, or about 10 hours of video.

✔ **The 32GB model** holds about 7,000 songs, 40,000 photos, or about 40 hours of video. (With 7,000 songs, you would have more than a week of nonstop music played around the clock.)

✔ **The 64GB model** holds about 14,000 songs, 90,000 photos, or about 80 hours of video.

Like the iPhone, the iPod touch lets you access the Web over a Wi-Fi Internet connection. After you're on Wi-Fi, you can then use the Safari app to browse the Web and interact with Web services, and the Mail app to send and receive e-mail. Stocks, Maps, and Weather are apps that show information from the Internet, and popular social networks such as Facebook and MySpace offer apps to connect you with your friends. You can also use the YouTube app to play YouTube videos on the Web. All these apps are supplied with your iPod touch, and you can download more apps by connecting to Wi-Fi and the Internet as I describe in Chapter 4, and touching the App Store icon, as I describe in Chapter 6.

Many of the apps you find listed at the App store are especially designed to take advantage of new features of the fourth-generation iPod touch. Like the iPhone 4, the fourth-generation iPod touch sports a three-axis gyro for measuring or maintaining orientation (used extensively by games), and a 3.5-inch, widescreen, multi-touch Retina display that offers a stunning 960-x-640–pixel resolution at 326 pixels per inch — so many pixels that the human eye can't distinguish individual ones. The newest iPod touch also offers a main camera on the back for recording HD (720p) video at up to 30 frames per second (with audio), and shooting photos at 960 x 720 pixel resolution. And you can use a front video camera for taking VGA-quality photos and making FaceTime video calls over the Internet.

In short, a fourth-generation iPod touch can do nearly everything an iPhone 4 can do, except make cellular-service phone calls or texting, use the 3G data network, or pinpoint its exact location with the Global Positioning System. Even so, the iPod touch can pinpoint its approximate location with Internet-based Location Services, and you can not only make FaceTime video calls, but also the equivalent of a phone call using the Skype app.

Twirling the iPod classic

The eighth-generation iPod classic model uses the same click wheel and buttons as the seventh-, sixth-, and fifth-generation models, combining the scroll wheel with pressure-sensitive buttons underneath the top, bottom, left, and right areas of the circular pad of the wheel. As of this writing, Apple provides a slim, 4.9-ounce 160GB model in black or silver.

The eighth-generation 160GB model holds about 40,000 songs, 25,000 photos, or about 200 hours of video, and its battery offers up to 36 hours of music playback, or 6 hours of video playback. The seventh-generation 120GB model holds about 20,000 songs or about 150 hours of video.

Going mano a mano with the iPod nano

Apple brought its multi-touch technology to the smallest screen possible. The sixth-generation iPod nano, only about a half-inch wide and high, pencil-thin, in a full spectrum of colors and clipable to your clothes, is the most fashionable iPod model yet. It plays music, audio podcasts, audio books, and the music portion of music videos.

This mini marvel (see Figure 1-2) offers a 1.54-inch color thin film transistor (TFT) display with 240 x 240 pixels of resolution to show crisp images of your album cover art, and includes a motion sensor so that you can shake it to shuffle songs. Apple offers an 8GB model that holds about 2,000 songs and a 16GB model that holds about 4,000 songs. It also offers an FM tuner for listening to radio and a pedometer to keep track of your footsteps.

Figure 1-2:
iPod nano
looks good
on you,
and plays
FM radio
as well as
music.

Each model offers a battery that can play up to 24 hours of music — all day and all of the night — or 5 hours of video.

The larger fifth-generation iPod nano also included a video camera and a built-in microphone, and plays videos — for details, visit this book's companion Web site.

Doing the iPod shuffle

If the regular iPod models aren't small enough to fit into your lifestyle or your budget, try the ultra-tiny 2GB iPod shuffle for $49 (see Figure 1-3). Its built-in clip lets you attach it to almost anything. The fourth-generation iPod shuffle has no display, but offers buttons on the front to control playback. This design keeps the size and weight to a minimum.

The iPod shuffle can also talk to you with the VoiceOver feature. Press the VoiceOver button on top of your iPod shuffle to hear the title and artist of the song. VoiceOver even tells you whether your battery needs charging.

The 2GB iPod shuffle holds about 500 songs, assuming an average of 4 minutes per song, using the AAC format at the High Quality setting for adding music (as described in Chapter 8). The battery offers up to 15 hours of power between charges.

Figure 1-3:
An iPod
shuffle is
the smallest
and least
expensive
iPod.

Comparing iPhone Models

The iPhone can not only phone home, but also monitor all your e-mail and browse the Internet with a full-page display, using a Wi-Fi network when it senses one. The touchscreen (see Figure 1-4) provides a rich set of icons for launching apps, and includes a full on-screen keyboard for entering text, numbers, and special symbols. The iPhone includes all the features of an iPod touch, and it's no slouch when it comes to acting like an iPod: It can play music, audio books, videos (such as TV shows, music videos, and even feature-length movies), and even podcasts. The iPhone 4 includes cameras front and back to shoot photos and videos and make FaceTime video calls, and it can display photos and set slide shows to music.

The 8GB, 16GB, and 32GB iPhone 4 models (introduced in June 2010) are slimmer and more powerful than the original iPhone, the iPhone 3G, and the iPhone 3GS. In addition to fast 3G data service, GPS mapping, and voice control, the iPhone 4 offers a visually stunning 960 x 640–pixel retina display for extremely crisp text and images, a higher-resolution camera for photos that also shoots HD video, and a front-facing video camera for making FaceTime video calls over the Internet. All iPhone models incorporate flash memory just like iPod touch, iPod shuffle, and iPod nano models.

The iPhone 4 built-in rechargeable lithium-ion battery offers up to 14 hours of talk time using the slower "E" (also known as Edge or 2G) cell network, or 7 hours using the faster 3G cell network (with 300 hours on standby). The iPhone 4 also offers up to 10 hours browsing the Internet on Wi-Fi or 6 hours using 3G, up to 10 hours playing video, and up to 30 hours playing music. All models offer Bluetooth for using wireless headphones and microphones when making phone calls.

Figure 1-4:
The iPhone 4 includes all the features of an iPod touch and can also phone home and shoot videos.

Comparing iPad Models

Douglas Adams, in the bestseller *The Hitchhiker's Guide to the Galaxy* (conceived in 1971 and published in 1979), introduced the idea of a handy travel guide that looked "rather like a largish electronic calculator," with a hundred tiny flat press buttons and a screen on which any one of a million 'pages' could be summoned at a moment's notice.

The iPad is an interstellar hitchhiker's dream come true. It's a new category of device — located somewhere between a Mac laptop and an iPod touch or iPhone in terms of its capabilities — that evolved from the iPhone design and uses the iPhone Operating System (iOS). The iPad models are 9.56 inches high, 7.47 inches wide, and only a half-inch thick. The iPad Wi-Fi model weighs 1.5 pounds, and the iPad 3G weighs 1.6 pounds. They offer all of the features of an iPod touch or iPhone, with the following differences:

- ✔ The larger touch-sensitive display size (1,024 x 768 pixels), which supports all of the iPhone OS gestures, also supports multi-finger gestures — apps can recognize multiple fingers (either yours or more than one user).

- ✔ The connection features are the same as the iPod touch and iPhone (except no phone calls) — the iPad offers Wi-Fi (like an iPod touch), and the iPad 3G offers both Wi-Fi and 3G Internet access (like an iPhone 3GS).

- ✔ Motion and location detection act the same way as an iPod touch or iPhone: the iPad offers Internet-based location (like an iPod touch), while the iPad 3G includes a hardware GPS (like an iPhone 3G or 3GS).

The iPad models, shown in Figure 1-5, use the same battery that offers up to 10 hours of using the Internet on Wi-Fi (9 hours on 3G), listening to music, or watching video. The iPad models come with the following flash memory capacities:

- ✔ **The 16GB model** holds about 3,500 songs, 20,000 photos, or about 20 hours of video.

- ✔ **The 32GB model** holds about 7,000 songs, 40,000 photos, or about 40 hours of video. (With 7,000 songs, you would have more than a week of nonstop music played around the clock.)

- ✔ **The 64GB model** holds about 14,000 songs, 90,000 photos, or about 80 hours of video.

Figure 1-5:
The iPad includes all the features of an iPod touch with a much larger screen.

Thinking Inside the Box

Don't destroy the elegantly designed box while opening your iPad, iPod, or iPhone. Before going any further, check the box and make sure that all the correct parts came with it. Keep the box in case, heaven forbid, you need to return the iPad, iPod, or iPhone to Apple — the box ensures that you can safely return it for a new battery or replacement.

The iPod touch, iPod classic, iPod nano, and iPhone are each supplied with a Dock Connector–to–USB cable. The cable connects your iPad, iPod, or iPhone (or its dock) to your computer or to the AC power adapter using a USB (Universal Serial Bus) connection — a way of attaching things to computers and bussing data around while providing power. The cable has a USB connector on one end and a flat dock connector on the other end to connect either to a dock or directly to an iPad, iPod, or iPhone. The iPod shuffle includes a special cable to connect to a USB power adapter or to your computer. The iPhone models come with a power adapter for recharging the battery, and the iPad comes with a special 10W power adapter.

The iPod touch, iPod classic, iPod nano, and iPhone are also supplied with stereo earphones (often called *earbuds*). (The iPad doesn't come with earphones, but you can use any of the earphones that work with an iPod or iPhone.)

Outside the box

There are a few things you may want to have around that are not in the box. For example, even though you don't really need an AC power adapter or dock — you can connect iPod models directly to your computer to recharge your battery — a power adapter or dock is useful for keeping the battery charged without having to connect the iPod to your computer.

The earbuds supplied with your iPod or iPhone may not suit your tastes, but you can find a hundred other headphone products that might. You can get all kinds of accessories, including headphones, speakers, the Apple Universal Dock, other docks, and AC power adapters, from the online Apple Store (www.apple.com/store), the physical Apple Store, or other stores such as Amazon.com and Fry's. Docks of various sizes, shapes, and functions are also available from vendors such as Belkin, Monster, and Griffin.

Computer and software not included

You still use a computer and iTunes to manage and backup the content on your iPad, iPod, or iPhone. These things are not in the box, obviously.

You've seen requirements before — lots of jargon about MB (megabytes), GB (gigabytes), GHz (gigahertz), and RAM (random access memory), sprinkled with names like Intel, AMD, and Mac OS X. Skip this section if you already know that your iPad, iPod, or iPhone works with your computer and you already have iTunes. But if you don't know whether it will work, and you don't have iTunes yet, read on.

The newest version of iTunes (as of this writing) is version 10.0.1. It makes sense to use the newest version, especially to activate any iPhone or iPod touch model, or to set up any iPod model. You also need the following:

✔ **A PC or Mac to run iTunes:** On a PC, iTunes version 10.0.1 requires Windows XP (with Service Pack 2) or a 32-bit edition of Windows 7 or Windows Vista. (You can use a 64-bit version of Vista if you also run the iTunes 64-bit installer — which you can download from the iTunes download page). While you can run iTunes 10.0.1 on a PC with a 1GHz Intel or AMD processor with a QuickTime-compatible audio card and a minimum of 512MB of RAM, you need at least a 2GHz Intel Core 2 Duo or faster processor and at least 1 GB of RAM to play HD-quality videos, an iTunes LP, or iTunes Extras from the iTunes Store. You also need a DirectX 9.0–compatible video card with 32MB of video RAM (64MB recommended) to watch video.

With a Mac, iTunes version 10.0.1 requires Mac OS X Version 10.5 or newer (Leopard , Snow Leopard, or newer version). Although you can run iTunes 10 on a Mac with an Intel, PowerPC G5 or G4 processor and at least 512MB of RAM, you need at least a 1GHz PowerPC G4, G5, or Intel processor to play Standard Definition video, or at least a 2GHz Intel Core 2 Duo or faster processor and at least 1 GB of RAM to play HD-quality videos, an iTunes LP, or iTunes Extras from the iTunes Store.

✔ **USB connection:** You need support for USB 2.0 (also called a *high-powered USB*) to connect your iPad, iPod, or iPhone.

For details about using USB or FireWire cables with older models, visit this book's companion Web site.

✔ **iTunes:** Make sure that you have the current version of iTunes — use the Automatic Update feature, which I describe in Chapter 2, to keep your iTunes software up to date. You can also download iTunes for Windows or the Mac from the Apple site (`www.apple.com/itunes/download`); it's free. See Chapter 2 for instructions.

Older iPod models, still available in stores and online, might include older versions of iTunes. You can download a newer version at any time to replace it.

✔ **QuickTime:** QuickTime comes with every Mac, and with iTunes for Windows. The iTunes installer for the PC installs the required version of QuickTime for Windows (Version 7.6.6 as of this writing), replacing any older version you might have. Macs have QuickTime preinstalled (Version 7.6 or newer is required), and Mac OS X automatically updates QuickTime if you use the Software Update feature of System Preferences on the Apple menu.

✔ **Internet connection:** Apple recommends a broadband Internet connection to buy content and stream previews from the iTunes Store, although it is possible with a dialup connection. At a minimum, you need some kind of Internet connection to download iTunes itself.

✔ **CD-R or DVD-R drive:** Without a disc burner, you can't burn your own discs. On a PC, you need a CD-R or DVD-R drive. On a Mac, you need a Combo or Super Drive (or compatible third-party disc burner) to burn your own discs.

Applying Power

All iPad, iPod, and iPhone models come with essentially the same requirement: power. You can supply power to your iPod or iPhone (and charge your battery at the same time) by using the provided cable and your computer, or you can use an optional AC power adapter that works with voltages in North America and many parts of Europe and Asia. (See Chapter 5 for information about plugging into power in other countries.) For an iPad, you may need to use the AC power adapter because many computers don't provide enough power through the USB connection to recharge the iPad battery.

Connecting your iPad, iPod, or iPhone

On the bottom of the iPad, iPod touch, iPod classic, iPod nano, or iPhone, you find a large connection called the *dock connection*. The dock connection mirrors the connection on the end of a dock — your iPad, iPod, or iPhone fits snugly in a dock, and the dock offers a dock connection for the cable to your computer.

To connect your iPad, iPod, or iPhone to your computer, plug the flat connector of the cable into the iPad, iPod, or iPhone dock connection (or the connection on the dock holding your iPad, iPod, or iPhone) and then plug the USB connector on the other end of the cable into the USB port on your computer.

The iPod shuffle is supplied with a special USB cable that plugs into the headphone connection of the iPod shuffle and draws power from the USB connection on the computer or from a USB power adapter. Plug one end of the included cable into the headphone connection of iPod shuffle and the other end into a USB 2.0 connection on your computer or power adapter.

A dock can be convenient as a base station when you're not traveling with your iPad, iPod, or iPhone because you can slip it into the dock without connecting cables. Just connect it to an Apple or a third-party dock and then use the cable supplied with your iPad, iPod, or iPhone to connect the dock to your computer or power adapter. You can pick up a dock at an Apple Store, order one online, or take advantage of third-party dock offerings. Some docks, such as the Apple Universal Dock, keeps your iPod classic or iPod nano in an upright position while connected, and the iPad Keyboard Dock keeps an iPad in an upright position and includes a physical keyboard for typing and activating features. Some docks also provide connections for a home stereo or headphones, and some docks offer built-in speakers.

You can connect the USB end of the supplied cable to either the Apple (or third-party USB) power adapter for power, or to the computer's USB 2.0 port for power. When you first connect your iPad, iPod, or iPhone to the computer, iTunes starts up and begins the setup and syncing process (see Chapter 2). After syncing, the computer continues to provide power through the USB 2.0 port to the iPad, iPod, or iPhone (although it may not be enough power to recharge an iPad).

Why USB 2.0? What happened to 1.0? Most PCs and all current Macs already have USB 2.0, which is all you need to sync an iPad, iPod, or iPhone with your computer. Although you can use a low-speed USB 1.0 or 1.1 connection to sync an iPod or iPhone, it's slower than molasses on a subzero morning for syncing.

To find out more about previous generations of iPods and iPhones, including detailed information about USB and FireWire cables and connections, visit this book's companion Web site.

Don't use another USB device in a chain, and don't use a USB hub to connect your iPad, iPod, or iPhone unless the hub is a *powered* hub — a hub with a separate power source, in other words. Note that a USB keyboard typically acts like a USB 1.1 hub, but older ones can't provide power to an iPad, iPod, or iPhone.

Turning it on and off

Touch any button to turn on an iPod classic. To turn off an iPod classic, press and hold the Play/Pause button. To keep an iPod classic from turning on by accident, you can lock it with the Hold switch on the top. The Hold switch locks the iPod buttons so that you don't accidentally activate them — slide the Hold switch so that it exposes an orange layer underneath. To unlock the buttons, slide the Hold switch so that it hides the orange layer underneath.

If your iPod classic shows a display but doesn't respond to your button-pressing, don't panic. Just check the Hold switch and make sure that it's set to one side so that the orange layer underneath disappears (the normal position).

To turn on an iPod shuffle, slide the three-way switch to expose the green layer underneath. To turn it off, slide the three-way switch to hide the green layer. With the three-way switch or On/Off switch, iPod shuffle models don't need a Hold switch.

To turn on a sixth-generation iPod nano, press the Sleep/Wake button on top. Press it again to turn it off. To conserve battery life, the screen goes dark anyway if you don't touch it for a while — press the Sleep/Wake button to turn it back on.

To turn on or awaken the iPad, iPod touch, or iPhone, press the Sleep/Wake button on top, or the Home button on the front. The screen shows the message `Slide to unlock` — slide your finger across this message to unlock the iPad, iPod touch, or iPhone.

To put an iPad, iPod touch, or iPhone to sleep, press the Sleep/Wake button. This reduces the power consumption to a tiny trickle (just enough to allow the software to respond to a quick touch, and in the case of the iPhone, to respond to phone calls). Putting the iPad, iPod touch, or iPhone to sleep also locks its controls just like a Hold switch.

You can turn the iPad, iPod touch, or iPhone completely off by holding down the Sleep/Wake button for about two seconds, until you see the Slide to Power Off slider; then slide your finger across the slider to turn it off. You can then turn it back on by pressing and holding the Sleep/Wake button. To save battery power, you should plug the iPad, iPod touch, or iPhone into

AC power or your computer before turning it back on from a completely off state. (For battery details, see the next section in this chapter.)

iPods can function in temperatures as cold as 50 degrees and as warm as 95° F (Fahrenheit), but they work best at room temperature (closer to 68° F). If you leave your iPad, iPod, or iPhone out in the cold all night, it might have trouble waking, and it might even display a low-battery message. Plug the iPad, iPod, or iPhone into a power source, wait until it warms up, and try it again. If it still doesn't wake up or respond properly, try resetting the iPad, iPod, or iPhone, as I describe in Chapter 21.

Facing Charges of Battery

The iPad, iPod, and iPhone models are supplied with built-in rechargeable batteries that are based on the most innovative battery technologies for portable devices:

- ✔ The iPod shuffle uses a lithium-polymer battery that offers 10 hours of music-playing time.

- ✔ The iPod nano uses a lithium-ion battery that offers 24 hours of music-playing time.

- ✔ The iPod classic uses a lithium-ion battery that offers 36 hours of music playback or 6 hours of video or photo display with music.

- ✔ The iPod touch uses a lithium-ion battery that offers 40 hours of music-playing time, or 7 hours of video, browsing the Internet using Wi-Fi, or displaying photo slide shows with music.

- ✔ The iPhone models use lithium-ion batteries. The iPhone 4 offers up to 40 hours of music-playing time, 10 hours of video-playing time, or 6 hours of slideshows with music; the iPhone 3GS offers 30 hours of music-playing time and the same for video and slideshows. However, depending on your network settings, practical battery time can vary widely. The iPhone models can operate for 300 hours on standby (waiting for calls) if you do nothing else with them. You also find different power requirements for different networks:

  - All iPhone models offer the AT&T 2G network in the United States for calling (which includes Edge for data transfer). The iPhone 4 gives you about 14 hours of talk time; you get 12 hours on an iPhone 3GS, or 10 hours on an iPhone 3G.

  - The iPhone 4 offers 10 hours of browsing the Internet using Wi-Fi and 6 hours using 3G; the iPhone 3GS offers 9 hours and the iPhone 3G 5 hours using Wi-Fi, and both the iPhone 3G and 3GS offer 5 hours of browsing using 3G. You can turn off 3G to use 2G by choosing Settings⇨General⇨Network and tapping the On button for the Enable 3G option.

✔ The iPad (both models) use a mammoth 25-watt-hour lithium-polymer
battery — about five times larger than the iPhone battery — that offers
up to 10 hours of playing music, watching videos, and browsing the
Internet using Wi-Fi, or 9 hours using 3G.

To find out more about the batteries in previous generations of iPods, visit
this book's companion Web site.

Keep in mind that playback battery time varies depending on how you use
your iPad, iPod, or iPhone — if you mix Web browsing and picture-taking
with video playback on an iPhone, or video shooting and playback on an iPad
nano, you have less battery time than if you just played music.

Recharging your battery

The iPad, iPod, or iPhone battery recharges automatically when you connect
it to a power source. For example, it starts charging immediately when you
insert it into a dock that's connected to a power source (or to a computer
with a powered USB connection).

It takes only four hours to recharge the battery fully for all iPad, iPod classic,
and iPhone models, and only three hours for an iPod nano or iPod shuffle.
Note, however, that it may take longer to recharge an iPad when it is connected to your computer. The fastest way to recharge an iPad is with the
included 10W power adapter. It will also recharge, but more slowly, when
attached to a computer through a high-power USB connection (as found on
recent Macs) or with an iPhone power adapter. When attached to a computer
through a standard USB (most PCs or older Macs), the iPad recharges, but
only when it's in sleep mode.

Need power when you're on the run? Look for a power outlet in the airport
terminal or hotel lobby and plug in with your AC power adapter — the iPod
nano battery fast-charges to 80 percent capacity in 1.5 hours, and the other
iPad, iPod, and iPhone models fast-charge in 2 hours. After the fast-charge, the
battery receives a trickle charge until fully charged.

A battery icon with a progress bar in the upper-right corner of the iPad, iPod,
or iPhone display indicates how much power is left. When you charge the
battery, the battery icon displays a lightning bolt. The battery icon is completely filled in when the battery is fully charged, and it slowly empties into
just an outline as the battery is used up. You can also display the battery
power percentage in the icon on an iPad, or next to the icon on an iPhone,
by choosing Settings⇨General⇨Usage, and tapping the Off button for Battery
Percentage to turn it on (tap On to turn it off).

You can check the battery of an iPod shuffle by turning it on or by connecting it to your computer. You can check the battery status without interrupting playback by quickly turning the iPod shuffle off and then on again. The tiny battery status light next to the headphone connector tells you how much charge you have:

- **Green:** The iPod shuffle is fully charged (if connected to a computer) or charged at least 50 percent.

- **Orange:** The iPod shuffle battery is still charging (if connected to a computer) or is as low as 25 percent. If the iPod shuffle is connected to your computer and blinking orange, this means that iTunes is synchronizing it — don't disconnect the iPod shuffle until it stops blinking.

- **Red:** Very little charge is left and you need to recharge it.

If no light is visible, the iPod shuffle is completely out of power, and you need to recharge it to use it.

To hear the VoiceOver feature speak your battery status ("full," "75 percent," "50 percent," "25 percent," or "low"), click and hold the center button of the earbud controls.

In iTunes, the battery icon next to your iPod shuffle's name in the Devices section of the source pane shows the battery status. The icon displays a lightning bolt when the battery is charging and a plug when the battery is fully charged.

The built-in, rechargeable battery in an iPad, iPod, or iPhone is, essentially, a life-or-death proposition. After its dead, it can be replaced, but Apple charges a replacement fee plus shipping. If your warranty is still active, you should have Apple replace it under the warranty program (which may cost nothing except perhaps shipping). Don't try to replace it yourself unless you don't mind invalidating the warranty.

Keeping an iPad, iPod, or iPhone in a snug carrying case when charging is tempting but also potentially disastrous. The device needs to dissipate its heat, and you could damage it by overheating it and frying its circuits, rendering it as useful as a paperweight. To get around this problem, you can purchase one of the heat-dissipating carrying cases available in the Apple Store. See Chapter 5 for more on accessories.

If you don't use your iPad, iPod, or iPhone for a month, even if it is connected to power and retaining a charge, it can still become catatonic. Perhaps it gets depressed from being left alone too long. At that point, it may not start — you have to completely drain and recharge the battery. To drain the battery, disconnect your iPad, iPod, or iPhone from power for 24 hours. Then, to fully recharge the battery, connect it to power for at least 4 hours without using it (or longer if you are using it).

Maintaining battery mojo

You have several ways to keep your battery healthy. I recommend a lean diet of topping off your iPad, iPod, or iPhone battery whenever it is convenient.

Using and recharging 100 percent of battery capacity is called a *charge cycle.* You can charge the battery many times, but there is a limit to how many full-charge cycles you can do before needing to replace the battery.

Each time you complete a charge cycle (100 percent recharge), it diminishes battery capacity slightly. Apple estimates that the battery loses 20 percent of its capacity (meaning it holds 80 percent of the charge) after 400 full-charge cycles for an iPod or iPhone, or 1,000 full-charge cycles for an iPad. Recharging your battery when it's only half empty does not count as a full-charge cycle, but as half a charge cycle. That means you can use half its power one day and then recharge it fully, and then use half the next day and recharge it fully again; this would count as one charge cycle, not two.

It's a good idea to *calibrate* the battery once soon after you get your iPad, iPod, or iPhone.

That is, run it all the way down (a full discharge) and then charge it all the way up (which takes at least four hours for an iPad, iPod touch, iPhone, or iPod classic, or three hours for an iPod nano or iPod shuffle). Although this doesn't actually change battery performance, it does improve the battery gauge so that the gauge displays a more accurate reading. This calibration occurs anyway if you fully recharge the battery, but if you've never done that, you can calibrate it by disconnecting the iPad, iPod, or iPhone from power for 24 hours to make sure that the battery is empty, and then fully recharging the battery.

iPad, iPod, and iPhone batteries typically last three years or more, but are vulnerable to high temperatures, which decrease their life spans considerably. Don't leave your iPad, iPod, or iPhone in a hot place, such as on a sunny car dashboard, for very long (don't leave it out in the rain, either — water can easily damage it).

For a complete description of how Apple's batteries work, see the Apple Lithium-Ion Batteries page at www.apple.com/batteries.

Saving power

The iPod classic and older models include a hard drive, and whatever causes the hard drive to spin causes a drain on power. iPod nano, iPod shuffle, iPod touch, iPad, and iPhone models use a flash drive, which uses less power but still uses power when playing content. The iPad, iPod touch, and iPhone also use power accessing the Internet, running applications, receiving push notifications (see Chapter 19 for details), using Bluetooth devices, and in the case of the iPhone, making and receiving calls. Keeping these activities to a minimum can help you save power.

The following are tips on saving power while using your iPad, iPod, or iPhone:

✔ **Pause.** Pause playback when you're not listening to music or watching video. Pausing (stopping) playback is the easiest way to conserve power, especially with an iPod shuffle.

✔ **Lock it (with the iPad, iPod nano, iPod touch, or iPhone).** Press the Sleep/ Wake button on top to immediately put it to sleep and lock its controls to save battery power. You can set your iPad, iPod touch, or iPhone to automatically go to sleep by choosing Settings➪General➪Auto-Lock from the Home screen, and choosing 1 Minute, 2 Minutes, 3 Minutes, 4 Minutes, or 5 Minutes (or Never, to prevent automatic sleep).

✔ **Hold it (with the iPod classic).** Flip the Hold switch on the iPod classic to the locked position (with the orange layer showing underneath) to make sure that controls aren't accidentally activated. You don't want your iPod playing music in your pocket and draining the battery when you're not listening.

✔ **Back away from the light.** Turn down the brightness on an iPod touch or iPhone by tapping Settings➪Brightness, on an iPod nano by tapping Settings➪General➪Brightness, or on an iPad by tapping Settings➪Brightness & Wallpaper, and dragging the brightness slider to the left. Use the backlight sparingly on the iPod classic — select Backlight Timer from the iPod Settings menu to limit backlighting to a number of seconds, or set it to Off. (Choose Settings from the main menu.) Don't use the backlight in daylight if you don't need it.

✔ **Don't ask and don't tell where you are (with an iPad, iPod touch, or iPhone).** Turn off Location Services if you aren't using apps that need it. Choose Settings➪General➪Location Services from the Home screen, and touch On for the Location Services option at the top to turn it Off. (You can also turn on or off Location Services for each app that uses it — see Chapter 4 for details.)

✔ **Let the postman ring twice (with an iPad, iPod touch, or iPhone).** Check e-mail less frequently. You may want to change Push and Fetch settings to be less frequent. See Chapter 19 for details.

✔ **Turn off 3G (with an iPad 3G, iPhone 3G or iPhone 3GS, iPhone 4).** Turn off 3G in any areas that don't offer a strong 3G signal. On an iPhone 3G, 3GS or 4, choose Settings➪General➪Network and tap the On button for the Enable 3G option to turn it off. You can still make and receive calls with the 2G network, but the iPhone will stop using so much power continually searching for 3G. On an iPad 3G, choose Settings➪Cellular Data and tap the On button for the Cellular Data option to turn it off.

✔ **Tune out Bluetooth (with an iPad, iPod touch, or iPhone).** Turn off Bluetooth (choose Settings➪General➪Bluetooth and touch the On button to turn it off) if you're not using a Bluetooth device.

✔ **Drop in from the Internet (with an iPad, iPod touch, or iPhone).** Turn off Wi-Fi when not browsing the Internet: Choose Settings➪Wi-Fi and touch the On button to turn it off.

✔ **Turn it off completely.** To turn off an iPod nano, press the Sleep/Wake button. To turn off an iPod classic, press and hold the Play/Pause button. To turn off an iPod shuffle, slide the switch to the off position, hiding the green layer underneath the switch. Although you can put an iPad, iPod touch, or iPhone to sleep by pressing the Sleep/Wake button, you can also turn it completely off by holding down the Sleep/Wake button for about two seconds, until you see the Slide to Power Off slider; then slide your finger across the slider to turn it off.

Keep in mind that starting up an iPad, iPod touch, or iPhone that was completely turned off takes quite a bit of power — more than if it woke from sleep. If you do turn it off, plug it into AC power or your computer before turning it back on.

✔ **You may continue.** Play songs continuously without using the iPad, iPod, or iPhone controls. Selecting songs and using Previous/Rewind and Next/Fast Forward require more energy. Also, turn off your iPad, iPod, or iPhone equalizer (EQ) if you don't need it (see Chapter 15).

Chapter 2

Setting Up iTunes and Your iPad, iPod, or iPhone

*i*Tunes manages your content and apps and syncs your personal information, content, and apps with your iPad, iPod, or iPhone. Although you can download content and apps directly from the iTunes Store or App Store to your iPad, iPod touch, or iPhone, you can't edit the content information (such as the artist and album title) on these devices. You also need a way to import music from CDs, convert media files into iPad, iPod, or iPhone formats, and make a backup of your content library. iTunes does all this and more, and provides a quick and easy browsing experience for accessing the iTunes Store and App Store from your computer.

This chapter explains how to set up your iPad, iPod, and iPhone with iTunes on a Mac or a Windows PC. iTunes installs the iPod software that controls the iPod nano, iPod classic, and iPod shuffle, or the iOS operating system software that runs inside the iPad, iPod touch, and iPhone — iTunes immediately recognizes the type of iPad, iPod, or iPhone you've connected, and installs the correct software.

Installing iTunes

Setting up iTunes is a quick and easy process. The most up-to-date version of iTunes as of this writing is version 10.0.1. However, software updates occur rapidly, so you may end up installing a newer version by the time you read this. (If you already have iTunes installed, see Chapter 21 for instructions on updating it.) You can visit the Apple Web site to download the most up-to-date version of iTunes, which recognizes all iPad, iPod, and iPhone models.

Installing on a Windows PC

Before installing iTunes, make sure that you're logged on as a Windows administrator user. Quit all other applications before installing and be sure to disable any antivirus software.

The iTunes installer also installs the newest version of QuickTime, replacing any older version you might have. *QuickTime* is the Apple multimedia development, storage, and playback technology. Although Windows users aren't required to use QuickTime beyond its use by iTunes, QuickTime is a bonus for Windows users because it offers digital video playback for QuickTime movies on the Internet.

To install iTunes for Windows, follow these steps:

1. **Download the iTunes installer from the Apple site.**

    Browse the Apple Web site (www.apple.com/itunes) and click the Download iTunes Free Download button, as shown in Figure 2-1. You need to enter an e-mail address. Follow the instructions to download the installer (iTunesSetup.exe file) to your hard drive. (A crucial step here is picking a location on your hard drive to save the file and *remembering* that location.)

Figure 2-1: Download the newest version of iTunes from the Internet.

2. Run the iTunes installer.

Double-click the `iTunesSetup.exe` file to install iTunes. At the Welcome screen, click the Next button. Apple's license agreement appears in the installer window. Feel free to scroll down to read the agreement, if only to appreciate legal minds at work. Whatever you do, you must select the option to accept the agreement, or the installer goes no further.

3. Select the option to accept the terms of the license agreement and then click the Next button.

After clicking Next (which is active only if you accept), the installer displays the iTunes installation options, as shown in Figure 2-2.

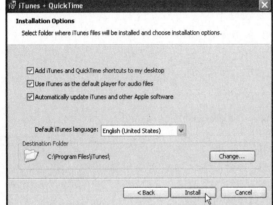

Figure 2-2:
Choose
iTunes
installation
options.

4. Choose your iTunes installation options.

You can turn the following options on or off (as shown in Figure 2-2):

- *Add iTunes and QuickTime Shortcuts to My Desktop:* You can install shortcuts for your Windows desktop for iTunes and the QuickTime Player.

- *Use iTunes as the Default Player for Audio Files:* I suggest turning this option on, allowing iTunes to be the default audio content player for all audio files it recognizes. If you're happy with your audio player, you can deselect this option, leaving your default player setting unaffected.

- *Automatically update iTunes and other Apple software:* Turn this option on so that iTunes can inform you when its software needs to be updated. This option automatically performs the function of choosing Help➪Check for iTunes Updates (see Chapter 21 for details).

5. **Choose the default language for iTunes.**

   The installer assumes that you want English (U.S.), so if you want to use a different language, you need to select it from the drop-down menu.

6. **Choose the destination folder for iTunes.**

   By default, the installer assumes that you want to store the program in the Program Files folder of your C: drive. If you want to use a different folder, click the Change button to use Windows Explorer to locate the desired folder.

7. **Click the Install button to finish.**

   After you click Install, the installer finishes the installation and displays the Complete dialog.

8. **Click the Finish button.**

   Restarting your Windows PC after installing software is always a good idea.

iTunes and QuickTime are now installed on your PC. To start using iTunes, double-click the iTunes desktop shortcut or use your Start menu to locate iTunes and launch it.

The first time you launch iTunes, yet another Apple license agreement appears. You must click the Agree button to continue (or cancel). After clicking Agree, iTunes displays the iTunes Setup Assistant — to get started, click the Next button.

Installing on a Mac

As a Mac user, you should already have iTunes installed because all Macs sold since 2003 come preinstalled with iTunes and Mac OS X. The most up-to-date version of iTunes as of this writing is version 9.2.1.

The version of iTunes that's provided with the Mac might be the newest version; then again, it might not be. If iTunes displays a dialog with the message that a new version of iTunes is available and asks whether you would like to download it now, choose Yes to download the new version. Mac OS X not only downloads iTunes but also installs it automatically — after asking you for the administrator's password, of course.

 You can set your Mac to automatically download the latest version of iTunes when it becomes available. Choose Preferences from the iTunes menu, click the General tab, and select the Check for Updates Automatically check box at the bottom of the General preferences to turn it on.

You can also set your Mac to check for all system software and Apple applications (including iTunes). Choose System Preferences from the Apple menu, and then choose Software Update from the System Preferences window. Select the Check for Updates check box to turn it on, and select Daily, Weekly, or Monthly from the pop-up menu. You can also click the Check Now button to check for a new version immediately. If one exists, it appears in a window for you to select. Click the check mark to select it, and then click the Install button to download and install it.

If you want to manually install iTunes on your Mac or manually upgrade the version you have, browse the Apple Web site (www.apple.com/itunes) to get it. You can download iTunes for free.

To install iTunes manually on your Mac, visit this book's companion Web site.

After installing iTunes, launch it by double-clicking the iTunes application or clicking the iTunes icon on the Dock. The first time you launch iTunes, yet another Apple license agreement appears. You must click the Agree button to continue (or cancel). After clicking Agree, iTunes displays the iTunes window with links to tutorials on buying and importing music.

Setting Up Your iPad, iPod, or iPhone

When you connect a new iPad, iPod, or iPhone for the first time, iTunes displays the Register and Set Up screen. Follow these steps to set up the device:

1. **With iTunes open, connect your iPad, iPod, or iPhone to the computer with a USB cable.**

   iTunes recognizes the iPad, iPod, or iPhone and opens the Register and Set Up screen to get you started.

2. **Click the Continue button (or click the Register Later button to skip the registration process).**

   iTunes displays the software license agreement. You can scroll down to read it if you want. You must choose to accept the agreement, or the installer goes no further.

3. **Select the option to accept the terms at the end of the license agreement and then click the Continue button.**

   After clicking Continue (which is active only if you accept), iTunes lets you register your iPad, iPod, or iPhone with Apple online so that you can take advantage of Apple support. iTunes displays a screen for entering your Apple ID; a membership ID for the MobileMe (formerly .Mac) service is also valid. If you purchased your iPad, iPod, or iPhone directly from Apple or have an Apple iTunes Store account, you already have an Apple ID. Enter that ID and password and then click the Continue button to swiftly move through the registration process — Apple automatically recognizes your purchase. If you bought your iPad, iPod, or iPhone elsewhere or you don't have an Apple ID or MobileMe ID, select the I Do Not Have an Apple ID radio button and then click the Continue button to get to the page for entering your iPad, iPod, or iPhone serial number and your personal information. Fields marked with an asterisk (*) are required, such as your name and e-mail address.

If you don't already have an iTunes Store account, the Setup Assistant is going to ask you to set up such an account now, as part of your iPad, iPod, or iPhone setup. Chapter 6 has all the details on setting up an iTunes Store account.

4. **Click Continue to advance through each screen in the registration process, and then click Submit at the end to submit your information.**

5. **(iPad, iPod touch, or iPhone only) If you've synced an iPad, iPod touch, or iPhone previously on the same computer, choose whether to use its settings by restoring from its backup, or to set up the device as new.**

   After clicking Submit, iTunes checks to see if you have ever backed up an iPad, iPod touch, or iPhone before. If you never backed up an iPad, iPod touch, or iPhone before, skip to Step 6. If you've synced one of these devices previously as I describe in Chapter 8 (and you haven't deleted its backup as I describe in Chapter 21), iTunes gives you the following choices:

   • **Set Up As a New iPod:** Select this option if you want to set the iPad, iPod touch, or iPhone up as new, and then click Continue. iTunes displays a screen that lets you enter a name for your iPod touch, as shown in Figure 2-3.

   • **Restore From the Backup Of:** Select this option, and pick an iPad, iPod touch, or iPhone from the pop-up menu, to restore the previous device's name and settings. Then click Continue, and skip Steps 6 and 7 (you're done). Your automatic sync settings are restored from the previous backup, and you can change them as I show in Chapters 8 and 9.

6. **Enter a new name for your iPod or iPhone.**

   iTunes displays a screen that lets you enter a name for your iPad, iPod, or iPhone, as shown in Figure 2-3 for an iPod touch, and Figure 2-4 for an iPod nano.

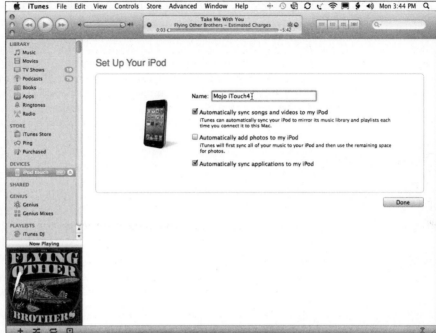

Figure 2-3:
Give your
iPod touch
(or iPad
or iPhone)
a name
and set
automatic
options.

Figure 2-4:
Give your
iPod nano
a name
and set
automatic
options.

7. Set the automatic options, and then click the Done button (on a Mac) or the Finish button (in Windows).

When it comes to setting automatic options, here's the deal:

- *Automatically Sync Songs and Videos (iPad, iPod classic, iPod touch, and iPhone):* If you want to copy your entire iTunes music and video library, leave the Automatically Sync Songs and Videos option selected. This option creates a mirror image of your music and video library on the device, including all playlists and audio files. (You can always change this setting later; see Chapter 8.) If your iPad, iPod classic, iPod touch, or iPhone can't hold your entire library, iTunes chooses songs for you, based on your ratings and how often you've played the songs. (To find out how to add ratings, see Chapter 11.) If you want to control which portion of your library to copy to the iPad, iPod classic, iPod touch, or iPhone, deselect this option and turn to Chapter 8 for synchronization details.

- *Automatically Sync Songs (iPod nano and iPod shuffle):* If you leave the Automatically Sync Songs option selected, iTunes copies a random selection of songs to the device. You can always choose to sync your iPod nano or iPod shuffle with a different selection as I describe in Chapter 8.

- *Automatically Add Photos:* Select this option to copy all the photos in your photo library to your iPad, iPod, or iPhone (not included with the iPod shuffle). (See Chapter 17 for information about synchronizing and playing photo libraries.) Leave it deselected if you want to transfer photos later. You can also choose the Pictures folder or choose another folder in the Sync Photos From pop-up menu (refer to Figure 2-3).

- *Automatically Sync Applications (iPad, iPod touch, and iPhone):* Select this option to copy all applications in your iTunes library to your device.

- *Enable VoiceOver (iPod shuffle):* Select this option to enable the VoiceOver kit. VoiceOver tells you the name of the song you're playing (as well as your battery status) and lets you choose from a spoken menu of playlists. See Chapter 15 for details.

After finishing setup, your iPad, iPod, or iPhone name appears in the iTunes source pane (the left column) under the Devices subheading.

If you chose the option to automatically synchronize your songs and videos, or restored your iPad, iPod, or iPhone from a backup set to automatically sync your songs and videos, your iPad, iPod, or iPhone fills up with content from your iTunes music library.

Don't want to add content now? If you deselect the automatically synchronize option, you can still add songs and videos later, along with podcasts, audio books, and other things — either manually or automatically, as I describe in Chapter 8.

After setting up your iPad, iPod, or iPhone (and syncing if you chose the sync options), disconnect the device from your computer by *ejecting* it. To eject your iPad, iPod, or iPhone, click the eject button next to its name (refer to Figure 2-4) in the Devices section of the source pane. You can then connect the iPad, iPod, or iPhone to its dock or power adapter to continue recharging its battery.

After ejecting the iPad, iPod, or iPhone, wait for its display to show the main menu or the OK to disconnect message. You can then disconnect it from the computer. Never disconnect an iPad, iPod, or iPhone before ejecting it because such bad behavior might cause it to freeze and require a reset. (If that happens, see Chapter 21 for instructions.)

Getting Started with iTunes

With iTunes, you not only have a digital jukebox that lets you add CDs and a video player that lets you add video (as I show in Chapter 7), but also a browser for Apple's online stores to download tons of content and apps. And after you've organized your content items and apps in iTunes, you can put them on your iPad, iPod, or iPhone and carry them with you.

iTunes helps you manage your songs and albums, audio books, TV shows, movies, and other videos from the iTunes Store and other sources; electronic books (e-books) and apps from the App Store; and e-books from the iBook Store (I describe these Apple online stores in Chapter 6, and how to copy into your iTunes library items from other sources, including audio CDs, in Chapter 7). You can also subscribe to *podcasts* that transfer audio or audio/video episodes, such as weekly broadcasts, automatically to your iTunes library from the Internet or through the iTunes Store. You can even use iTunes to listen to Web radio stations and add your favorite stations to your music library. You can also use iTunes to burn songs onto an audio CD and organize backup copies of your media library.

As if that weren't enough, iTunes gives you the power to organize content into playlists, as I describe in Chapter 13. (You can even set up dynamic, smart playlists that reflect your preferences and listening habits.) iTunes even has a built-in equalizer with preset settings for all kinds of music and listening environments, as I show in Chapter 12.

The Mac and Windows versions of iTunes are virtually identical, with the exception that dialogs and icons look a bit different between the two operating systems. You also find a few other differences, mostly related to the different operating environments. The Windows version lets you import unprotected Windows Media (WMA) songs; the Mac version, like other iLife applications, can integrate its library directly within iPhoto to use with slide-shows, iMovie to include in movies, iWeb to include in Web pages, and iDVD to include in menus for DVDs. Nevertheless, as Apple continues to improve iTunes, the company releases upgrades to both versions at the same time, and the versions are free to download.

Opening the iTunes Window

You can run iTunes anytime (with or without an iPad, iPod, iPhone, or Apple TV) to build and manage your library of music, audio books, podcasts, Web radio stations, TV shows, and other videos. You don't have to connect your iPad, iPod, or iPhone until you're ready to transfer content to it (as I describe in Chapter 8).

When you launch iTunes, your library and other sources of content appear. Figure 2-5 shows the iTunes window on a PC running Windows showing the column browser with the Album Listview, which shows album covers. To find out more about the column browser and Album List view, see Chapter 10.

The Mac and Windows versions of iTunes offer the same functions and view-ing options, including the *cover browser* (also known as Cover Flow). Figure 2-6 shows the iTunes window on the Mac with the cover browser open, dis-playing the cover art for albums — to learn how to use the cover browser, see Chapter 10. Both versions offer the Ping Sidebar for the Ping social music network (shown in Figure 2-5 before signing up for Ping, and in Figure 2-6 after signing up for Ping), which I describe later in this chapter. iTunes also provides the Speakers pop-up menu for choosing a remote speaker system — it is set to the default computer speakers in Figure 2-5, and set to Express Buddy in Figure 2-6 (an AirPlay-compatible Airport Express hub with speak-ers), which I explain in Chapter 12.

iTunes offers multiple views of your library and your sources for content, as well as controls for organizing, importing, and playing content, as follows:

  ✔ **Source pane:** Displays the source of your content, handily divided into the following sections:

    • *Library:* Includes your music, movies, TV shows, podcasts, books (audio books and e-books), apps (iPhone, iPod touch, and iPad applications and iPod games), ringtones, educational lessons from iTunes U, and all available radio stations.

    • *Store:* Includes the iTunes Store, the Ping social network for iTunes users, and your Purchased or Downloads list (if you've purchased items or have recently downloaded items).

Source pane

Rewind

Play/Pause

Forward

Eject

Volume control   Status pane

View buttons   Genius Sidebar

Search field

Figure 2-5:
The iTunes
window on
a PC set to
Album List
view with
the column
browser
showing.

Show/Hide
artwork

Artwork Column   List pane

Speakers menu

Column Browser

Genius button

Add
playlist

Repeat

Show/Hide Genius Sidebar

Shuffle

Artwork pane

- *Devices:* Includes audio CDs and any iPad, iPods (such as *iPod* in
  Figure 2-5 and *Mojo iTouch4* in Figure 2-6), iPhones, and Apple TV
  devices that are connected to your computer.

- *Eject button:* This button appears next to the name of an audio CD, iPad, iPod, or iPhone in the source pane (refer to Figure 2-5). Clicking the eject button, um, *ejects* a CD or an iPad, iPod, or iPhone. However, whereas a CD actually pops out of some computers, iPad, iPods, and iPhones act like hard drives, and ejecting them simply removes *(unmounts)* the drives from the system so that you can disconnect them.

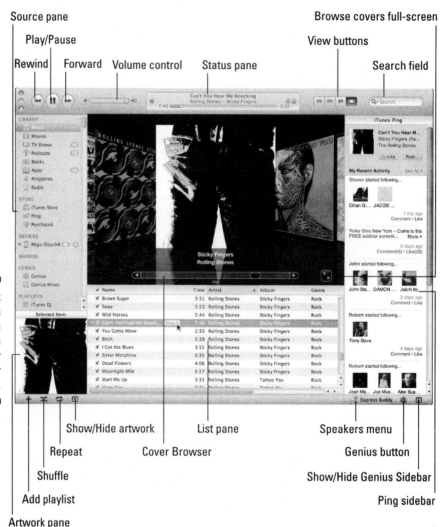

Figure 2-6: The iTunes window on a Mac with the cover browser open.

- *Shared:* Includes iTunes libraries on your home network that you can share iTunes Store content with, as I describe in Chapter 6.

- *Genius:* Includes Genius mixes and your Genius playlists, which I describe in Chapter 13.

- *Playlists:* Includes the automatic tune-selector iTunes DJ (see Chapter 12 for details) and your own playlists (see Chapter 13 for more info).

✔ **Cover browser:** Also called Cover Flow, the cover browser lets you flip through your cover art to choose songs (refer to Figure 2-6). You can use the slider to move swiftly through your library, or you can click to the right or left of the cover in the foreground to step forward or backward in your library. I show this in more detail in Chapter 10.

✔ **List pane:** Depending on the source that's selected in the source pane under Library, Store, Devices, Shared, Genius, or Playlists, the list pane (refer to Figure 2-5) displays the content from that source. For example, choosing a playlist shows the contents of that playlist in the list pane, while choosing TV Shows in the Library section displays the TV shows in your iTunes library in the list pane.

✔ **View buttons:** The four buttons in the upper-right corner change your view of the list pane to show a list (List view), an album list with cover art (Album List view), a grid of cover art images (Grid view), or the cover browser (Cover Flow).

✔ **Column browser:** To see the column browser, choose View⇨Column Browser⇨Show Column Browser. To hide the column browser, choose View⇨Column Browser⇨Hide Column Browser.

✔ **Search field:** Type in this field to search your library. You can also use the search field to peruse a playlist or to look within the iTunes Store.

✔ **Status pane:** When content is playing, you can see the artist name, piece title (if known), and the elapsed time displayed in this pane. When synchronizing, you see a progress bar. If more than one operation is happening at the same time (such as playing music and synchronizing), you can see either status display by clicking the tiny right arrow in the status pane.

✔ **Player buttons — Forward/Next, Play/Pause, and Previous/Rewind:** Use these buttons to control the playback of content in iTunes.

✔ **Volume control:** You can change the volume level in iTunes by dragging the volume control slider in the upper-left section of the iTunes window to the right to increase the volume or to the left to decrease it. The maximum volume of the iTunes volume slider is the maximum set for the computer's sound, which you set separately. See Chapter 12 for more about setting volume levels on your computer.

- ✔ **Playlist buttons — Add, Shuffle, Repeat:** Use these buttons to add play-lists, and randomly shuffle or repeat playback of playlists.

- ✔ **Show/Hide artwork button:** Use this button to display or hide artwork (either your own or the artwork supplied with purchased songs and videos).

- ✔ **Speakers pop-up menu:** Use this pop-up menu near the lower-right corner of the iTunes window to select a different speaker system than the computer's speakers (see Chapter 12). This pop-up menu appears only if you choose Preferences (from the iTunes menu on a Mac or the Edit menu in Windows), click the Devices tab, and turn on the Look for Remote Speakers Connected with AirPlay option. If iTunes locates such speakers, the pop-up menu appears.

- ✔ **Genius button:** The Genius button, located in the lower-right corner of the iTunes window to the left of the Show/Hide Ping Sidebar button, generates a Genius playlist of songs from your library that go great with the song you selected. The Genius button appears gray unless you have selected a song — see Chapter 14 for details. After clicking the Genius button, the Genius playlist appears and is automatically selected in the source pane in the Playlists section.

- ✔ **Show/Hide Ping Sidebar button:** Use this button to display or hide the Ping Sidebar.

- ✔ **Ping Sidebar:** The Ping Sidebar (refer to Figure 2-6) shows you the music-downloading activities of the friends you follow, and the music talked about by the artists you follow. You have obligation to buy any-thing, and you can dispense with it if it bothers you — you can open or close the Ping Sidebar by clicking the boxed-arrow Show/Hide Ping Sidebar button in the lower-right corner of the iTunes window. (See the next section for details.)

If you don't like the width of the source pane, you can adjust it by drag-ging the vertical bar between the source and list panes. You can also adjust the horizontal bar between the song listing in the list pane and the column browser. To resize the iTunes window on a Mac, drag diagonally from the lower-right corner. In Windows, drag the edges of the window horizontally or vertically.

Using Ping

Are you gaga over Lady GaGa? Loco for Yo-Yo Ma? Jubilant over John Legend? Frantic about Michael Franti? Or still crazy for Clapton after all these years? All the information you need is a just a click away in Ping, the social music network that is part of iTunes. Ping lets you follow your favorite artists to see what they've been up to, and follow your friends as they download music from the iTunes Store and post messages about songs in their iTunes libraries.

The Ping Sidebar appears after you click the Show/Hide Genius Ping Sidebar button (refer to Figure 2-5). Click the Learn More button to learn more about it, or select Ping in the Store section of the source pane, and then click Turn on Ping to get started. iTunes then displays a dialog for you to sign in with your Apple ID to your iTunes Store account (to learn about setting up an iTunes account or signing in, see Chapter 6).

Once signed in, you see your profile page. You can edit your profile to include a photo, your location, a brief description, and the genres you most like in music. Scroll down the profile page to add the music you like — you can pick options to automatically display all music you like, rated, reviewed, or purchased, or manually pick albums to display from your library. You can enter artist or album names in a search field to search for music you like.

Scroll down further to set your privacy settings. You can choose to allow people to follow you (or not), and check the option to require your approval first before they can follow you. When finished, click the Save button in the lower-right corner of the profile page.

After you are on Ping, your recent activity page appears. You can click People to see the people you follow or the people who follow you. To find people, enter names in the search field under the Find People heading on the recent activity page. You can also click the Email button under the search field to invite your friends by e-mail.

A Follow (or Stop Following) button appears with every person's name and description. Click on a person to see that person's profile, recent activity (such as the songs downloaded, reviews, likes, and comments). Click Featured to see featured artists in Ping that you can follow.

You can immediately start liking songs in your iTunes library or in the iTunes Store. A Ping button appears next to the song when you select it (refer to Figure 2-6; the cursor points to the Ping button next to "Can't You Hear Me Knocking" by the Rolling Stones in the list pane). Click the Ping button to see a pop-up menu of choices. Choose Like to like the song, Post to post the song with a message, or Show Artist Profile to show the artist's profile page in Ping. You can also choose to show the artist, album name, or song title in the iTunes Store, and use the Like or Post buttons on the artist or album page. Ping artist messages also appear in the iTunes app on an iPod touch or iPhone. (See Chapter 6 for iTunes Store and iTunes app details.)

If you show the Ping Sidebar (refer to Figure 2-6), the song you selected appears at the top along with Like and Post buttons. Below the selected songs are thumbnails and messages of your friends and artists' recent activities in Ping.

Ping is a great way to discover music in the iTunes Store, because you can download from the store any song that any of your friends liked or posted messages about. Ping is not a comprehensive social network like Facebook or MySpace — it uniquely complements those networks by letting you hook up only with the friends who like the same type of music, and with the artists who make that music.

Chapter 3

Putting Your Finger On It

· ·

In This Chapter

▶ Touching and gesturing on an iPad, iPod nano, iPod touch, or iPhone

▶ Typing on the iPad, iPod touch, or iPhone

▶ Thumbing through iPod classic menus

· ·

The iPad, iPod, and iPhone are all about convenience. Apple designed the iPod classic and iPod shuffle models to be held in one hand so that you can perform simple operations by thumb. Even if you're all thumbs when pressing small buttons on tiny devices, you can still thumb your way to iPod heaven. The iPod shuffle's VoiceOver feature complements this arrangement by announcing each song, so you can quickly jump around.

With an iPad, iPod nano, iPod touch, or iPhone, your fingers do the walking. You can make gestures, such as flicking a finger to scroll a list quickly, or sliding your finger to scroll slowly or drag a slider (such as the volume slider). On an iPod nano you can double-tap a photo to zoom into it and see more detail, and then drag the image to position the part you want to see in the center of the screen. On an iPad, iPod touch, or iPhone, pinch with two fingers to zoom out of a photo, or pull apart with two fingers (also known as *unpinch*) to zoom in to the photo to see it more clearly.

This chapter gives you a quick tour of the iPad, iPod, and iPhone models, including the menus of an iPod classic, the iPod shuffle controls, and all the touch-and-gesture tricks to make your iPad, iPod nano, iPod touch, or iPhone dance and sing. I also give you a complete tour of one of the most unique features of the iPad, iPod touch, and iPhone: the on-screen keyboard.

Tapping Your iPad, iPod touch, or iPhone

The iPad, iPod touch, or iPhone responds to tapping, flicking, and sliding your finger(s), among other gestures (such as shaking, tilting, two-finger tapping, and so on). One tap is all you need to run an app or select something, but sometimes you have to slide your finger to scroll the display and see more selections.

Sticky fingers are not recommended. To clean your iPad, iPod touch, or iPhone, make sure to unplug all cables and turn it off. (See Chapter 1.) Use a soft, slightly damp, lint-free cloth to wipe it clean. See Chapter 22 for cleaning tips.

Sliding to the Home screen

The first message you see on an iPad, iPod touch, or iPhone display (besides the time of day and the date) is `Slide to unlock` — to get started, you have to unlock the iPad, iPod touch, or iPhone by sliding your finger across the message. After the unit is unlocked, your Home screen appears in all its glory. (See Figure 3-1 for an iPod touch and iPhone, and Figure 3-2 for an iPad.)

There's no place like Home — it's the screen where you start. After you tap an icon, a new screen appears with selections and icons that are different for each app. Press the physical Home button below the screen (not shown in the figures) at any time to go to back to the Home screen.

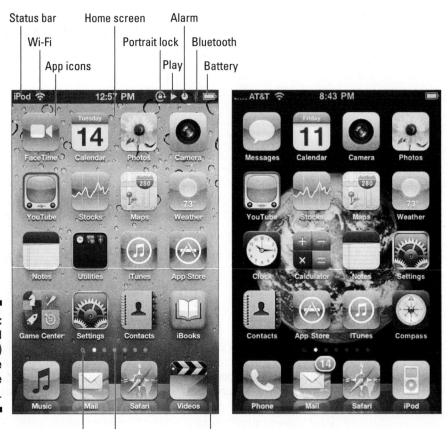

Figure 3-1: The iPod touch (left) and iPhone (right) Home screen.

Figure 3-2:
The iPad
Home
screen
(landscape
mode).

Apps you download from the App Store (as I describe in Chapter 6) show up as icons on your Home screen. You can also save Web "clips" (page references) to your Home screen as icons that take you directly to those Web pages (as I describe in Chapter 18). When you add enough apps and Web clips so that they no longer all fit on the first page of the Home screen, the iPod touch or iPhone automatically creates more Home screens to accommodate them, and the iPad automatically creates a second Home screen for apps. (See the section "Cleaning Up Home Screens on an iPad, iPod touch, or iPhone," later in this chapter, to find out how to organize your icons into folders and rearrange icons on your Home screens.)

The bottom row of the Home screen (refer to Figure 3-1 for an iPod touch or iPhone, and Figure 3-2 for an iPad) is called the *dock*. Icons in the dock remain on the screen when you switch from one Home screen to another. You can change the apps in the dock, as I show in "Cleaning Up Home Screens on an iPad, iPod touch, or iPhone" later in this chapter.

The tiny dots above the dock show how many Home screens you have, and also indicate which screen you're viewing. To switch to another Home screen, flick with your finger left or right, or tap a dot in the row of dots (the far-left dot is actually a magnifying glass icon for the Search screen).

Press the Home button under the screen to go to back to the first Home screen. To go to any other Home screen, tap one of the dots above the dock on any Home screen — for example, to go to Home screen 4, tap the fourth dot to the right of the magnifying glass icon.

Tapping the apps from Apple

The iPad, iPod touch, and iPhone Home screen (refer to Figure 3-1) offers the following icons for apps supplied by Apple for free:

- ✔ **FaceTime (iPod touch):** Make FaceTime video calls to other people that have FaceTime (currently fourth-generation iPod touch and iPhone 4 models) using Wi-Fi. See Chapter 20 for details.

- ✔ **Safari:** Use the Safari Web browser.

- ✔ **Phone (iPhone):** Make and receive mobile phone calls and FaceTime calls (see Chapter 20 for FaceTime).

- ✔ **Messages (iPhone):** Send and receive SMS text messages by phone.

- ✔ **Mail:** Check and send e-mail.

- ✔ **Calendar:** View your calendar.

- ✔ **Contacts:** View your contacts.

- ✔ **YouTube:** List and select videos from YouTube.

- ✔ **Stocks (iPod touch and iPhone):** Check the prices for financial stocks, bonds, and funds (iPod touch and iPhone only).

- ✔ **Maps:** View maps and get driving directions.

- ✔ **Weather (iPod touch and iPhone):** View the weather in multiple cities (iPod touch and iPhone only).

- ✔ **Clock (iPod touch and iPhone):** View multiple clocks and use the alarm clock, timer, and stopwatch (iPod touch and iPhone only).

- ✔ **Compass (iPhone):** View a compass showing your direction (iPhone 3GS and iPhone 4 only).

- ✔ **Calculator (iPod touch and iPhone):** This app is a regular calculator for adding, subtracting, multiplying, dividing, and so on. Also, if you hold the iPod touch or iPhone horizontally, it becomes a scientific calculator.

- ✔ **Notes:** Add text notes.

- ✔ **Voice Memos:** Record using the built-in microphone (iPad and iPhone) or the Apple earbud microphones.

- ✔ **Utilities (iPod touch):** This is a folder on the iPod touch Home screen containing the Clock, Calculator, and Voice Memos apps (see descriptions above). For details on creating your own Home screen folders, see "Organizing apps into folders" in this chapter.

✔ **Settings:** Adjust settings for Wi-Fi, sounds, brightness, Safari, and other apps, as well as apply other settings for the iPad, iPod touch, or iPhone itself.

✔ **Music (iPod touch):** Select playlists, artists, songs, albums, and more (including podcasts, genres, composers, audio books, and compilations). The Music icon also offers Cover Flow browsing, as I describe in Chapter 15.

✔ **Videos (iPad and iPod touch):** Select videos by type (movies, music videos, TV shows, or video podcasts).

✔ **iPod (iPad and iPhone):** Select playlists, artists, songs, videos, and more (including podcasts, genres, composers, audio books, and compilations). The iPod icon also offers Cover Flow browsing on an iPhone, as I describe in Chapter 15. On an iPhone, use the iPod icon to also select videos.

✔ **Photos:** Select photos by photo album or select individual photos in the Photo Library.

✔ **Camera (iPod touch and iPhone):** Snap a photo (iPhone and iPhone 3G), or shoot video (fourth-generation iPod touch, iPhone 3GS and iPhone 4). See Chapter 17 for details.

✔ **App Store:** Go to Apple's online App Store to download other Apple and third-party apps.

✔ **Game Center (iPod touch and iPhone):** Discover and play games online with your friends.

✔ **iTunes:** Go to the iTunes Store to purchase content.

Additionally, you can download Apple's free iBooks app to read electronic books (e-books) from Apple's iBook store on your iPad, iPod touch, or iPhone.

You find one more icon for an app that you can activate in Settings, if you have the appropriate Nike shoes and the Nike+ iPod Sport Kit, sold separately. See Chapter 22 for details.

Touching and gesturing

With the iPad, iPhone, or iPod touch, it's touch and go. These models respond to gestures you make with your fingers:

✔ **Drag with your finger:** Scroll up or down lists slowly.

✔ **Flick up or down:** Swipe your finger quickly across the surface to scroll up or down lists quickly.

- **Touch and hold:** Touch and hold and object in order to drag it, or while scrolling, touch and hold to stop the moving list.

- **Flick from left to right or right to left:** Quickly swipe your finger across the screen to change screens or application panes (Home screens, Cover Flow when browsing music, Weather, and other apps).

- **Single tap:** Select an item.

- **Double tap:** Zoom in or out with Safari, Maps, and other applications.

- **Two-finger single tap:** Zoom out in Maps.

- **Pinch:** Zoom out.

- **Unpinch:** Zoom in.

Searching for anything

A tiny magnifying glass icon for searching appears to the left of the dots above the dock on the Home screen. Tap this icon, or flick with your finger to the right, to show the Search screen. The Search function is similar to the Spotlight Search feature of Mac OS X. You can then type in a search term and immediately see suggestions.

Shake, rattle, and roll

Your iPad, iPod touch, or iPhone can sense motion with its built-in accelerometer, and the fourth-generation iPod touch and iPhone 4 can sense orientation with its three-axis gyro. When you rotate it from a vertical view (portrait) to a horizontal view (landscape), the iPad, iPod touch, or iPhone detects the movement and changes the display accordingly. This happens so quickly that you can control a game with these movements.

For example, Pass the Pigs is a dice game in which you shake three times to roll your pigs to gain points. In the Labyrinth game, you tilt your iPad, iPod touch, or iPhone to roll a ball through a wooden maze without falling through the holes. And you can shake, rattle, and roll your way around the world in Yahtzee Adventures as you rack up high scores.

And if that's too tame for you, try Chopper, a helicopter game in which you need to complete your mission and return to base while avoiding enemy fire from tanks and bazooka-wielding madmen. You tilt the iPad, iPod touch, or iPhone to fly and touch the screen to drop bombs or fire the machine gun.

Xhake Shake lets you shake, flip, rub, and tap your iPad, iPod touch, or iPhone to challenge your hand-eye responses. And for scrolling practice, try Light Bike (loosely based on the Disney movie *Tron*), in which you scroll to maneuver a light bike from a third-person perspective against three computer-controlled light bikes. And infants can join the fun: Silver Rattle shows a screen that changes color and rattles with every shake. Big Joe Turner would be proud.

Search looks through contacts, calendars, e-mail (the To, From, and Subject fields, but not the message content), the content (songs, videos, podcasts, and audio books), the text in the Notes app, and text messages. Tap a contact, calendar entry, e-mail, note, or text message suggestion to open it, or tap the song, video, podcast, or audio book suggestion to play it.

You can set which types of information to search through, and the order of information types to search first. On a fourth-generation iPod touch, iPhone 3GS, or iPhone 4, choose Settings⇨General⇨Spotlight Search from the Home screen; on an iPad, older model iPod touch, or iPhone 3G, choose Settings⇨General⇨Home, and at the bottom of the Home settings screen, tap Search Results on an iPad, or Spotlight Search on an iPod touch or iPhone 3G. Tap any information type (such as Contacts, Music, Video, Notes, and so on) to remove the check mark, which removes that type of information from the search; tap the information type again to bring back the check mark and include it in the search. To change the order of information types to search, touch and hold an information type, and then drag it to a new position in the list.

Checking the status bar

The iPad, iPod touch, or iPhone shows its current state in the status bar at the top of the screen (refer to Figure 3-1 for an iPod touch or iPhone, or Figure 3-2 for an iPad). The icons mean the following:

- ✔ **iPod:** Just in case you forgot you had an iPod touch in your hands (very existential). On an iPad 3G or iPhone, you see the cascading bars of cell-phone service coverage (on an iPad 3G, the cell service is for data only).

- ✔ **Wi-Fi:** This icon says that the iPad, iPod touch, or iPhone is connected to a Wi-Fi network. The more arcs you see in the icon, the stronger the connection to the network. To find out more about setting up Wi-Fi with Internet in your home, see Chapter 4.

- ✔ **E or 3G:** This icon tells you that your iPad 3G or iPhone is connected to either the Edge (E) or 3G cellular data service (3G is available for iPhone 3G, iPhone 3GS, and iPad 3G models).

- ✔ **Airplane mode:** This icon shows if airplane mode is turned on (iPad 3G, fourth-generation iPod touch, and iPhone) — in this mode, you can't access the Internet or use Bluetooth devices. Note that you can turn Wi-Fi and Bluetooth back on while in airplane mode, so that you can use the airline's Wi-Fi (if offered). (Not visible in Figure 3-1 or Figure 3-2.)

- ✔ **Network activity:** This icon twirls to show that data is traveling from the network to your iPad, iPod touch, or iPhone (or vice versa). (Not visible in Figure 3-1 or Figure 3-2.)

✔ **VPN:** If you have special network settings that access a virtual private network (VPN), this icon shows up to tell you that you are connected to it. See Chapter 4 for details. (Not visible in Figure 3-1 or Figure 3-2.)

✔ **Lock:** You see this icon whenever the iPad, iPod touch, or iPhone is locked. (The Slide to unlock message also appears on the screen.) (Not visible in Figure 3-1 or Figure 3-2.)

✔ **Bluetooth:** This icon appears only if Bluetooth is turned on. If Bluetooth is on and a device, such as a headset or keyboard, is connected, the icon is white; if it is on but nothing is connected, it turns gray.

✔ **Location Services:** This icon appears if an app is using Location Services to determine the location of the iPod touch. See Chapter 4 for details. (Not visible in Figure 3-1 or Figure 3-2.)

✔ **Portrait lock:** This icon appears if you locked the iPad, fourth-generation iPod touch, iPhone 3GS, or iPhone 4 in portrait orientation. See "Switching orientation" in this chapter for details.

✔ **Play:** This icon tells you that a song, audio book, or podcast is playing (in case you didn't know — maybe you took your headphones off).

✔ **Alarm:** This icon appears if you set an alarm. See Chapter 4 for details.

✔ **Battery:** The Battery icon shows the battery level or charging status. See Chapter 1 for details.

Multitasking your apps (iPod touch, iPhone 3GS, or iPhone 4)

On the fourth-generation iPod touch and the iPhone 3GS and iPhone 4, multiple apps can stay in memory and run simultaneously. Only one app runs in the *foreground* — where the action occurs — while all other apps hang out in the *background*. For example, audio services like Pandora work in the background to keep playing music from the Web while you run another app in the foreground. Other examples are voice-prompted navigation apps, Internet calling apps, and apps that perform long downloads — they keep working while you're on a call or using another app in the foreground.

You can quickly move the currently running app to the background, and switch to another background app, by double-clicking the Home button. The four most recently used apps in the background appear in the bottom row of the screen, as shown in Figure 3-3 (left side). Tap any app on this row to immediately switch to that app and move it to the foreground. You can also flick left to see more apps that are running in the background, and tap any one of them.

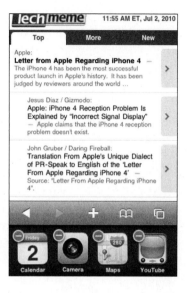

Figure 3-3:
Switch to
another app
(left) and
remove an
app from
the recent
background
(right).

While running any app, or while viewing any Home screen, you can double-click the Home button to see the bottom row of apps in the background. You can also remove an app from the bottom row, terminating the app so it no longer runs in the background — touch and hold the app icon until all the icons in the bottom row start wiggling as if they were doing the jailhouse rock, with a circled minus (-) sign in the top left corner of each app's icon, as shown in Figure 3-3 (right side). Tap the circled minus (-) sign to remove the app. You can free as many as you like. When finished, press the Home button once to stop the icons from wiggling. (The app appears again in the row of recently opened background apps the next time you run it and switch to another app.)

Switching orientation

The iPad, iPod touch, and iPhone Home screens appear in portrait orientation, as do most apps. However, many apps, including Safari and Mail, change the orientation to landscape when you quickly rotate the iPad, iPod touch, or iPhone. For example, to view a Web page in landscape orientation in Safari, rotate the device sideways. Safari automatically reorients and expands the page. To set it back to portrait, rotate the device again. You may prefer landscape for viewing Web pages or entering text with the onscreen keyboard, which is wider in landscape orientation.

You can lock the display of an iPad, iPod touch, or iPhone in portrait orientation so that it doesn't jump to landscape even when you rotate the device. To lock the orientation on an iPad, push the lock button (on the side of the iPad above the volume buttons) down. To unlock the orientation, push the lock button up.

To lock into portrait orientation on an iPod touch or iPhone, double-click the Home button to see the bottom row of apps in the background, and then flick the bottom of the screen from left-to-right to show the Music player controls and portrait lock button. Tap the portrait lock button to lock the iPod touch or iPhone into portrait orientation. The portrait lock icon appears in the status bar (refer to Figure 3-1, left side) when the orientation is locked into portrait.

Cleaning Up Home Screens on an iPad, iPod touch, or iPhone

It's easy to go crazy in the App Store and end up with a mess of apps across several Home screens on your iPad, iPod touch, or iPhone. Fortunately you can organize your apps into folders, rearrange your app icons over your Home screens, and even create additional Home screens to hold them.

To rearrange your iPad, iPod touch, or iPhone app icons within a Home screen or over several Home screens, or to organize them into folders, touch and hold any icon until all the icons begin to wiggle. (That's right; it looks like they're shakin' their booties.) After rearranging icons or organizing folders of icons, press the Home button to stop all that wiggling, which saves your new arrangement for your Home screens.

You can also delete apps you downloaded from the App Store by tapping the circled X that appears inside the icon as it wiggles. A warning appears, telling you that deleting the app also deletes all of the app's data. You can tap Delete to delete the app, or Cancel. You can then stop the physical Home button to stop the icons from wiggling, or continue to rearrange icons and organize them into folders.

Rearranging icons on your Home screens

After you have your icons dancing as I describe previously, you can drag a wiggling icon to a new position on the Home screen, and the other icons move to accommodate, creating a new arrangement.

To move a wiggling icon to the next Home screen, drag it to the right edge of the screen; to move it to the previous Home screen, drag it to the left edge. If there is no Home screen on the right, your iPad, iPod touch, or iPhone creates a new one. You can flick to go any Home screen and drag more wiggling icons to other Home screens. You can create up to eleven Home screens.

While the wiggling icons are doing their show, you can also change the icons in the dock. On an iPad, you can drag two more icons into the dock to make a total of six, and also drag any icon out of the dock and then drag another in to replace it. On an iPod touch or iPhone, you are limited to four icons — but you can drag any icon out of the dock and then drag another one in to replace it.

To stop all that wiggling, press the Home button, which saves your new arrangement.

To reset your Home screens to the default arrangement, thereby cleaning up any mess you may have made on them, choose Settings⇨General⇨Reset from the Home screen. On the Reset screen, tap Reset Home Screen Layout.

Organizing apps into folders

You can also organize your app icons into folders on your Home screens so that you can find them more easily. Folders also make it easier to find categories of apps — you can add all your social networking apps to a Social folder, or all your news-gathering apps into a News folder.

While your icons are wiggling (as I describe previously), drag the first app icon you want to include in the folder onto the second app icon you want to include. The system creates a new folder, including the two app icons, and shows the folder's name, which is based on the first icon you dragged (for example, if you drag a "news" app like NYTimes (The New York Times app) over another "news" app such as AP Mobile (the AP newswire app), the folder is called News as shown in Figure 3-4, left side). You can then tap the folder's name field and use the keyboard to enter a different name, as shown in Figure 3-4 (right side).

To close a folder, tap outside the folder, or press the Home button to stop rearranging your app icons.

To add another app icon to a folder, touch and hold an app icon to start the icons wiggling again (if they're not already wiggling), and drag the app icon onto the folder. To move an app icon out of a folder, start the icons wiggling again if they're not already, tap the folder to open it, and then drag the icon out of the folder. To delete a folder, move all the icons out of it. The folder is deleted automatically when empty.

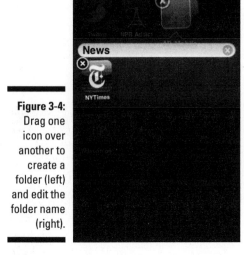 

Figure 3-4:
Drag one
icon over
another to
create a
folder (left)
and edit the
folder name
(right).

You can put up to 12 app icons into a folder. Like individual icons, folders can be rearranged by dragging them around the Home screens. You can also drag folders to the dock.

Tickling the Keyboard on an iPad, iPod touch, or iPhone

One trick that's sure to amaze your friends is the ability to whip out your iPad, iPod touch, or iPhone and type notes, contact information, calendar entries, map locations, stock symbols, e-mail messages, and Web site addresses (and even cell-phone text messages on an iPhone). You can also make selections for pop-up menus that appear on Web pages. You can do all this with the on-screen keyboard.

Tap a text entry field, such as the URL field for a Web page in Safari (as I describe in Chapter 18) or the text of an e-mail message (as I describe in Chapter 19), and the on-screen keyboard appears. Although you can touch-type on an iPad the same way as a regular keyboard, the iPod touch and iPhone screens are smaller — so you may want to practice with just one finger, and as you get used to it, try also using your thumb.

Typing into Notes

You can practice your technique using the Notes app. Tap Notes on the Home screen and the on-screen keyboard appears, as shown in Figure 3-5. (If you've already saved notes, a list of notes appears — tap the + button in the upper-right corner to type a new note.)

Figure 3-5: The keyboard layout for letters (left), numbers (center), and symbols (right).

Tap the keys, and as you type, each letter appears above your thumb or finger. If you tap the wrong key, slide your finger to the correct key. The letter isn't entered until you lift your finger from the key.

 You can start a new sentence quickly by double-tapping the spacebar to insert a period followed by a space. The keyboard automatically capitalizes the next word after you type a period, a question mark, or an exclamation point.

 Don't like what you just typed? Shake your iPad, iPod touch, or iPhone, and a message appears with the Undo Typing and Cancel buttons. Tap Undo Typing to undo the last bit of typing you did.

To enable caps lock (locking the keyboard to uppercase letters), choose Settings⇨General⇨Keyboard and then tap the Off button next to Enable Caps Lock to turn it on. (Tap it again to turn it off.) You can then double-tap the Shift key to turn on caps lock (uppercase letters). The Shift key turns blue, and all letters you type are uppercase. Tap the Shift key again to turn caps lock off.

To save your note, tap Done in the upper-right corner. A list of Notes appears with the last-modified date attached to each note. You can also delete a note by choosing the note and tapping the Trash icon at the bottom of the note. Notes can be synchronized back to your computer's e-mail program — see Chapter 9.

You can e-mail notes to others (and also transfer notes to your computer by e-mailing them to an e-mail address you receive e-mail with on your computer). Choose the note from the Notes screen and tap the letter icon at the bottom of the note to display a ready-made e-mail message that contains the text of your note — all you need to do is enter the e-mail address. See Chapter 19 for details on sending the message.

Typing numbers and symbols

To enter numbers, symbols, or punctuation, tap the .?123 key at the lower-left corner of the keyboard (refer to Figure 3-5, left side). This changes the keyboard layout to numbers (as shown in Figure 3-5, center). To return to the alphabetical keys, tap the ABC key.

To enter symbols with the keyboard, tap the .?123 key for the number layout (refer to Figure 3-5, left side) and then tap the #+= key (refer to Figure 3-5, center) to change the layout to symbols, as shown in Figure 3-5 (right side).

Here's a trick you can use to switch to the numeric keyboard layout and back to alphabetical layout automatically to type a number and continue typing letters: Touch and hold down the .?123 key and then slide your finger over the keyboard to the number you want. Release your finger to select the number. The keyboard immediately reverts back to alphabetic keys so that you can continue typing letters.

Need to use an accent mark? For instance, the word *café* should really have an accent mark over the *e,* and there may even come a day when you need to include a foreign word or two in a note — lycée or Autowäsche or también, for example. Although you can switch the language for the keyboard (as I describe in Chapter 22), you can also include variations of a letter by using the English keyboard. Touch and hold your finger on a letter (such as *e*) to show a row of keys that offer variations on the letter. Slide your finger over the row to highlight the variation you want and then release your finger to select it.

Editing text and handling word suggestions

Yes, you can edit your mistakes. To edit text in an entry field, touch and hold to see the circular magnifier, which magnifies portions of the text view as shown in Figure 3-6 (left side).

Before releasing your finger, slide the magnifier to the position for inserting text. You can then tap keys to insert text, or you can use the delete key — the key sporting the X — to remove text.

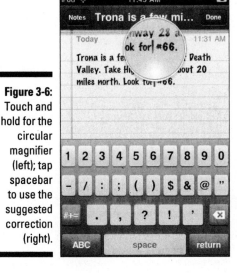 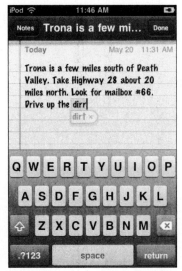

Figure 3-6: Touch and hold for the circular magnifier (left); tap spacebar to use the suggested correction (right).

The intelligent keyboard automatically suggests corrections as you type, as shown in Figure 3-6, right side (some languages only). You don't need to accept the suggested word — just continue typing. If you do want to accept it, tap the spacebar, a punctuation mark, or the Return key. Your iPad, iPhone, or iPod touch fills in the rest of the word.

To reject the suggested word, finish typing the word or tap the X next to the suggestion to dismiss it. Each time you reject a suggestion for the same word, your iPad, iPod touch, or iPhone keeps track and eventually adds the word you've been using all along to its dictionary. The iPad, iPod touch, or iPhone includes dictionaries for English, English (UK), French, French (Canada), German, Japanese, Spanish, Italian, and Dutch. The appropriate dictionary is activated automatically when you select a particular international keyboard. (See Chapter 22 for details about international keyboards.)

You can turn off suggestions by choosing Settings⇨General⇨Keyboard from the Home screen and tapping On for Auto-Correction. (On changes to Off when you tap it.)

Copying (or cutting) and pasting

You can copy or cut a chunk of text and paste it into another app — for example, you can copy a paragraph from a note in Notes and paste it into an e-mail message in Mail.

Double-tap a word to select it for copying or cutting. The word appears selected with handles on either end of the selection and a Cut/Copy/Paste bubble above it, as shown in Figure 3-7 (left side). You can then tap Cut (to cut the text) or Copy (to copy the text) in preparation for pasting it elsewhere.

You can also select the nearest word, or the entire text, by touching an insertion point. The Select/Select All/Paste bubble appears (refer to Figure 3-7, center). Tap Select to select the nearest word (left or right of the insertion point) or Select All to select all the text, and the Cut/Copy/Paste bubble appears (refer to Figure 3-7, right side).

Figure 3-7: Double-tap a word (left), or tap to insert and tap Select (center) to select all the text (right).

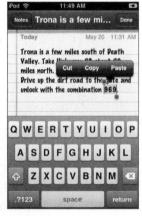 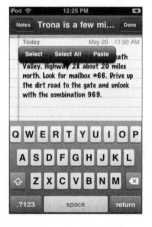 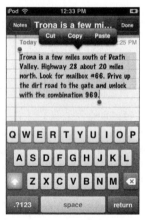

To make a more precise selection, double-tap a word as previously described and then drag one of the handles by sliding your finger. A rectangular magnifier appears, as shown in Figure 3-8 (left side), which magnifies portions of the text view so that you can drag the handle more precisely. When you remove your finger to stop dragging, the Cut/Copy/Paste bubble appears (refer to Figure 3-8, right side). You can then tap Cut or Copy.

To paste the text you just cut or copied, open a note (or create a new note) in Notes, create a new e-mail message, or open any app that lets you enter text. (For details on creating a new e-mail message, see Chapter 19.) Touch an insertion point for pasting the text. The circular magnifier appears (as shown in Figure 3-9, left side), which magnifies portions of the text view so that you can mark the insertion point precisely. When you remove your finger, the Cut/Copy/Paste bubble appears (refer to Figure 3-9, center), or if text is already in the message, the Select/Select All/Paste bubble appears. Either way, you can then tap Paste to paste the text at that point (refer to Figure 3-9, right side).

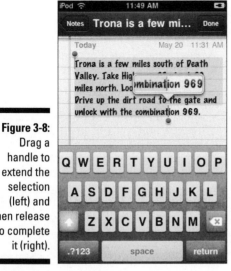
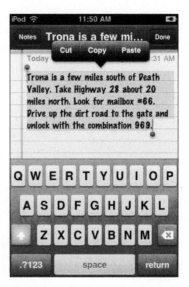

Figure 3-8:
Drag a handle to extend the selection (left) and then release to complete it (right).

Need to undo the last cut or paste? Shake your iPad, iPod touch, or iPhone, and a message appears with the Undo Cut (or Undo Paste) and Cancel buttons. Tap Undo Cut (or Undo Paste) to undo the last operation.

Figure 3-9:
Touch to insert (left) and tap Paste (center) to paste the text (right).

You can use Copy, Cut, and Paste in Safari to copy portions of a Web page (see how in Chapter 18), in Mail to copy portions of an e-mail message (see Chapter 19), or even in Calendar to copy the details of an event (see Chapter 20).

Setting keyboard options

To set keyboard options, choose Settings⇨General⇨Keyboard from the Home screen. The Keyboard settings screen appears, with options for Auto-Correction, Auto-Capitalization, Enable Caps Lock, and the Shortcut for inserting a period.

Tap On to turn off Auto-Correction if you don't want the keyboard to suggest typing corrections.

Auto-Capitalization automatically capitalizes the next word after you type a period, question mark, or exclamation point (punctuation that ends a sentence). It also automatically capitalizes after you tap the Return key. The assumption is that you're starting a new sentence or new line of text that should begin with a capital letter. Tap On to turn this feature off if you want; tap Off to turn it back on.

To turn on caps lock (locking the keyboard to uppercase letters), tap the Off button next to enable Caps Lock. (Tap it again to turn it off.) You can then double-tap the Shift key to turn on caps lock (uppercase letters). The Shift key turns blue, and all letters you type are uppercase. Tap the Shift key again to turn caps lock off.

The shortcut for inserting a period is to double-tap the spacebar, which inserts a period followed by a space. The assumption is that you want to finish a sentence and start the next one. Tap On to turn this feature off if you want; tap Off to turn it back on.

To find out how to turn on and use multiple international keyboards, see Chapter 22.

Tapping Your iPad nano

You control the iPod nano in a similar fashion as the iPod touch and iPhone: by tapping and swiping. After turning on the iPod nano, the first Home screen appears, as shown in Figure 3-10, with dots along the bottom indicating the number of Home screens. As you swipe left or right, you move to the next Home screen — and the dot representing the current screen is highlighted.

Figure 3-10:
The iPad
nano's
first Home
screen.

The icons on the Home screen represent choices for listening to your synced music or podcasts, or for using other features like the Clock (with its Stopwatch and Timer functions), or Photos to display your synced photos. The iPod nano offers the following icons on its Home screens:

- ✔ **Playlists:** Lists the playlists synced from your iTunes library or created on the iPod nano. See Chapter 8 about syncing playlists and Chapter 15 about creating playlists on your iPod nano.

- ✔ **Now Playing:** Provides quick access to the currently playing audio. See Chapter 15 for details.

- ✔ **Artists:** Lists songs synced from your iTunes library, organized by artist, as I describe in Chapter 15.

- ✔ **Genius Mixes:** Lists the Genius Mixes synced from your iTunes library. (That's right, Chapter 15 again.)

- ✔ **Radio:** Opens the FM radio tuner, when you connect earphones to iPod nano. See Chapter 16 for details on playing the radio.

- ✔ **Podcasts:** Lists the podcasts synced from your iTunes library. Chapter 16 has the details.

- ✔ **Photos:** Displays the photos synced from your computer. See Chapter 17 for details.

- ✔ **Settings:** Opens settings for the iPod nano features, many of which I cover in Chapter 4.

- ✔ **Songs:** Lists songs synced from your iTunes library, in alphabetical order. See Chapter 15 for browsing songs.

- ✔ **Albums:** Lists albums synced from your iTunes library, in alphabetical order. Chapter 15 explains browsing by album, and Chapter 8 shows you how to sync albums.

- ✔ **Genres:** Lists songs by genre.

- ✔ **Composers:** Lists songs by composer.

- **Fitness:** Opens the built-in pedometer and workout history, and Nike + iPod features if a Nike + iPod receiver or supported gym equipment is connected to your iPod nano.

- **Clock:** Opens the clock, stopwatch, and timer.

- **iTunes U:** Lists iTunes U collections synced from your iTunes library (it doesn't appear unless you synced iTunes U collections — see Chapter 6 about the iTunes U section of the iTunes Store).

- **Audiobooks:** Lists audiobooks synced from your iTunes library (it doesn't appear unless you synced audiobooks, which I describe in Chapter 8).

- **Voice Memo:** This appears if you have voice memo recordings on your iPod nano, or you've connected earbuds with a microphone. It opens the controls for recording and managing voice memos.

To find out how to record voice memos, visit this book's companion Web site (see the Introduction for details).

Tap an icon to open it. You can then tap choices in menus, and swipe sideways to move to the next or previous screen. Continually swiping right from any menu or choice (such as the Clock or the Now Playing screen) takes you to the first Home screen. You can also touch and hold anywhere on the screen (except on an icon or control) to return to the Home screen.

Touch and hold an icon to rearrange icons on Home screens — when the icons begin to jiggle, drag them into a new order and then press the Sleep/ Wake button to save the new arrangement.

The icons in the status bar at the top of the iPod nano screen tell you what's happening:

- The play icon (right-facing triangle) shows that a song, podcast, audio- book, or iTunes U episode is playing.

- The pause icon (two vertical bars) shows that a song, podcast, audio- book, or iTunes U episode is paused.

- The radio beacon icon shows that the radio is playing.

- The sneaker icon shows that the pedometer is turned on and counting steps.

- The battery icon shows the battery level or charging status.

You can rotate the iPod nano screen so it's easier to see when you clip it to your clothing or something. Place two fingers on the screen and rotate in the direction you want the screen to rotate, until the screen faces the way you want.

Thumbing Your iPod classic or iPod shuffle

The circular click wheel on iPod classic makes scrolling through an entire music collection quick and easy. With your finger or thumb, scroll clockwise on the wheel to scroll down a list or counterclockwise to scroll up. As you scroll, options on the menu are highlighted. Press the Select button at the center of the wheel to select whatever is highlighted in the menu display.

The main menu for iPod classic offers the following selections:

- **Music:** Select playlists, artists, albums, songs, genres, composers, or audio books. You can also select Cover Flow to browse by cover art or choose Search to search for a song or album title or artist (as I describe in Chapter 15).

- **Videos:** Select videos by video playlist or by type (movies, music videos, or TV shows), as I demonstrate in Chapter 16.

- **Photos:** Select photos by photo album or select all photos in the Photo Library (as I show in Chapter 17).

- **Podcasts:** Select podcasts by title and then select podcast episodes. Find out more in Chapter 16.

- **Extras:** View the clock, set time zones for clocks, set alarms and the sleep timer, use the stopwatch, and view contacts and your calendar, as I show in Chapter 4.

- **Settings:** Adjust menu settings, the backlight timer, the clicker, the date and time, and so on (see Chapter 4). You can also set the iPod's EQ (see Chapter 15).

- **Shuffle Songs:** Play songs from your music library in random order.

- **Now Playing:** This selection appears only when a song is playing — it takes you to the Now Playing display.

The iPod classic click wheel has pressure-sensitive buttons underneath the top, bottom, left, and right areas of the circular pad that tilt as you press them. These buttons perform various tasks for song, podcast, audio book, and video playback. Here they are, in clockwise order from the top:

- **Select:** Press the Select button at the center of the wheel to select whatever is highlighted in the menu display.

- **Menu:** Press once to go back to the previous menu. Each time you press, you go back to a previous menu until you reach the main menu.

- **Next/Fast Forward:** Press once to skip to the next item. Press and hold Next/Fast Forward to fast-forward.

- **Play/Pause:** Press to play the selected item. Press Play/Pause when the item is playing to pause the playback.

- **Previous/Rewind:** Press once to start an item over. Press twice to skip to the previous item (such as a song in an album). Press and hold to rewind.

The buttons and click wheel on the iPod classic can do more complex functions when used in combination:

- **Turn on the iPod.** Press any button.

- **Turn off the iPod.** Press and hold the Play/Pause button.

- **Reset the iPod.** You can reset the iPod if it gets hung up for some reason. (For example, it might get confused if you press the buttons too quickly.) See Chapter 21 for instructions on how to reset your iPod.

- **Change the volume.** While playing a song (the display reads Now Playing), adjust the volume by scrolling the click wheel. Clockwise turns the volume up; counterclockwise turns the volume down. A volume slider appears on the iPod display, indicating the volume level as you scroll.

- **Skip to any point in a song, video, audio book, or podcast.** While playing an item (the display reads Now Playing), press and hold the Select button until the progress bar appears to indicate where you are, and then scroll the click wheel to move to any point in the song. Scroll clockwise to move forward and counterclockwise to move backward. Press the Select button again to see lyrics for the song (if available). Find out more about using these controls in Chapter 16.The iPod shuffle offers the following buttons on its front side:

- **Plus (+) and minus (-) buttons (top and bottom):** Press plus (+) to increase the volume, or minus (-) to decrease the volume.

- **Next/Fast Forward (right side):** Press once to skip to the next item. Press and hold Next/Fast Forward to fast-forward.

- **Play/Pause (center):** Press to play the selected item. Press Play/Pause when the item is playing to pause the playback.

- **Previous/Rewind (left side):** Press once to start an item over. Press twice to skip to the previous item (such as a song in an album). Press and hold to rewind.

To discover advanced iPad, iPod, and iPhone techniques, such as customizing your menus, visit the Tips section of the author's Web site at www.tony bove.com.

Chapter 4

Choosing Settings for Your iPad, iPod, or iPhone

In This Chapter

▶ Setting the time, date, clock, alarm, timer, and stopwatch

▶ Changing the brightness, wallpaper, sound effects, and other settings

▶ Locking your iPad, iPod, or iPhone with a combination passcode

▶ Connecting your iPad, iPod touch, or iPhone with the Internet

*T*he iPad, iPod, and iPhone offer settings you can adjust for daily operation, in order to save battery power, change sound effects, lock it up for protection, connect to the Internet, determine your location, and so on. You can also use an iPod or iPhone as a timekeeper to help you keep track of your personal life — setting an alarm, using the stopwatch, and displaying clocks of different time zones for traveling. And if you worry that your iPad, iPod, or iPhone might fall into the wrong hands, consider setting a combination lock.

This chapter covers settings for all iPad, iPod, and iPhone models, including those that are specific to the iPad, iPod touch, and iPhone, such as setting the brightness of the display, choosing the *wallpaper* (a stylin' background when it's locked), knowing your location, and placing restrictions on downloading and playing content. You also find out how to connect an iPad, iPod touch, or iPhone to a Wi-Fi or cellular data service network for Internet access.

This chapter also shows you how to set the backlight, the click sound, and even the display font for an iPod. I also show you how to check your calendar and your contacts on an iPod classic or iPod nano.

There's No Time Like the Right Time

Your iPad, iPod, or iPhone may already be set to the correct time, date, and time zone, depending on where you bought it (except, of course, the iPod shuffle, which doesn't offer these features). The iPad and iPhone set the time and date automatically after you connect them to your computer, the Internet, or the cellular service. Other iPod models set the time and date when you set them up on your computer.

If you need to change the time zone, time, or date, you can do that yourself at any time (sorry for the pun). You can even set how the time appears in the status bar at the top of the screen.

On an iPad, iPod touch, or iPhone

To set the date and time for an iPad, iPod touch, or iPhone, follow these steps:

1. **Choose Settings⇨General⇨Date & Time from the Home screen.**

   On an iPod touch, the Date & Time menu appears with the 24-Hour Time, Time Zone, and Set Date & Time options. On an iPad or iPhone, you see the 24-Hour Time and Set Automatically options, with Set Automatically set to On.

2. **(Optional) If you'd rather see military time, tap the Off button for the 24-Hour Time option to turn it on.**

   With the 24-hour display, 11 p.m. is displayed as 23:00:00 and not 11:00:00. To turn off the 24-Hour Time option, tap the On button.

3. **iPad and iPhone only: Turn off the Set Automatically option in order to set the time and date manually.**

   The Set Automatically option is turned on by default for the iPad and iPhone. If this is okay with you, skip to Step 10 (you're done). If not, touch the On button to turn the Set Automatically option to Off, so that you can set the time and date manually. After turning off the Set Automatically option, two new options appear: Time Zone and Set Date & Time.

4. **Tap the Time Zone option to set the time zone.**

   The on-screen keyboard appears; see Chapter 3 for instructions on how to use it. Type the name of the city you're in (or, if you're in the middle of nowhere, the nearest big city) and then tap the Return button on the keyboard. Your iPad, iPod touch, or iPhone looks up the time zone for you.

5. **Tap the Date & Time button in the upper-left corner of Time Zone screen to finish and return to the Date & Time menu.**

6. **Tap the Set Date & Time option.**

   Tapping the Date field brings up a slot-machine-style date wheel — the Date & Time screen, which fills the entire iPod touch or iPhone screen, as shown in Figure 4-1. On an iPad, the Date & Time screen pops up underneath the Date & Time option.

7. **Slide your finger over the wheel to select the month, day, and year.**

   Slide until the selection you want appears in the gray window on the slot-machine wheel.

8. **Tap the Time field to bring up a time wheel.**

   Slide your finger over the wheel to set the hour, minutes, and AM or PM.

Figure 4-1: Slide the wheel of fortune to set the month, day, and year (left) and time (right).

9. **To finish, return to the Date & Time menu.**

   On an iPod touch or iPhone, tap the Date & Time button in the upper-left corner of the Date & Time screen (refer to Figure 4-1). On an iPad, tap outside the Date & Time pop-up screen.

10. **Tap the General button in the upper-left corner of the Date & Time menu to return to the General menu.**

On an iPod nano or iPod classic

To set the date and time on an iPod nano or iPod classic, follow these steps:

1. **Press the Menu button on an iPod classic for the main menu, or swipe an iPod nano to the right until you see the first Home screen.**

2. **Choose Settings⇨Date & Time on an iPod classic, or swipe left one Home screen, tap Settings⇨General, and then tap Date & Time.**

   The Date & Time menu appears, with selections for setting the date, time, time zone, and 24-hour clock. The Time in Title option appears for an iPod classic to display the time in the menu title bar; the Time On Wake and Clock Face options appear on an iPod nano.

3. **(Optional) Choose Time Zone.**

   Skip this step and the next step if the time zone already set is correct. After choosing Time Zone, a map appears on an iPod classic with a red dot set to your current time zone on the map. On an iPod nano, a list of countries appears.

4. **(Optional) Scroll to choose a time zone on an iPod classic, or tap a country and then a city (or state) on an iPod nano.**

   Skip this step if the time zone is correct; otherwise, on an iPod classic, move the red dot to another zone by scrolling the click wheel — the red dot jumps from one region of the map to another, and the time zone appears below the map. Press the Select button to choose a zone. On an iPod nano, tap a country in the country list, and then tap a city (or state) for its time zone. After selecting the time zone, the Date & Time menu appears again.

5. **Choose Date from the Date & Time menu.**

   The Date display appears with the month field highlighted on an iPod classic. On an iPod nano, the date appears as a slot machine with the month, the day, and the year cylinders you can scroll with your finger.

6. **Change the field setting on an iPod classic by scrolling the click wheel, or the slot machine on an iPod nano by scrolling the cylinders.**

   Scroll clockwise on an iPod classic to go forward and counterclockwise to go backward. Slide your finger up or down to scroll each cylinder on an iPod nano.

7. **Press the Select button on a iPod classic, or tap the Done button on an iPod nano, after scrolling to the appropriate setting.**

   On an iPod classic, the next date field is now highlighted. On an iPod nano, the Date & Time menu appears, and you can skip to Step 9.

8. **iPod classic only: Repeat Steps 6 and 7 for the day and year.**

   After you finish scrolling and then selecting the Year field, the Date & Time menu appears automatically.

9. **Choose Time from the Date & Time menu.**

   On an iPod classic, the Time display appears with the Hour field highlighted. On an iPod nano, the time appears as a slot machine with the hour, the minute, and the AM/PM cylinders you can scroll with your finger.

10. **Change the field setting on an iPod classic by scrolling the click wheel, or the slot machine on an iPod nano by scrolling the cylinders.**

    Scroll clockwise on an iPod classic to go forward and counterclockwise to go backward. Slide your finger up or down to scroll each cylinder on an iPod nano.

11. **Press the Select button on a iPod classic, or tap the Done button on an iPod nano, after scrolling to the appropriate setting.**

    On an iPod classic, the next date field is now highlighted. On an iPod nano, the Date & Time menu appears.

12. **iPod classic only: Repeat Steps 10 and 11 for minutes and AM/PM.**

    After finishing the AM/PM field, the Date & Time menu appears again.

To show military time (so that 11 p.m. is displayed as 23:00), choose the 24-Hour Clock option in the Date & Time menu on an iPod classic and press the Select button to turn it on. The option changes from 12-hour to 24-hour. To switch back, press the Select button again. On an iPod nano, tap the Off button next to the 24-Hour Clock option in the Date & Time menu to turn it on; tap On to turn it off.

 To display the time on the menu title bar of an iPod classic, scroll to the Time in Title option in the Date & Time menu and then press the Select button to turn this option on. To stop showing the time on the menu title bar, press the Select button again to toggle it to Off.

 You can display the iPod nano's Clock face every time you wake up the iPod nano — tap Off next to the Time On Wake option in the Date & Time menu to turn on the Clock display. When you wake your iPod nano, the Clock appears; swipe right to go back through the Now Playing screen to the Home screens. You can also switch the Clock's face from white to black — tap Clock Face in the Date & Time menu, and then tap White or Black.

Rock Around the Clocks

You can always know what time it is — just look at the time on the Home screen of an iPad, iPod touch, or iPhone, or on the main menu title bar of an iPod classic or the Clock face of an iPod nano. But you can also know what time it is in *other* time zones by displaying multiple clocks — using Apple's Clock app or a third-party app on an iPod touch or iPhone, or a third-party app (such as The World Clock) on an iPad, or Clocks in the Extras menu of an iPod classic. (Sorry, the iPod nano has only one clock, and iPod shuffles don't offer clocks.)

Alarms can be useful for waking up or just gearing up for an appointment; a stopwatch can help you exercise, and a timer can help you cook. You can set an alarm and run a stopwatch on an iPod classic, and use the Stopwatch and Timer features of Clock on an iPod nano (you can use the Timer as an alarm). On an iPhone or iPod touch, you can use the Clock app or a third-party app to do all three — alarm, stopwatch, and timer. On an iPad, you can use a third-party app, such as Tunemark Radio to set a radio station for your alarm, and Giant Timer to run a stopwatch.

Checking the time in Paris and Bangkok

With the Clock app on an iPod touch or iPhone, or the Clocks option in the Extras menu of an iPod classic, you can display clocks with different time zones, which is useful for traveling halfway around the world (or calling someone who lives halfway around the world).

To add clocks on an iPod touch or iPhone, tap the Clock icon on the Home screen and then tap the World Clock icon along the bottom of the display. It takes only two steps to add a clock:

1. **Touch the plus (+) button in the upper-right corner of the display.**

   The on-screen keyboard appears with a text entry field.

2. **Type a city name on the keyboard, and tap Return (or tap Cancel next to the text entry field to cancel).**

   The iPod touch or iPhone looks up the city's time zone to display the clock. (For details on how to use the on-screen keyboard, see Chapter 3.)

The initial clock and any clocks you add sport a daytime face (white background and black hands) from 6 a.m. to 5:59 p.m., as shown in Figure 4-2 (left side), and a nighttime face (black background with white hands) from 6 p.m. to 5:59 a.m. If you add more clocks than can fit on the screen, you can flick to scroll the screen to see them.

Figure 4-2:
Add more clocks for other time zones (left) and add an alarm (right).

To remove a clock, tap the Edit button in the upper-left corner of the display (refer to Figure 4-2, left side) and then tap the circled minus (–) button next to the clock to delete it.

To create more clocks, edit the clocks, or delete additional clocks with an iPod classic, follow these steps:

1. **Choose Extras➪Clocks from the main menu, and highlight a clock.**

   One or more clocks appear (depending on how many you have created), showing the present time and location. If you have more than one clock and you want to edit one of them, scroll the click wheel to highlight the clock you want to edit.

2. **Press the select button on the iPod to select the clock.**

   The Add and Edit options appear, along with a Delete option if you have more than one clock.

3. **Scroll the click wheel to select Add, Edit, or Cancel (or Delete if you have more than one clock already) and press the select button.**

   If you select Add or Edit, a list of geographical regions appears in alphabetical order, from Africa to South America. If you select Delete, the clock is deleted, and you can skip the following steps.

4. **Scroll the Region list, choose a region, and press the select button.**

   The City menu appears with a list of cities in the region in alphabetical order.

5. **Scroll the City list, choose a city, and then press the select button.**

   You return to the list of clocks. You now have added a new clock (or edited a clock if you selected the Edit option).

Getting alarmed

Time is on your side with your iPod or iPhone. On an iPod touch or iPhone, you can set *multiple* alarms to go off on different days and set a variety of tones and sounds for your alarms that play through its speaker. On an iPod classic, you can even assign a playlist to an alarm to play through external speakers or headphones.

To set alarms on an iPod touch or iPhone, follow these steps:

1. **Tap the Clock icon on the Home screen and tap the Alarm icon along the bottom of the display.**

2. **To add an alarm, tap the plus (+) button in the upper-right corner of the display.**

   The Add Alarm screen appears, as shown in Figure 4-2 (right side), with options and a slot-machine-style wheel for setting the alarm time.

3. **Slide your finger over the wheel to set the hour and minute, and a.m. or p.m.**

   Slide until the selection you want appears in the gray window on the slot-machine wheel.

   Now you can set some optional features, or you can skip to Step 8 and be done with it.

4. **(Optional) Tap the Repeat option to set the alarm to repeat on other days.**

   You can set it to repeat every Monday, Tuesday, Wednesday, Thursday, Friday, Saturday, and/or Sunday. (You can select multiple days.)

5. **(Optional) Tap the Sound option to select a sound for the alarm.**

   A list of sounds appears; touch a sound to set it for the alarm.

6. **(Optional) Tap the On button to turn off the Snooze option, or tap it again to turn it back on.**

   With the Snooze option, the iPod touch or iPhone displays a Snooze button when the alarm goes off, and you tap Snooze to stop the alarm and have it repeat in 10 minutes (so that you can snooze for 10 minutes).

7. **(Optional) Tap the Label option to enter a text label for the alarm.**

   The label helps you identify the alarm in the Alarm list.

8. **Tap the Save button in the upper-right corner to save the alarm.**

When the alarm goes off, your iPod touch or iPhone displays the message `You have an alarm` (and the date and time), along with the Snooze button if the Snooze option is turned on (refer to Step 6). Slide your finger to unlock the iPod touch or iPhone to stop the alarm's sound, or tap the Snooze button to stop the alarm temporarily and let it repeat 10 minutes later. (When it goes off again, slide the unlock slider to turn it off — don't tap the Snooze button again; you're late for work!)

To delete an alarm on an iPod touch or iPhone, tap the Clock icon on the Home screen and tap the Alarm icon along the bottom of the display. In the Alarm list, tap the alarm you want to trash and then tap the Edit button in the upper-left corner of the display. The alarm appears with a circled minus (–) button next to it; tap this button and then tap the red Delete button that appears to delete the alarm.

An iPod classic can do more than play a beep sound for the alarm — you can set a playlist, which you can hear by connecting the iPod to speakers or a stereo (or headphones, if you sleep with headphones on). To set an alarm on an iPod classic, follow these steps:

1. **Choose Extras⇨Alarms from the main menu.**

   The Create Alarm and Sleep Timer options appear on the Alarms main menu.

2. **Choose Create Alarm and press the Select button.**

   The Alarms submenu appears.

3. **Highlight the Alarm option and press the Select button to turn it on.**

4. **Choose Date from the Alarms submenu.**

   The Date display appears with the month field highlighted.

5. **Change the field setting by scrolling the click wheel.**

   Scroll clockwise to go forward and counterclockwise to go backward.

6. **Press the Select button after scrolling to the appropriate setting.**

   The next field is now highlighted.

7. **Repeat Steps 5 and 6 for the day and year.**

   After you finish scrolling and then selecting the Year field, the Alarms submenu appears automatically.

8. **Choose Time from the Alarms submenu.**

   The Time display appears with the Hour field highlighted.

9. **Change the field setting by scrolling the click wheel.**

   Scroll clockwise to go forward and counterclockwise to go backward.

10. **Press the Select button after scrolling to the appropriate setting.**

    The next field is now highlighted.

11. **Repeat Steps 9 and 10 for minutes and AM/PM.**

    After finishing the AM/PM field, the Alarms submenu appears again.

12. **Choose Repeat from the Alarms submenu and choose a repeat multiple.**

    You can choose to set the alarm to go off once, every day, weekdays, weekends, every week, every month, or every year. After choosing a repeat multiple, the Alarms submenu appears again.

13. **Choose Alert from the Alarms submenu and choose a tone or a playlist.**

    The Tones and Playlists options appear in the Alerts submenu. Choose Tones to select a beep, or set Tones to None (no sound) if you want the iPod to display the alarm without making a sound. Choose Playlists to select a playlist (or None for no sound). After choosing a tone or a playlist, the Alerts submenu appears again; press Menu to go back to Alarms.

14. **Choose Label from the Alarms submenu to set a label to identify this alarm.**

    You can set labels for your alarms so that you can identify them easily in the Alarms main menu. Select a label from the prepared list, which includes labels such as Wake Up, Work, Class, Appointment, and so on. After choosing a label, the Alarms submenu appears again.

15. **Press Menu to return to the Alarms main menu, which now includes your new alarm with its label in a list of alarms under the Sleep Timer heading.**

You can create as many alarms, at different dates and times, as you need. To delete an alarm, select the alarm from the list on the Alarms main menu. The Alarms submenu appears with a list of options. Choose Delete.

When the alarm goes off, your iPod classic displays an alarm message along with the Dismiss and Snooze buttons. Choose Dismiss or Snooze by scrolling the click wheel and then select it by pressing the Select button. Dismiss stops the alarm's sound, whereas Snooze stops the sound temporarily and repeats it 10 minutes later.

Timing your steps

You can set an hour-and-minute timer for anything — baking cookies, baking CDs, or baking in the sun on the beach. The timer built into the Clock app on your iPod touch or iPhone and the Clock feature of the iPod nano continues running even when playing music or running other apps. You might want to use a timer to see whether a set of activities — playing songs, playing videos, selecting from menus, and running apps — occurs within a specific time. (If you need to use seconds as well as minutes and hours, try using the stopwatch, which I describe in the next section.)

To use the timer on an iPod touch or iPhone, follow these steps:

1. **Tap the Clock icon on the Home screen.**

    The Clock display appears.

2. **Tap the Timer icon along the bottom of the Clock display.**

    The timer wheel for minutes and hours appears, along with the Start button.

3. **Flick the timer wheel to set the timer in hours and minutes.**

4. **Tap the When Timer Ends button and then tap a sound to use when the timer is up.**

5. **Tap Set in the upper-right corner of the display to set the sound (or Cancel in the upper-left corner to cancel the sound).**

6. **Tap Start to start the timer.**

The timer runs backward. You can touch Cancel to cancel the timer or wait until it runs out. When it runs out, the iPod touch or iPhone plays the sound (if a sound is set) and presents an OK button. Tap OK to stop the sound.

On an iPod nano, the Clock offers the Timer screen, which you can use to set an alarm, or to set a sleep timer that turns off the iPod nano automatically. To use it, follow these steps:

1. **Tap Clock on the iPod nano's fourth Home screen (you may have to swipe left to get to it).**

   The clock appears.

2. **Swipe left twice to see the Timer screen.**

   The Timer screen shows two cylinders you can flick to set the hours and minutes.

3. **Flick the hours and minutes cylinders to set the timer.**

   To use the Timer as an alarm, set it to the number of hours and minutes before the alarm should go off.

4. **(Optional) To set the alert sound, tap the "i" in the lower right corner of the Timer screen, tap a sound, and then tap Set.**

   A list of sound effects appears (by default, the sound is set to Marimba). Tap an alert sound, and then tap Set.

5. **Tap Start to turn the timer on.**

   The timer runs backward. You can touch Stop on the Timer screen to cancel the timer, or wait until it runs out. When it runs out, the iPod nano plays the sound over the headphones and presents an OK button.

6. **Tap OK to stop the sound and timer.**

Using the stopwatch

You can use a stopwatch with a lap timer for timing exercises, jogging, racing laps, seeing how long it takes the bus to travel across town, or finding out how long your friend takes to recognize the song you're playing. Whatever you want to measure with accurate time to the tenth of a second, the stopwatch is ready for you.

Even while you're running the stopwatch, you can still use the iPod or iPhone to play music, videos, audio books, and podcasts. When you play a video, the stopwatch continues to count as usual; when you switch back to the stopwatch display, the video automatically pauses.

To use the stopwatch on an iPod touch or iPhone, follow these steps:

1. **Tap the Clock icon on the Home screen, and tap the Stopwatch icon along the bottom of the display.**

   A stopwatch appears with Start and Reset buttons and 00:00.00 (minutes, seconds, and fractions of seconds) as the stopwatch counter.

2. **Tap the Start button to start counting.**

   The stopwatch starts counting immediately; the left button changes to Stop and the right button changes to Lap.

3. **(Optional) Tap the Lap button to mark each lap.**

   Tap the Lap button to record each lap. Repeat this step for each lap — Clock creates a list of lap times.

4. **Tap the Stop button to stop counting.**

   The counter stops counting. The left button changes to Start, and the right button changes to Reset. You can resume the count from where you left off by tapping Start, or you can start the count again from zero by tapping Reset.

To use the stopwatch on an iPod nano, follow these steps:

1. **Tap Clock on the iPod nano's fourth Home screen (you may have to swipe left to get to it).**

   The clock appears.

2. **Swipe left once to see the Stopwatch screen.**

   The Stopwatch screen shows zero time and Start and Reset buttons.

3. **Tap Start to start the stopwatch.**

The stopwatch starts counting immediately; the Start button changes to Stop and the Reset button changes to Lap. To record lap times, tap Lap after each lap. To pause the stopwatch, tap Stop. Tap Start to resume.

To reset the stopwatch, tap Reset when the stopwatch is paused. However, you may want to review lap times before you start a new session — tapping Reset deletes the information. To review lap times first, tap the icon (with two horizontal bars) next to the time in the status bar. The last session's statistics appear. You can then tap Reset to start a new session.

To use the stopwatch on an iPod classic, follow these steps:

1. **Choose Extras➪Stopwatch from the main menu.**

   A stopwatch appears with the Play/Pause icon.

2. **Press the Select button to start counting.**

   The stopwatch starts counting immediately.

3. **(Optional) Press the Select button to mark each lap.**

   Press the Select button to record the current lap time while counting resumes accurately for the next lap. Repeat this step for each lap.

4. **Press the Play/Pause button to stop counting, and then press the Menu button.**

   The Stopwatch menu appears. The menu now includes the Current Log option to show the lap timings for the stopwatch session. Also included are previous stopwatch session logs. The iPod saves the stopwatch results in a session log for convenience, so you don't have to write them down.

5. **Select Resume to resume counting or New Timer to start a new stopwatch session.**

   You can resume the stopwatch session from where you left off, or you can start a new stopwatch session.

6. **(Optional) Read your stopwatch logs by choosing Current Log or the date of a previous log on the Stopwatch menu.**

7. **(Optional) Delete your stopwatch logs by choosing Clear Logs on the Stopwatch menu.**

Setting the sleep timer

As you can with a clock radio sleep timer, you can set your iPod or iPhone to play music or videos for a while before going to sleep.

To set the timer on the iPhone or iPod touch as a sleep timer, first follow the instructions in the section "Timing your steps" earlier in this chapter. Then touch the When Timer Ends button and touch Sleep iPod at the top of the list to put the iPod touch or iPhone to sleep when the timer ends. Touch Set in the upper-right corner of the display to set the Sleep iPod option (or Cancel in the upper-left corner to cancel). Finally, touch Start to start the timer. You can then play music or videos until the timer ends and the iPod touch or iPhone automatically goes to sleep.

You can use the Timer on an iPod nano to set a sleep timer. Flick to set the hours and minutes as I describe in "Timing your steps" earlier in this chapter, and then tap the "i" in the lower right corner of the Timer screen. Tap Sleep iPod, and then tap Set. Tap Start when you're ready to start the timer.

To set the sleep timer on an iPod classic, choose Extras from the main menu; then choose Alarms⇨Sleep Timer. A list of intervals appears, from 0 (Off) to 120 minutes (2 hours). You can select a time amount or the Off setting (at the top of the list) to turn off the sleep timer. After the iPod shuts itself off or you turn it off, the preference for the Sleep Timer is reset to the default status, Off.

Using the iPod nano pedometer

A pedometer counts each step you take by detecting the motion, measuring your progress and motivating you to exercise more. The iPod nano offers a pedometer that uses the built-in accelerometer to keep track of your steps. For more accurate results, keep the iPod nano in your pocket or in the iPod nano Armband while using the pedometer. Even so, pedometers also record movements other than walking, such as tying your shoes or shakin' your booty, so don't expect complete accuracy.

To use the pedometer for the first time, follow these steps:

1. **Tap Fitness on the fourth Home screen, and then tap Pedometer.**

   Before using the pedometer, you need to set it to your correct weight. The Choose Weight screen appears with the weight in three cylinders (units, decimals, and either pounds or kilograms).

2. **Set your correct weight and tap Done.**

   You can flick the cylinders to set the weight, and then tap Done. The Pedometer screen appears with zero steps and a Start button.

3. **Tap Start to start the pedometer.**

   You can leave it on so that the pedometer counts all the steps you take all the time. To stop it, tap Stop on the Pedometer screen.

The pedometer icon appears in the status bar to indicate that it's on. It runs in the background until you stop it, so you can listen to music and walk about while it counts your steps. After midnight, any steps you take are automatically tracked for the new day, so you can leave the pedometer on all the time and get an accurate daily count.

To view your pedometer history, tap Fitness on the fourth Home screen, and then tap History. You can then tap Personal Bests or Workout Totals. Sessions listed by date show details of start and stop times, distance, steps, and calories burned for each session.

You can also set a daily step goal. Tap Settings on the second Home screen, and then tap Pedometer. Tap Daily Step Goal, and then tap the Off button to turn it on. A screen appears with cylinders for the number of steps, which you can flick to set. Tap Done to set the goal.

If your weight changes, you can update the pedometer in your iPod nano with your new weight: Tap Settings on the second Home screen, and then tap Pedometer. Tap Weight, and then set your weight as I describe above in Step 2.

Setting the Passcode for Your Lock

You can set a passcode for the iPad, iPod touch, iPod classic, or iPhone to lock it and thereby prevent others from navigating through your content (not available for the iPod nano or iPod shuffle). Setting a passcode also turns on data protection for an iPad, iPod touch, iPhone 3GS, or iPhone 4, which uses your passcode as the key for encrypting mail messages and their attachments. (Data protection may also be used by some apps.) *Note:* The lockup works only when your iPad, iPod, or iPhone is not attached to a computer.

An iPad, iPod touch, or iPhone locks itself when it goes to sleep, and as you already know, you have to slide your finger over the unlock message to wake it up. But you can also set this passcode to keep the iPad, iPod touch, or iPhone protected from access after waking up — so that you need to supply the passcode.

If you're playing music when your iPod classic is locked, the music continues playing — and you can even use the Play/Pause button to pause and resume playback — but if you set a passcode, no one can navigate the iPod classic or even change the volume without providing the passcode.

To conserve power, you can force your iPad, iPod touch, or iPhone to go to sleep by pressing the Sleep/Wake button — but you still need the passcode (if you set one) to use it after waking it up. Similarly, you can force an iPod classic to go to sleep by pressing the Play/Pause button, but you still need the passcode to unlock it. When the iPad, iPod, or iPhone awakens, it remembers everything — including its passcode.

Don't bother to call Apple to see whether the company can unlock your iPad, iPod, or iPhone for you. If you can't enter the correct passcode, or attach it to the computer you set it up on, your only recourse is to restore the iPad, iPod, or iPhone to its factory conditions — see Chapter 21.

To set a passcode for your iPad, iPhone, or iPod touch, follow these steps:

1. Choose Settings⇨General⇨Passcode Lock from the Home screen.

The Passcode Lock screen appears with the Simple Passcode and Turn Passcode On options.

2. **To use a four-number passcode, leave the Simple Passcode option turned on; if you want to use a more complex alphanumeric password as a passcode, tap On for Simple Passcode to turn it Off.**

3. **Tap Turn Passcode On at the top and enter the passcode.**

   If you left the Simple Passcode option turned on in Step 2, you see a calculator-style keypad — enter a four-number passcode by touching numbers in the keypad. If you turned off the Simple Passcode option in Step 2, you see a full keyboard — enter an alphanumeric password as a passcode using the keyboard. If you change your mind, tap the Cancel button to cancel the operation.

4. **Enter the same passcode again to confirm the passcode.**

   After reentering the passcode, the Passcode Lock screen appears with the Turn Passcode Off, Change Passcode, Require Passcode, Voice Dial (iPhone only), and Erase Data options.

5. **Choose Passcode options.**

   • You can Turn Passcode Off to turn it off, or Change Passcode to change it. You need to enter the passcode to do either.

   • You can set the Require Passcode option to Immediately, After 1 Minute, After 5 Minutes, After 15 Minutes, After 1 Hour, or After 4 Hours.

   • You can turn Voice Dial on or off for an iPhone. Voice Dial is normally on; as a security measure you may want to turn it off, so that the iPhone must be unlocked with the passcode first.

   • You can turn On or Off the Erase Data option. This option erases all the information and content on the iPad, iPod touch, or iPhone after 10 successive failed passcode attempts.

6. **When you're done, tap General to return to the General menu.**

The passcode screen appears immediately after you slide the Slide to unlock message. After correctly entering the passcode, the iPad, iPod touch, or iPhone unlocks.

To unlock a passcode-locked iPad, iPod touch, or iPhone, you must enter the same passcode, or restore the iPad, iPod touch, or iPhone to its original factory settings, as I describe in Chapter 21. Restoring erases everything — this is, of course, a measure of last resort, and should only be performed on the computer you synced it with, so that you resync it to your iTunes library.

To set a passcode (combination lock) for your iPod classic, follow these steps:

1. **Choose Extras⇨Screen Lock⇨Lock.**

   The Screen Lock icon appears with your combination lock set to zeros.

2. **Select the first number of the passcode by scrolling the click wheel.**

   While you scroll with your iPod, the first digit of the passcode changes. You can also press the Previous/Rewind or Next/Fast Forward button to scroll through numbers.

3. **Press the Select button to pick a number.**

   This sets your choice for the first number and moves on to the next number of the passcode. Repeat this step for each number of the passcode. When you pick the last number, the message `Confirm Combination` appears.

4. **Confirm the passcode.**

   Repeat Steps 2 and 3 for each number of the passcode to confirm it. After confirming, your iPod is locked.

On a locked iPod classic, the lock icon appears if you press any key. To unlock the iPod after locking it, press any button and then repeat Steps 2 and 3 to enter each number of the passcode. After correctly entering the passcode, the iPod classic unlocks and returns to the last viewed screen.

To reset the passcode, first unlock the iPod, and then choose Extras⇨Screen Lock⇨Reset Combination, and then repeat Steps 2 through 4. To turn off the lock, reset the combination to all zeroes.

If you don't know the passcode, attach the iPod classic to the computer you used to set it up and synchronize it with iTunes. When you disconnect it after synchronizing with iTunes, the iPod classic is no longer locked with a passcode.

Getting Personal

Your future might be so bright that you gotta wear shades, but your iPad, iPod, or iPhone display might not be bright enough. You can change the timer for the backlight on an iPod classic and set the brightness of the display on all models, as well as set the contrast of the black-and-white displays of older models.

You have plenty of other settings to consider, in order to give your iPad, iPod touch, or iPhone a personal touch. Besides wallpapering the display of your iPad, iPod touch, or iPhone, you can set keyboard clicks and alert sounds to indicate that e-mail has arrived, that something in your calendar needs attention, and so on. You can also wallpaper your iPod nano.

If you share your iPad, iPod touch, or iPhone with children or adults who act like children, you may want to place restrictions that prevent explicit music from the iTunes Store from being displayed in playlists, prevent the use of apps such as YouTube, or stop any access to the iTunes Store or App Store. Your iPad, iPod touch, or iPhone can let you do that, too.

Adjusting the backlight of your iPod classic

The iPod classic and older iPods use a display backlight that turns on when you press a button or use the click wheel and then turns off after a short amount of time. You can set the backlight on the iPod classic to remain on for a certain interval of time. From the main menu, choose Settings⇨Backlight. A menu appears, giving you the options of 2 seconds, 5 seconds, 10 seconds, 15 seconds, 20 seconds, 30 seconds, and Always On. Select one by scrolling to highlight the selection and then press the Select button.

Using the backlight drains an iPod battery; the longer you set the interval, the more frequently you need to recharge the battery.

To set the backlight to *always* be on, choose Always On. If you want the backlight to *always* be off, choose Always Off. If you set it to always be off, the backlight doesn't turn on automatically when you press any button or use the click wheel — and the display is much darker, of course.

Brightening and wallpapering

To adjust the brightness of the display for an iPod classic, choose Settings⇨ Brightness. The Brightness screen appears with a slider that shows the brightness setting, which ranges from low (a quarter-moon icon) to high (a bright sun icon). Scroll clockwise to increase the brightness (toward the bright sun) and counterclockwise to decrease the brightness (toward the moon).

To adjust the brightness of an iPad, iPod touch, or iPhone, first tap the Settings icon on the Home screen and then tap Brightness on the Settings screen of an iPod touch or iPhone, or Brightness & Wallpaper on an iPad. To adjust the brightness on an iPod nano, tap Settings⇨General⇨Brightness from the second Home screen.

The Brightness screen appears with a slider that shows the brightness setting, which ranges from low (a dim sun icon) to high (a bright sun icon). Slide the brightness slider's knob with your finger to the right to increase the brightness (toward the bright sun) and to the left to decrease the brightness (toward the dim sun). Of course, the brighter the screen, the more power is drawn from the battery.

On an iPod nano's Brightness screen, tap Restore to Default to set the brightness back to its default setting (a bit dimmer than half).

The Brightness screen on an iPad, iPod touch, or iPhone includes the Auto-Brightness option, which helps you conserve battery power in light conditions that don't require a bright display. It uses a built-in ambient light sensor above the earpiece (above the touch screen on the front of the iPad, iPod touch, or iPhone display) to adjust the brightness automatically for current light conditions. Auto-Brightness makes the display appear relatively bright depending on your Brightness setting — if you set it to be dimmer than normal, Auto-Brightness adjusts it to current light settings to be dimmer than normal. The Auto-Brightness option is usually turned on, but you can touch the On button to turn it to Off if you want.

While you're at it, why not wallpaper your display? You can make your iPad, iPod touch, or iPhone display different stylish wallpaper backgrounds for your lock screen and Home screen — one wallpaper image appears on the lock screen and another appears behind the icons on your Home screens (or you can use the same image for both). You can also put up photos or other images from your photo library as your wallpaper choices. On an iPod nano you can set a colorful pattern as your wallpaper on the Home screens.

To set the wallpaper on an iPod touch or iPhone, choose Settings⇨Wallpaper from the Home screen; on an iPad, choose Settings⇨Brightness & Wallpaper from the Home screen. You can then tap the lock screen and Home screen thumbnail that appears to show a menu of wallpaper options.

On the wallpaper options menu, you can choose from among stylish built-in wallpaper images by tapping the Wallpaper button at the top. You can also choose from the photo library you synchronized with your iPad, iPod touch, or iPhone by tapping Photo Library or a photo album, or you can choose photos saved on your iPad by tapping Saved Photos, and on your iPod touch or iPhone by tapping Camera Roll. (For more about photos, see Chapter 17.)

On an iPod touch or iPhone, tap a thumbnail to select an image for your wallpaper or tap the Wallpaper button in the upper-left corner to return to the Wallpaper menu. After tapping a thumbnail, your iPod touch or iPhone displays the Move and Scale screen, which lets you optionally pan the image by dragging your finger, and optionally zoom in or out of the image by pinching and unpinching with your fingers. Tap the Set Wallpaper button to set the image as your wallpaper or tap Cancel to cancel.

On an iPad, tap a thumbnail to select the image for your wallpaper, or tap the Back button to the Wallpaper menu. After tapping a thumbnail, the image appears along with the Set Lock Screen, Set Home Screen, Set Both, and Cancel buttons along the top. Tap Set Lock Screen to set the image for the lock screen only, or Set Home Screen to set it for the Home screen only, or Set Both to set the image to both at once.

Sound effects and ringtones

Don't want to hear the iPad, iPod touch, or iPhone keyboard click while you type, or hear the snap noise as you swipe your finger over the "unlock" message? You can set which events can trigger sound effects as well as the volume of the sound effect. Choose Settings➪ Sounds from the iPod touch or iPhone Home screen, or Settings➪General➪Sounds from the iPad Home screen. You can then turn the sounds for new mail, sent mail, calendar alerts, locking and unlocking, and using the on-screen keyboard. Tap On to turn off the sound for each option (or vice versa).

The click wheel of an iPod classic makes a clicking sound you can hear through its tiny speaker. You can turn it off by choosing Settings from the main menu, and then selrecting Clicker once so that Off appears next to it on the right. Selecting Clicker again turns it back on.

When someone calls your iPod touch or iPhone with FaceTime (see Chapter 20 for details), it plays a ringtone just like a cell phone.

You can decide what the ringtone sound should be by choosing a built-in ring-tone, or downloading ringtones based on popular songs from the iTunes Store, or making them yourself using a sound-editing program such as GarageBand on a Mac. After downloading ringtones from the iTunes Store, or importing the ringtones to the Library section of the iTunes source pane, you can sync the ringtones with your iPod touch or iPhone as I show in Chapter 8.

You can also assign individual ringtones to people in your Contacts list, so that you can tell by the ringtone who's calling — see Chapter 20 for details.

To set the ringtone, choose Settings➪Sounds from the iPod touch or iPhone Home screen, and tap Ringtone. You can then select a built-in ringtone, or if you synced ringtones from iTunes, you can select a synced ringtone.

Drag the volume slider above the Ringtones setting to adjust the volume of the ringtone and alert sounds. If you turn on the Change with Buttons option under the volume slider on an iPod touch, you can also use the volume buttons on the side of the iPod touch to set and change the volume.

Location, location, location

Perhaps nothing is more personal than your physical location. With Location Services on your iPad, iPod touch, or iPhone, apps like Maps (and lots of third-party apps like Google Earth, SkyOrb, Foursquare, Loopt, and various travel apps) can grab this physical location information and use it to help you find things closer to you. For example, the Maps app can find your location on the map, which is very useful for getting directions (see Chapter 20).

An iPad, iPod touch, or iPhone can find itself in the physical world with varying precision depending on the model. The iPad 3G, iPhone 3G, iPhone 3GS, and iPhone 4 offer the Global Positioning System (GPS), which uses orbiting satellites to pinpoint their locations in a range of 10 to 100 meters. The earlier-model iPhone, the iPad Wi-Fi, and the iPod touch can triangulate their locations with scary precision as well, even though these models don't offer GPS — they leverage the most extensive Wi-Fi reference database in the world. You need to be connected to Wi-Fi to use Location Services on an iPad Wi-Fi or iPod touch (see the section "Going Online with your iPad, iPod touch, or iPhone," later in this chapter).

You can turn Location Services on or off by choosing Settings⇨General⇨ Location Services from the Home screen, and then tapping the Off button for Location Services at the top of the screen to turn it on, or the On button to turn it off.

The Location Services setting at the top of the screen turns on the services for all apps. You can also decide which apps can use Location Services. Each app you used that requested your location within the last 24 hours appears in the Location Services screen, showing whether Location Services has been turned on or off for that app. Tap the On button for each app to turn it off for that app.

 Turn Location Services off if you are not using apps that make use of it, to conserve battery power. After turning it off, your iPad, iPod touch, or iPhone prompts you to turn it back on if you run an app that makes use of Location Services (such as Maps).

Setting restrictions

Are you lending your iPad, iPod touch, or iPhone to a youngster (or an adult acting like one)? You may want to set restrictions that

- ✔ Prevent access to explicit music, podcasts, and videos according to ratings.
- ✔ Prevent the use of apps such as YouTube and Safari.
- ✔ Prevent installation of new apps.

✔ Restrict use of the Camera app (see Chapter 17 about taking pictures or capturing video on an iPod touch or iPhone).

✔ Restrict other features, such as FaceTime on a fourth-generation iPod touch or iPhone 4.

✔ Disallow in-app purchases.

✔ Stop access to the iTunes Store or App Store.

Choose Settings⇨General from the Home screen and then tap Restrictions to see the Restrictions screen. Tap Enable Restrictions and then set up a restrictions passcode (which is separate from your Passcode Lock passcode). Enter a four-number passcode by touching numbers on the calculator-style keypad. (If you change your mind, tap the Cancel button to cancel the operation.) Then enter the same passcode number again to confirm the passcode, and the restrictions are enabled and appear ready for you to change.

Set the restrictions you want by tapping each control's On switch to turn it off. By default, all controls are on, which means that usage is allowed (not restricted). Turn off a control to restrict its use.

If you restrict access to Safari, YouTube, the Camera, the iTunes Store, and/ or the App Store (for installing apps), those icons are removed from the Home screen so that they can't be accessed. If you turn off Location, location data is no longer provided to applications. Restricted content does not appear when accessing the iTunes Store. To access the icons and the restricted content, you need to turn off the restrictions first (or turn off all restrictions).

You can turn In-app Purchases On or Off, choose a ratings system based on your country, and set restrictions based on the chosen ratings system for music, podcasts, movies, TV shows, and apps. For example, tap Music & Podcasts and turn Explicit On (to allow explicit material) or Off (to keep it clean). To allow movies rated PG-13 and lower (PG, G) but not R or NC-17, tap Movies and then tap PG-13 to set the limit. For TV shows, you can set the limit based on their ratings (TV-G, TV-MA, and so on).

For Apps, you can set the age limit, such as 4+ (essentially anyone), 9+ (must be at least nine), 12+ (must be 12 or older), and 17+ (must be 17 or older).

To turn off all restrictions, choose Settings⇨General⇨Restrictions and then enter the passcode. Tap Disable Restrictions and then reenter the passcode. Your iPad, iPod touch, or iPhone is now free.

Setting notifications

The Notifications setting appears in the Settings menu of your iPad, iPod touch, or iPhone if you've installed an app that uses the Apple Push Notification service. Push notifications are used by apps to let you know about new information, such as messages, even when the app isn't running (see Chapter 19 for more about the Push feature).

Notifications differ depending on the app — some notify you with alerts (text or sound), and some also display a numbed badge on the app icon (for example, to show that you have messages on Facebook or MySpace). You can control what type of notification you receive from each app, and you can also turn notifications off or on.

It's a good idea to turn notifications completely off if you are trying to conserve battery life.

To turn notifications on or off, choose Settings⇨Notifications to see the Notifications screen. Tap On next to Notifications to turn it off, or tap Off to turn it back on. You can also specify the type of notification for each app: select the app, and then tap the options on or off for alerts, sounds, or icon badges.

Going Online with your iPad, iPod touch, or iPhone

Going online means connecting to the Internet — using either a Wi-Fi network, or the Edge or 3G data services offered by AT&T (the Edge data service from AT&T is available on all iPhones and the iPad 3G, and 3G is available on the iPad 3G, iPhone 3G, iPhone 3GS, and iPhone 4). To surf the Web, check e-mail, or use the iTunes Store or App Store (or any other app that uses the Internet) on your iPad, iPod touch, or iPhone — or to use Location Services on your iPad Wi-Fi, iPod touch, or earlier-model iPhone — you must first connect to the Internet.

An iPad, iPod touch, or iPhone can join Wi-Fi networks at home, at work, or at Wi-Fi hotspots around the world. Although some public Wi-Fi networks are free, others require logging in first, and still others require logging in and supplying a credit card number. Still others are detected but locked — if you select a locked network, a dialog appears asking for a password.

If you don't have Wi-Fi at home but you do have a broadband Internet connection (such as cable or DSL), I recommend buying an AirPort Express or AirPort Extreme, available in the Apple Store — you can then connect your Internet connection to the AirPort to extend Internet access over Wi-Fi throughout your home.

If you use an iPad 3G or iPhone, AT&T offers wireless data services for connecting to the Internet that are either included as part of your iPhone/AT&T bill or billed separately (as with an iPad 3G). Although all iPhone models and the iPad 3G can use the Edge data service, the faster 3G service is also available for the iPad 3G, iPhone 3G, iPhone 3GS, and iPhone 4.

Turning Wi-Fi on or off

To turn Wi-Fi on, choose Settings➪Wi-Fi from the Home screen to display the Wi-Fi Networks screen. Tap the Off button for the Wi-Fi setting to turn it on (tap it again to turn it off).

When Wi-Fi is turned on, your iPad, iPod touch, or iPhone detects and automatically acquires a Wi-Fi signal you've used before, or it can detect one or more signals in the area and present them in a list for you to choose. The list of available Wi-Fi networks appears below the Wi-Fi setting, as shown in Figure 4-3.

Figure 4-3:
Enable Wi-Fi and then choose a Wi-Fi network.

If your iPad, iPod touch, or iPhone isn't already connected to Wi-Fi, it's set by default to look for networks and ask whether you want to join them whenever you use something that requires the network (such as Safari, YouTube, Mail, and so on). You can stop your iPad, iPod touch, or iPhone from looking and asking: Scroll down to the end of the list of Wi-Fi networks on the Wi-Fi Networks screen and then tap the On button for the Ask to Join Networks option to turn it off. You can still join networks manually, but you won't be interrupted with requests to join networks.

You should turn off Wi-Fi if you're not using it to save battery power and to keep your iPhone or iPod touch from automatically receiving e-mail (you can also change your Push settings to stop automatic e-mail — see Chapter 19). Choose Settings➪Wi-Fi and then tap the On button for the Wi-Fi setting to turn it off.

Choosing a Wi-Fi network

You can scroll the list of networks on the Wi-Fi Networks screen to choose one. You can scroll quickly by flicking your finger or scroll slowly by dragging up or down, but however you scroll, you choose a Wi-Fi network by tapping its name. Networks are named by their administrators. (If you set up your own home Wi-Fi, you get to name yours whatever you want.)

When connected to a Wi-Fi network, your iPad, iPod touch, or iPhone displays the Wi-Fi icon in the status bar at the top of the display. This also indicates the connection strength — the more arcs you see in the icon, the stronger the connection.

If a Lock icon appears next to the Wi-Fi network name, it means that the network is locked and you need a password. When you select a locked network, the iPad, iPod touch, or iPhone displays an Enter Password screen and the on-screen keyboard. Tap out the password using the keyboard. (For details on how to use the on-screen keyboard, see Chapter 3.) Tap Join to join the network or tap Cancel in the upper-right corner to cancel joining.

To join a Wi-Fi network that requires either a credit card or an account for you to log into, select the network and then use Safari to open the network's Web page. (For more on using Safari, see Chapter 18.) The first Web page you see is typically the login page for the service (for example, a commercial Wi-Fi service or a hotel service). Follow the instructions in Chapter 18 for interacting with Web pages and entering information.

Your iPad, iPod touch, or iPhone remembers most Wi-Fi connections and their passwords, and automatically uses one when it detects it within your range. If you've used multiple Wi-Fi networks in the same location, it picks the last one you used.

You can also stop your iPad, iPod touch, or iPhone from automatically joining a Wi-Fi network — such as a paid or closed Wi-Fi service that somehow got hold of your device and won't let you move on to other Web pages without typing a password. See Chapter 22 for this tip.

Using 3G on an iPad 3G, iPhone 3G, iPhone 3GS, or iPhone 4

You can usually connect your iPhone to the Internet using the relatively slow Edge cellular data service from AT&T. In addition, you can use the faster 3G cellular data service on an iPad 3G, iPhone 3G, iPhone 3GS, and iPhone 4. You don't have to log in; the services are active unless you turn them off.

You need to set up cellular data service on an iPad 3G before using it. Choose Settings⇨Cellular Data, and then follow the instructions to type in your user information, select a plan, and enter your credit card information. To monitor your data usage, choose Settings⇨Cellular Data and tap View Account. 3G is available in most areas, and the slower Edge service is typically available if 3G is not. When active, you see the E icon (signifying Edge) or the 3G icon in the status bar next to AT&T.

You may want to turn 3G cellular services off on your iPhone 3G, iPhone 3GS, or iPhone 4, or all cellular services on your iPad 3G, to save battery power, especially when you're connected through Wi-Fi because you don't need both at the same time. On an iPhone 3G, 3GS, or 4, choose Settings⇨General⇨Network from the Home screen, and at the top of the Network screen, touch On for the Enable 3G option to turn it Off. On an iPad 3G, choose Settings⇨Cellular Data, and then touch On for the Cellular Data option to turn it Off. Don't forget to turn it back On when you need cellular data service.

Chapter 5

Going Mobile

*P*ut on "Eight Miles High" by the Byrds while cruising in a plane at 40,000 feet. Watch the "Lust for Life" music video by Iggy Pop on a bus heading out of Detroit. Ride the rails listening to "All Aboard" by Muddy Waters, followed by "Peavine" by John Lee Hooker. Or cruise on the autobahn in Germany with Kraftwerk. When you go mobile with your iPad, iPod, or iPhone, it provides high-quality sound and excellent picture quality no matter how turbulent the environment.

If you can't plug your iPad, iPod, or iPhone into a power source while it's playing, you can use the battery for quite a while before having to recharge. You can find all the accessories that you need to travel with an iPad, iPod, or iPhone in the Apple Store at www.apple.com. This chapter is all about using your iPad, iPod, or iPhone on the road with accessories.

Connecting Headphones and Portable Speakers

Apple designed the iPad, iPod, and iPhone to provide excellent sound through headphones or earphones. From the headphone/line-out connection, though, the iPad, iPod, or iPhone can also play sound through portable speaker systems. The speaker systems must be self-powered or able to work with very little power (just like headphones and earphones do) and allow audio to be input via a 3.5mm, stereo mini-plug connection.

Looking at specs, you notice that iPad, iPod, and iPhone models include a small amplifier that's plenty powerful enough to deliver audio through the headphone/line-out connection. All current models, including the iPod shuffle, have a frequency response of 20 to 20,000 Hz (hertz), which provides distortion-free sound at the lowest or highest pitches. (In this case, hertz has nothing to do with rental cars. A *hertz* is a unit of frequency equal to one cycle per second.) At pitches that produce frequencies of 20 cycles per second or 20,000 cycles per second (and everything in between), the iPad, iPod, or iPhone responds with distortion-free sound. (The iPad includes built-in stereo speakers that produce excellent sound without the need for external speakers.)

Portable speaker systems typically include built-in amplifiers and a volume control, and they usually offer a stereo mini-plug that you can attach directly to the iPad, iPod, or iPhone headphone/line-out connection or to a dock headphone/line-out connection. To place the external speakers farther away from the iPad, iPod, or iPhone, use a stereo mini-plug extension cable, which is available at most consumer electronics stores. These cables have a stereo mini-plug on one end and a stereo mini-socket on the other.

Some portable speaker systems, such as the DLO Portable Speakers (www. dlo.com) or the Bose SoundDock Portable digital music system (www.bose. com, see Figure 5-1), provide a convenient dock connection for playing audio.

Figure 5-1:
The Bose SoundDock Portable speaker system.

To get optimal sound quality when using a portable speaker system equipped with volume controls, set your iPad, iPod, or iPhone volume to about half or three-quarters, and then raise or lower the volume of your speaker system.

When you travel, take an extra pair of headphones (or earphones) and a splitter cable, which is available in any consumer electronics store (for example, the Monster iSplitter is available in the Apple Store). That way, you can share music from one device with someone on the road.

For a very portable stereo system that fits in your pocket, try the Motorola EQ5 Wireless Travel Stereo Speaker (`http://direct.motorola.com/hellomoto/EQ5/`). It uses Bluetooth to connect to your iPad, iPod touch, or iPhone. And for a portable stereo system that offers big sound on a rechargeable battery and is perfect for environments like the beach or a boat, check out the Sonic Impact i-P23 speaker system (available from Amazon or Google Products). It includes universal adapters for all dockable iPod and iPhone models and an audio input connection for connecting your computer or an audio player. The double-duty case is a durable cover that acts as a speaker cabinet for both speakers to give the speakers better bass response.

Playing Car Tunes

I always wanted to be able to fill up a car with music just as easily as filling it up with fuel without having to carry dozens of cassettes or CDs. With an iPad, iPod, or iPhone, an auto-charger to save on battery power, and a way to connect the iPad, iPod, or iPhone to your car's stereo system, you're ready to pump music. (Start your engine and queue up "Getting in Tune" and then "Going Mobile" by The Who.) You can even go one step further and get a new BMW, Toyota, or similarly equipped car that offers an iPod or iPhone dock cable installed and integrated into the car's stereo system so that you can control the iPod or iPhone from your car stereo — including handy controls on the steering wheel.

Here are your options when it comes to playing your iPad, iPod, or iPhone music through a car stereo:

- **Use your car's AUX mini-port (if you have one).** Many cars offer AUX (auxiliary) line-in audio input to play an auxiliary device through the car's stereo system. You can connect a mini-plug cable directly to the iPad, iPod, or iPhone headphone connection and then to the AUX input. You can then get an iPad, iPod, or iPhone power adapter for your car's lighter socket, or plug directly into a 110-volt socket if your vehicle offers one. This method works great with rental cars that are supplied with AUX mini-ports.

- **Install an iPod-ready or iPhone-ready stereo.** BMW, Mercedes-Benz, Toyota, Honda, and many other auto companies offer car stereo options and models that are iPod-ready or iPhone-ready. You connect your iPod or iPhone through a dock connection, and you can control the iPod or iPhone from your car stereo's head unit. This method offers the best sound quality.

- **Use your car's cassette player.** If your car has a cassette player, use a standard cassette adapter and an iPad, iPod, or iPhone power adapter for your car's lighter socket. For a semi-permanent installation, you can add a car mount to keep your iPad, iPod, or iPhone secure. Cassette adapters offer medium quality that's usually better than wireless adapters.

✔ **Use your radio and a wireless adapter.** Use a wireless adapter that plays your iPad, iPod, or iPhone as if it were a station on your FM radio dial. Some car mounts offer built-in wireless adapters. This might be your only inexpensive choice if you don't have a cassette deck. *Note:* Wireless adapters might not work well in cities where FM stations crowd the radio dial. Also, when picking out an FM transmitter for an iPad, make sure that it meets the iPad's higher 10w power requirement.

✔ **Install an audio and power connection.** Custom-install an interface for your car stereo that offers high-quality, line-in audio input and power. Some custom interfaces enable you to control the iPod or iPhone from your car stereo's head unit. For example, Toyota offers an integration kit for plugging an iPod into the car glove box and using either the steering wheel or usual audio system controls.

Using built-in or custom installations

Premium car manufacturers are introducing cars that are *iPod-ready* and/or *iPhone-ready,* including an iPod or iPhone interface for the car stereo system that uses the dock connector cable that's compatible with all iPod and iPhone models. For example, BMW offers such a model with audio controls on the steering wheel. Mercedes-Benz, Volvo, MINI Cooper, Nissan, Alfa Romeo, and Ferrari all also offer iPod-ready models. In addition, car stereo manufacturers (such as Alpine and Clarion) offer car audio systems with integrated iPod interfaces; see Figure 5-2.

You may be able to swap a higher-fidelity car stereo for a car you are about to purchase — or you may want to replace your car stereo simply for this purpose. The Sony CDX-GT630UI is a typical iPod-and iPhone-ready car stereo that lets you connect either device with a USB cable and controls the iPod or iPhone through its head unit in the dashboard.

If you can't afford an iPod-ready or iPhone-ready car or new car stereo, you can opt for a custom installation of an iPod or iPhone interface for your existing car stereo and car power (such as using a custom cable interface for a CD changer, which a skilled car audio specialist can install in your dashboard). For example, Dension (www.dension.com) offers the Gateway series of products for controlling iPod and iPhone models and auxiliary devices in a car.

Using auxiliary input and power adapters

If you're lucky enough to have a car with an AUX (auxiliary) line-in connection on its stereo, you can use that to pipe the sound from your iPad, iPod, or iPhone into your car stereo. All you need is a mini-plug cable to connect directly to the iPad, iPod, or iPhone headphone connection and then to the AUX line in. You can then adjust the volume on both the iPad, iPod, or iPhone, and the car stereo.

Figure 5-2:
An iPod-
integrated
car stereo
installation.

For an iPad, iPhone, or iPod touch, you can use Belkin's Mini-Stereo Link Cable or Monster's iCable for Car, which are designed specifically to fit the headphone connection.

You still need to provide power for the iPad, iPod, or iPhone (unless you don't mind using up battery power while playing content in your car). Although some new vehicles (particularly SUVs and cars, such as the Toyota Matrix mini–station wagon) offer 110-volt power outlets you can use with your Apple-supplied battery charger, most cars offer only a lighter/power socket that requires a power adapter to use with your iPad, iPod, or iPhone. Be careful to pick the right type of power adapter for your car's lighter/power socket.

Belkin (www.belkin.com) offers the Auto Kit for $39.99, and it includes a car power adapter with a convenient socket for a stereo mini-plug cable (which can connect directly to a car stereo if the stereo has a mini-socket for audio input). The adapter includes a volume-adjustable amplifier to boost the sound coming from the iPod or iPhone before it goes into the cassette adapter or car stereo. If you don't need the extra volume control, you can get a less expensive car power adapter, the Mobile Power Cord for iPod, for $19.99 from Belkin. The Radtech ProCable AutoPower (www.radtech.us) is one of many that meet the power requirements for an iPad.

See also the section "Setting up car mounts" for more power choices because some car mounts include power.

Using cassette player converters

Until you get an iPod-ready or iPhone-ready car or car stereo, or one with an AUX line-in, you can use a cassette-player adapter to connect with your car stereo. (I describe wireless connectivity later, in the section "Connecting by wireless radio.") Many car stereos have a cassette player, and you can buy a cassette adapter — the Sony CPA-9C Car Cassette Adapter, for example — from most consumer electronics stores. The cassette-player adapter looks like a tape cassette with a mini-plug cable (which sticks out through the slot when you're using the adapter). Adapters work with most front-loading and side-loading cassette decks — it's the same shape as a cassette — as long as the cable doesn't prevent its loading.

First connect the mini-plug cable directly to the iPad, iPod, or iPhone head-phone connection. Then insert the adapter into the cassette player, being careful not to get the cable tangled inside the player.

One inherent problem with this approach is that the cable that dangles from your cassette player looks unsightly. You also might have some trouble eject-ing the adapter if the cable gets wedged in the cassette-player door. Overall, though, this method is the best for most cars because it provides better sound quality than most wireless methods.

Don't forget — you still need a car power adapter to supply power, which I describe in the previous section.

Setting up car mounts

Even with an AUX line-in connection or a cassette adapter, and a power adapter, you still have at best only a clumsy solution that dangles wires. Attached to these wires, your iPad, iPod, or iPhone needs a secure place to sit while your car moves because you don't want it bouncing around and you certainly don't want to hold it in your hands while driving (which is illegal in some states).

You can fit an iPod securely in position in a car without getting a custom installation. The TuneDok ($29.99) from Belkin (www.belkin.com) holds your iPod securely and fits into your car's cup holder. The TuneDok ratchet-ing neck and height-adjustment feature lets you reposition the iPod to your liking. The cable-management clip eliminates loose and tangled cables, and the large and small rubber base and cup fit most cup holders.

For the iPod touch or iPhone, you may want a car mount that puts the dis-play in reach for tapping. The $29.99 Kensington Power Port Car Mount (http://us.kensington.com) provides a 4.5-inch flexible arm you can adjust for optimal positioning, and a swivel head for horizontal or vertical ori-entation. It also plugs into the car's lighter/power socket to provide power.

For an iPad, consider the ModulR (`http://modulrcase.com`), which comes with a range of interchangeable accessory attachments — one accessory lets you attach the iPad to a car's seat headrest, so that someone in the back seat can watch video or surf the Web. RAM Mounting Systems (`www.ram-mount.com`) offers the $34.46 RAM POD I and other products for mounting an iPad, and Scosche Industries (`www.scosche.com`) offers the iKit for installing the iPad with a rotating dock at the end of a ball-joint mounted in the dash.

MARWARE (`www.marware.com`) offers an inexpensive solution for both car use and personal iPod or iPhone use. The Car Holder ($6) attaches to the dashboard of your car or windshield and lets you attach an iPod or iPhone that's wearing one of the MARWARE Sportsuit covering cases. (See the section "Dressing Up Your iPod and iPhone for Travel," later in this chapter.) The clip on the back attaches to the Car Holder.

ProClip (`www.proclipusa.com`) offers mounting brackets for clip-on devices. The brackets attach to the dashboard, and you can install them in seconds. After you install the bracket, you can use different custom holders for the iPod or iPhone models or for cell phones and other portable devices.

Connecting by wireless radio

A wireless music adapter lets you play music from your iPad, iPod, or iPhone on an FM radio with no connection or cable. However, the sound quality might suffer a bit from radio interference. I always take a wireless adapter with me whenever I rent a car because even if a rental car has no AUX line-in connection or cassette player (ruling out the use of my cassette adapter), it probably has an FM radio.

You can use a wireless adapter in a car, on a boat, or even on the beach with a portable radio. I even use it in hotel rooms with a clock radio.

To use a wireless adapter, follow these steps:

1. **Set the wireless adapter to an unused FM radio frequency.**

   Some adapters offer only one frequency (typically 87.9 MHz). Others offer you a choice of several frequencies: typically 88.1, 88.3, 88.5, and 88.7 MHz. Some even let you pick any FM frequency. If given a choice, choose the frequency and set the adapter according to its instructions. Be sure to pick an unused frequency — a frequency that's being used by an FM station in range of your radio is sure to interfere with your iPod signal.

2. **Connect the wireless adapter to the iPod or iPhone headphone/line-out connector or to the line-out connector on an iPod car dock.**

   The wireless adapter acts like a miniature radio station, broadcasting to a nearby FM radio. (Sorry, you can't go much farther than a few feet, so no one else can hear your Wolfman Jack impersonation.)

3. **Tune to the appropriate frequency on the FM dial.**

Tune any nearby radio to the same FM frequency that you chose in Step 1.

You need to set the adapter close enough to the radio's antenna to work, making it impractical for home stereos. You can get better-quality sound by connecting to a home stereo with a cable.

Don't be surprised if the wireless adapter doesn't work as well in cities — other radio stations might cause too much interference.

Here are a few wireless adapters I have no trouble recommending:

✔ **TRAFFICJamz** ($12.99) from Newer Technology (www.newertech.com) is both a charger and a transmitter that works with all model iPods.

✔ **iTrip** ($49.99) from Griffin Technology (www.griffintechnology. com) automatically finds the three clearest frequencies wherever you are and saves them for you as presets, and can be controlled with the free iTrip Controller App on an iPod touch or iPhone to choose presets or tune manually using a tuning wheel. The Griffin 2010 iTrip Auto FM transmitter works with the iPad.

✔ **TuneCast Auto Live with ClearScan for iPhone and iPod** ($79.99) from Belkin (www.belkin.com) quickly scans and finds the best FM frequency with one push of a button — it is the only FM transmitter with GPS-assisted scanning. The free ClearScan Live app for iPod touch or iPhone lets you control scanning.

✔ **Monster iCarPlay Wireless 800 FM Transmitter** ($89.95) from Monster Cable (www.monstercable.com) offers a power adapter as well as excellent-quality playback for iPad, iPod, or iPhone. You can select radio frequencies of 88.1, 88.3, 88.5, 88.7, 88.9, 89.1, 89.3, or 89.5 MHz. Although a bit more expensive, this product offers excellent sound quality.

✔ **TransDock micro with IntelliTune** ($59.99) from Digital Lifestyle Outfitters (www.dlo.com) for iPod models scans for open FM frequencies automatically and sports a cool dial for adjusting your settings and manually tuning the frequency.

When picking out the FM transmitter, make sure that it meets the iPad's higher 10w power requirement.

Dressing Up the iPad, iPod, and iPhone for Travel

Lots of stylin' accessories are available for dressing your iPad, iPod, or iPhone up for travel. You can find different types of protective gear — from leather jackets to aluminum cases — in many different styles and colors in your local Apple Store or the online Apple store.

For starters, Apple offers access to hundreds of products from other suppliers on its iPod Accessories page for iPod and iPhone models (`www.apple.com/ipod/accessories.html`) and its iPad Accessories page for iPad models (`www.apple.com/ipad/accessories.html`) — follow the Shop link to go directly to Apple's online store to view product details and make purchases. Some are designed primarily for protecting your iPad, iPod, or iPhone from harm; others are designed to provide some measure of protection while also providing access to controls.

On the extreme end of the spectrum are hardened cases that are ready for battlefields in deserts or jungles — the Humvees of protective gear, if you will. Matias Corporation (`http://matias.ca/armor`) offers versions of the sturdy Matias Armor case ($29.95) for each iPod and iPhone model, which offers a hard, resilient metal exoskeleton that can withstand the abuse of bouncing down a flight of metal stairs without letting your iPod or iPhone pop out. The iPad Defender Series Case from OtterBox (`www.otterbox.com`) offers three layers of hardcore protection and a back polycarbonate cover you can snap over the face to protect the display.

Business travelers can combine personal items into one carrying case. The Leather Folio ($29.99) cases from Belkin (`www.belkin.com`) for iPod classic and iPod touch models are made from fine-grain leather that even Ricardo Montalban would rave about. The cases can also hold personal essentials, such as business and credit cards. The HipCase cases ($29.99) from DLO (`www.dlo.com`) let you stash credit cards and other essentials along with your iPod or iPhone, and include sturdy leather-covered belt clips.

On the sporty side, MARWARE (`www.marware.com`) offers the Sportsuit Convertible cases ($12.99) for iPod and iPhone models, with a patented belt-clip system, offering interchangeable clip options for use with the MARWARE Car Holder or with an armband or belt. The neoprene case has vulcanized rubber grips on each side and bottom for a no-slip grip as well as plastic inserts for impact protection, offering full access to all the device's controls and connections while it's in the case. MARWARE also offers the $44.99 Eco-Flip flip-top and Eco-Vue folio cases for iPad models.

Using Power Accessories

If you want to charge your iPad, iPod, or iPhone battery when you travel abroad, you can't count on finding the same voltage that exists in your home country. You can use your Apple power adapter, or your computer, to recharge your iPad, iPod, or iPhone. However, you need to plug it into an outlet somewhere. Fortunately, power converters for different voltages and plugs for different outlets are available in most airport gift shops, but the worldly traveler might want to consider saving time and money by getting a travel kit of power accessories from the Apple Store or from a consumer electronics store.

I found several varieties of power converter kits for world travel in my local international airport, but they were pricey — check your local Radio Shack or consumer electronics store first, or try Amazon.com or MacMall.com. Most kits include a set of AC plugs with prongs that fit different electrical outlets around the world. You can connect the Apple power adapter for the iPad, or the power adapters for the iPod or iPhone, to these adapters. The AC plugs typically support outlets in North America, Japan, China, the United Kingdom, Continental Europe, Korea, Australia, and Hong Kong. You should also include at least one power accessory for use with a standard car lighter, such as car chargers from Belkin (www.belkin.com), Kensington (www.kensington.com), or Newer Technology (www.newertech.com).

One way to mitigate the battery blues is to get an accessory that lets you use replaceable alkaline batteries — the kind that you can find in any convenience store — in a pinch. The TunePower Rechargeable Battery Pack for iPod ($79.99) from Belkin (www.belkin.com) lets you power an iPod Classic or older-model iPod with standard AA alkaline replaceable batteries even when your internal iPod battery is drained.

The $79.95 mophie Juice Pack Air Case and Rechargeable Battery for iPhone 3G and iPhone 3GS, and soon (as of this writing) for the iPhone 4, (www.mophie.com) is a unique power accessory that doubles as a hard-shell case. With its rechargeable external battery concealed inside the protective form-fitting case, it drains its own battery before it moves on to the one in your iPhone, conserving your iPhone battery power.

Part II
Filling Up Your Empty Cup

The 5th Wave   By Rich Tennant

"It's like any other pacemaker, but it comes with an internal iPod docking accessory."

In this part . . .

Part II shows you how to fill up your iPad, iPod, or iPhone with extreme content and killer apps using iTunes.

✓ Chapter 6 shows how to get content and apps from the online iTunes Store and App Store. You set yourself up with an account and then download music, videos, TV shows, movies, podcasts, and audio books, as well as apps for the iPad, iPod touch, and iPhone. You also find out how to download tunes and applications directly to your iPad, iPod touch, or iPhone.

✓ In Chapter 7 you discover how to rip music CDs and import other audio files as well as audio books, videos, and podcasts into your iTunes library.

✓ Chapter 8 describes synchronizing your iPad, iPod, or iPhone with your iTunes library, as well as how to manually manage the contents of an iPad, iPod, or iPhone.

✓ Chapter 9 describes automatically synchronizing your iPad, iPod, or iPhone with calendars and contacts using iTunes and MobileMe. It also covers managing and synchronizing e-mail accounts, bookmarks, and notes on your iPad, iPod touch, or iPhone.

Chapter 6

Shopping at the iTunes Store

· ·

In This Chapter

▶ Setting up an account with the iTunes Store

▶ Previewing and buying songs, TV shows, movies, and audio books

▶ Browsing, previewing, and downloading podcasts

▶ Buying music, podcasts, and apps directly with your iPad, iPod touch, or iPhone

· ·

*A*pple set the standard for content downloads by offering the easiest, fastest, and most cost-effective service for buying content online. The iTunes Store accounts for more than 25 percent of all music sold in the U.S. alone. And that's not all — you can purchase or rent TV shows and movies, including HD movies, and you can download TV shows, music videos, podcasts, educational material, applications, and games to use with your iPad, iPod, or iPhone.

The iTunes Store includes the App Store, which offers free and commercial iPad, iPod touch, and iPhone applications. You can find apps in just about every category you can think of, including gaming, social networking, sports, business, and more. The store also includes games for the iPod nano and iPod classic.

iTunes even connects you to other iTunes Store buyers with its Ping social network for music, which I describe in Chapter 2. You can follow artists, follow your friends to learn what music interests them, and learn about concerts and events near you. Ping makes it easy to discover and download new music in the iTunes Store and keep up on your friends' tastes in music.

You can also download free or commercial content and apps directly to an iPad, iPod touch, or iPhone wirelessly from the Internet. The entire iTunes Store, including the App Store, is available right at your fingertips, and the iBook Store is available on the iPad through the free iBooks app, which is also available for downloading to an iPhone or iPod touch. This chapter shows you how to sign in and take advantage of what these stores have to offer.

The iTunes Store also offers parental controls that let you disable various sections as well as limit the purchase of various content based on MPAA/TV ratings. To learn more about managing your iTunes Store account, visit this book's companion Web site.

Visiting the iTunes Store

You can visit the iTunes Store on your computer by connecting to the Internet, launching iTunes, and clicking iTunes Store in the Store section of the source pane.

You can also click an iTunes Store link on Apple's Web site, or a similar link on any other Web sites that are iTunes affiliates with songs for sale (such as www.rockument.com). The link automatically launches iTunes, if you have it, and opens the iTunes Store. If you don't have iTunes, the link takes you to a Web page for the content and offers a button to click to download and install iTunes (see Chapter 2 for details on installing iTunes).

As of this writing, the iTunes Store offers millions of songs you can freely copy and play on other devices. Until recently, many of the songs were copy-protected — you could only play them on up to five different authorized computers and use them on iPods, iPhones, or Apple TVs. Now, all songs and albums are provided in the iTunes Plus format, which offers higher sound quality *without* copy protection. You can play iTunes Plus songs on any player that supports the AAC format and on an unlimited number of computers, and you can burn an unlimited number of CDs with them.

You can buy audio books as well as episodes and entire seasons of TV shows, and you can purchase them in advance, so you see them immediately. First-run movies are available for rent or purchase. iTunes also offers tons of free content in the form of *podcasts,* which are similar to syndicated radio and TV shows, but you can download and play them at your convenience on your computer and on your iPad, iPod, iPhone, and Apple TV. iTunes even offers free lectures, language lessons, and audio books with educational content in its iTunes U section.

Like with most online services, the music that you buy online isn't as high in audio quality as music on a commercial CD, although most people can't tell the difference when playing the music on car stereos or at low volume. The quality of the music sold in the iTunes Store is comparable with the quality you get when ripping CDs or importing songs using the MP3 or AAC format. You also get song information, such as artist, song titles, the album title, and cover artwork. The iTunes Store also offers albums with an immersive visual experience (referred to as *iTunes LP*) that includes liner notes, pictures, video, animation, and lyrics. Some albums are provided with the electronic equivalent of a complete jewel case booklet that you can print yourself.

To find out more about renting movies and TV shows and about audio encoding formats, visit this book's companion Web site.

If you already have your iTunes program open, you have at least three choices when it comes to opening the iTunes Store:

> ✔ **Click iTunes Store in the Store section of the source pane.** The iTunes Store home page opens, as shown in Figure 6-1.

✔ **Click any link in the Ping Sidebar.** The iTunes Store home page opens and automatically switches your source pane selection to iTunes Store. The Ping Sidebar offers suggestions based on the music your friends are downloading; see Chapter 2 for details.

✔ **Click the Ping button in iTunes.** Click the Ping button next to a song to see a pop-up menu which includes options to show the artist, album name, or song title in the iTunes Store.

The iTunes Store uses the iTunes list pane to display its wares. You can check out content to your heart's content, although you can't buy content, download free content, or rent movies and TV shows unless you have an iTunes Store account set up.

The iTunes Store also provides tabs and buttons on a black bar above the List pane. The left and right triangle buttons work just like the back and forward buttons of a Web browser, moving back a page or forward a page, respectively. The button with the Home icon takes you to the iTunes Store home page. (Refer to Figure 6-1.)

Figure 6-1:
The iTunes Store home page.

List pane (showing iTunes Store)

Setting Up an Account

One important task that you must do in iTunes on your computer is set up your iTunes Store account. You need an account to download free or commercial content and apps to your computer as well as to use the iTunes and App Store apps on your iPad, iPod touch, or iPhone. To create an iTunes Store account, follow these steps:

1. **In iTunes, click the iTunes Store option in the Store section of the source pane.**

   The iTunes Store home page appears (refer to Figure 6-1), replacing the list pane.

2. **Click the Sign In tab in the upper-right area of the window to either create an account or sign in to an existing account.**

   When you're logged in to an iTunes account, the account name appears in place of the Sign In tab.

   After you click the Sign In tab, iTunes displays the account sign-in dialog.

   If you already set up an account with the iTunes Store with the MobileMe (formerly .Mac) service or with other Apple services (such as the Apple Developer Connection or Apple's online store), you're halfway there. Type your ID and password and then click the Sign In button. Apple remembers the personal information that you put in previously, so you don't have to reenter it every time you visit the iTunes Store. If you forgot your password, click the Forgot Password button, and iTunes provides a dialog so that you can answer your test question. If you answer correctly, iTunes e-mails your password to you.

3. **Click the Create New Account button.**

   iTunes displays a new page that welcomes you to the iTunes Store.

4. **Click the Continue button on the iTunes Store welcome page.**

   After you click Continue, the terms of use appear with the option at the end to agree to the terms. If you don't select the option to agree, iTunes continues to display the terms until you agree or click the Cancel button.

5. **Select I Have Read and Agree to the iTunes Terms and Conditions and click the Continue button.**

   iTunes displays the personal account information page of the setup procedure, with text fields to enter your e-mail address, password, and other information.

6. **Fill in your personal account information.**

   Type your e-mail address into the Email Address field. Make up a password, and enter it twice — in the Password field and in the Verify field. Then enter a question and answer that you can easily remember (in case you forget your password). Finally, enter your birth date and options for receiving e-mail from Apple. Don't forget the password you made up — you need it to access the store from your iPad, iPod touch, or iPhone as well as from your computer or another computer.

7. **Click the Continue button and then enter your credit card information.**

The entire procedure is secure, so you don't have to worry. The iTunes Store keeps your personal information (including your credit card information) on file, and you don't have to type it again.

8. **Click the Continue button to finish the procedure.**

The account setup finishes and returns you to the iTunes Store home page. You can now use the iTunes Store to purchase and download content to play in iTunes and use on any iPad, iPod, iPhone, or Apple TV.

 Click Change Country under the Manage list at the bottom of the iTunes Store page to choose online stores in other countries. For example, the iTunes Store in France displays menus in French and features hit songs and TV shows for the French market. If you've set up your account in only one country (such as the United States), you have to set an account up again for the country you're switching to, in order to purchase content in that country's store. You can set up multiple accounts in multiple countries, and Apple takes care of credit card transactions and currency conversions.

Cruising the Multimedia Mall

The iTunes Store home page is loaded with specials and advertisements to peruse. You can preview any song in the iTunes Store for up to 30 seconds. Some movies offer one-minute previews and movie trailers you can view for free, and TV shows and audio books can offer up to 90 seconds. If you have an account set up, you can buy and download content immediately, including movies for rent.

Browsing songs and albums

To look at music in more depth, click the Music tab in the black bar above the list pane — refer to Figure 6-1. You can also pick a music genre by clicking the down-arrow button that appears next to the Music tab when your pointer appears over the tab. After clicking an album or selecting an advertisement for an album, the album's page appears with a description and other links, as shown in Figure 6-2. You can then click the Buy Album button, or the Buy buttons for individual songs, as I describe in "Buying and Downloading Media" later in this chapter.

Figure 6-2:
An iTunes
Store page
showing an
iTunes LP
album.

With all Buy buttons in the store, you can click the down-arrow button attached to it (refer to Figure 6-2) to see options such as Like and Post (for Ping), Gift This Song (or Album), Add to Wish List, Tell a Friend (by e-mail, for albums or entire pages), Copy Link (so that you can Paste it in a text file or message), Share on Facebook, and Share on Twitter. With a Buy button for an individual song, you can also choose Other Versions to see other versions of the song.

What if you're looking for particular music in a particular genre? You can browse the iTunes Store by genre and artist name in a method similar to browsing your iTunes library.

To browse the iTunes Store, choose View⇨Column Browser⇨Show Column Browser, or click the Browse link in the Quick Links column on the right side of the iTunes Store home page. iTunes displays the store's offerings categorized by type of content (such as Music), and it displays music by genre and subgenre — and within each subgenre, by artist and album. Select a genre in the Genre column, then a subgenre in the Subgenre column, then an artist in the Artist column, and finally an album in the Album column, which takes you to the list of songs from that album that are available to preview or purchase, as shown in Figure 6-3.

You can play music in your iTunes library while browsing the iTunes Store, as I do in Figure 6-3 — I'm playing Elvis while searching for more Elvis.

Figure 6-3:
Browse the
iTunes Store
for music by
genre, artist,
and album.

To see more information about the album that it came from, click the content
link (one of the gray-circled arrow buttons in the list pane):

- Clicking the arrow in the Artist column takes you to the artist's page of
  albums.
- Clicking the arrow in the Album column takes you to the album page.
- Clicking the arrow in the Name column takes you to album page with the
  song highlighted.

My only complaint about browsing by artist is that artists are listed alphabetically by first name. For example, you have to look up Elvis Presley under *Elvis*
and not *Presley*.

To preview a song, click the song title in the list pane and then click the play
button (or press the spacebar) or double-click the song.

By default, the previews play on your computer off the Internet in a stream,
so you might hear a few hiccups in the playback. Each preview lasts about 30
seconds. Just when you start really getting into the song, it ends. If the song
is irresistible, though, you can buy it on the spot — for details, see the section "Buying and Downloading Media," later in this chapter.

Power searching

If you're looking for DMB's "That Song That Jane Likes" or know specifically what to search for, type it into the Search Store field in the upper-right corner of the iTunes window; this lets you search the iTunes Store for just about anything. You can type part of a song title or artist name to quickly display results from the iTunes Store in the list pane.

If you're serious about your content and you truly desire the power to search for exactly what you want, click the Power Search link in the Quick Links column on the right side of the iTunes Store home page (or choose Store⇨Search).

The Power Search page appears. You can choose the type of content to search through by choosing from a pop-up menu under the page title at the top: All Results (search all types), Music, Movies, TV Shows, Apps, Audiobooks, Podcasts, or iTunes U (part of the iTunes Store that offers free lectures, language lessons, and audio books).

For example, choose Music to power-search only for music and music videos (refer to Figure 6-4). The entry fields for Artist, Composer, Song, Album, and Genre appear. You can fill in some of or all these fields, or just fill in part of any field if that's all you know — such as the Composer (Bob Dylan) and part of the song title ("Takes a Lot") in Figure 6-4. After you fill in as much as you want, click the Search button in the top-right corner. Albums, movies, music videos, and other items found appear on the page as well as a song list.

Celebrities tell all (and so can you)

Do you want to be influenced? Do you want to know what influenced some of today's celebrities and buy what they have in their music collections? Choose the Music tab at the top of the iTunes Store page to go to the Music page. Scroll down the Music page and click a celebrity name in the Celebrity Playlists section of the More in Music column on the right to go to that celebrity's page. A typical celebrity playlist offers about an album's worth of songs from different artists. You can preview or buy any song in the list, or follow the music links to the artist or album page.

The Music page advertises some of the celebrity playlists, but a lot more are available. To see all the celebrity playlists, go to the More in Music column on the right side of the Music page and click the See All link to the right of the Celebrity Playlists section title. You arrive at the Celebrity Playlists page. You can use the Sort By pop-up menu in the upper-right corner to sort the list by Most Recent or by Title (which is usually the celebrity's name).

You can also be influenced by other buyers and do a little influencing yourself. Go to the Music page, and click the iMix link in the More to Explore column at the bottom right corner of the page to check out playlists that have been contributed by other consumers and published in the iTunes Store (such as my own "Country Blues Roots" iMixes). iMixes offer 30-second previews of any songs in the iMix playlists.

To find out how to publish your own iMix playlist, visit this book's companion Web site.

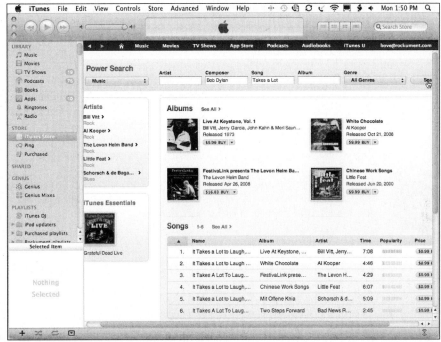

Figure 6-4:
Use Power
Search to
refine your
search in
the iTunes
Store.

Browsing movies, TV shows, music videos, and audio books

The uncool thing about video stores — besides the weird people who hang out in them — is the lack of a comfortable way to preview videos before you buy them. Instead, go to the iTunes Store online to preview movies and TV shows before you buy them (and before you rent a movie) — and then go ahead and buy or rent them from the iTunes Store. Most shows offer 30 seconds of previewing time, and many movies offer trailers that are even longer.

To find TV shows, movies, music videos, or audio books, you can

✔ Click the TV Shows, Movies, or Audiobooks tab in the black bar at the top of iTunes Store page. You can also click the down-arrow button next to each tab to browse by genre.

✔ For music videos, click the down-arrow button next to the Music tab and then select Music Videos from the pop-up menu.

✔ Use the column browser (refer to Figure 6-3). You can then select Audiobooks, Movies, Music Videos, or TV Shows from the iTunes Store column and then pick a genre.

To preview a TV show, movie, or music video, click the title in the list pane and then click the play button (or press the spacebar). (Movies, music videos, and TV shows are all just videos on the computer, so I use the term *videos* from now on.)

The video plays in the iTunes window, in the artwork pane in the lower-left corner of the iTunes window, in a separate window, or full-screen, depending on your playback settings. (See Chapter 12 for details.) Click the iTunes play/pause, forward/next, and previous/rewind buttons to control playback and use the iTunes volume slider to control the volume, just like with songs. For more details about playing videos in iTunes, see Chapter 12.

Most movie pages offer a View Trailer button — click it to view the theatrical trailer for the movie. To return to the movie page, click Close Preview under the lower-right corner of the trailer picture.

Browsing and subscribing to podcasts

Podcasting is a popular method of publishing audio and video shows to the Internet, enabling people to subscribe to a feed and receive the shows automatically. Similar to a tape of a radio broadcast, you can save a podcast episode and play it back at your convenience, both in iTunes on your computer and on your iPad, iPod, or iPhone. You can also burn an audio podcast episode to an audio CD or MP3 CD.

By *subscribing,* I mean listing the podcast in the Podcasts section of the Library section of the source pane, so that new episodes are downloaded automatically. It's like a magazine subscription that's updated with a new issue every month or so. Your copy of iTunes automatically finds new podcast episodes and downloads them to your computer.

A podcast episode can be anything from a single song to a commentary-hosted radio show; a podcaster, like a broadcaster, provides a stream of episodes over time. Thousands of professional and amateur radio and video shows are offered as podcast episodes. Video podcasts are also called *videocasts* or *vodcasts.*

The iTunes Podcast page in the iTunes Store lets you browse, find, preview, and subscribe to podcasts, many of which are free. To find podcasts in the iTunes Store, do one of the following:

> ✔ **Click the Podcasts tab in the black bar at the top of the iTunes Store page.** The iTunes Store displays the Podcast page, with advertisements for popular podcasts and a list of Top Podcasts in the far-right column. You can click the down-arrow button next to the Podcasts tab to choose specific categories.

You can also get to the Podcast page by clicking Podcasts in the iTunes source pane and then clicking Podcast Directory at the bottom of the list pane.

✔ **Browse all podcasts in a particular category.** Use the column browser (refer to Figure 6-3) and then select Podcasts in the iTunes Store column. Select options from the Category column and Subcategory column.

✔ **Search for a podcast by name or keyword.** You can type a search term into the Search Store field in the upper-right corner of the iTunes window to find any podcasts or other content items that match. You can also use the Power Search feature, described earlier in this chapter in the section "Power searching."

You can also find podcasts outside of iTunes Store on the Internet. To find out how to add podcasts to iTunes manually from the Internet, visit this book's companion Web site.

After you select a podcast, the iTunes Store displays the podcast's specific page in the iTunes Store, showing all available podcast episodes. To select, play, and subscribe to a podcast, follow these steps:

1. **Choose a podcast in the iTunes Store.**

   The iTunes Store offers a description and a Subscribe button to receive new podcasts. The page also lists the most recent podcast episodes. You can click the *i* icon on the far-right listing margin to display separate information about each podcast episode.

2. **To preview the podcast, click an episode title and then click the play button or press the spacebar.**

   You can play a preview of any episode in the list. iTunes plays the episode for about 90 seconds, just like a Web radio station streaming to your computer. To jump ahead or play the entire episode, you must first subscribe to the podcast. By subscribing, you enable automatic downloading of episodes to your computer.

3. **Click the Subscribe (or Subscribe Free) button on the podcast page to subscribe to the podcast.**

   In typical Apple fashion, iTunes first displays an alert to confirm that you want to subscribe to the podcast.

4. **Click the OK button to confirm.**

   iTunes downloads the podcast to your computer and switches to Podcasts in the Library section of the source pane. iTunes displays your newly subscribed podcast in the list pane. See Chapter 12 for details on playing podcasts in iTunes.

5. (Optional) Get more episodes of the podcast.

When you subscribe to a podcast, you get the current episode. However, a podcast probably has past episodes still available. To download any free or commercial episodes, click the Free or Buy button at the far right side of the episode.

You can play the podcast, incorporate it into playlists, and make copies and burn CDs as much as you like.

Updating podcasts

Many podcast feeds provide new material on a regular schedule. iTunes can check these feeds automatically and update your library with new podcast episodes. You can, for example, schedule iTunes to check for new podcast episodes — such as news, weather, traffic reports, and morning talk shows — before you wake up and automatically update your iPad, iPod, or iPhone.

To check for updates manually, select Podcasts in the Library section of the source pane and then click the Refresh button in the lower-right corner of the Podcasts pane, which appears if podcasts need to be updated. All subscribed podcast feeds are updated immediately when you click Refresh, and iTunes downloads the most recent (or all) episodes, depending on how you set your podcasts preferences to schedule podcast updates.

To change your podcast settings so that iTunes can check for new podcasts automatically, click the Settings button at the bottom of the Podcasts pane to display the Podcast Settings dialog. You can change the settings for each podcast separately by choosing the podcast in the Settings For pop-up menu. The settings are as follows:

- ✔ **Check for New Episodes:** Choose to check for podcasts every hour, day, week, or manually — whenever you want.

- ✔ **Settings For:** Choose which podcast in your iTunes library you are scheduling updates for, or choose Podcast Defaults to apply these settings to all podcasts in your library.

- ✔ **When New Episodes Are Available:** You can download the most recent one (useful for news podcasts), download all episodes (useful for podcasts you might want to keep), or nothing so that you can use the Refresh button to update manually as you need.

- ✔ **Episodes to Keep:** Choose to keep all episodes, all unplayed episodes, the most recent episodes, or previous episodes.

Keeping unplayed episodes is a useful way to organize your news podcasts. If you've played an episode (or a portion of it), you likely don't need it anymore, but you probably do want to keep the ones you haven't played yet. With this setting, iTunes automatically deletes the ones you've played.

If you sync podcasts automatically to your iPad, iPod, or iPhone, as I describe in Chapter 8, don't set the Episodes to Keep pop-up to All Unplayed Episodes — use All Episodes instead. This is why: If you listen to part of a podcast episode on your iPad, iPod, or iPhone and then sync the device, the podcast episode disappears from iTunes (because it is no longer unplayed). If the episodes are still out there on the Internet, you can recover them by choosing Download All for the When New Episodes Are Available option.

Buying and Downloading Media

As you select multimedia content, you can purchase the items and download them to your computer immediately. All you need to do is click the Buy button in the far-right column of the item, whether it is a song, a TV show episode, or an audio book. (You might have to scroll your iTunes Store window to see the far-right column.) You can also click the Buy Album button in an album advertisement.

The iTunes Store may prompt you to log in to your account after you click the Buy button (unless you just recently logged in). It then displays a warning dialog to make sure that you want to buy the item, and you can then complete your purchase by clicking the Buy button, or cancel. After clicking the Buy button, iTunes downloads the item and, after downloading, it appears in your iTunes library. You can continue buying items while downloading, and because you already logged in, the iTunes Store complies immediately without asking again for a password. The iTunes Store keeps track of your purchases over a 24-hour period and charges you for a total sum rather than for each single purchase.

You can see the list of all the items that you purchased by selecting the Purchased playlist under the iTunes Store option in the source pane. The list pane changes to show the items you purchased.

Each time you buy content, you get an e-mail from the iTunes Store with the purchase information. It's nice to know right away what you bought.

Changing other iTunes Store preferences

You can change iTunes Store preference settings by choosing iTunes⇨Preferences on the Mac or by choosing Edit⇨Preferences in Windows. In Preferences, click the Store tab. The Store preferences appear as follows:

✔ **Automatically Check for Available Downloads:** Set this preference to automatically check for uncompleted downloads from the iTunes Store and finish them (see the next section for details).

✔ **Automatically Download Prepurchased Content:** If you purchase an iTunes Pass for TV show episodes, set this preference so that when the episodes become available, iTunes automatically downloads them.

✔ **Automatically Download Missing Album Artwork:** Set this preference to download cover art from the iTunes Store for albums and songs you import from other sources (such as audio CDs).

✔ **Use Full iTunes Window for iTunes Store:** Set this preference to display the store in a full window, rather than just the list pane.

Resuming interrupted downloads

All sales are final; you can't return the digital merchandise. However, the download must be successful — you have to receive it all — before the iTunes Store charges you for the purchase. If for any reason the download is interrupted or fails to complete, your order remains active until you connect to the iTunes Store again.

iTunes remembers to continue the download when you return to iTunes and connect to the Internet. If for some reason the download doesn't continue, choose Store➪Check for Available Downloads to continue the interrupted download.

Your downloads are automatically transferred to the Purchased playlist, but during the downloading process, a Downloads choice appears in the source pane under Purchased, which you can select to check its progress. After selecting Downloads, you can click the Pause All button to pause downloads, and later, click Resume All to resume downloads. You can also click the pause button at the right side of each item's row to pause the downloading of a single item; click it again to resume downloading that item. You can also prioritize the order of downloading by dragging items into a different order in the Downloads window.

Appearing at the App Store

Got an iPad, iPod touch, or iPhone? You can get loads of free and commercial applications (called *apps*) that run on your iPad, iPod touch, and iPhone — in most cases, the same app, or versions of it, run on all three types of devices.

To visit the App Store, click the App Store tab in the black bar at the top of the iTunes Store page (refer to Figure 6-1) to find the apps. The App Store page appears, as shown in Figure 6-5. Click the iPhone button at the top to see iPhone and iPod touch apps, or click the iPad button to see iPad apps. Some apps that appear in both areas of the store are built as a single version that runs on iPhone (and iPod touch) and iPad models, and some are built as separate versions for the iPhone (and iPod touch) and the iPad.

Figure 6-5:
Find iPad
and iPhone
(including
iPod touch)
apps in the
App Store
section of
the iTunes
Store.

Click an app's icon to go to the information page for that app, which may also contain reviews and a slide show depicting the app in all its glory. The information page offers the Buy App button (to purchase and download a commercial app) or the Free App button (to download a free app). Click the Buy App or Free App button to download the app to your iTunes library. Downloaded apps appear in the Apps section of your iTunes library — click Apps in the Library section of the source pane to see their icons.

When an app you downloaded is updated, iTunes informs you — the message Update Available appears at the bottom of the Apps section with an arrow link that takes you to the My Apps Update page in the iTunes Store, with icons of the apps to update. Click the Get Update button next to each app to download the update, which automatically replaces the previous version of the app.

You can also update your apps directly on your iPad, iPod touch, or iPhone — see "Updating apps you've downloaded" later in this chapter.

The iTunes Store also offers colorful "click wheel" games to play on your iPod classic or nano, such as Mini Golf, Monopoly, Mahjong, Tetris, and Sudoku — visit this book's companion Web site for details.

Shopping with your iPad, iPod touch, or iPhone

The entire iTunes Store and App Store are both available right at your fingertips on your iPad, iPod touch, or iPhone. You can search for, browse, and preview songs and videos; make purchases; and download content and apps. Whatever you buy on the iPad, iPod touch, or iPhone is automatically copied to your iTunes library the next time you synchronize it with your computer, as I describe in Chapter 8 — as long as you don't delete it directly from your device for syncing (to find out how to delete apps directly from your Home screens, see Chapter 3).

You can use iTunes to set up an iTunes Store account first if you don't already have one, and then sign in to the account, as I describe in the section "Setting Up an Account," earlier in this chapter — and you need to remember your password. Then sync your iPad, iPod touch, or iPhone to iTunes as I describe in Chapter 8. After syncing your iPad, iPod touch, or iPhone so that it has your account information, you shouldn't have to bother with it again, and you are able to download items from the iTunes Store and App Store on your iPad, iPod touch, or iPhone from then on.

You can also create or sign into an iTunes account directly on an iPad, iPod touch, or iPhone, and view your account information: Choose Settings⇨Store from the Home screen. To sign into an existing account, tap Sign In and type your account name and password. If your iPad, iPod touch, or iPhone is already synced with your account, the View Account button appears in place of Sign In — tap View Account to see account information. To create one or more accounts directly on your iPad, iPod touch, or iPhone, tap Create New Account. Confirm your country or region and touch Next. Tap Agree to the terms of service, and then enter the information on the New Account screen with the on-screen keyboard. Tap Next to continue through the setup screens to finish setting up your account.

To use the iTunes Store and App Store on your iPad Wi-Fi or iPod touch, you must first connect to the Internet (see Chapter 4 for details). Be sure you have an iTunes Store account set up (see the section "Setting Up an Account," earlier in this chapter).

Browsing and downloading content

To go to the iTunes Store on an iPad, iPod touch, or iPhone, tap the iTunes icon on the Home screen. The store screen appears on an iPod touch or iPhone with Music, Videos, Search, Podcasts (see the next section), and More icons along the bottom, as shown in Figure 6-6 (left side). The store screen appears on an iPad with Music, Movies, TV Shows, Podcasts (see the next section), Audiobooks, iTunes U, and Downloads icons along the bottom, and a Search field in the top-right corner.

Here's the lowdown on the icons:

✔ **Tap the Music icon** to see featured music. To search through genres, tap the Genres button and choose a genre. Tap any song to hear a preview.

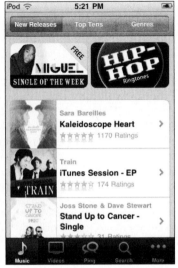 

Figure 6-6:
The iTunes Store (left) and App Store (right) on an iPod touch or iPhone.

✔ **Tap the Videos icon** on an iPod touch or iPhone to see featured movies, TV shows, and music videos.

✔ **Tap the Ping icon** to sign in and use the Ping social network for music. To find out more about Ping, see Chapter 2.

✔ **Tap the Movies or TV Shows icon** on an iPad to see featured movies or TV shows.

✔ **Tap the Search icon** to search the store and then tap the entry field to bring up the on-screen keyboard. Type the search term and tap the Search button to search the store.

✔ **Tap the Podcasts icon on an iPad** to . . . er, well, I explain that one in the next section.

✔ **Tap the Audiobooks, iTunes U, or Downloads icon** on an iPad to select audio books, iTunes U lessons, or Downloads, which shows you the progress of your downloads from the store.

✔ **Tap the More icon** on an iPod touch or iPhone for more choices, including Audiobooks, Podcasts, iTunes U, and Downloads.

To buy a song, tap the price and then tap Buy Now. Enter your password and tap OK.

Purchased songs are added to a Purchased playlist on your iPad, iPod touch, or iPhone, and they're included in your Purchased playlist in iTunes. iTunes automatically syncs songs and albums purchased on your iPad, iPod touch, or iPhone to your iTunes library when you connect it to your computer so that you have a backup.

Some albums offer bonus content, such as liner notes, which are downloaded to your iTunes library on your computer, but not to your iPad, iPod touch, or iPhone. An alert appears on your iPad, iPod touch, or iPhone if you've previously purchased one or more songs from an album. Tap Buy if you want to purchase the entire album, or tap Cancel if you want to buy the remaining songs on the album individually.

If you lose your network connection or turn off your iPad, iPod touch, or iPhone while downloading, the download pauses and then resumes when you reestablish connection with the Internet. If you go back to your computer, iTunes can complete the download operation to your iTunes library. To make sure that you received all downloads to your iPad, iPod touch, or iPhone, use iTunes on your computer and choose Store⇨Check for Available Downloads.

Browsing and downloading podcasts

If you'll recall, podcasts are audio and video episodes designed to be downloaded to your iPad, iPod touch, or iPhone. Most podcast episodes are free. On the store screen, tap the Podcasts icon to see podcasts available for downloading from the iTunes Store directly to your iPad, iPod touch, or iPhone.

You can also view categories of podcasts by tapping Categories in the upper-right corner of the Podcasts screen on an iPod touch or iPhone, or the upper-left corner on an iPad. You can also see the top ten in each category by tapping Top Tens at the top of the screen of the iPod touch or iPhone, or Top Charts on an iPad.

After selecting a podcast, a list of episodes appears. Tap the Free button (or Buy button for paid podcasts) next to an episode, enter your password, and then tap OK to start downloading the podcast episode. To return to the iTunes Store music screen on an iPod touch or iPhone, tap the Music button in the upper-left corner of the screen that lists the podcast episodes.

Browsing and downloading apps

Tap the App Store icon on the Home screen to grab some apps. The Store screen appears on an iPod touch or iPhone with the Featured, Categories, Top 25, Search, and Updates icons along the bottom (refer to Figure 6-6, right side). On an iPad, the Store screen appears with the Featured, Top Charts, Categories, and Updates icons along the bottom of the screen, and a Search field in the top-right corner of the screen. Here's how to use them:

- ✔ **Tap the Featured icon** for featured apps. You can then tap What's Hot to see the most popular apps based on downloads, or tap New to see the newest apps. On an iPod touch and iPhone, tap Genius to see suggested apps based on the ones you already have; on an iPad, tap Release Date to list apps by release date.

- ✔ **Tap Categories** to browse by category, and then tap a category, such as Games, to see a list of all games by popularity.

- ✔ **Tap the Top 25 icon** on an iPod touch or iPhone, and then tap Top Paid to see the top 25 paid apps by popularity, or tap Top Free to see the top 25 free apps.

- ✔ **Tap the Top Charts icon** on an iPad to see the top paid apps by popularity and the top free apps.

- ✔ **Tap the Search icon** to search the store, and tap the entry field to bring up the on-screen keyboard. Type the search term and tap Search to search the store. Suggestions pop up right away; for example, if you search for *Tony's Tips* in the App Store, my app "Tony's Tips for iPhone Users Manual" appears in the list of suggestions.

- ✔ **Tap the Updates icon** . . . wait, forget I said that. I cover that icon in the *next* section, so check that out if you want details.

These buttons show lists of apps. Tap an app to view its information screen, and then tap the Price button (for a paid app) or Free button (for a free app) to download the app. The Price or Free button changes to the Install button. Tap Install and then enter your password and tap OK.

You can also tap the Tell a Friend button on the app's information screen to send the app information in an e-mail. See Chapter 19 for details on how to send the e-mail.

Your iPad, iPod touch, or iPhone displays the Home screen with the icon for the new app as it loads. As soon as the Loading message is replaced by the name of the app, the app is ready to be tapped.

Updating apps you've downloaded

The App Store on your iPad, iPod touch, or iPhone notifies you if any of your apps have been updated — a number appears in the Updates icon along the bottom row of icons. When an update is available, use it. Updates fix bugs and introduce new features you may want.

Tap the Updates icon to see the list of updated apps. To update an app, tap the app in the list to see the app's information screen and then tap the Update button. The Update button changes to the Install button. Tap Install and then enter your password and tap OK. The update replaces the previous version of the app as it loads into your iPad, iPod touch, or iPhone.

Sharing iTunes Purchases in Your Home Network

Say your daughter just downloaded an album from the iTunes Store on her computer, which connects to your computer over a home network. You'd like to have a copy of it in your computer's iTunes library as well. Rather than painstakingly copying the music files from computer to computer, you can use the Home Sharing feature to share the purchased content. With Home Sharing, you can browse the iTunes libraries of up to five authorized computers on your home network, copy over from those libraries anything you want, and automatically add new purchases made on any of the computers to your own library.

Home Sharing is linked to a single iTunes Store account, which is perfect if you use one account for family purchases. In order to share purchased content that is copy-protected, such as movies and TV shows, you must first choose Store⇨Authorize Computer and enter your account and password for each computer's iTunes library whose purchased content you want to share (up to five computers can be authorized at once). You can share non-protected content without authorizing the computers. (To deauthorize a computer, choose Store⇨Deauthorize Computer.)

The Home Sharing feature actually copies the media files from one computer to another. It is not the same as sharing an iTunes library over a network to stream music from one computer to others. To learn more about the network-sharing features of iTunes and how to manage your iTunes account, including authorizing and deauthorizing computers, visit this book's companion Web site.

To turn on Home Sharing, click Home Sharing in the Shared section of the source pane and sign into your iTunes account. Do the same for each computer's iTunes library that you want to share.

After signing into your account in Home Sharing, and after signing into your account on another computer's iTunes library in Home Sharing, the other computer's library appears in the Shared section the source pane, as shown in Figure 6-7. Click the shared library to see it in the list pane.

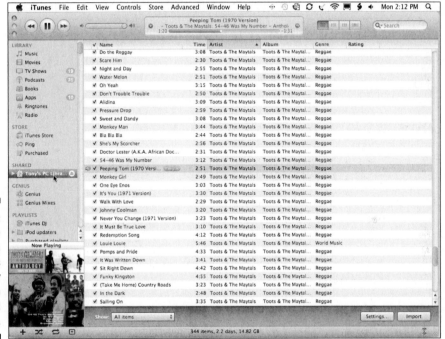

Figure 6-7: With Home Sharing, the other iTunes library appears in the Shared section.

You can show all the items in the shared library, or just the items that are *not* in your library so that you can see what you're missing — choose All Items or Items Not in My Library from the Show pop-up menu in the bottom left corner of the list pane (refer to Figure 6-7).

To import an item from the shared library to your library, select the item in the shared library, and then click the Import button in the bottom right corner of the list pane (refer to Figure 6-7). You can also drag items, albums, and artists directly over the Library section of the source pane to copy them to your library.

You can set up Home Sharing so that purchases made with the shared iTunes library on other computers are automatically copied to your iTunes library. Click Settings in the lower right corner of the list pane (refer to Figure 6-7), and then select the content categories for automatic transfer: Music, Movies, TV Shows, Books, and Applications.

To stop sharing a library on another computer, click the Eject button next to the library name (refer to Figure 6-7), or choose Controls⇨Disconnect "*library name*" (or press ⌘-E on a Mac or Ctrl-E in Windows).

Chapter 7

Bringing Content into iTunes

. . . .

. . . .

*I*f iPad, iPods, and iPhones were spaceships, iTunes would be the space station they dock with to get supplies. iTunes is the central repository of all content. You can bring your music from audio CDs into iTunes to preserve the music forever in digital format and play the music on your iPad, iPod, iPhone, or Apple TV without having to fumble for discs. You can import sound and video files downloaded from the Internet into iTunes to keep all your content organized, and then you can take your content with you in your iPad, iPod, or iPhone by syncing the device to iTunes (as I show in Chapter 8).

In this chapter, I show you not only how to import music from audio CDs, but also how to import music and videos from the Internet or other sources into your iTunes library. You get started in the simplest way possible: using iTunes to play music tracks on a CD, before importing the CD's music. You can use iTunes just like a jukebox, only better — you don't have to pay for each song you play, and you can play some of or all the songs on an album in any order.

Playing CD Tracks in iTunes

iTunes needs content. You can get started right away by ripping music from CDs into your library, as I describe in "Importing Audio CDs" in this chapter. For more instant gratification, though, you can play music right off the CD first, before importing it. Maybe you don't want to put the music into your library just yet. Maybe you just want to hear it first, as part of your Listen First, Rip Later plan.

To play a CD, insert any music CD — or even a CD-R that someone burned for you — into your computer. After you insert the CD, iTunes displays a dialog that asks whether you want to import the CD into your library — you can click the Yes button to import now, or the No button to do nothing yet. Click No if you want to play the CD first, or if you want to change your import settings (as I show you how to do in "Importing Audio CDs," later in this chapter).

If you're connected to the Internet, iTunes displays the track information for each song automatically. If the track information doesn't appear, you can grab it from the Internet, or edit it yourself (see Chapter 11 for details).

When you play a CD in iTunes, it's just like using a CD player. To play a CD, select a track and click the play button. The play button then turns into a pause button, and the song plays. When the song finishes, iTunes continues playing the songs in the list in sequence until you click the pause button or until the song list ends. You can skip to the next or previous song by using the arrow keys on your keyboard or by clicking the forward button or the back button (next to the play button). You can also double-click another song in the list to start playing it.

You can press the spacebar to perform the same function as clicking the play button; pressing it again is just like clicking the Pause button.

The status pane above the list of songs tells you the name of the artist and the song title as well as the elapsed time of the track. When you click the artist name, the artist name is replaced by the album name. The time on the left of the slider is the elapsed time; the time on the right is the duration of the song. When you click the duration, it changes to the remaining time; click it again to return to the song's duration.

You can rearrange the order of the tracks to automatically play them in any sequence you want, similar to programming a CD player. When you click the up arrow at the top of the first column in the list pane, it changes to a down arrow, and the tracks appear in reverse order. To change the order of tracks that you're playing in sequence, just click and hold the track number in the leftmost column for the song; then drag it up or down in the list.

To skip tracks so that they don't play in sequence, deselect the check box next to the song names. iTunes skips deselected songs when you play the entire sequence.

You can repeat an entire CD by clicking the repeat button below the source pane on the left side of the iTunes window (or choosing Controls⇨Repeat All). When it's selected, the repeat button shows blue highlighting. Click the repeat button again to repeat the current song (or choose Controls⇨Repeat One). The button changes to include a blue-highlighted numeral 1. Click it once more to return to normal playback (or choose Controls⇨Repeat Off).

The shuffle button, located to the left of the repeat button, plays the songs on the CD in random order, which can be fun. You can then press the arrow keys on your keyboard or click the back and forward buttons to jump around in random order.

Eject a CD by clicking the eject icon next to the CD name in the source pane or by choosing Controls⇨Eject Disc. You can also right-click the CD name and choose Eject from the contextual menu that appears.

Importing Audio CDs

Bringing music tracks from a CD into iTunes is called *ripping* a CD (audio programmers *do* have a sense of humor). *Ripping,* in technical terms, is extracting the song's digital information from an audio CD and wrapping it, or *encoding* it, in a particular digital audio file format such as the AAC or MP3 format, explained later in this chapter. The format and its settings affect the sound quality and the space occupied by the song file on the computer and the iPad, iPod, or iPhone. They also affect the song's compatibility with other types of players and computers.

If this is your first time ripping a CD, you may want to change the default import format settings in order to improve sound quality or to reduce the amount of disk space occupied by songs. After setting them, your import format and settings stay the same until you change them again. Also, before ripping any CD, you may want to edit the song information, as I describe in Chapter 11, or set the Gapless Album option, which I describe in the section called, "Don't fall into the gaps" later in this chapter.

How easy is it to rip a CD? After you've set your importing format and chosen its settings (or decide to use the default format and its settings), just pop an audio CD into your CD-ROM/DVD drive. Click the Yes button to rip your CD into iTunes and, without further ado, your CD tracks are absorbed into your iTunes library.

If you want to edit the song information, set the Gapless Album option, or change import formats and settings, click the No button to make your changes first. Then start the rip, as I describe in the section "Let it rip" later in this chapter.

Changing import preferences and settings

To change your import preferences, format, and settings, or to change the way iTunes rips — whether it rips right away, asks first, or automatically ejects afterward — follow these steps:

1. **Choose iTunes⇨Preferences⇨General on a Mac or Edit⇨Preferences⇨ General in Windows.**

   The iTunes Preferences dialog opens, showing the General preferences, including the When You Insert a CD pop-up menu and the Import Settings button.

2. **Choose what action iTunes should take for the When You Insert a CD option in the General preferences.**

   Choose one of the following actions on the pop-up menu for when you insert an audio CD, as shown in Figure 7-1:

   - *Show CD:* iTunes does nothing else. This preference is ideal if you regularly edit the song information first, as I describe in Chapter 11, or need to change the format and settings when importing different CDs.

   - *Begin Playing:* See "Playing CD Tracks in iTunes" earlier in this chapter for details on playing CDs.

   - *Ask to Import CD:* iTunes displays the dialog that asks whether you want to import the CD. This preference is ideal if you think you may want to change the format and settings or edit the song information on a per-CD basis.

   - *Import CD:* iTunes uses the current import format and settings and automatically imports the CD. This preference is useful if you want to use the same import format and settings every time.

   - *Import CD and Eject:* iTunes automatically imports and then ejects the CD, making way for the next one. This preference is useful for importing a batch of CDs and you want to use the same import format and settings for the entire batch.

3. **Make sure that the Automatically Retrieve CD Track Names from Internet check box is checked (if not, click to select it).**

   This preference, underneath the When You Insert a CD preference, is selected by default — but make sure that the box is checked. iTunes automatically grabs the song titles, artist names, album titles, and so on directly from the Internet, as I describe in Chapter 11.

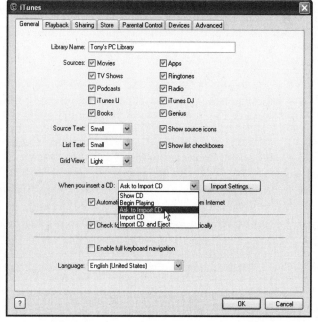

Figure 7-1:
Set the
appropri-
ate action
for iTunes
after a CD is
inserted.

4. **Click the Import Settings button in the General preferences.**

   The Import Settings dialog appears, as shown in Figure 7-2.

5. **Make your changes, guided by my suggestions that follow, and then click the OK button.**

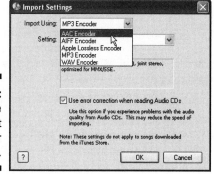

Figure 7-2:
Change
your import
settings for
ripping CDs.

The Import Settings dialog offers the following choices:

- ✔ **Import Using:** Set this pop-up menu to choose the import format. This choice is perhaps the most important, and I describe it in more detail later in this section.

- ✔ **Setting:** This offers different settings depending on your choice of format. For example, in Figure 7-3, the AAC Encoder for the AAC format is already selected, and I'm in the process of choosing the iTunes Plus setting, which is the quality setting for music available in the iTunes Store. Set this pop-up menu to the iTunes Plus or High Quality setting for most music, or choose Custom to choose a custom setting. The Spoken Podcast setting is for lower-quality voice recordings. See the following bulleted list for more information about encoders and settings and how they affect quality and file size.

- ✔ **Use Error Correction When Reading Audio CDs:** Although you'll reduce importing speed, select this check box to use error correction if you have problems with audio quality or if the CD skips. (Not every skipping CD can be imported even with error correction, but it might help.)

Figure 7-3:
Change the
quality set-
ting for the
encoder you
chose for
importing.

For a quick and pain-free ripping session, choose from among the following formats in the Import Using pop-up menu, based on how you plan to use the music:

- ✔ **AAC Encoder:** I recommend encoding music into the AAC format for almost all uses except for burning another audio CD. (AIFF, Apple Lossless, or WAV is better if you plan to burn another audio CD at the highest quality with the songs you ripped, and MP3 is the only format to use for MP3 CDs and other MP3 players.) For music, choose the High Quality or iTunes Plus settings from the Setting pop-up menu.

- ✔ **AIFF Encoder:** Use AIFF if you plan to burn the song to an audio CD using a Mac (use WAV for Windows), or use it with a DVD project. AIFF offers the highest possible quality, but it takes up a lot of space (about

10MB per minute). Choose the Automatic option from the Setting pop-up menu for best results. Don't use AIFF for songs that you intend to transfer to your iPad, iPod, or iPhone, or to an MP3 CD.

You can rip a CD as many times as you want, and use a different format for each version, as long as you modify the album name or song title to identify each version. For example, you might rip *Sgt. Pepper's Lonely Hearts Club Band* with the AAC Encoder for use in your iPad, iPod, or iPhone. You might then rip it again after changing the encoder to the higher-quality Apple Lossless or AIFF Encoder, using a different album name (such as Sgt. Pepper-2), for burning onto an audio CD. After burning the CD, you can delete Sgt. Pepper-2 to reclaim the hard drive space.

✔ **Apple Lossless Encoder:** Use the Apple Lossless format for songs that you intend to burn onto audio CDs as well as for playing on an iPad, iPod, or iPhone. The music is imported at the highest quality, with compression that doesn't lose any information (which is why it is called *lossless*). The files are just small enough (about 60–70 percent of the size of the AIFF versions) that they don't hiccup on playback on the iPad, iPod, or iPhone.

✔ **MP3 Encoder:** Use the MP3 format for songs that you intend to burn on MP3 CDs or that you intend to use with MP3 players or your iPad, iPod, or iPhone — it's universally supported. If you use MP3, I recommend choosing the Higher Quality option from the Setting pop-up menu.

✔ **WAV Encoder:** WAV is the high-quality sound format that's used on PCs (like AIFF on Macs), but it also takes up a lot of space (about 10MB per minute). Use WAV if you plan on burning the song to an audio CD or using WAV with PCs. Choose the Automatic option from the Setting pop-up menu for best results. Don't use WAV for songs that you intend to transfer to your an MP3 player or to an MP3 CD; use MP3 instead.

To find out more about audio encoding formats, how to adjust custom settings to reduce space and increase audio quality, and how to convert songs from one format to another (and what problems to look out for when doing so), visit this book's companion Web site.

Don't fall into the gaps

Some CDs — particularly live concert albums, classical albums, rock operas (such as The Who's *Tommy*), and theme albums (such as *Sgt. Pepper's Lonely Hearts Club Band* by The Beatles) — are meant to be played straight through, with no fading between the songs.

Fortunately, you can turn on the Gapless Album option for multiple songs or for an entire album. With the Gapless Album option set in iTunes, songs play seamlessly one to the next. You can also play these songs seamlessly on your iPad, iPod, or iPhone (except iPod models older than sixth-generation).

To turn on the Gapless Album option for an entire CD before importing it, follow these steps:

1. **Click the No button if the import dialog appears (to postpone importing).**
2. **Select the CD title in the source pane.**

   The CD title appears in the source pane under Devices.
3. **Choose File➪Get Info.**

   The CD Info dialog opens.
4. **Select the Part of a Gapless Album check box and then click the OK button.**

To turn on the Gapless Album option for multiple songs on the CD but not the entire CD, follow these steps:

1. **Follow Steps 1 and 2 in the preceding list.**
2. **Select the songs in the list pane.**

   From the album, select the songs that you want to play continuously (such as the first two songs of *Sgt. Pepper*).

   To select multiple songs, click the first one, press and hold ⌘ on a Mac or Ctrl in Windows, and click each subsequent song. To select consecutive songs, click the first one, hold down the Shift key, and click the last one.
3. **Choose File➪Get Info and then click the Yes button in the warning dialog about editing multiple items.**

   The Multiple Item Information dialog opens.
4. **Click the Options tab for the Options pane.**
5. **Select Yes from the Gapless Album pop-up menu.**

   After choosing Yes on the pop-up menu, a check mark appears next to the Gapless Album option to indicate that it has changed.
6. **Click the OK button to close the Multiple Item Information dialog and update the options for the selected songs.**

For older iPod models, or as an alternative to using the Gapless Album option, you can use the Join Tracks option when ripping a CD to join the tracks in your iTunes library so that they play seamlessly on an iPod or iPhone. To join tracks, select the tracks and choose Advanced➪Join CD Tracks. You can join tracks only when ripping a CD, not afterward.

Let it rip

After changing your import settings and preferences, you're ready to rip. To rip a CD, follow these steps:

1. **Insert an audio CD into your computer's CD-ROM/DVD drive.**

   The dialog appears asking whether you want to import the CD into your library, with Yes and No buttons.

2. **Click Yes to import (and skip to Step 5) or No to set options first.**

   Click the No button to set preferences and import settings as described in the previous section, and then click the Import Settings button in the lower right corner of the list pane. See the previous section for changing your import settings. You may also want to click No to set songs to be skipped, or if you see unnamed tracks rather than the proper track, artist, and album names in the list pane (see Chapter 11 to fix song information or grab it from the Internet).

3. **(Optional) Deselect the check boxes next to any songs on the CD that you don't want to import.**

   iTunes imports only the songs that have check marks next to them; when you remove the check mark next to a song in the list pane, iTunes skips that song.

   Be sure to set your import settings and the Gapless Album option to your liking before actually ripping the CD.

4. **Click the Import CD button.**

   The Import CD button appears next to the Import Settings button in the lower-right corner of the list pane after you insert a CD. The status display shows the progress of the operation. To cancel, click the small *x* next to the progress bar in the status display.

5. **When all the songs are imported, choose Controls⇨Eject Disc to eject the disc.**

   In the list pane, iTunes displays an orange, animated waveform icon next to the song that it's importing. When iTunes finishes importing each song, it replaces the waveform icon with a check mark, as shown in Figure 7-4. (On a color monitor, the check mark is green.) iTunes chimes when it finishes the import list.

You can also eject the CD by clicking the eject button next to the disc name in the Devices section of the source pane. Mac users can press the eject button on the upper-right corner of the Mac keyboard.

Figure 7-4:
iTunes
shows a
check mark
to indicate
that it's
done ripping
the song.

Adding Audio Files

If you already have music, audio books, or other audio files — MP3, AAC, AIFF, or WAV files — that you downloaded or copied to your hard drive, you can simply drag them over the Library section of the source pane of the iTunes window to bring them into your library. If you drag a folder or disk icon, all the audio files that it contains are added to your iTunes library (and if you drag it into the Playlists section of the source pane, a playlist is created — see Chapter 13 for details). You can also choose File⇨Add to Library on a Mac, or File⇨Add File to Library and File⇨Add Folder to Library on a Windows PC, as an alternative to dragging. For details on where iTunes stores the file, see Chapter 14.

MP3 CDs are easy to add because they're essentially data CDs. Simply insert them into your CD-ROM drive, open the CD in the Finder, and drag and drop the MP3 audio files into the iTunes window — no need to rip, in other words. Downloaded audio files are even easier — just drag and drop the files into iTunes. If you drag a folder or CD icon, all the audio files it contains are added to your iTunes library.

Adding Videos

Besides purchasing and downloading videos from the iTunes Store, as I describe in detail in Chapter 6, you can also download video files (files that end in .mov, .m4v, or .mp4) from the Internet, or copy them from other computers and bring them into iTunes. From iTunes, you can sync them to your iPad, iPod, iPhone, and Apple TV after converting them into a format that looks best for those devices.

To convert a video for use with an iPod or iPhone, select the video (see Chapter 10 for browsing instructions) and choose Advanced⇨Create iPod or iPhone Version. To convert a video for use with an iPad or with Apple TV, choose Advanced⇨Create iPad or Apple TV Version. The selected videos are automatically copied when you convert them, leaving the originals intact.

To find out more about bringing videos, including MPEG files, from other sources into iTunes and converting videos for use with iPad, iPods, iPhones, and Apple TV, visit the tips section of the author's Web site (www.tonybove.com).You can drag a video file into iTunes just like an audio file. Drag each video file from the Mac Finder or Windows Desktop to the Library section of the source pane, or directly to a playlist in the Playlists section of the source pane, or to the list pane. The video files that you import into iTunes show up in the Movies section of your iTunes library — click Movies in the Library section of the source pane to see them. You can use iTunes to change the media type (for example, to change a video file from Movie to Music Video) — see Chapter 11 for details.

Video files are organized in folders and stored in the iTunes Media library on your hard drive just like audio files — see Chapter 14 for details.

Chapter 8

Getting in Sync with Your iTunes Library

• •

In This Chapter

▶ Synchronizing your iPad, iPod, or iPhone with your iTunes library

▶ Choosing what to sync and what not to sync

▶ Copying content directly to, or deleting from, your iPad, iPod, or iPhone

• •

*i*Tunes is the all-knowing, all-powerful synchronizer, the software you use to put content and apps on your iPad, iPod, or iPhone.

Synchronizing your iPad, iPod, or iPhone with iTunes means automatically copying content and apps to the device. It also means keeping the device up to date with all or part of your iTunes library. The sync operation also keeps an iPad, iPod touch, or iPhone up to date with your iTunes Store account information so that you can download items from the iTunes Store or App Store directly to your iPad, iPod touch, or iPhone. Not only that, but the content you obtain from the stores with one account can be synced with all the iPads, iPods, and iPhones you have at no extra cost.

If you make changes in iTunes to content you synced to the iPad, iPod, or iPhone, those changes are automatically carried over to the iPad, iPod, or iPhone when you sync it with iTunes again. Your iPad, iPod, or iPhone mirrors the content of your iTunes library, or as much of the content as will fit — and iTunes can make assumptions if the entire library won't fit, or give you options to be more selective, as I describe in this chapter.

You also use iTunes to sync Apple TV, which lets you play your iTunes library content on an HDTV audio-video system. To find out more about Apple TV, visit this book's companion Web site.

When you first set up your iPad, iPod, or iPhone, you can choose the option to sync your entire iTunes library automatically. From that point on, your iPad, iPod, or iPhone synchronizes with your entire library automatically, right after you connect it to your computer. (See Chapter 2 for details on setting up your iPad, iPod, or iPhone.)

The full, everything-but-the-kitchen-sync approach works well if your combined iTunes library and photo library are small enough to fit in their entirety on your iPad, iPod, or iPhone. For example, if your iTunes and photo libraries combined are less than 29GB and you have a 32GB iPod touch, sync everything. (You can see the size of your iTunes library in GB, or *gigabytes,* at the bottom of the iTunes window in the center.) Syncing everything copies your entire library, and it's just as fast as copying individual items (if not faster) because you don't have to select the items to copy.

If your iTunes library has more content than your iPad, iPod, or iPhone can hold, you can make decisions about which parts to sync. You can select options to synchronize music, TV shows, movies, and so on. For example, you can copy all your songs and audio books, but only some of your TV shows, none of your movies, and only the podcasts you haven't heard yet.

This chapter also describes how to copy songs, videos, podcasts, and audio books directly to your iPad, iPod, or iPhone using the manual method. You can even combine automatic syncing with manual methods to build your iPad, iPod, or iPhone library as you see fit.

If you store photos in an iPhoto library on a Mac, or in a program (such as Adobe Photoshop Album) in Windows, you can set up your iPad, iPod, iPhone, or Apple TV with the option to copy your entire photo library. See Chapter 17 for details.

Syncing with Your iTunes Store Account

You can sync your iPad, iPod touch, or iPhone with your iTunes Store account information in advance, so that you don't have to manually sign in with your iPad, iPod touch, or iPhone before downloading from the iTunes Store or App Store. (You can also manually sign in or create an account on your iPad, iPod touch, or iPhone, as I show in Chapter 6.)

If you were signed in to your iTunes Store account when you initially set up and synced your iPad, iPod touch, or iPhone, the store account information was also synchronized. If not, or if you want to resync your store information, visit the iTunes Store and sign in to your account first, before syncing your iPad, iPod, or iPhone.

You don't have to buy anything; just signing in to the store provides all the info you need for syncing an iPad, iPod touch, or iPhone with the iTunes Store account. (If you haven't set up your iTunes Store account yet, flip back to Chapter 6, do the deed, and then sign in by clicking the Sign In tab in the upper-right area of the iTunes window.)

After signing into your account, go ahead and follow the steps in the next sections to sync your iPad, iPod, or iPhone — "Syncing Everything," "Choosing What to Sync," or "Manually Managing Music and Videos."

After syncing to your account, your iPad, iPod touch, or iPhone always syncs any purchased content or apps you download directly to it with your iTunes library whenever you connect it to your computer — that way you don't lose any content or apps if, heaven forbid, something happens to your iPad, iPod touch, or iPhone.

Syncing Everything

Follow these five easy steps to sync all the content and apps in your iTunes library to an iPad, iPod, or iPhone:

1. **Connect the iPad, iPod, or iPhone and select its name when it appears in the Devices section of the source pane.**

   iTunes displays the sync options to the right of the source pane, with tabs for each page of sync options.

2. **Click the Summary tab to see the Summary page, if it is not already selected.**

   The Summary page shows how much space on the device is occupied by content and how much is still free. (See Figure 8-1.)

3. **If the iPad, iPod, or iPhone isn't already synchronizing, click the Sync button in the lower-right corner to synchronize it.**

   Most likely your iPad, iPod, or iPhone is already set to automatically synchronize with iTunes after connecting it. After clicking the Sync button (or if iTunes is automatically syncing), the iTunes status pane tells you that iTunes is syncing.

   If you haven't made any sync selections, the default is to copy everything in your iTunes library to your iPad, iPod, or iPhone. (Only the music, audio books, and audio podcasts in your library are copied to an iPod shuffle.)

   If your iPad, iPod, or iPhone is not set to automatically synchronize, or even if synchronization is going on, you can select content to sync, as I describe later in this chapter, and click Apply to start re-syncing again with the new settings.

4. **Wait for the synchronization to finish and then click the eject button next to the iPad, iPod, or iPhone name in the source pane.**

   You should always wait until the iTunes status pane (at the top) displays that the synchronization is complete.

5. **Disconnect your iPad, iPod, or iPhone from your computer.**

   That's it. Your iPad, iPod, or iPhone is now synchronized.

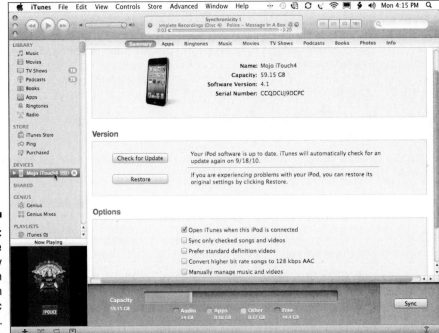

Figure 8-1:
The
Summary
page for an
iPod touch
offers sync
options.

Your iTunes library is the main library for your content, while the library in your iPad, iPod, or iPhone is like a satellite holding some or all of the same content. If you make changes in your iTunes library after syncing the iPad, iPod, or iPhone, those changes are automatically copied over to the iPad, iPod, or iPhone when you sync again — unless you manually manage content, as I describe in "Manually Managing Music and Videos" in this chapter. That means if you delete an album or video from your iTunes library, that album or video is also deleted from your iPad, iPod, or iPhone the next time you sync. You can also delete items directly from your iPad, iPod, or iPhone without changing your iTunes library — see "Deleting items on your iPad, iPod, or iPhone" later in this chapter.

You probably don't need to know anything else in this chapter about synchronizing with content — unless your iTunes library and additional photo library are too large to fit, or you want to be more selective about which content to synchronize.

iTunes backs up your synchronization settings for each iPad, iPod, and iPhone that you connect from the last time when you synchronized the device.

Photos you've organized in a photo library (such as iPhoto on a Mac, or Adobe Photoshop Elements on a Windows PC) are also copied over. See Chapter 17 for details.

If your iTunes library is too large to fit on your iPad, iPod, or iPhone, iTunes decides which songs and albums to include by using the ratings that you set for each song. (To find out how to set ratings, see Chapter 11.) If your iPad, iPod, or iPhone already has photos on it, iTunes asks whether you want to delete them to gain more space. After clicking the Yes or No button, iTunes tries its best to fit everything. If it has to cut something, though, it skips copying new photos and displays the message `Some photos were not copied`.

You can squeeze more songs onto an iPad, iPod, or iPhone if you convert them to a lower-bit-rate format — and you can do this on the fly while syncing (although it can dramatically increase sync time; large libraries might need to be synced overnight). Select the Convert Higher Bit Rate Songs to 128 kbps AAC option (refer to Figure 8-1). As a result, the songs take up less space on the iPad, iPod, or iPhone than they occupy in your iTunes library.

If you're still short of space even after skipping photos, iTunes displays a warning about the lack of free space, and it asks whether you want to disable podcast synchronization and let iTunes create a selection of songs in a playlist based on ratings and playback counts in iTunes. (See Chapter 13 for details on using playlists.)

 ✔ **If you click the Yes button,** iTunes creates a new playlist (titled "*Your device name* Selection," as in "My iPod touch Selection") and displays a message telling you so. Click the OK button, and iTunes synchronizes your iPad, iPod, or iPhone using the new playlist. iTunes also sets your iPad, iPod, or iPhone to synchronize music automatically by playlist, as I describe in the next section.

 ✔ **If you click the No button,** iTunes updates automatically until it fills your iPad, iPod, or iPhone without creating the playlist.

From that point on, your iPad, iPod, or iPhone synchronizes with your iTunes library automatically, right after you connect it to your computer.

To prevent an iPad, iPod, or iPhone from automatically synchronizing, press ⌘-Option (Mac) or Ctrl-Alt (Windows) while you connect the device; then keep pressing until the iPad, iPod, or iPhone name appears in the iTunes Source pane. You can then change the iPad, iPod, or iPhone sync setting to manually manage music and videos, as I describe later in this chapter.

If you connect an iPad, iPod, or iPhone previously linked to another computer to *your* computer, iTunes displays a message warning you that clicking the Yes button replaces its content with the content from your computer's library. If you don't want to change the content on the iPad, iPod, or iPhone, click No. If you click Yes, iTunes erases the device and synchronizes it with your computer's library. To avoid this warning, first set the iPad, iPod, or iPhone sync settings to manually manage music and videos, as I describe later in this chapter, on the same computer the device was previously synced with.

Choosing What to Sync

If you have a massive content library that doesn't fit on your iPad, iPod, or iPhone, you can go the selective route, choosing which content to automatically sync with your iTunes library. By synchronizing selectively, you can still make your iPad, iPod, or iPhone match at least a subset of your iTunes library. If you make changes to that subset in iTunes, those changes are automatically made in the device when you synchronize again.

You don't have to sync to one massive library in iTunes — you can create several subsets of your main library (sublibraries) so that each sublibrary could be small enough to fit on a certain type of device. To find out how to manage multiple iTunes libraries, visit the tips section of the author's Web site (www.tonybove.com).

Syncing everything but the kitchen

You can decide which items you *don't* want to synchronize and simply not include them by first *deselecting* them one by one in your iTunes library. (If you have a large iTunes library, this may take some time — you may find it easier to synchronize by playlists, artists, and genres, as I show in the next section.)

By default, all content items are selected — a check mark appears in the check box next to the item. To deselect an item in your iTunes library, click the check box next to the item so that the check mark disappears. To reselect an item, just click the check box again.

You can quickly select (or deselect) an entire album by showing the column browser (choose View⇨Column Browser⇨Show Column Browser) and selecting the album. Then press ⌘ (Mac) or Ctrl (Windows) while selecting (or deselecting) a single song in the album in the list pane.

After you deselect the items you don't want to transfer, connect your iPad, iPod, or iPhone to your computer and select its name when it appears in the Devices section of the Source pane (refer to Figure 8-1). Then select the Sync Only Checked Songs and Videos check box. The Sync button changes to Apply — click the Apply button.

iTunes restarts synchronization and deletes from the iPad, iPod, or iPhone any items in the library that are deselected, to save space, before adding back in the items in the iTunes library that are selected. That means the items you deselected are now *gone* from your iPad, iPod, or iPhone — replaced by whatever items were selected. Of course, the items are still in your iTunes library. Wait for the synchronization to finish and then click the eject button next to the iPad, iPod, or iPhone name in the Source pane.

Getting picky about playlists, artists, and genres

You can include just the items that are defined in playlists, including Genius playlists, and/or just specific artists. Syncing by playlists, artists, and genres is a great way of syncing vast amounts of music without syncing the entire library. (To find out how to create playlists, see Chapter 13.)

For example, you can create four playlists that contain all essential rock, folk, blues, and jazz albums, and then select all four, or just one, two, or three of these playlists to sync with your iPad, iPod, or iPhone, along with everything by specific artists (such as Frank Zappa, who doesn't fit into these categories).

After connecting your iPad, iPod, or iPhone to your computer, select its name when it appears in the Devices section of the source pane (refer to Figure 8-1). Then click the Music tab of the sync options. The Music sync options page appears, as shown in Figure 8-2.

By default, the Entire Music Library option is checked, unless you are manually managing music as I describe later in this chapter. To change your sync options, select the Sync Music check box.

Figure 8-2:
Sync only
the selected
playlists,
artists, and
genres.

If you are manually managing music, a message appears asking if you are sure that you now want to sync music — and that all content already on your iPad, iPod, or iPhone will be replaced. Click the Sync Music button to go ahead (or Cancel to cancel), which returns you to the Music sync options page.

To choose playlists, artists, and genres to sync with the iPad, iPod, or iPhone, click the Selected Playlists, Artists, and Genres option at the top of the Music sync options page (refer to Figure 8-2). You can then select each playlist from the Playlists list, each artist from the Artists list, and (if you scroll the Music sync options page) each genre from the Genres list. You can choose any number of playlists, artists, and genres. (In Figure 8-2, I selected some playlists in the Playlists column along with Joe Cocker and Ry Cooder in the Artists column.) Finally, click the Apply button to apply changes (or Revert to cancel), and click the Sync button if synchronization hasn't already started automatically.

iTunes copies only what you've selected in the Playlists, Artists, Genres, and Albums columns of the Music sync options page. If you also select the Include Music Videos check box (as I do in Figure 8-2), iTunes includes music videos listed in the playlists (except, of course, for an iPod shuffle, which doesn't play video). For an iPad, iPod touch, or iPhone, you can also select the Include Voice Memos check box to sync your voice memos from the Voice Memo app with iTunes. (See Chapter 20 for details on using Voice Memo.)

You can also automatically fill up the rest of your iPad, iPod, or iPhone free space with random songs (after syncing your selected playlists, artists, and genres) by selecting the Automatically Fill Free Space With Songs option. iTunes randomly chooses the music as I describe in the latter part of the "Syncing Everything" section in this chapter.

If you select the Sync Only Checked Songs and Videos check box on the Summary page sync options (refer to Figure 8-1), only selected items are copied. iTunes ignores items that are not selected, even if they're listed in the chosen playlists, artists, and genres for synchronization.

Picking podcast episodes and books

You can get picky about which podcast episodes should be copied during synchronization, and even which parts of audio books. When syncing an iPad, iPod touch, or iPhone that already has Apple's iBooks app installed, you can also choose which electronic books to sync and use with iBooks.

Clicking the Podcasts tab of the sync pages presents options for choosing podcast episodes to include. (You can include audio podcasts to sync with an iPod shuffle, but not video podcasts.)

Connect your iPad, iPod, or iPhone to your computer, and select its name when it appears in the Devices section of the source pane (refer to Figure 8-1). Then click the Podcasts tab. The Podcasts sync options page appears, as shown in Figure 8-3. Click the Sync Podcasts option at the top.

The Podcast sync options let you choose unplayed or recently added episodes (as shown in Figure 8-3). Select the Automatically Include ____ Episodes Of ____ check box; choose a modifier from the first pop-up menu, such as All Unplayed or 10 Most Recent; and then choose All Podcasts or Selected Podcasts from the second pop-up menu. If you chose Selected Podcasts, you can select a podcast in the Podcasts column below these options, and then select specific episodes in the Episodes column (which may already be selected depending on your choices in the pop-up menus).

For example, in Figure 8-3, I'm automatically synchronizing the 10 most recent episodes of selected podcasts — which automatically selects The Flying Other Brothers-Music Podcast (all three new episodes). I'm also selecting two episodes of the Rockument podcast.

Finally, click the Apply button to apply changes, and click the Sync button if synchronization hasn't already started automatically.

Figure 8-3:
Sync the 10 most recent episodes of selected podcasts and a few episodes of another podcast.

Clicking the Books tab of the sync pages presents options for choosing audio books. If you have the iBooks app installed on your iPad, iPhone, or iPod touch, you also have options for choosing e-books. To sync books, follow these steps:

1. **Connect your iPad, iPod, or iPhone to your computer, and select its name when it appears in the Devices section of the source pane (refer to Figure 8-1).**

2. **Click the Books tab.**

   The Books sync options page appears with options for syncing audio books, and additional options for syncing e-books if you have iBooks installed on your iPad, iPhone, or iPod touch.

3. **To sync audio books, click the Sync Audiobooks option, and then click one of the following sync options:**

   • Choose All Audiobooks to sync all of them.

   • Choose Selected Audiobooks, and then choose entire audio books in the Audiobooks column on the left, or select an audio book on the left and then choose specific parts of the audio book in the right column.

4. **To sync e-books for use with iBooks, click the Sync Books option, and then click one of the following sync options:**

   • Choose All Books to sync all of them.

   • Choose Selected Books, and then click the check boxes next to the books you want to sync.

5. **After choosing sync options, click Apply to apply changes and click the Sync button if synchronization hasn't already started automatically.**

After syncing podcast episodes, audio books, or e-books, you can continue listening or reading from where you left off on your computer or other synchronized device. For example, if you were reading an e-book using the iBooks app on an iPad, and synced the iPad with iTunes, and then synced your iPod touch with iTunes, you can continue reading with the iBooks app on your iPod touch from where you left off on the iPad.

Choosing movies and TV shows

Movies and TV shows take up a lot of space, so if you limit the movies and TV episodes you synchronize with your iPad, iPod, or iPhone, you gain extra space for more music, audio books, podcasts, and photos. (This section doesn't apply to the iPod shuffle, which doesn't play movies or TV shows.)

To get choosy about movies, connect your iPad, iPod, or iPhone to your computer, and select its name when it appears in the Devices section of the source pane (refer to Figure 8-1). Then click the Movies tab of the sync options. The Movies sync options page appears with the Sync Movies and Automatically Include options at the top.

Select the Sync Movies check box, and then select the Automatically Include ___ Movies check box; choose a modifier from the pop-up menu, such as All, 1 Most Recent, All Unwatched, or 10 Most Recent Unwatched. If you choose any option other than All, you can then select specific movies from the list below the option.

To pick only the TV episodes you want, click the TV Shows tab of the sync options. The TV Shows sync options page appears, as shown in Figure 8-4.

Select the Automatically Include ___ Episodes Of ___ check box; choose a modifier from the first pop-up menu, such as All, All Unwatched, or 5 Most Recent; and then choose All Shows or Selected Shows from the second pop-up menu. If you chose Selected Shows, or deselect the Automatically Include option, you can select shows in the Shows column below these options, and then select specific episodes in the Episodes column. For example, in Figure 8-4, I'm synchronizing two episodes of *Star Trek: The Original Series*.

After choosing sync options, click the Apply button to apply changes and click the Sync button if synchronization hasn't already started automatically.

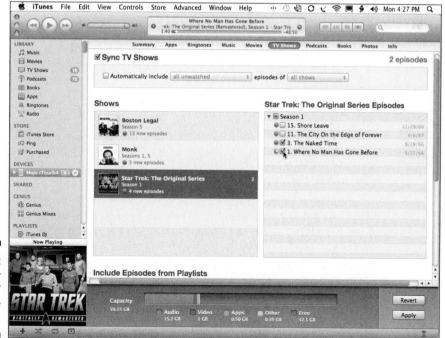

Figure 8-4:
Sync only selected TV show episodes.

Syncing and arranging apps

Your iPad, iPod touch, or iPhone is set by default to sync all the apps in your iTunes library. iTunes automatically skips any app that doesn't belong on the device (such as an iPad app when you are syncing an iPod touch), and displays a warning about any other app it skips for other reasons (such as not having a proper authorization code). Because most apps don't take up a lot of space, I recommend simply letting iTunes do its thing and sync all the apps that belong on the device.

However, you can selectively choose apps to synchronize. Follow these steps:

1. **Connect your iPad, iPod, or iPhone to your computer, and select its name when it appears in the Devices section of the source pane (refer to Figure 8-1).**

2. **Click the Apps tab of the sync options.**

    The Apps sync options page appears, as shown in Figure 8-5.

3. **Click the Sync Apps option if it is not already selected.**

4. **From the list box on the left (refer to Figure 8-5), select the app's check box for each app that you want to synchronize.**

    You can scroll the list box to see all your apps — and you can click the Sort button at the top to toggle sorting the list by Name, Kind, Category, Date, or Size. For example, in Figure 8-5, I am switching from Sort by Kind to Sort by Category.

To quickly select or deselect specific apps in the list box, use the arrow keys on your keyboard (up and down) to move from app to app and press the spacebar to check or uncheck each app.

You can set iTunes to automatically sync to your iPad, iPod, or iPhone all new apps that you acquire from the App Store using iTunes, without having to selectively choose them. Scroll the Apps sync options page to the bottom and select the Automatically Sync New Apps option. Deselect this option to prevent iTunes from automatically syncing all new apps.

Although you can rearrange and delete apps on your iPad, iPod touch, or iPhone Home screens directly, as I describe in meticulous detail in Chapter 3, you can also do this in iTunes while syncing. Click the thumbnail image of any Home screen on the far right side of the Apps sync options page to view the app icons on that Home screen, and then click and drag the app icons to the positions you want, or select an app icon and click the circled X in the upper-left corner to delete the app. You can even drag an app from the list box to its precise position on a Home screen to sync that app.

Figure 8-5:
Sort the list
of apps and
then select
apps to
sync.

To organize apps into folders, drag an app icon on top of another in the
Home screen on the right side of the Apps options page. For example, in
Figure 8-6, I dragged the NPR Addict app over the NYTimes app in Home
screen 5 to create the News folder, which I can then rename if I want to.

If you use apps that can share files between your computer and your iPad,
iPod touch, or iPhone — such as Stanza with its library of electronic books,
or Pages on the iPad for word processing — scroll the Apps sync options all
the way down to the bottom to see the File Sharing section. Select the app in
the Apps column on the left. You can then save a document or file on your
computer by selecting it in the right column, clicking the Save To button, and
then browsing for a location on your hard drive to save it. You can also copy
a document or file onto your iPad, iPod touch, or iPhone by clicking the Add
To button, browsing for the file, and clicking Open. The file is automatically
copied to the iPad, iPod touch, or iPhone to use with the app.

After choosing sync options, click the Apply button to apply changes and
click the Sync button if synchronization hasn't already started automatically.

Figure 8-6:
Organize
apps into
folders
on Home
screens.

Syncing ringtones

You can purchase ringtones from the iTunes Store using iTunes on your computer, and synchronize them with your iPod touch or iPhone to use with FaceTime calls. To selectively choose ringtones for your iPod touch or iPhone, follow these steps:

1. **Connect your iPod touch or iPhone to your computer, and select its name when it appears in the Devices section of the source pane (refer to Figure 8-1).**

2. **Click the Ringtones tab of the sync options.**

   The sync options appear for ringtones.

3. **Click Sync Ringtones at the top of the page if the option is not already turned on.**

4. **Click the All Ringtones option, or click the Selected Ringtones option and then select each ringtone to synchronize in the Ringtones box.**

   You can scroll the list box to see all your ringtones. Click the check box to select one.

5. **Click Apply to apply changes and then click the Sync button if synchronization hasn't already started automatically.**

iTunes erases any previous ringtones in the iPod touch or iPhone and copies only the ringtones you selected in Step 4.

Manually Managing Music and Videos

If your entire library is too big for your iPad, iPod, or iPhone, or you want to guarantee that you have some free space left on your iPad, iPod, or iPhone, you may want to copy individual items directly. By setting your iPad, iPod, or iPhone to manually manage music and videos, you can add content to the device directly via iTunes, and you can delete content on the device as well. You can even copy some songs or videos from another computer's iTunes library without deleting any content from your iPad, iPod, or iPhone.

To set your iPad, iPod, or iPhone to manually manage music and videos, first connect it to your computer. Then follow these steps:

1. **Select the iPad, iPod, or iPhone name in the Devices section of the iTunes source pane.**

   After selecting the name, the Summary page appears, displaying the sync options (refer to Figure 8-1).

2. **Select the Manually Manage Music and Videos check box (on an iPod shuffle, select Manually Manage Music).**

   iTunes displays a message for iPod nano and iPod classic models (and older models) warning you that manually managing music and videos also requires manually ejecting the iPod before each disconnect.

3. **Click the OK button for the warning and click the Apply button to apply the change.**

Copying items directly to your iPad, iPod, or iPhone

After setting your iPad, iPod, or iPhone to manually manage music and videos, you can select and drag music and videos — songs, albums, audio books, music videos, movies, and TV shows — to your iPad, iPod, or iPhone name in the source pane. (Similarly, after setting an iPod shuffle to manually manage music, you can select and drag music, audio books, and audio podcasts to the iPod shuffle name.)

You can drag the media from its section in the iTunes library or from an existing playlist, or drag an entire playlist. To do so, follow these steps:

1. **In the iTunes source pane, select the source of your media.**

   You might select Music in the Library section, for instance, or a playlist in the library.

   You can select music in your library using List, Album List, Grid, or Cover Flow view (see Chapter 10 for browsing details), or select songs in a playlist.

2. **Drag items (such as one or more songs or an album) directly from your iTunes library or playlist over the iPad, iPod, or iPhone name in the Devices section of the source pane.**

   You can drag individually selected songs or an entire album from Cover Flow view, List view, Album List view (see Figure 8-7), or Grid view. When you drag an album cover or album title, all the songs in the album are copied. If you drag a playlist name from the Source pane to the iPad, iPod, or iPhone name, all the songs associated with the playlist copy along with the playlist itself.

Figure 8-7: Drag songs to an iPod touch (Mojo iTouch).

3. **Wait for the copying to finish, and then click the eject button next to the iPad, iPod, or iPhone name in the Source pane to eject it.**

4. **Disconnect your iPad, iPod, or iPhone from your computer.**

Deleting items on your iPad, iPod, or iPhone

When you manually manage music and videos on an iPad, iPod, or iPhone (or manage music on an iPod shuffle), you can also delete content from the iPad, iPod, or iPhone. Set the option to manually manage music and videos (if it isn't set that way already) and then follow these steps:

1. **In the source pane, click the triangle to the left of the iPad, iPod, or iPhone name to expand its library.**

   The iPad, iPod, or iPhone library sections appear in the source pane (Music, Movies, TV Shows, and other sections), followed by playlists. The library is indented underneath the iPad, iPod, or iPhone name.

2. **Click any content type in the iPad, iPod, or iPhone library to see the items.**

   The content items appear in the list pane to the right of the source pane.

3. **Select an item and press Delete/Backspace or choose Edit⇨Delete.**

   iTunes displays a warning to make sure that you want to do this; click the OK button to go ahead or the Cancel button to stop. If you want to delete a playlist, select the playlist underneath the iPad, iPod, or iPhone name in the Source pane and then press Delete/Backspace or choose Edit⇨Delete.

Autofill it up

You can also automatically fill your iPad, iPod, or iPhone while managing music and videos manually. Autofill randomly picks songs from your entire iTunes library or from a playlist you select in the iTunes source pane.

Autofill is especially useful for copying random songs to an iPod shuffle every time you connect it to your computer. Eventually, you can shuffle through everything in your library if you so wish by randomly autofilling your iPod shuffle every time you sync.

Set the option to manage music and videos on the iPad, iPod, or iPhone, or to manually manage music on the iPod shuffle (if it isn't set that way already). Then follow these steps:

1. **In the source pane, click the triangle to the left of the iPad, iPod, or iPhone name to expand its library.**

   The iPad, iPod, or iPhone library sections appear in the source pane (Music, Movies, TV Shows, and other sections), followed by playlists. The library is indented underneath the iPad, iPod, or iPhone name.

2. **Select Music under the iPad, iPod, or iPhone name in the Devices section of the source pane.**

   The music on your iPad, iPod, or iPhone appears in the list pane, along with the Autofill pane along the bottom, as shown in Figure 8-8.

3. **Choose your source of music from the Autofill From pop-up menu.**

   You can choose a playlist, as I did in Figure 8-8 (I switched from the White Shoe playlist to the Purchased smart playlist), or choose the Genius option or a Genius playlist (which I describe in Chapter 13), or Music for the entire music library. If you choose a playlist or Genius playlist, Autofill uses only the playlist or the Genius feature as the source to pick random songs. After choosing your source of music, iTunes creates a playlist and displays it in the list pane.

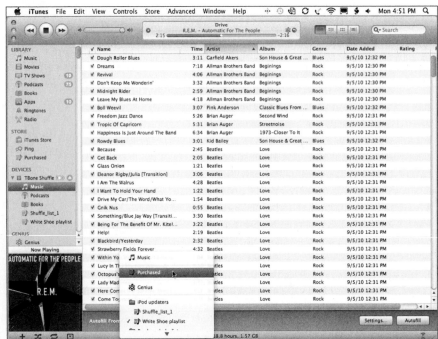

Figure 8-8:
Autofill an iPod shuffle from an iTunes playlist.

4. **(Optional) Click the Settings button to set options and then click the OK button.**

   After clicking the Settings button, the Autofill Settings dialog appears. You can choose to replace all the items on the iPad, iPod, or iPhone, to choose items randomly, or to choose higher rated items more often

5. **Click the Autofill button to start copying songs.**

   iTunes copies the contents of the Autofill playlist to your iPad, iPod, or iPhone.

6. **Wait for the copy operation to finish and then click the eject button.**

   Always wait until the iTunes status pane tells you that the copying is finished.

Chapter 9

Syncing Mail, Calendars, Contacts, and Bookmarks

*Y*ou may choose an iPod classic to play music and videos on the road, but you may also find it useful for viewing the personal information — contacts, appointments, and events — that you manage on your home or office computer. The iPod classic and older models offer *one-way* synchronization of personal information from your computer to the iPod. (The iPod shuffle and fourth-generation iPod nano don't hold personal information, so this chapter isn't relevant for them.)

The iPad, iPod touch, or iPhone can take care of all aspects of your digital life: It can send and receive e-mail, save your notes, keep track of your calendar, sort your contacts, and save bookmarks to all your favorite Web sites as you browse them. You can also add personal info directly to your iPad, iPod touch, or iPhone, and synchronize that information back with your computer, which is *two-way* synchronization.

If you're a road warrior, you may want to fill your iPad, iPod, or iPhone with your personal information. This chapter shows you how.

Organizing Your Personal Info

You already manage your contacts, calendars, e-mail, and Web bookmarks with applications on your computer. Now you can use iTunes to synchronize your iPod classic or iPod nano with these calendars and contacts, or your iPad, iPod touch, or iPhone with these calendars, contacts, e-mail accounts, notes, and bookmarks.

If you're a Mac user, you have it easy: You can use the Address Book application to manage your contacts, iCal for calendars, Mail for e-mail and notes, and Safari for Web bookmarks. All these applications are provided free with Mac OS X. You can also sync contacts from Microsoft Entourage, Yahoo! Address Book, and Google Address Book, and sync calendars from Entourage.

If you're a Windows user, you can sync your contacts with Microsoft Outlook 2003 or 2007, Yahoo! Address Book, Google Address Book, Windows Address Book (Outlook Express), or Vista Contacts. You can sync calendars and notes with Outlook and sync bookmarks with Microsoft Internet Explorer or Apple's Safari for Windows.

The iPad, iPod touch, and iPhone can also use the Exchange ActiveSync protocol to sync e-mail, calendars, and contacts with Microsoft Exchange Server 2003 Service Pack 2 or Exchange Server 2007 Service Pack 1. For many e-mail accounts, the settings automatically appear, like magic.

If you signed up for Apple's MobileMe service (formerly the .Mac service, now www.me.com), you can automatically keep your iPad, iPod touch, and iPhone synchronized along with several computers and other iPad, iPod touch, and iPhone models, all at once, with the latest e-mail, bookmarks, calendar entries, and contacts, as I describe in the section "Going MobileMe to Sync Your iPad, iPod touch, or iPhone," later in this chapter.

What's cool about "cloud computing" Web services like MobileMe, Microsoft Exchange, and Yahoo! Mail is that their e-mail services *push* e-mail messages to your computer and your iPad, iPod touch, or iPhone so that they arrive immediately, automatically. Some, like Comcast, offer their own apps (the Comcast Mobile app, for example) to receive pushed messages. Other types of e-mail account services let you *fetch* e-mail from the server — you must first select the account in Mail on your iPad, iPod touch, or iPhone before it can actually retrieve the e-mail.

You probably already know how to manage your calendar activities and your contacts on your computer. In fact, you're probably knee-deep in contacts, and your calendars look like they were drawn up in the West Wing. If not, visit the tips section of my Web site (www.tonybove.com) for advice on using MobileMe and on adding and editing contacts and calendar information on your Mac (with Address Book and iCal) or Windows computer (with Outlook).

Syncing Your Personal Info Using iTunes

You use iTunes to synchronize an iPod classic with calendars and contacts on your computer.

With an iPad, iPod touch, or iPhone, you can sync your personal information using iTunes, or a push service such as MobileMe or Microsoft Exchange. You can switch between iTunes and the push service anytime you want. MobileMe and Microsoft Exchange get their write-ups in the next section, and this section tackles the iTunes method.

To synchronize your iPad, iPod, or iPhone with contacts, calendars, e-mail accounts, notes, and bookmarks by using iTunes, follow these steps:

1. **Connect the iPad, iPod, or iPhone and select its name when it appears in the Devices section of the source pane.**

   iTunes displays the iPad, iPod, or iPhone sync options to the right of the source pane.

2. **Click the sync options' Info tab for an iPad, iPod touch, or iPhone, or the Contacts tab for an iPod classic (or older model).**

   The Info sync options page appears for the iPad, iPod touch, or iPhone (see Figure 9-1 for an iPod touch), offering the Contacts, Calendars, Mail Accounts, Other (bookmarks and notes), and Advanced sections. (At the top is a link to information about the MobileMe service if you are not already using it for syncing.)

   If you have an iPod classic or older model, what you see is the Contacts and Calendars synchronization options page with the same options.

3. **Select the option to synchronize contacts.**

   On a Mac: Select the Sync Address Book Contacts check box (shown in Figure 9-1). With an iPad, iPod touch, or iPhone, you also have the option to sync with Yahoo! Address Book — click the Configure button to enter your login information. An option to sync with Microsoft Entourage appears for the iPad, iPod touch, iPhone, iPod nano, or iPod classic if you have Entourage's identity database set up on your Mac.

   For help with Entourage identities on a Mac, see www.entourage.mvps. org/database/.

   On a Windows PC: Select the Sync Contacts With option and choose Yahoo! Address Book, Windows Address Book, Google Contacts, or Outlook from the pop-up menu.

4. **Select the All Contacts option or select the Selected Groups option and choose which groups to synchronize.**

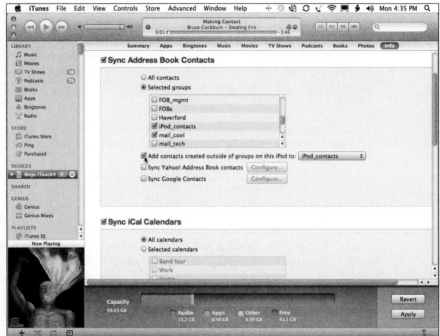

Figure 9-1:
Synchronize
contacts
and
calendars.

You can synchronize all contacts or just selected groups of contacts (such as the "iPod_contacts" and "mail-cool" groups selected in Figure 9-1). To choose groups, select the check box next to each group in the list; scroll the list to see more groups.

If you make changes on an iPad, iPod touch, or iPhone, iTunes automatically keeps all contacts you've selected synchronized with your computer's application. You can also set the Add Contacts Created Outside of Groups option to a particular group, so that contacts created on your iPad, iPod touch, or iPhone outside of groups are assigned to this group.

5. **Scroll the page and select the option to synchronize calendars.**

On a Mac, select the Sync iCal Calendars check box (shown in Figure 9-1); an option to sync with Microsoft Entourage also appears if you have the application on your Mac. On a Windows PC, select the Sync Calendars With option and choose Outlook from the pop-up menu.

6. **Select the All Calendars option. (Alternatively, if you're using iCal with Mac OS X, select the Selected Calendars option and choose the calendars to synchronize.)**

In Windows, you can synchronize all calendars with Microsoft Outlook, but you don't have the option to sync only selected calendars. (The Selected Calendars option is grayed out.) With iCal in Mac OS X, you can synchronize all calendars or just those you select. To choose specific calendars, select the check box next to each calendar in the list.

The iPad, iPod touch, and iPhone include the Do Not Sync Events Older Than *xx* Days option, in which you can set the *xx* number of days (see the top of Figure 9-2 for this option, which is at the very bottom of the Calendars section).

Unless you are using an iPad, iPod touch, or iPhone, you can skip to Step 12.

7. **To synchronize e-mail accounts with an iPad, iPod touch, or iPhone, scroll down to the Mail Accounts section and select the Sync Mail Accounts option.**

   The Mail Accounts section, shown in Figure 9-2, appears below the Calendars sections on the Info sync options page. On a Mac, select the Sync Mail Accounts option. On a Windows PC, choose Outlook or Outlook Express from the pop-up menu for the Sync Mail Accounts From option.

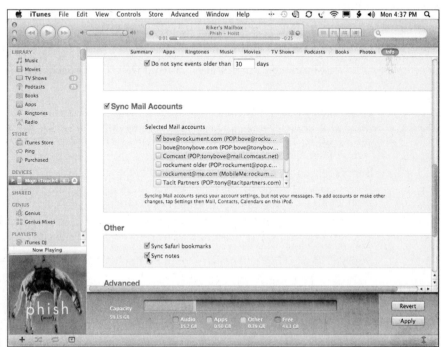

Figure 9-2: Synchronize e-mail accounts with an iPod touch (or iPhone).

8. **Choose the e-mail accounts you want to sync with your iPad, iPod touch, or iPhone.**

   After selecting the Sync Mail Accounts option in Step 7, a list of e-mail accounts appears in the box below. To choose accounts, select the check box next to each account in the list; scroll the list to see more e-mail accounts.

9. **To synchronize Web bookmarks with your iPad, iPod touch, or iPhone, scroll down to the Other section and select the Sync Bookmarks option.**

   On a Mac running OS X, the option is Sync Safari Bookmarks; on a Windows PC, iTunes offers a pop-up menu to choose Internet Explorer or Safari.

10. **To synchronize notes on your computer with an iPad, iPod touch, or iPhone, select the Sync Notes option in the Other section.**

    You can sync the notes you create in the Notes app on your iPad, iPod touch, or iPhone with the Mail application on a Mac or with Outlook on a Windows PC. Select the Sync Notes option on a Mac; on a Windows PC, choose Outlook from the pop-up menu for the Sync Notes With option.

11. **Click the Apply button to apply the changes. (Alternatively, click the Revert button to cancel the changes.)**

    iTunes starts to synchronize your iPad, iPod, or iPhone.

12. **Wait for the sync to finish and then click the eject button next to the iPad, iPod, or iPhone name in the source pane to eject device.**

    Wait until the iTunes status pane (at the top) displays the message Sync is Complete.

After setting the synchronization options, every time you connect your iPad, iPod, or iPhone, iTunes automatically synchronizes it with your personal sync options.

Synchronizing an e-mail account to your iPad, iPod touch, or iPhone copies *only* the e-mail account setup information; the messages are retrieved by the iPad, iPod touch, or iPhone over the Internet. Whether the messages in your inbox appear on your iPad, iPod touch, or iPhone *and* on your computer depends on the type of e-mail account you have and how you've configured it — for example, if you delete on your computer an e-mail message from a push account (such as MobileMe), or from an account set up to delete messages on the server as soon as you delete them on your computer, the message also disappears from any iPad, iPod touch, and iPhone configured to use that account.

If you select a calendar or a group of contacts to be synchronized on a Mac and later want to remove that particular calendar or group of contacts, deselect the calendar (see the preceding Step 6) or the group (see the preceding Step 4) and then click the Apply button to resynchronize. iTunes synchronizes only the group of contacts and calendars selected, removing from the iPad, iPod, or iPhone any that aren't selected.

iTunes also offers Advanced options at the bottom of the Info page for the iPad, iPod touch, or iPhone. Use these options to sync your iPad, iPod touch, or iPhone from scratch to replace all contacts, calendars, notes, mail accounts, or bookmarks. You can choose which ones you want to replace by selecting the check box next to each option. iTunes replaces the information once, during the next sync operation. After that operation, these Advanced options are automatically turned off.

Going MobileMe to Sync Your iPad, iPod touch, or iPhone

MobileMe synchronizes MobileMe e-mail accounts, along with contacts, calendars, and bookmarks, on a Web server on the Internet — also known as *the cloud.* You can then keep your iPad, iPod touch, or iPhone synchronized to the cloud wirelessly, without having to connect it to your computer.

Your iPad, iPod touch, or iPhone can receive pushed e-mail, contacts, calendars, and bookmarks from the MobileMe cloud as long as it is awake (meaning that the screen is on or the device is connected to your computer or to a power adapter).

The place to start organizing your information is usually your computer. However, if you've already entered contacts and calendars on your iPad, iPod touch, or iPhone, sync the contacts and calendars from your iPad, iPod touch or iPhone with iTunes first, as I describe in the previous section. Then sync your computer with MobileMe, and then your iPad, iPod touch, or iPhone with MobileMe.

Make sure that the information you synchronize the very first time to MobileMe is the correct, complete information. You should synchronize your primary source with MobileMe — typically your computer, which has the newest info — *before* synchronizing your iPad, iPod touch, or iPhone with MobileMe.

MobileMe first makes its appearance when you set up your iPad, iPod touch, or iPhone: An advertisement appears with buttons to try MobileMe. If you skipped the ad (like many people do), you can go back and try MobileMe by following these steps:

1. **Connect the iPad, iPod touch, or iPhone to your computer and select its name when it appears in the Devices section of the source pane.**

   iTunes displays the sync options to the right of the source pane.

2. **Click the Info tab.**

   The Info sync options page appears, offering the MobileMe setup button at the top.

3. **Click the Set Up Now button.**

   iTunes jumps to your browser to open the MobileMe setup page on the Apple Web site. Here you can find out all about MobileMe, click the Free Trial button, or log in if you already have an account. Apple also provides step-by-step instructions for setting up MobileMe on your computer and syncing with your iPad, iPod touch, or iPhone — or you can read all about it in the next few sections.

After setting up your MobileMe account on a Mac or Windows PC as described in the next sections, you turn on your MobileMe account on your iPad, iPod touch, or iPhone, as I describe in section "Setting Up Mail Accounts on Your iPad, iPod touch, or iPhone," later in this chapter. You can set up and turn on your MobileMe account on all the iPads, iPods, and iPhones you have.

Setting up on a Mac

Setting up MobileMe is easy on a Mac: When you sign in to MobileMe for the first time, MobileMe automatically configures Mac OS X Mail on your Mac to send and receive e-mail from your MobileMe account and to synchronize contacts from Address Book and calendars from iCal. If you already set up your iPad, iPod touch, or iPhone with a Mac and MobileMe service, automatic synchronization should already be set up on that Mac.

If not, you can set up a Mac to sync with MobileMe at any time. Follow these steps:

1. **Choose System Preferences from the Apple menu, choose MobileMe, click the Account tab, and sign in.**

2. **Click the Sync tab.**

   The Sync options for MobileMe appear, as shown in Figure 9-3.

3. **Select the Synchronize with MobileMe check box and then choose a sync interval from the pop-up menu. (Refer to Figure 9-3.)**

   For the most frequent updates, choose Automatically to sync with MobileMe every 15 minutes. You can instead choose Manual to sync only when you click the Sync Now button.

4. **Select the check boxes to choose information to sync with MobileMe.**

   You can choose to sync just contacts, calendars, bookmarks, or mail accounts, or all of them. (You can also sync other items, such as Dashboard Widgets, Dock Items, Keychains, and Mail Rules and Signatures, for use with other Macs, but these are not synced to your iPad, iPod touch, or iPhone.)

Figure 9-3:
Sync
options for
MobileMe
on a Mac.

5. **Click the Sync Now button if you chose Manually (otherwise syncing begins automatically).**

   The sync commences. To make sure that your data has synced, go to www.me.com, log in, and click the Contacts and Calendar icons along the top row of icons on the left.

Setting up in Windows

Download and install on your PC the latest version of MobileMe Control Panel for Windows, available from http://support.apple.com/downloads. MobileMe Control Panel is required to set up and manage MobileMe syncing and manage iDisk settings on a Windows PC.

To set up a Windows PC to sync with MobileMe or to check your sync settings or sync immediately, follow these steps:

1. **From the Windows Start menu, open Control Panel and choose MobileMe Control Panel.**

   The MobileMe panel appears with tabs along the top.

2. **Click the Account tab for the Account pane (if it isn't already visible) and log in with your MobileMe member name and password if you aren't already logged in.**

3. **Click the Sync tab.**

   The sync options appear, as shown in Figure 9-4.

4. **Select the Sync with MobileMe check box and then select a sync interval.**

   For the most frequent updates, choose Automatically to sync with MobileMe every 15 minutes. You can instead choose Manual to sync only when you click the Sync Now button.

5. **Select the check boxes to sync your contacts, calendars, and bookmarks, and then use the drop-down lists to choose which Windows applications you want to use when syncing with these items.**

6. **Click the Sync Now button.**

Figure 9-4:
Sync
options for
MobileMe
on a
Windows
PC.

The sync starts. To make sure that your data has synced, go to www. me.com, log in, and click the Contacts and Calendar icons along the top row of icons on the left.

If you use Microsoft Outlook in conjunction with Microsoft Exchange Server, MobileMe won't sync contacts or calendars with Outlook — use Exchange Server instead. See the section "Setting Up Mail Accounts on Your iPad, iPod touch, or iPhone," later in this chapter.

When you sync upon a cloud

If your contacts or calendar entries show up in duplicate or triplicate in your computer or on your iPad, iPod touch, or iPhone, as if they were stuck inside of MobileMe with the memory blues again, you probably need to overwrite the data in the MobileMe cloud.

Selecting items to synchronize may not overwrite all the data in the cloud. To overwrite the data stored in the cloud with the data on your computer, open MobileMe (in System Preferences on a Mac or Control Panel in Windows), click the Sync tab, and then click the Advanced button. (Refer to Figure 9-3 for a Mac or Figure 9-4 for Windows.) Select the computer you are syncing from in the list at the top and then click Reset Sync Data.

In the dialog that appears, choose an option from the Replace pop-up menu:

✔ On a Mac, you can choose All Sync Info, or Bookmarks, Calendars, or Contacts. (The other choices on the pop-up menu — Key Chains, Mail Accounts, and so on — don't copy over to the iPad, iPod touch, or iPhone but are useful for keeping other computers synchronized.)

✔ In Windows, you can choose All Sync Info, or Bookmarks, Calendars, or Contacts.

After choosing an option from the Replace pop-up menu, click the arrow underneath the Cloud icon to change the animation so that the data arrow points from the computer to the cloud. Finally, click the Replace button.

This action replaces the data in the MobileMe cloud with the data on your computer. You can also use these steps to go in reverse — replace the data on your computer with the data in MobileMe. To do this, click the arrow so that the animation points the arrow from the cloud to the computer.

Setting Up Mail Accounts on Your iPad, iPod touch, or iPhone

To set up a Mail account on your iPad, iPod touch, or iPhone, including a MobileMe e-mail account (with contacts, calendars, and bookmarks) or a Microsoft Exchange account, follow these steps:

1. **Choose Settings⇨Mail, Contacts, Calendars from the Home screen.**

   The Mail, Contacts, Calendars settings screen appears, with the Accounts section at the top, as shown in Figure 9-5 (left side).

2. **Tap the Add Account button and then tap the account type from the list of account types that appears.**

   Your choices are Microsoft Exchange, MobileMe, Gmail, Yahoo! Mail, AOL, or Other, as shown in Figure 9-5 (right side). After tapping the account type, the New Account screen appears for Exchange, MobileMe, Gmail, Yahoo! Mail, and AOL accounts, and the Other screen appears for Other accounts.

Figure 9-5:
Tap Add
Account
(left) to see
the list of
account
types (right).

3. **Enter your account information as follows:**

   Generally speaking, you need to enter your name, username, password, and optional description by tapping next to a field's name (such as Name or Address) to display the keyboard. Then use the keyboard to enter the information and tap Return on the keyboard to finish entering. As you tap Return, the next field appears ready for you to enter information, until you reach the last field. Tap Return to finish entering information.

   • *MobileMe, Gmail, Yahoo! Mail, or AOL:* Enter your name, username, password, and an optional description on the New Account screen, and then tap Save in the upper-right corner to save account information. Your iPad, iPod touch, or iPhone verifies the account; if the account can't be verified, the message `Cannot Get Mail` appears, indicating that the username or password is incorrect (which may be the case, or perhaps a network problem prevented proper connection). Tap OK and try Steps 2 and 3 again (or tap Cancel to cancel). If the account is verified, you're done for a Gmail, Yahoo! Mail, or AOL account and you can skip the rest of these steps — the Mail, Contacts, Calendars settings screen appears with the new account listed in the Accounts section.

For MobileMe, your iPad, iPod touch, or iPhone displays your account's settings screen.

- *Microsoft Exchange:* Enter your name, username, domain (optional), password, and an optional description on the New Account screen, and then tap Next in the upper-right corner to save the account information and move on to the Exchange account's settings screen. Microsoft's Autodiscovery service kicks in to check your username and password to determine the address of the Exchange server. If it can't find the server's address, a dialog appears for you to enter it — enter the complete address in the Server field and tap Save.

- *Other:* Tap Add Mail Account on the Other screen for an IMAP (Internet Message Access Protocol) or POP (Post Office Protocol) account. The New Account screen appears; enter your name, user-name, password, and an optional description, and then tap Save in the upper-right corner to save the account information. The iPad, iPod touch, or iPhone searches for the account on the Internet and displays the New Account settings screen.

4. **Set your mail account settings on the New Account settings screen as follows:**

- *MobileMe or Exchange:* Turn on any of or all the items you want to sync: Mail, Contacts, Calendars, and Bookmarks (MobileMe only). If you sync these items using your MobileMe or Exchange account, syncing them in iTunes is turned off. Any of these items on your iPad, iPod touch, or iPhone are replaced by the MobileMe or Exchange account versions. (You can always return to the account setting's screen to turn them off to enable syncing with iTunes.) For Exchange, you can set how many days of e-mail you want to sync to your iPad, iPod touch, or iPhone. Tap Save in the upper-right corner to finish and save your settings.

- *Other:* Tap IMAP or POP on the New Account settings screen, depending on the type of e-mail account you have — ask your e-mail service provider if you don't know. Then enter or edit the account information, including the server names and your user name and password for incoming and outgoing mail. (Get this information from your service provider if you don't know it.) Tap Save in the upper-right corner to finish and save your settings. The Mail, Contacts, Calendars settings screen appears with the new account listed in the Accounts section.

5. **When the Sync or Cancel warning appears for MobileMe or Exchange accounts, tap Sync (or Cancel).**

When you tap the Sync button, MobileMe or Exchange overwrites any existing contacts, calendars, and bookmarks on your iPad, iPod touch, or iPhone (or the subset of these that you chose in Step 4). The Mail, Contacts, Calendars settings screen appears with the new account listed in the Accounts section.

6. **Tap Fetch New Data (refer to Figure 9-5, left side), and tap Off for Push to turn it on (if it isn't already on).**

   That's it! Your iPad, iPod touch, or iPhone syncs automatically from this point on, with data pushed or fetched from the e-mail account depending on your push and fetch settings. (For details, see Chapter 19.)

Changing and Deleting Mail Accounts

You can temporarily turn off a Mail account on your iPad, iPod touch, or iPhone, change its settings, or delete it from your iPad, iPod touch, or iPhone.

To turn off a Mail account in your iPad, iPod touch, or iPhone temporarily, or change account settings, choose Settings⇨Mail, Contacts, Calendars from the Home screen and then touch the account in the Accounts section to see that account's settings screen. You can then change your account's settings, including the items that are synced to your iPad, iPod touch, or iPhone with a MobileMe or Microsoft Exchange account.

To delete the account, scroll down and tap Delete Account. Deleting a Mail account from an iPad, iPod touch, or iPhone doesn't affect the e-mail account or its settings on your computer.

Part III
Managing Your Library

The 5th Wave   By Rich Tennant

"It's a fully furnished, 3-bedroom house that's designed to fit perfectly over your iPod."

In this part . . .

As soon as you start building your iTunes library, you'll want to know how to organize all your content, add or change the content information, add ratings, build playlists, burn CDs, and make a backup of your library.

✓ Chapter 10 describes how to browse your iTunes library, change the list view options, sort your content, and search for songs, artists, albums, music videos, audio books, movies, TV shows, apps, and games.

✓ Chapter 11 shows you how to add or edit the information (such as the artist or title), add or change the artwork, and add ratings for each content item.

✓ Chapter 12 describes how to play music, audio books, videos, and podcasts in your iTunes library.

✓ Chapter 13 shows you how to build regular playlists, smart playlists, and genius playlists of songs and albums in iTunes.

✓ Chapter 14 is a guide to burning audio CDs, MP3 CDs, and data CDs and DVDs, as well as copying media files and making backup copies of your iTunes library.

Chapter 10

Searching, Browsing, and Sorting in iTunes

*Y*ou rip a few CDs, buy some songs and movies from the iTunes Store, and you're hooked. You keep adding more and more content to your library and forget how to find items you added last month. It's time to discover how to organize your content and navigate your iTunes library.

The iTunes library can hold an almost unlimited number of files, depending on how much space you have on your computer's hard drive. But even if you keep your iTunes library down to the size of what fits on your iPad, iPod, or iPhone, you still have a formidable collection at your fingertips. If your content collection is getting large, organize it to make finding songs, audio books, podcasts, and videos easier. After all, finding U2's "I Still Haven't Found What I'm Looking For" is a challenge, even in a library that fits on an 8GB iPod nano.

This chapter shows you how to search, browse, and sort your iTunes library. You can find any content item in seconds. You can also change the viewing options to make your library's display more useful, such as displaying songs sorted by artist, album, genre, or other attributes, or sorting TV shows by season or episode.

Browsing Your Library Content

As you know, the iTunes window provides the list pane on the right side and the source pane on the left side (refer to Chapter 2 for figures showing Mac and Windows versions). The list pane offers a view of your library and content, depending on which sources of content you choose in the source pane on the left side. The choices in the source pane are as follows:

✔ **Library section:** Select Music, Movies, TV Shows, Podcasts, Books, Apps, Ringtones, or Radio. By default, iTunes doesn't display iTunes U. To see iTunes U, or to change the options listed in the Library section, choose iTunes⇨Preferences (Mac) or Edit⇨Preferences (Windows), click the General tab at the top of the Preferences window, and select or deselect the Show options depending on what you want to display. Click the OK button to accept the changes.

  • *Music:* Lists the entire library of songs and music videos purchased, downloaded, ripped, or copied into the library.

  • *Movies:* Lists the movies downloaded from the iTunes Store and video files you've added to your library.

  • *TV Shows:* Lists TV shows downloaded from the iTunes Store. (This list includes video files you've imported and then changed to TV Show in the Media Kind popup of the Options pane of the Info dialog — see Chapter 11 for details on adding or changing the media type.)

  • *Podcasts:* Lists the podcasts you've subscribed to. (See Chapter 7 for details on subscribing to and browsing podcasts.)

  • *Books:* Lists the audio books downloaded from the iTunes Store or from Audible.com or other sources, and electronic books downloaded from the iBooks store. (To include audio files you've ripped or imported, see Chapter 11 for details on changing the Media Kind pop-up of the Options pane of the Info dialog.)

  • *Apps:* Lists the iPad, iPod touch, and iPhone apps downloaded from the App Store or iTunes Store, and iPod games downloaded from the iTunes Store.

  • *Ringtones:* Lists the ringtones downloaded from the iTunes Store or from other sources, as well as those created in GarageBand on a Mac and added to your iTunes library.

  • *Radio:* Lists the Internet radio stations you can play. Radio station content is streamed to your computer but not stored in your library.

  • *iTunes U:* Courseware, lectures, and other items downloaded from or subscribed to in the iTunes U section of the iTunes Store.

✓ **Store section:** The iTunes Store and Ping (see Chapter 6).

✓ **Devices section:** Your iPad, iPod, iPhone, and Apple TV appear listed here when connected, as well as an audio CD when inserted into your computer. When you select a device such as an iPod, iTunes displays the summary page with synchronization options. See Chapter 8 for details on navigating the library on an iPad, iPod, or iPhone set for managing content manually.

✓ **Shared section:** Shared iTunes libraries for sharing content on your home network appear here, as I show in Chapter 6.

✓ **Genius section**: The Genius Mix and any of the Genius playlists you generate appear in this section. See Chapter 13 for details on using the Genius Mix and Genius playlists.

✓ **Playlist section:** Smart playlists and regular playlists appear in this section. Also appearing in this section is iTunes DJ, which lets you continually change a playlist of random songs. See Chapter 12 for details on iTunes DJ, and Chapter13 for the player's guide to playlists.

Overwhelmed by all the content in the list pane? Try browsing. iTunes offers four view buttons in the upper-right corner for browsing your content in the list pane:

✓ **List** (the List view button on the left, or choose View⇨As List) shows items in a list. For details on what you can do in List view, see "Browsing songs by artist and album" in this section.

✓ **Album List** (the Album List view button, or choose View⇨As Album List) shows items in a list sorted by album with album cover art. For details on what you can do in Album List view, see "Browsing songs by artist and album" in this section.

✓ **Grid** (the Grid view button, or choose View⇨As Grid) shows thumbnail cover art images in a grid, as shown in Figure 10-1. You can select a thumbnail of an album to select the album. Double-click a thumbnail to display a list of albums with an artwork column. Switch the focus of your browsing by clicking the Albums, Artists, Genres, and Composers tabs along the top.

✓ **Cover Flow** (the Cover Flow button on the right, or choose View⇨As Cover Flow) shows the cover browser, also known as Cover Flow, as described in the next section.

In List or Album List view, choose View⇨Column Browser⇨Show Column Browser to show the browser, which displays columns you can browse to easily find items. To make the browser disappear and see your content in a full list, choose View⇨ Column Browser⇨Hide Column Browser.

Album List   Cover Flow

List   Grid

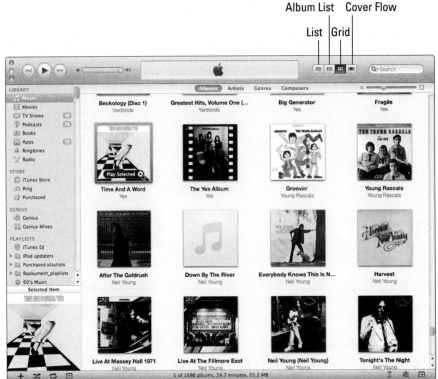

Figure 10-1:
Browse
music in
Grid view.

Browsing by cover art with Cover Flow

Does viewing a cover whet your appetite for the music, story, or video inside? Of course it does. Covers provide a context that simply can't be put into words or conveyed by sound. One fantastic innovation of iTunes is how it integrates cover art from albums, books, podcasts, and videos with your library so that you can flip through your content to find items based on the artwork. Figure 10-2 shows the iTunes window using Cover Flow view to display the Music portion of the iTunes library.

To select Cover Flow, click the rightmost of the four view buttons in the upper-right corner of the iTunes window (refer to Figure 10-1). You can also show the cover browser by choosing View⇨As Cover Flow.

Cover Flow lets you flip through your cover art to select music, movies, TV shows, podcasts, books, and apps. (The cover browser doesn't work with ringtones or radio stations.) Just drag the slider under the cover art to scroll swiftly through your library, or click to the right or left of the foreground cover art to move forward or backward, respectively. When you scroll or click through cover art, the content items in the list pane also change.

Double-click the foreground cover art to start playing the first item — whether it's an album's first song, a movie, the first chapter of an audio book, or the first episode of a TV show (but not an e-book or app, which can't be played in iTunes).

Click the browse full-screen button (refer to Figure 10-2) to display Cover Flow, um, full-screen. You can still click a cover to select an album, click within each cover to move forward and backward, and use the cover browser's slider to navigate your library. iTunes also offers a volume control slider to set the audio volume while browsing full-screen cover art. Press Esc (Escape) or click the browse full-screen button (with its arrows pointing inward) in the lower-right corner of the display to stop displaying the cover browser full-screen and return to the iTunes window.

Figure 10-2: Browse music using Cover Flow view.

Browse full screen

To fill your library automatically with cover art, get yourself an iTunes Store account (if you don't already have one). Log in to your account; choose Advanced⇨Get Album Artwork. iTunes grabs the cover art not only for content downloaded from the iTunes Store — including movies, TV shows, audio books, and podcasts — but also for CDs you ripped, provided that the albums are also available in the iTunes Store. Even if you downloaded or ripped only one song of an album, you get the album's cover art for that song.

You can also get your cover art from other places that sell CDs, audio books, and DVDs (including Amazon.com) or even scan it from the actual CDs, DVDs, or books. You can then add cover art from a scanned or downloaded image file to any content item in your iTunes library, as I describe in Chapter 11. The optimal size for cover art is 300 x 300 pixels.

Browsing songs by artist and album

To select List view, click the leftmost of the four view buttons in the upper-right corner of the iTunes window (refer to Figure 10-1). You can also choose View⇨As List. To choose Album List view, click the Album List view button to the right of the List view button.

To browse music in your library in List view or Album List view, select Music in the source pane in the Library section. The List and Album List views show the title of each song in the Name column, the artist or band name in the Artist column, and the title of the album in the Album column. To browse the list, choose View⇨Column Browser⇨Show Column Browser. To hide the browser, choose View⇨Column Browser⇨Hide Column Browser.

The column browser organizes music content into Genres, Artists, Albums, Composers, and Groupings columns — you can choose which columns to display by choosing View⇨Column Browser⇨Genres, View⇨Column Browser⇨Artists, and so on — to select each category to show (or deselect each category to remove). For example, in Figure 10-3, I'm using Album List view, and I included only the Genres, Artists, and Albums columns in the column browser. (For a peek at what List view looks like without the column browser, see Figure 10-5.)

The column browser appears in the leftmost column (as shown in the Windows version of iTunes in Chapter 2) by default or if you choose View⇨Column Browser⇨On Left. The Genres, Artists, and Albums columns appear from left to right, with the song list in the far right column. When you select an album, iTunes displays only the songs for that album in the far right column.

You can switch the column browser to appear in the top part of the list pane, as shown in Figure 10-3, if you choose View⇨Column Browser⇨On Top. This view, which is the traditional " browse" mode of earlier versions of iTunes, is useful if your display is not very wide. Select a genre in the Genres column to see artists in that genre in the Artists column, or select All at the top of the Genres column to see all artists for all genres. When you select an artist in the Artists column, the album titles appear in the Albums column (on the right). When you select an album, iTunes displays only the songs for that album in the list pane below the column browser.

To see the songs for more than one album from an artist at a time, press ⌘ (Mac) or Ctrl (Windows) while clicking each album name.

Figure 10-3:
Select an artist in the column browser to see the list of albums for that artist.

After selecting an album in the Albums column, the songs in the list pane are listed in the proper album track order, just as the artist, producer, or record label intended. (You can even edit the song information easily in this view. I describe how to get and edit track information in wondrous detail in Chapter 11.)

To browse all the songs in your library, select All at the top of each of the columns — Genres, Artists, and Albums. You can also switch to Grid view (refer to Figure 10-1) or to Cover Flow view (refer to Figure 10-2) to show the album cover art.

Browsing books and podcasts

If you don't see Books in the Library section of the source pane, choose iTunes⇨Preferences (Mac) or Edit⇨Preferences (Windows), click the General tab at the top of the Preferences window, select the Books option next to the Show heading, and click the OK button. The Books option then appears in the source pane in the Library section.

To browse the audio books in your library, and iPad/iPhone/iPod touch e-books you downloaded with the iBooks app, select Books in the source pane. In Grid view, the cover art for e-books appear first, followed by audio books. You can browse book titles and authors with the column browser in

List view, or browse cover art in Cover Flow view. The List, Album List, and Cover Flow views mix e-books with audio books. Both List and Album List views show the title of each book in the Name column and the author's name in the Authors column. Audio books are organized into parts and typically include part numbers in their titles.

To browse podcasts, select Podcasts in the Library section of the source pane. You can browse podcast episodes with the column browser in List or Album List view, or browse cover art in Grid view or Cover Flow view. You can then see the episodes of a podcast by clicking the podcast, and in List or Album List view, by clicking the triangle next to the podcast name. For details on playing episodes, see Chapter 12.

The List and Album List views show the title of each podcast and its episodes in the Podcast column. The mysterious blue dot next to a podcast means that you haven't played one or more episodes of the podcast yet. (The same blue dot appears next to each unplayed episode.) As soon as you start listening to or watching a podcast, the dot turns into a half-moon until you complete the episode (accompanied by the theme of *The Twilight Zone*).

Browsing movies, videos, and TV shows

To browse movies, select Movies in the Library section of the source pane. Most video files you add to your library from sources other than the iTunes Store are classified as movies, and some, such as EyeTV recordings, are classified as TV shows — but you can change their media type as I describe in Chapter 11 so that, for example, a video shows up as a TV show or music video, rather than a movie. You can also find in the Movies listing those movies and short films you downloaded from the iTunes Store.

You can browse movies, TV shows, and videos with the column browser in List or Album List views, or browse cover art in Grid view or Cover Flow view. The Grid view and the Cover Flow view show the first key frame of the movie or the box cover art for the movie.

You can browse TV shows by selecting TV Shows in the Library section of the source pane. The List and Album List views show the episode title, show title, and season number. The column browser in List or Album List view organizes TV shows by Genres, Shows, and Seasons. The Grid and Cover Flow views show the promotional cover art for the TV show.

Browsing apps and iPod games

The apps you download for your iPad, iPod touch, or iPhone, along with the games you download for your iPod classic or iPod nano (or older model iPod), show up in the Apps section of your iTunes library. Apps for the iPad, iPod touch, and iPhone are available in the App Store, and "click wheel" games for the iPod nano, iPod classic, and older fifth-generation models are in the iTunes Store (see Chapter 6 for glorious details). And although you can't run the apps or play the games in iTunes, you can browse the list of apps and games you downloaded.

To browse your iPad, iPod touch, and iPhone apps, as well as iPod classic and iPod nano "click wheel" games, select Apps in the source pane. The Grid and Cover Flow views show the promotional cover art for the app or game. Grid view separates the apps into sections for iPad, iPhone and iPod touch apps (which run on all three devices), iPhone and iPod touch Apps (which run on both devices), iPad Apps (which run only on the iPad models), and iPod Games (click-wheel games for iPod nano, iPod classic, and older fifth-generation models).

Visit this book's companion Web site for details on how to play click-wheel games on your iPod classic or iPod nano.

Displaying Content in List Pane

To display your content in the list pane as a list, click the left view button (refer to Figure 10-1) or choose View⇨As List. Choose View⇨Column Browser⇨ Show Column Browser to show the column browser in List view, or choose View⇨Column Browser⇨Hide Column Browser to hide it. You can also choose Album List view (click the Album List view button to the right of the List view button, or choose View⇨As Album List) to display cover art in the list pane.

The column headings in the List pane have different meanings for the following types of content:

- **Songs and music videos:** The Name is the title of the song; the Artist is the band, artist, or performer. The Album is the title of the CD or vinyl record on which the song appeared. For music videos, the Name is typically the title of a song in the music video. If you download a song or album from the iTunes Store that has multiple artists on different songs but is not a compilation, the Album Artist is the artist for the entire album.

- **Podcasts:** The Name is the title of the podcast episode (as in "Ballad Roots of California Folk-Rock"), the Artist is the name of the podcast author (as in Tony Bove) or producer (such as Chicago Public Radio), and the Album is the name of the podcast (as in Rockument).

- **Audiobooks:** The Album is typically the book's title (as in *Fear and Loathing in Las Vegas*), and the Name is typically the title of one of the parts (as in *Fear and Loathing in Las Vegas*–Part 1 of 3).

✔ **TV shows:** The Name is the name of the TV show episode (as in "Mr. Monk and the Airplane"), the Artist is the name of the show (as in *Monk*), and the Album is the season (as in *Monk*, Season 1).

iTunes lets you customize the List pane (which also appears below the Cover Flow view). For music, the list starts out with the Name, Time, Artist, Album, and more columns. You might have to drag the horizontal scroll bar along the bottom of the list pane to see all these columns. You can display more, less, or different columns.

Customize the columns in the following ways:

✔ **Make a column wider or narrower.** While you move your cursor over the divider between two columns, the cursor changes to a vertical bar with opposing arrows extending left and right; you can click and drag the divider to change the column's width.

✔ **Change the order of columns.** Click a column heading and drag the entire column to the left or right.

You can't change the position of the Name column and the narrow column to its left, which displays indicators and shows the playlist order.

✔ **Add or remove columns.** You can add or remove any column except Name and the playlist order for music, TV shows, podcasts, books, ringtones, or radio stations:

a. Select the type of content in the source pane in the Library section (Music, TV Shows, Podcasts, Books, Ringtones, or Radio) and choose View➪View Options.

b. Select the columns that you want to appear in the list from the View Options dialog (as shown in Figure 10-4, left side, for Music, and right side for TV Shows).

Figure 10-4: Change the view options for music (left) and TV shows (right).

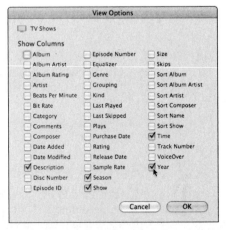

You can also change which columns are visible by Control-clicking (on a Mac) or right-clicking (in Windows) any column heading in the list in either Browse or List view.

Enabling the Kind column in the View Options dialog can help you keep track of different kinds of files, such as songs encoded in the AIFF, AAC, WAV, Apple Lossless, or MP3 formats, or videos encoded in the QuickTime or MPEG formats.

Sorting Content by the View Options

With just a little know-how, you can use the view options to sort the listing of content items. You can sort items not only by name or album but also by composer, the date the items were added to the library, or other information that you can add to an item (as I describe in Chapter 11).

At the very least, you can sort the content by the column headings you now use. You can also add other column headings (as I describe in the previous section) and sort with them.

For example, clicking the Time column heading reorders the items by their duration in *ascending order,* from shortest to longest. If you click the Time heading again, the sort is in *descending order,* which is reversed, starting with the longest item. You can sort by any column heading, such as Artist, Album, Track, Date Added, and Ratings.

You can tell whether the sort is in ascending or descending order by the little arrow indicator in the heading. When the arrow points up, the sort is in ascending order; when pointing down, it's in descending order.

You can always sort a list using the old standby, alphabetical order (with numbers, special characters, and blank spaces sorting to the end). Click the Artist heading to sort the items in the list by artist name in alphabetical order (arrow pointing up). Click it again to sort the list in reverse alphabetical order (arrow pointing down).

iTunes also lets you sort the song list via the Album column. Click the word "Album" to switch to "Album by Artist" which groups albums by artist and then lists them alphabetically. You can then click the little arrow indicator to sort in ascending or descending order, or click "Album by Artist" to switch back to "Album".

iTunes keeps track of the songs, books, TV shows, and podcasts you skip — not to be polite, just to be useful. You can use this feature to sort the Music, TV Shows, and Books lists of your library in list view, thereby making it easier to select and delete the items you skip. Add the Skips column in the View Options dialog (refer to Figure 10-5) to your list, as I describe in "Changing the view options" earlier in this chapter, and then click the column's heading to sort the list by the number of skips.

Searching for Content

Because your iTunes library will most likely grow, you might find the usual browsing and scrolling methods that I describe earlier in this chapter too time-consuming. Let iTunes find your content for you!

If you want to search the entire library with the column browser open in List or Album List view, select All at the top of the Genres and Artists columns to browse the entire library before typing a term in the Search field. Or, if you prefer, choose View⇨Column Browser⇨Hide Column Browser to show the List or Album List view without the browser (for a peek at what List view by itself looks like, see Figure 10-5).

Locate the Search field — the oval field in the upper-right corner — and follow these steps:

1. **Click in the Search field and enter several characters of your search term.**

   Use these tips for successful searching:

   - *Specify your search* with a specific title, artist, or album.

   - *Narrow your search* by typing more characters. Using fewer characters results in a longer list of possible songs.

   - *Case doesn't matter, nor do whole words.* The search feature ignores case. For example, when I search for *miles,* iTunes finds a long list that includes "Eight Miles High," "Forty Miles of Bad Road," and "She Smiles like a River," as well as everything by Miles Davis.

2. **Look through the results, which display while you type.**

   The search operation works immediately, as shown in Figure 10-5, displaying any matches in the Name, Artist, and Album columns.

3. **Scroll through the search results and then click an item to select it.**

To back out of a search so that the full list appears again, you can either click the circled X in the Search field (which appears after you start typing characters) or delete what you typed. You then see the entire list in the list pane, just like before you began your search. All the items are still there and remain there unless you explicitly remove them. Searching manipulates only your view of the items.

Figure 10-5:
Search for
anything by
typing any
part of the
name, artist,
album, or
title.

Finding the Content's Media File

Getting lost in a large library is easy. While you browse your library, you might want to return quickly to view the current item playing. While your file plays, choose View⇨Go to Current Song (or press ⌘-L on a Mac or Ctrl-L in Windows as a shortcut). iTunes shows you the item that's playing.

You can also show the location of the media file for any content item. This trick comes in handy when you want to open the media file's folder. On a Mac, choose File⇨Show in Finder (or press ⌘-R); in Windows, choose File⇨Show in Windows Explorer (or press Ctrl-R). iTunes gives control to the operating system (Mac or Windows), which displays the folder that contains the media file.

Showing Duplicate Items

Because your library will grow, you'll probably want to check for duplications. Some songs that appear on artist CDs also appear on compilation or soundtrack CDs. If you rip them all, you could have duplicate songs that take up space on your hard drive. You might even have duplicate videos and audio books.

On the other hand, maybe you want to find different versions of the same song by the same artist. Even when the songs appear on different albums, iTunes can quickly find all the songs with the same title by the same artist.

To show duplicate items in the list, choose File⇨Display Duplicates. iTunes displays all the duplicate items in the list pane in the order of the last sort. (For example, if you last sorted by Album, the items appear in Album order.) If you're using the column browser in List view, you see all the duplicate items in artist order. Click the artist to see the duplicate items specifically for that artist.

To stop showing duplicate items and return to your previous view, click the Show All button below the list of duplicates, or choose File⇨Display All.

Deleting Content

Deleting content might seem counterproductive when you're trying to build your iTunes library, but sometimes you just have to do it — for example, if you ripped a CD twice and you want to delete the duplicates, or if you simply need to remove content and store it elsewhere.

After selecting a media category (such as Music, Movies, TV Shows, and so on) in the Library section in the source pane, you can select any content item and delete it by pressing Delete/Backspace (or choosing Edit⇨Delete). You can select an artist for the artist's entire *oeuvre,* or an album to select the entire album, and then delete it. You can also select a single TV show episode and then choose Edit⇨Delete All to delete all episodes.

You can select a single episode of a podcast and then choose Edit⇨Delete All to delete all episodes but keep the podcast itself so that you are still subscribed to the podcast. If you delete the podcast, you remove it from your library, and you have to resubscribe to it to get it back. If you delete an episode, you can get it back by clicking the Get button next to the episode.

Deleting a content item from the iTunes library removes the item from your library, but it doesn't remove it from your hard drive until you agree. In the first warning dialog that appears, click the Remove button to remove the selected items from the library or click the Cancel button. iTunes then displays a second warning about moving the files that are still in the iTunes Music folder to the Trash (Mac) or Recycle Bin (Windows). You can click the Move to Trash button on a Mac, or the Move to Recycle Bin button in Windows, to trash the item. Click Keep File to keep it in your music folder, or click Cancel to cancel the operation.

If you choose to move the content to the Trash or Recycle Bin, the content is not yet deleted from your hard drive — you can recover the files by copying them out of the Trash or Recycle Bin, or you can empty them to delete them permanently.

You can delete multiple items in one clean sweep. Press Shift while you click a range of items. Alternatively, press ⌘ (Mac) or Ctrl (Windows) when you click individual items to add them to the selection. Then press Delete/Backspace (or choose Edit➪Delete).

You can delete items from playlists yet keep the items in your library. When you delete an item from a playlist, the item is simply deleted from the list — not from the library. You can delete entire playlists as well without harming the content in the library. (See Chapter 13 for more information about playlists.)

Chapter 11

Adding and Editing Information in iTunes

---

*O*rganization depends on information. You expect your computer to do a lot more for you than just store a song with *Track 01* as the only identifier. Not only can iTunes retrieve the song's track information from the Internet, but it can also find the cover art for you.

Adding all the information for your iTunes content seems like a lot of trouble, but you can get most of the information automatically from the Internet — and without all that pesky typing. Adding track information is important because you certainly don't want to mistakenly play Frank Zappa's "My Guitar Wants to Kill Your Mama" when trying to impress your classical music teacher with the third movement of Tchaikovsky's *Pathétique Symphony,* do you? And because videos you make yourself or convert from other sources don't have this automatic information, you have to enter *some* description to tell them apart.

This chapter shows you how to add information to your content library in iTunes and edit it for better viewing so that you can organize your content by artist, album name, genre, composer, and ratings. You can then use this information to sort your content in the list pane by clicking the column headings. This chapter also describes how to add cover art for navigating your library in Cover Flow view, Grid view, and List view with the Artwork column.

Retrieving Song Information from the Internet

Why bother entering information if someone else has already done it for you? You can easily get information about most music CDs from the Internet (that is, assuming you can connect to the Internet). The online database available for iTunes users holds information for millions of songs on commercial CDs and even some bootleg CDs.

When you pop a commercial music CD into your computer running iTunes, iTunes automatically looks up the track information for that CD on the Internet and fills in the information fields (name, artist, album, and so on). You don't need to do anything to make this happen. You can also edit the information after iTunes fills in the fields.

If your computer doesn't access the Internet automatically, you might want to turn off automatic information retrieval. To turn off the retrieval of track information, choose iTunes➪Preferences (Mac) or Edit➪Preferences (Windows), and then click the General tab (if it's not already selected). Deselect the Automatically Retrieve CD Track Names from Internet option near the bottom of the dialog and click OK.

You can retrieve song information manually — when you're ready to connect to the Internet. After connecting to the Internet, choose Advanced➪Get Track Names.

Entering Content Information

You have to enter the information for certain media, including CDs that aren't known by the database, custom CD-Rs, and videos and audio books that you bring into iTunes from sources other than the iTunes Store. No big deal, though; just follow these steps:

1. **Click directly in the information field (such as Artist).**

2. **Click again so that the mouse pointer toggles to an editing cursor — but not so quickly that the track starts playing.**

3. **Type text directly into the information field.**

After grabbing the song information from the Internet or typing it, iTunes keeps track of the information for the CD even if you just play the CD without importing it. The next time you insert the CD into the same computer with the user account, the song information is automatically filled in.

You can submit the content information you entered to the online database for iTunes, so that others who insert the same CD can benefit from your edits. Visit this book's companion Web site for details on using the Gracenote database at www.gracenote.com.

Editing the Information

Retrieving ready-made song information from the Internet is a great help, but you might not always like the format it comes in. Maybe you want to edit artist and band names or other information, such as removing *The* from the beginning of band names, such as The Who, The Band, The Beatles, and The Beach Boys. Even though these names sort correctly (in alphabetical order, under their proper names), I dislike having *The* before the band name, so I routinely remove it.

You might also want to change the information that is supplied by the iTunes Store for the content you download. And if you obtain your content from other sources, you might need to add information for the first time.

You can edit the content information by clicking directly in the specific track's field (such as the Artist field) and then clicking again so that the mouse pointer toggles to an editing cursor. You can then select the text and type over it — or use the Copy, Cut, and Paste commands on the Edit menu — to move tiny bits of text around within the field. As you can see in Figure 11-1, I changed the Artist field from *Hartford, John* to *John Hartford.*

You can edit the Name, Artist, Album, Genre, and Ratings fields in the list. However, editing this information by choosing File⇨Get Info is easier. Keep reading to find out why.

Editing multiple items at once

Editing in the content list is fine if you're editing the information for one item, but typically you need to change all the tracks of an audio CD. For example, if a CD of songs by Bob Dylan is listed with the artist as *Dylan, Bob,* you might want to change all the songs at once to *Bob Dylan.* Changing all the information in one fell swoop is fast and clean, but like most powerful shortcuts, you need to be careful because it can be dangerous.

Follow these steps to change a group of items at once:

1. **Select a group of content items by clicking the first item and then pressing Shift while you click the last item.**

   All the items between the first and last are highlighted. You can extend a selection by Shift-clicking other items or add to a selection by ⌘-clicking (Mac) or Ctrl-clicking (Windows). You can also remove items already selected by ⌘-clicking (Mac) or Ctrl-clicking (Windows).

2. **Choose File⇨Get Info or press ⌘-I (Mac) or Ctrl-I (Windows).**

   A warning message displays:

   ```
   Are you sure you want to edit information for multiple
   items?
   ```

   Speed-editing the information in multiple items at once can be dangerous for your library organization. If, for example, you change an informational snippet for one item in a selected group (the song or movie title, for example), the corresponding snippet for all items in the selected group is going to change as well! Be careful about what you edit when using this method.

3. **Click the Yes button to edit information for multiple items.**

   The Multiple Item Information dialog appears, as shown in Figure 11-2.

4. **Edit the field you want to change for all the items.**

   When you edit a field, a check mark appears automatically in the check box next to the field. iTunes assumes that you want that field changed in all the selected items. Make sure that no other check box is selected except the ones for the fields that you want.

5. **Click the OK button to make the change.**

   iTunes changes the field for the entire selection of items.

Solo artists show up sorted by first name when listed alphabetically, unless you add a sort field for the artist. The Sorting tab allows you to add sort fields — for example, you can add the artist name "Hartford, John" in the Sort Artist field, as I do in Figure 11-3, for the John Hartford songs so that they show up in the "H" artists (as if the artist is "Hartford, John") rather than in the "J" artists when sorted alphabetically. To make this change for multiple songs, follow Steps 1-3 above, and then click the Sorting tab. Then edit the sort field as shown in Figure 11-3 and click OK. To make this type of change for a single song or other content item, see the next section.

Figure 11-1:
Click inside a field to edit the information.

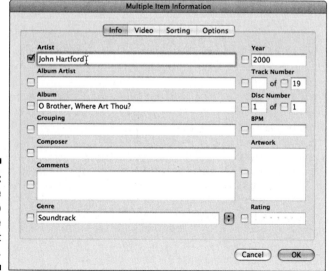

Figure 11-2:
Change the field info for multiple items at once.

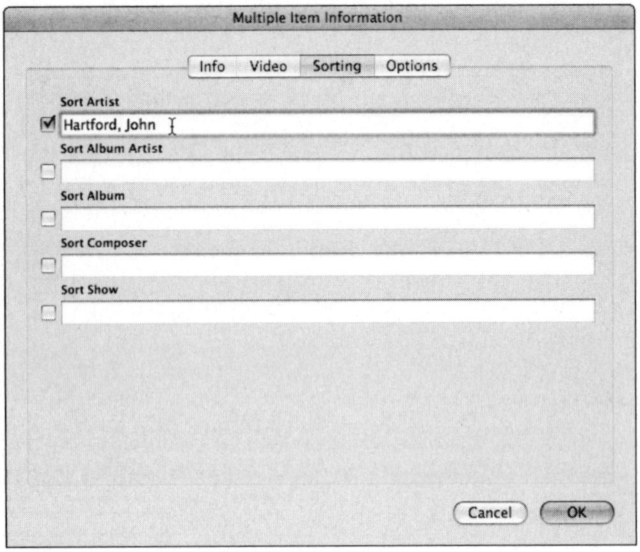

Multiple Item Information

Info   Video   Sorting   Options

Sort Artist

☑ Hartford, John

Sort Album Artist

☐

Sort Album

☐

Sort Composer

☐

Sort Show

☐

Cancel   OK

Figure 11-3:
Change the artist sort field so that the artist is listed alphabetically by last name.

Editing fields for a single item

Although the track information grabbed from the Internet is enough for identifying a song in your iTunes library, some facts — such as composer credits — might not be included. Adding composer credits is usually worth your effort because you can then search and sort by composer and create playlists based on the composer. Videos (movies, TV shows, and music videos), podcasts, and audio books might also have information in their fields that you want to change or have blank fields that could use some helpful information.

You may want to change the Album Artist field, or fill it in if it's blank, for certain songs on compilation albums or music from box sets. iTunes offers both Artist and Album Artist fields for a song so that you can include the album artist name if it's different — such as the artist name for a compilation album that features songs by different artists (for example, a "duet" album by an artist who brings in other guest artists). You can also change the list view options (as I describe in Chapter 10) to include the Album Artist field as a column for sorting the song list.

To get a look at (and edit) what the online database provided about an item, first select the item and then choose File➪Get Info (or press ⌘-I on a Mac or Ctrl-I in Windows).

When you select one item, its information dialog appears and your edits affect only one item; when you select multiple items, the Multiple Item Information dialog appears and your edits affect multiple items.

A selection's information dialog offers the following tabs:

✔ **Summary:** The Summary tab offers useful information about the media file format and location on your hard drive, the file size, and the digital compression method (along with bit rate, sample rate, and other settings).

✔ **Info:** The Info tab allows you to change the name, artist, composer, album, genre, year, and other information. You can also add comments, as shown in Figure 11-4.

✔ **Video:** The Video tab lets you enter information to describe the video. The information fields are set up for TV shows, including the title of the show, episode number and ID, and season number, but you can skip them for movies and music videos and just add a description. You can also edit the description of a podcast, which appears in the Video tab's Description field.

✔ **Sorting:** The Sorting tab allows you to add information to sort fields that affect how your library content appears in sorted lists. For example, you can add a different name for the artist in the Sort Artist field to the right of the Artist field, such as *Dylan, Bob* for *Bob Dylan,* so that Dylan appears in the "D" section (rather than the "B" section) of the artists when sorted alphabetically. Information from the Info tab appears on the left side, and you can add the alternative sort field on the right side. You can even add a Show field for the title of a concert or some other use. Choose View⇨View Options to select the sort field as a list view option, and then you can sort your content in list view by using the sort field (such as sorting by Show).

✔ **Options:** The Options tab, as shown in Figure 11-5, offers the following:

- *Volume Adjustment:* You can set the volume for a song, video, podcast, or audio book in advance so that it always plays at that volume (or lower, if your overall iTunes or iPad/iPod/iPhone volume is set lower). Drag the slider to the right to increase the volume adjustment up to 100% (twice the usual volume); drag the slider to the left to decrease the volume adjustment to –100% (half the usual volume). For more details on setting the volume in advance, see Chapter 12.

- *Equalizer Preset:* Choose an equalizer preset for an item. See Chapter 12 for details on using the Equalizer in iTunes, and Chapter 15 on how you can use an Equalizer preset to control how an item sounds on your iPad, iPod, or iPhone.

- *Media Kind:* Set (or change) the type of media. For example, after importing a video, you can change its Media Kind to movie, TV show, or music video. See "Changing the media type" in this section for details.

- *Rating:* Assign up to five stars to an item as a rating. (See how in the next section.)

- *Start Time and Stop Time:* Set the start and stop times for an item. You can use these options to cut unwanted intros and outros of a song (such as announcers, audience applause, and tuning up), or to skip opening credits or commercials of movies. You can also use it in conjunction with the Convert feature to split an item (or, in the parlance of record label executives and artists, split a track) into multiple items (tracks).

Visit this book's companion Web site for details on setting start and stop times and using the iTunes equalizer.

- *Remember Playback Position:* Set this option for an item so that when you select and play the item, iTunes resumes playing it from where you left off. This option is usually turned on for audio books, movies, and TV shows.

- *Skip When Shuffling:* Set this option for an item to be skipped from Party Shuffle.

- *Part of a Gapless Album:* Set this option for an item to be played back without a gap between songs. (See Chapter 7 to find out about the gaps between songs.)

✔ **Lyrics:** The Lyrics tab offers a text field for typing or pasting lyrics (or any text). Some songs in the iTunes Store are supplied with lyrics — you can find them here.

You can view lyrics on an iPad, iPod touch, or iPhone by starting a song and then, while the song is playing, tapping the song's album cover. To see lyrics on an iPod nano or iPod classic, start playing a song and then press the Select button several times until you see the lyrics. On an iPod nano, the first press shows the scrubber bar, the second shows ratings, the third shows the Shuffle slider, and the fourth shows the lyrics. If you press the Select button too many times, the iPod returns to the Now Playing display.

✔ **Artwork:** The Artwork tab allows you to add or delete artwork for the item. See the upcoming section "Adding Cover Art."

You can apply the entry of a sort field on the Sorting tab to all the tracks of the same album or to all tracks by the same artist, album artist, composer, or show. After changing the sort field for an item on the Sorting tab, select the item in List view, Control-click (Mac) or right-click (Mac or Windows) the item to display the contextual menu, and then choose Apply Sort Field. Click Yes to make the change.

To move through an album one item at a time when using Get Info (without closing and reopening the information dialog), click the Previous or Next buttons in the lower-left corner of the dialog.

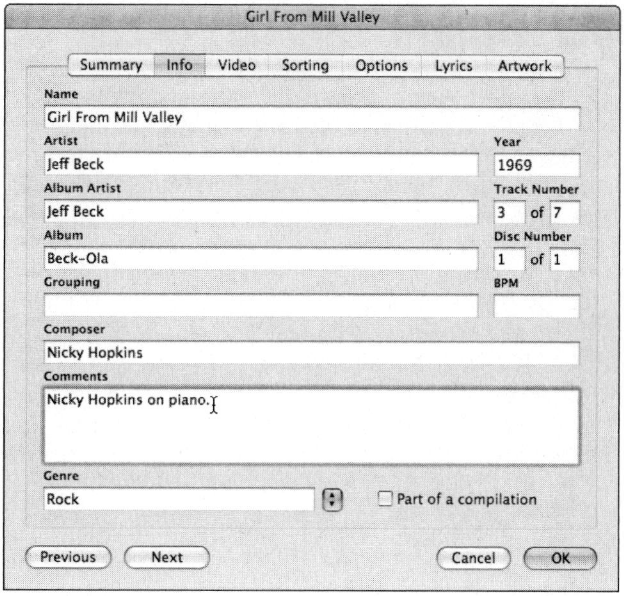

Figure 11-4:
View and
edit infor-
mation from
the Info tab.

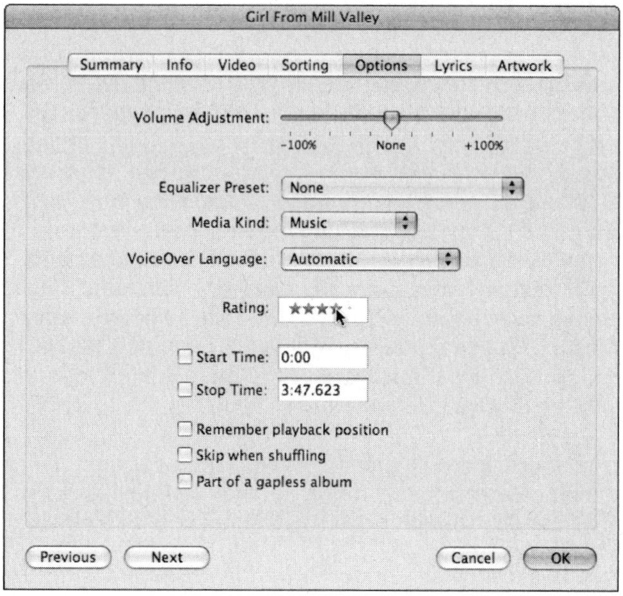

Figure 11-5:
Add a rating
to a song
from the
Options tab.

Adding a rating

iTunes allows you to rate your content. The cool thing about ratings is that they're *yours*. You can use ratings to mean anything you want. For example, you can rate songs based on how much you like them, whether your mother would listen to them, or how they blend into a work environment. You can also rate videos based on your watching habits, as well as audio books and podcasts.

To add a rating to a content item, click the Options tab (refer to Figure 11-5) and drag inside the My Rating field to add stars. The upper limit is five stars (for the best). You can also select the item and choose File➪Rating to assign a rating to an item, or display a Ratings column in list view to assign ratings. (See Chapter 10 for details on changing the view options.)

You might have noticed the My Top Rated playlist in the Playlists section of the source pane. This playlist is an example of a *smart playlist* — a playlist that updates when ratings are changed. The My Top Rated playlist plays all the top-rated songs in your library. You can find out more about playlists in Chapter 13.

Changing the media type

If an audio book file imports as a song into your iTunes library, or a video file imports as a movie, or you want to change podcast episodes so that they show up as audio books or songs, you can change the media type for the content item.

To change the media type, first select the content item, choose File➪Get Info (or press ⌘-I on a Mac or Ctrl-I in Windows), and then click the Options tab (refer to Figure 11-5). You can then choose the option you want in the Media Kind pop-up menu. The options for the Media Kind menu change depending on the content item selected. You can change the selected song to Podcast, iTunes U lesson, Audiobook, or Voice Memo; the selected podcast episode to a song (Music), iTunes U lesson, Audiobook, or Voice Memo; the selected video podcast to a Movie, the selected video to a Music Video, Movie, TV Show, Podcast, or iTunes U lesson, and so on.

You can also change the media type for multiple items at once. Follow Steps 1-3 in "Editing multiple items at once" in this section, and then click the Options tab. You can then change the option in the Media Kind pop-up menu and click OK.

If you are changing a song to a podcast, use the episode title for Name (song title), the podcast publisher for Artist, and the podcast name for Album in the information dialog. Then click the Video tab in the information dialog and enter the podcast's description in the Description field.

Adding Cover Art

iTunes displays the cover art for your albums, videos, movies, TV shows, podcasts, books, audio books, and apps in the Cover Flow browser. (See Chapter 10 for details.) All current iPad, iPod, and iPhone models (except the iPod shuffle) display the cover art. So it makes sense to get the art, especially because it's free!

Items that you buy from the iTunes Store typically include an image of the album, book, or box cover art or a photo of the artist that serves as cover art, and apps from the App Store use a larger version of the app icon as the cover art. You can see the artwork in the lower-left corner of the iTunes window by clicking the Show/Hide Artwork button (the rightmost button in the row of four buttons at the bottom of the iTunes window on the left side). To fill your library automatically with cover art for the CDs you ripped, get yourself an iTunes Store account if you don't already have one. Log in to your account and then choose Advanced⇨Get Album Artwork. iTunes grabs the cover art not only for iTunes Store purchases, but also for CDs you ripped — provided that the albums are also available in the iTunes Store.

To download cover art for ripped CDs automatically after ripping them (without having to manually choose Advanced⇨Get Album Artwork each time), choose iTunes⇨Preferences on a Mac or Edit⇨Preferences in Windows, click the Store tab, and select the Automatically Download Missing Album Artwork option.

You can also get your cover art from other places that sell CDs, such as Amazon.com, or you can even scan them from the actual CDs. The optimal size for cover art is 300 x 300 pixels. Save it in a graphics format that iTunes (and its underlying graphics technology, *QuickTime*) understands — JPEG, GIF, PNG, TIFF, or Photoshop. With a Web browser, you can visit Web pages to scout for suitable art; just Control-click (Mac) or right-click (Mac or Windows) an image to download and save the image on your hard drive. With Safari on a Mac and some browsers (such as Firefox or Safari) in Windows, you can drag the image directly from the Web browser window into the iTunes art pane.

To add artwork to one or more items, select it (or them) in your iTunes library and do one of the following:

✔ **Drag the artwork's image file from a Desktop folder into the artwork viewing area (the lower-left corner of the iTunes window).**

To add artwork for an entire album (rather than just individual songs) or season of TV shows, first select the album or season in the column browser or select all the items in list view. Then drag the image file into the artwork viewing area.

✔ **Add artwork to a single item through the information window.**

Choose File⇨Get Info and then click the Artwork tab in the information dialog. Click the Add button, browse your hard drive or network for the image file, select the file, and then click the OK button.

✔ **Add artwork for multiple items in the Multiple Item Information dialog.**

Choose File⇨Get Info after selecting the items, enable the Artwork field (select its check box), and then drag a graphics file for the cover art from a Desktop folder to the Artwork well. Click the Yes button for the warning message to change the artwork.

See the section "Editing multiple items at once," earlier in this chapter to find out more about using the Multiple Item Information dialog.

To remove the artwork from an item, view the artwork in a larger window or resize the artwork, choose File⇨Get Info, and then click the Artwork tab. You can add a different image with the Add button, delete images with the Delete button, or resize images with the size slider.

Chapter 12

Playing Content in iTunes

· ·

In This Chapter

▶ Adjusting your computer volume

▶ Playing songs on your stereo through a wireless AirTunes connection

▶ Playing songs, podcasts, and audio books in iTunes

▶ Playing videos in iTunes

· ·

*I*f you like to entertain folks by spinning tunes and playing videos at home or at parties, iTunes could easily become your media jockey console. With iTunes, your computer is a mean multimedia machine that can mix sounds, photos, and videos. And even if you've never mastered a stereo system beyond adjusting the bass, treble, and volume, you can quickly and easily fine-tune the sound in iTunes, and even adjust the volume and equalizer settings for each song, video, audio book, and podcast.

But that's not all: You can also use iTunes to play video on your computer's display, or you can send it to a larger television or display monitor — even a video projector — to get a bigger picture. And if you've integrated Apple TV with your home audio system and television, you can use iTunes to feed music and video to Apple TV wirelessly, as I describe in this chapter.

To find out more about Apple TV, visit this book's companion Web site.

Changing the Computer's Output Volume

You can control the volume and other characteristics of the sound coming from your computer's speakers, headphones, or external speakers. Even if you connect your computer to a home audio system with its own volume and equalizer controls, it's best to get the volume correct at the source — your computer and iTunes — and then adjust the output volume as you please on your audio system or external speaker unit.

You control the volume by using your computer system's audio controls. iTunes also controls the volume, but that control is within the limits of the computer's volume setting. For example, if you set your computer's volume to half and set iTunes volume to full, you get half volume because the computer limits the volume to half. After the sound leaves your computer, you can adjust it further with the volume controls of your stereo system or external speakers.

Adjusting the sound on a Mac

Today's Macs come with built-in or external speakers and at least one headphone/line-out connection that you can use to connect external speakers or a stereo system. Mac OS X lets you configure output speakers and control levels for stereo speakers and multichannel audio devices.

To adjust the volume on your Mac, follow these steps:

1. **Choose System Preferences from the Apple menu or the Dock and then click the Sound icon.**

   Otherwise, press Option and a volume control key on your keyboard simultaneously as a shortcut. You can have iTunes open and playing music while you do this.

2. **In the Sound preferences pane that opens, click Output and select the sound output device.**

   If you have headphones (or external speakers attached to the headphones connection on your Mac), a Headphones option appears in the list of sound output devices. The External Speakers or Internal Speakers option may also appear for speakers connected through a line-out connection or built into the Mac.

3. **Adjust the volume.**

   You can do any of the following:

   - Drag the slider to adjust the volume while you listen to music.
   - Select the Mute check box to silence your Mac.
   - Drag the Balance slider to put more music in the left or right channel.

4. **Close the Preferences window, either by choosing System Preferences⇨Quit System Preferences, clicking the red button in the upper-left corner of the window, or pressing ⌘-Q.**

   The Sound preferences window isn't like a dialog: When you change settings, you can hear the effect immediately without having to click OK. (There isn't an OK button, anyway.)

For more information about using Mac OS X, see *Mac OS X Leopard For Dummies* or *Mac OS X Snow Leopard For Dummies* by my good friend Bob "Dr. Mac" LeVitus (published by Wiley).

Adjusting the sound in Windows

Windows 7, Windows Vista, Windows XP, and Windows 2000 let you configure output speakers and control levels for stereo speakers and multichannel audio devices.

Use the Sounds and Audio Devices Properties dialog to change the volume. To open this dialog, choose Start➪Control Panel, click the Sounds and Audio Devices icon, and then click the Volume tab. You can then drag to set the volume. You can also silence your PC by selecting the Mute check box.

For more information about adjusting sound on a PC, see *PCs For Dummies* by Dan Gookin (published by Wiley).

Using Remote Speakers

Say you want to play the music in your iTunes library, but your stereo system is across the room or in another room, and you don't want to extend wires to the stereo system. What you need is a wireless connection from your computer to your stereo system.

You can use an Apple AirPort Wi-Fi network in your home — such as AirPort Express by itself, or Apple TV with AirPort Extreme or Time Capsule. AirPort Express and Apple TV work with Apple's AirPlay technology, which lets you play your iTunes music through your stereo or powered speakers in any room of your house, without wires; with Apple TV, you can also play video. The only catch is that your computer must be within range of the Wi-Fi network or connected by an Ethernet cable. To find out more about setting up a wireless network or Apple TV for stereo playback, see "Using AirPlay or Apple TV for Wireless Stereo Playback" at the end of this chapter.

To play music, podcasts, audio books, or Web radio stations in your iTunes library on wireless speakers, first set your iTunes preferences to look for speakers connected wirelessly with AirPlay. Choose iTunes➪Preferences (Mac) or Edit➪Preferences (Windows) and click the Devices tab to show the Devices pane, shown in Figure 12-1. Select the Look for Remote Speakers Connected with AirPlay check box.

After selecting the Look for Remote Speakers option, you can also select the Allow iTunes Control from Remote Speakers option to control the iTunes volume from Apple TV or other remote speakers that can offer iTunes volume control.

After you select the option to look for AirPlay-connected speakers, the Speakers pop-up menu appears in the lower-right corner of the iTunes window (set to Computer, the default option). The Speakers pop-up menu includes any available wireless AirPlay networks, as shown in Figure 12-2. You can select the AirPlay network to play through speakers attached to it ("Express Buddy" in Figure 12-2), or select Apple TV to play through speakers attached to your Apple TV. From that point, iTunes plays the sound through the AirPlay network or Apple TV rather than through the computer.

You can also choose to play through multiple speakers, such as the Computer and Apple TV (or in Figure 12-2, "Express Buddy") at the same time. Choose Multiple Speakers in the Speakers pop-up menu (refer to Figure 12-2), and then choose the speaker systems to use in the dialog that appears. This dialog also provides a master volume slider you can drag to set the master volume for the multiple speakers.

To get back to playing sound through speakers connected to the computer (or through the computer's built-in speakers), choose Computer from the Speakers pop-up menu.

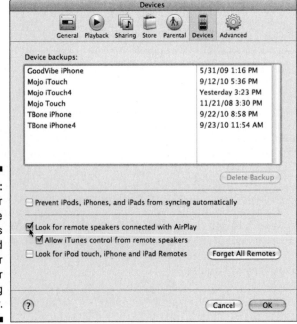

Figure 12-1:
Look for remote speakers connected to your computer using AirPlay.

Figure 12-2:
Choosing
the
AirTunes
network
"Express
Buddy"
from the
Speakers
menu.

Playing Songs

When you've found a song you want to play (see Chapter 10 for browsing and searching details), simply select it in the list pane and then click the play button. The play button toggles to a pause button while the song plays.

When the song finishes, iTunes continues playing the songs in the list in sequence until you click the pause button (which then toggles back into the play button) or until the song list ends. This setup is useful if you select an album, but not so great if you select a song at random and don't want to hear the next one. (Fortunately, you can arrange songs in playlists so that they play back in exactly the sequence you want; see Chapter 13 for details.)

You can skip to the next or previous song by pressing the right- or left-arrow key, respectively, or by clicking the forward or back button next to the play button. You can also double-click another song in the list to start playing it.

Press the spacebar to perform the same function as the play button; press the spacebar again to pause.

If you want to see the rest of your computer screen while playing music, you can minimize the iTunes screen to just the playback controls. On a Mac, choose Window⇨Zoom (or click the green button in the upper-left corner of the window); choose it again (or click the green button again) to zoom back out to full size. On a Windows PC, choose View⇨Switch to Mini Player (or press Ctrl-M); click the screen button (the middle button on the left side of the Mini Player) or press Ctrl-M to zoom back out to full size.

Grooving with the iTunes DJ

Playlists, as I describe in Chapter 13, are great for organizing music in the order that you want to play it, but you can have iTunes serve up songs at random. iTunes DJ (formerly Party Shuffle) is a dynamic playlist that automatically generates a semirandom selection in a list that you can modify on the fly. With iTunes DJ, you might even find songs in your library you forgot about or rarely play. iTunes DJ always throws a few rarely played songs into the mix.

To use iTunes DJ, follow these steps:

1. **Select iTunes DJ in the Playlists section of the source pane.**

   The iTunes DJ track list appears in place of the list pane, with the Source pop-up, Settings, and Refresh buttons at the bottom, as shown in Figure 12-3.

2. **Choose a source from the Source pop-up menu below the track list.**

   You can select Music (refer to Figure 12-3) to use the entire music portion of your library, or select any playlist as the source for music (including a smart playlist; see Chapter 13 for details). If you select a playlist, iTunes DJ limits its choices to songs from that playlist.

3. **(Optional) Click the Settings button, and options in the Settings dialog.**

   You can select options to control how many recently played songs and upcoming songs should remain in the iTunes DJ list, and to play higher rated songs more often. You can also allow guests to request songs with Apple's Remote app for iPod touch or iPhone.

   To find out more about iTunes DJ options, visit this book's companion Web site.

4. **(Optional) If you don't like the order of songs, you can rearrange them. If you dislike any songs, you can remove them.**

   You can rearrange the order of songs in the iTunes DJ playlist by dragging songs to different positions in the list. Remove songs by selecting them in the iTunes DJ playlist and pressing Delete/Backspace (or choosing Edit⇨Delete).

5. **Play the iTunes DJ playlist by selecting the first song (or any song) and then clicking the play button or pressing the spacebar.**

(When you pick a song in the middle to start playing, the songs before it are grayed out to show that they won't play.)

6. **Add, delete, or rearrange songs, even while iTunes DJ plays.**

While the iTunes DJ list plays, you can add songs in one of two ways:

- *Open iTunes DJ in a separate window by double-clicking iTunes DJ in the source pane.* You can then drag songs from the main iTunes window directly into position in the iTunes DJ track list.

- *Without opening iTunes DJ in a separate window, you can switch to the music portion of your library or a playlist and drag the song over iTunes DJ in the source pane.* When you add a song to iTunes DJ, it shows up at the end of the track list. You can then drag it to a new position.

You can add one or more albums to the iTunes DJ track list by dragging the albums; the songs play in album order. You can also add all the songs by an artist by dragging the artist's name. iTunes DJ acts like a dynamic playlist — you add, delete, and change the order of songs on the fly.

Figure 12-3: iTunes DJ spins random songs from your entire library or from a playlist.

Cross-fading song playback

DJs in clubs and on the radio often make a smooth transition from the ending of one song to the beginning of the next one. This is called a *cross-fade*. Ordinarily, iTunes is set to have a short cross-fade of one second (the time after the fade-out of the first song to the fade-in of the second), but you can adjust that if you like.

You can change the cross-fade by choosing iTunes⇨Preferences on a Mac or Edit⇨Preferences in Windows and then clicking the Playback icon. The Playback preferences appear, as shown in Figure 12-4.

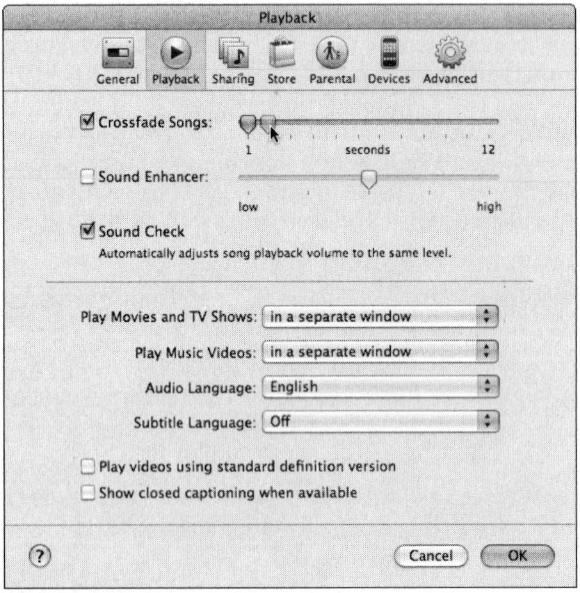

Figure 12-4:
Set the
cross-fade
between
songs
and other
playback
options.

> **Playback**
>
> General   Playback   Sharing   Store   Parental   Devices   Advanced
>
> ☑ Crossfade Songs:
> 1   seconds   12
>
> ☐ Sound Enhancer:
> low   high
>
> ☑ Sound Check
> Automatically adjusts song playback volume to the same level.
>
> Play Movies and TV Shows: [in a separate window ▲▼]
> Play Music Videos: [in a separate window ▲▼]
> Audio Language: [English ▲▼]
> Subtitle Language: [Off ▲▼]
>
> ☐ Play videos using standard definition version
> ☐ Show closed captioning when available
>
> (?)   (Cancel) (OK)

Select the Crossfade Songs preference, and then increase or decrease the cross-fade by dragging the slider. Each notch in the slider represents one second. The maximum amount of cross-fade is 12 seconds. With a longer cross-fade, you get more overlap from one song to the next; that is, the second song starts before the first one ends. To turn off the cross-fade, deselect Crossfade Songs.

Playing Podcasts

A podcast transfers audio or audio/video episodes, such as weekly broadcasts, automatically to your iTunes library from the Internet or through the iTunes Store (as I describe in episodic detail in Chapter 7). Podcasts that you subscribe to appear in the list pane when you select Podcasts in the Library section of the source pane. You can add podcast episodes to your library by subscribing to them in the iTunes Store (see Chapter 6).

To play the most recent podcast episode, select the Podcasts item in the Library section of the source pane, select a podcast in any view, and then click the play button. To play a specific podcast episode, follow these steps:

1. **Select the Podcasts item in the Library section of the source pane, and choose List, Album List, or Cover Flow view.**

2. **Select a podcast in List or Album list view or in the list under the Cover Flow view, and then click the triangle to see its episodes.**

   The triangle rotates, and a list of episodes appears beneath the podcast, as shown in Figure 12-5 (using List view).

3. **Select the podcast and then click the play button.**

   You can use the iTunes playback controls to fast-forward or rewind the podcast or play it from any point. The blue dot next to a podcast means that you haven't yet played it. As soon as you start listening to a podcast, the dot disappears.

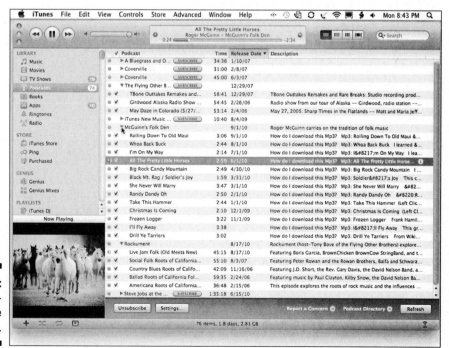

Figure 12-5: Open a podcast to see its episodes.

When you play a podcast, iTunes remembers your place when you stop listening to it, just like it remembers when you place a bookmark in an audio book or pause during a movie — even after quitting and restarting iTunes. iTunes resumes playing from that playback position when you return to the podcast to play it.

Some podcasts are enhanced to include chapter marks and photos. When you play an enhanced podcast in iTunes, a Chapters menu appears on the iTunes menu bar. Choose this menu to display the podcast's chapter marks, artwork, and chapter start times.

If the podcaster embedded a photo in an audio podcast file or included a link to a video from the file, the photo or video content appears in the Artwork pane.

Although you can drag a podcast into a playlist to include it in that playlist, you can also drag a podcast to the source pane to create a new playlist, as long as you drag it to an empty space in the Playlist section of the source pane (and not into another playlist). The new playlist takes on the name of the podcast. You can also add other podcasts to the new playlist and rename the playlist. For more information about playlists, see Chapter 13.

Playing Audio Books

You can store and play audio books, articles, and spoken-word titles just like songs in iTunes, and you can download titles from the iTunes Store (as I describe prolifically in Chapter 6). Choose Books in the Library section of the Source pane to see them. (To change the media type of audio books imported as songs into iTunes so that they appear in the Books section of your library, see Chapter 11.)

To play an audio book, select it just like you would a song (see details on browsing and listing content in Chapter 10) and then click the play button. You can use the iTunes playback controls to fast-forward or rewind the audio book or play it from any point.

Audio books from the iTunes Store are enhanced to include chapter marks. When you play any of these audio books in iTunes, the Chapters menu appears on the iTunes menu bar, just like it does for a podcast with chapters. Choose the Chapters menu to display and select the audio book's chapter marks.

Playing Videos

iTunes is versatile when it comes to playing videos — the TV shows, movies, video podcasts, and music videos you downloaded from the iTunes Store (see Chapter 6) as well as the video files you imported into iTunes from other sources (see Chapter 7).

To watch a video in iTunes, select it in your library (see details on browsing and listing movies, TV shows, and videos in Chapter 10) and then click the play button. Use the previous/rewind, play/pause, and forward/next buttons to control playback and the iTunes volume slider to control the volume, just like with songs.

By default, the video appears in the artwork pane in the lower-left corner of the iTunes window. If the artwork pane isn't visible, playing the video makes it appear. You can also make the artwork pane appear or disappear by clicking the Show/Hide Artwork button.

To watch a video in a separate window, click the video while it plays in the artwork pane. A separate window appears that includes a transparent QuickTime controls pane with buttons for controlling video playback, as shown in Figure 12-6. Click the play button at the center of the pane to play or pause, and then drag the slider to move forward or backward through the video. Click the rewind or fast forward button on either side of the play button in the controls pane to move backward or forward through a video. Click the "close window" button to close the window just as you would close a window with Mac OS X or Windows.

Figure 12-6:
Drag the
QuickTime
playback
slider
to move
forward or
backward
through a
video.

The transparent QuickTime controls pane disappears while the video plays, but you can make it reappear at any time by moving the cursor to the bottom center of the video window. The controls pane also offers a volume control slider to set the audio volume of the video, and the full-screen video button to change the video display to full-screen. (See the section "Playing a video full-screen," later in this chapter.)

You can resize the separate video window by dragging the lower-right corner of the window. You can also increase or decrease the window size from the View menu — choose View➪Video Size➪Increase Size or View➪Video Size➪ Decrease Size. To show the video window so that all of it fits on the screen choose View➪ Video Size➪Fit to Screen. Choose View➪ Video Size➪Actual Size to set the window back to the actual size of the video picture.

Changing video playback preferences

To change your iTunes preferences for playing movies, TV shows, and music videos, choose iTunes➪Preferences (Mac) or Edit➪Preferences (Windows), and click the Playback tab (refer to Figure 12-4). You can choose the following options separately for movies/TV shows and for music videos:

- ✔ In the Artwork Viewer, as described previously.

- ✔ In a Separate Window, as described previously and shown in Figure 12-6.

- ✔ In the iTunes Window — filling just the iTunes window, with the same transparent QuickTime controls pane used in a separate window as described previously (and shown in Figure 12-6).

- ✔ Full Screen or Full Screen (with Visuals), which fills the entire computer display. See the next section, "Playing a video full-screen" for details.

Playing a video full-screen

After you choose the Full Screen option from the Play Movies and TV Shows pop-up menu and/or the Play Music Videos pop-up menu as described in the previous section (refer to Figure 12-4), those videos fill the screen when they play, with a transparent QuickTime controls pane offering buttons for controlling video playback.

To change from watching a video in a separate window to a full-screen view, click the full-screen video button in the transparent QuickTime controls pane (refer to Figure 12-6). You can also choose View➪ Video Size➪Fit to Screen.

When you're playing a video in full-screen view, the following controls are available:

✔ **Esc (Escape):** Press to stop full-screen playback and return to the iTunes window.

✔ **Spacebar:** Press to pause playback. (Pressing the spacebar again resumes playback.)

✔ **Your mouse or pointing device:** Simply move these to display the transparent QuickTime controls pane and then click the full-screen video button (now with its arrows pointing inward) to stop full-screen playback and return to the iTunes window.

A cool party trick is to seamlessly mix music videos and music with visuals. To display a mixed playlist of music and videos (see Chapter 13 to create playlists), choose iTunes➪Preferences (Mac) or Edit➪Preferences (Windows). Then click the Playback tab and choose the Full Screen (with Visuals) option from the Play Music Videos pop-up menu (or even the Play Movies and TV Shows pop-up menu, if you include these in your playlist). When you play the mixed music-video playlist, iTunes automatically shows full-screen video for your videos and full-screen visuals for your music, seamlessly moving from one to the other.

To find out more about displaying visuals while playing music, and details about connections to home video and stereo equipment, visit this book's companion Web site.

Adjusting the Sound

Some songs are just too loud. I don't mean too loud stylistically, as in thrash metal with screeching guitars; I mean too loud for your ears when you're wearing headphones or so loud that the music is distorted. And some songs are just too soft; you have to increase the volume to hear them and then lower the volume to listen to louder songs. Videos, podcast episodes, and audio books can also vary greatly from loud to soft. To remedy these problems, you can set the volume in advance for these items. You can also soundcheck your entire music library to bring it in line, volume-wise.

Setting the volume in advance

With songs, audio books, podcast episodes, and videos that you already know are too loud (or too soft), consider setting the volume for those items in advance so that they always play with the desired volume adjustment. You can even set the volume for entire albums or podcasts.

To adjust the overall volume of a particular item in advance so that it always plays at that setting, perform the following steps:

1. **Select one or more items in your iTunes library.**

   To set the volume in iTunes for multiple songs, you can select an entire album or you can select all the songs. To set the volume for a whole podcast, select it instead of individual episodes.

2. **Choose File⇨Get Info.**

   The information dialog appears.

3. **Click the Options tab.**

   The Options pane of the information dialog appears, as shown in Figure 12-7. Drag the Volume Adjustment slider left or right to adjust the volume lower or higher. You can do this while playing the file.

4. **Click the OK button to finish.**

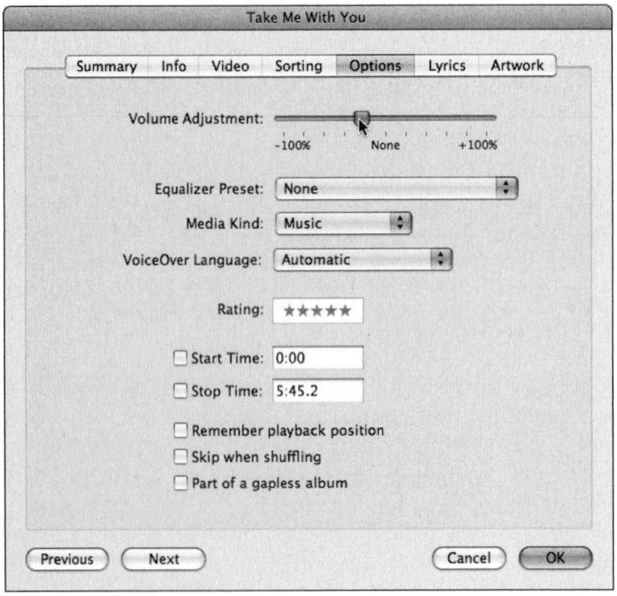

Take Me With You

| Summary | Info | Video | Sorting | **Options** | Lyrics | Artwork |

Volume Adjustment: ⎯⎯⎯⎯●⎯⎯⎯⎯
-100%   None   +100%

Equalizer Preset: [None ▾]

Media Kind: [Music ▾]

VoiceOver Language: [Automatic ▾]

Rating: ★★★★★

☐ Start Time: 0:00

☐ Stop Time: 5:45.2

☐ Remember playback position
☐ Skip when shuffling
☐ Part of a gapless album

(Previous) (Next)   (Cancel) (OK)

Figure 12-7:
Adjust the volume setting for a song here.

Equalizing the sound

The Beach Boys were right when they sang "Good Vibrations" because that's what music is — the sensation of hearing audible vibrations conveyed to the ear by a medium, such as air. Musicians measure pitch by the *frequency* of vibrations. When you increase the bass or treble, you're actually increasing the volume, or intensity, of certain frequencies. iTunes provides an equalizer to fine-tune the sound spectrum frequencies in a more precise way than with bass and treble controls. It increases or decreases specific frequencies of the sound to raise or lower highs, lows, and midrange tones.

You can use the iTunes equalizer (EQ) to customize playback for different musical genres, listening environments, or speakers. iTunes comes with more than 20 EQ presets of the most commonly used settings, including ones for specific music genres, such as classical and rock.

To choose an equalizer preset for a song, video, podcast, or audio book, select the item in the iTunes library, choose File⇨Get Info, and click the Options tab (refer to Figure 12-7). Click the Equalizer Preset pop-up menu to assign an EQ preset, and click the OK button. If something is playing, you hear the effect in the sound immediately after choosing the preset.

For even finer control, you can open the iTunes Equalizer window by choosing Window⇨Equalizer. You can then adjust frequencies by clicking and dragging sliders that look like mixing-board faders. You can also see what a preset actually does to the frequencies by clicking the Equalizer window's pop-up menu to select the same preset by name. The faders in the equalizer show you exactly what the preset does.

Find out more about tweaking the sound with the equalizer by visiting the Tips section of my Web site (www.tonybove.com).

Sound-checking and enhancing the volume

Because music CDs are manufactured inconsistently, discrepancies occur in volume. Some CDs play louder than others; occasionally, even individual tracks on a CD might vary.

You can standardize the volume level of all the songs in your iTunes library with the Sound Check option. This option has the added benefit of applying the same volume adjustment when you play the songs back on your iPad, iPod, or iPhone, as I describe in Chapter 15.

To enable Sound Check, follow these steps:

1. **Drag the iTunes volume slider to set the overall volume for iTunes.**

   The volume slider is located in the upper-left corner of the iTunes window, to the right of the play button.

2. **Choose iTunes⇨Preferences (Mac) or Edit⇨Preferences (Windows).**

   The iTunes Preferences dialog appears.

3. **Click the Playback tab.**

   The Playback preferences appear (refer to Figure 12-4).

4. **Select the Sound Check box.**

   iTunes sets the volume level for all songs according to the level of the iTunes volume slider.

5. Click the OK button.

The Sound Check option sets a volume adjustment based on the volume slider on all the songs so that they play at approximately the same volume.

The operation runs in the background while you do other things. If you quit iTunes and then restart it, the operation continues where it left off when you quit. You can switch Sound Check on or off at any time.

You can also improve the depth of the sound by enhancing high and low frequencies. Audiophiles and sound purists would most likely use the equalizer to boost frequencies, but you can use this brute-force method to enhance the sound. Follow these steps:

1. Choose iTunes⇨Preferences (Mac) or Edit⇨Preferences (Windows).

The iTunes Preferences dialog appears.

2. Click the Playback tab.

The Playback preferences appear (refer to Figure 12-4).

3. Select the Sound Enhancer check box and adjust the slider:

- *Increase the sound enhancement.* Dragging the Sound Enhancer slider to the right (toward High) is similar to pressing the loudness button on a car stereo or the equivalent of boosting the treble (high) and bass (low) frequencies in the equalizer.

- *Decrease the high and low frequencies.* Drag the slider to the left toward Low.

The middle setting is neutral, adding no enhancement — the same as disabling Sound Enhancer by deselecting its check box.

Using AirPlay or Apple TV for Wireless Stereo Playback

Apple's AirPlay technology works with its AirPort technology, which provides Wi-Fi networking for any AirPort-equipped Mac or wireless-capable PC that uses a Wi-Fi–certified IEEE 802.11b, 802.11g, or 802.11n wireless card or offers built-in Wi-Fi. For more about AirPort, see *Mac OS X Snow Leopard All-in-One For Dummies,* by Mark L. Chambers (published by Wiley).

If you already have a wireless network in place, you can add AirPort Express without changing anything. The AirPort Express wirelessly links to your existing wireless network without requiring any change to the network. You can even use several AirPort Express units — one for each stereo system or set of powered speakers, in different rooms.

All by itself, AirPort Express creates a Wi-Fi network. You can attach your Internet cable modem or other Ethernet network to AirPort Express to link your ready-made Wi-Fi network to the outside world. You can also take AirPort Express on the road to use in hotel rooms to share an Internet connection among wireless computers.

To use AirPlay and AirPort Express, follow these steps:

1. **Follow the instructions to install the software supplied with AirPort Express.**

2. **Connect your stereo or a set of powered speakers to the AirPort Express audio port.**

   You can use an optical digital or analog audio cable. (Both are included in the AirPort Express Stereo Connection Kit available from the Apple Store.) Which cable you use depends on whether your stereo or set of powered speakers has an optical digital or analog connection.

3. **Plug AirPort Express into an electrical outlet.**

   Use the AC plug that came with AirPort Express or the power extension cord included in the AirPort Express Stereo Connection Kit. AirPort Express turns on automatically when connected to an electrical outlet. The status light glows yellow while AirPort Express is starting up. When it is fully up and running, the light turns green.

On your computer, set your iTunes preferences to look for speakers connected wirelessly with AirPlay, following the instructions in "Using Remote Speakers" earlier in this chapter.

The AirPort Express is small enough to fit in the palm of your hand, and it travels well because all it needs is a power outlet. You can take your laptop and AirPort Express to a friend's house or party, connect the AirPort Express to the stereo system and a power outlet, and then use your laptop anywhere in its vicinity to play DJ. You can even use portable powered speakers in a hotel room without wires and use a hotel room's LAN-to-Internet access with an AirPort Express to connect your wireless computer and other wireless computers in the room to the Internet.

You can use any computer with iTunes to play its library content (audio *and* video) through Apple TV to your home entertainment system without your having to synchronize that library's content — meaning that you don't have to change the content that is already synchronized with your Apple TV. That way, if you invite a friend over with her laptop, you can quickly play any tune in her laptop's library without changing the synchronized content from your computer. You can play anything in an iTunes library, even if your Apple TV is already filled with synchronized content.

To find out how to synchronize your Apple TV, visit this book's companion Web site.

Chapter 13

Organizing iTunes Content with Playlists

*T*he ability to play any set of songs in a specific order is one of the joys of using iTunes. A *playlist* is a list of the items that you want, organized in the sequence that you want to play them. For example, you can make a playlist of love songs from different albums for a romantic mood, or surf songs for a trip to the beach.

You can also organize playlists for different operations, such as burning a CD, or syncing content to your iPad, iPod, iPhone, or Apple TV. I create playlists that combine songs from different albums based on themes or similarities. For example, I sync a set of jazz playlists with my iPhone for cruising around in the city at night, a set of classic rock playlists with my iPod shuffle for jogging in the morning, a set of playlists of short films mixed with TV shows with my iPad for a long airplane ride, and a playlist of rain songs to celebrate rainy days.

You can even create a *smart playlist,* which automatically includes items in the playlist based on the criteria you set up and also removes items that don't match the criteria. The information included in iTunes (see Chapter 11) is very useful for setting up the criteria. For example, you can define the criteria for a smart playlist to automatically include songs from a particular artist or songs that have the highest rating or fit within a particular musical genre.

Creating Playlists

Playlists are important for managing your content library. For example, you need to create a playlist in order to burn a CD (as I show in Chapter 14), and you may want to synchronize your iPad, iPod, or iPhone using playlists (as I describe in Chapter 8). They can also make it easier to find items you like without searching the entire library for them. You can create playlists of individual songs or entire albums. You can also include audio books, TV shows, videos, podcast episodes, and Web radio stations in playlists.

To create a playlist, follow these steps:

1. **Click the add playlist (plus "+" sign) button (in the lower-left corner of the iTunes window under the source pane) or choose File⇨New Playlist.**

   This step creates a new, untitled playlist in the Playlists section of the Source pane named, appropriately enough, *untitled playlist,* highlighted and ready to rename.

2. **Give the playlist a new descriptive name.**

   You can begin typing a new name and press Return (or just click somewhere else) to save the name. (If the playlist name wasn't highlighted first, click once to select it and then click the name again so that the text cursor appears; doing so highlights the playlist name, making it ready for you to type the new name.)

   After you type the new name, iTunes automatically sorts it into alphabetical order in the Playlists section of the Source pane (underneath the smart playlists).

   You can rename a playlist at any time by clicking its name twice and typing a new one.

3. **Select a source, such as Music or Podcasts, in the Library section of the Source pane and then drag items from the library to the playlist.**

   Drag one item at a time or drag a group of items, dropping them onto the playlist name in the source pane. The initial order of items in the playlist is based on the order in which you drag them to the list. You can add all the podcast episodes to a playlist by dragging the podcast name, or you can open it to reveal its episodes (see Chapter 12 for details) and drag separate episodes to the playlist rather than the entire podcast.

4. **Select the playlist in the Playlists section of the source pane to play it.**

   After selecting a playlist, the items in the playlist appear in the list pane. Select any item in the playlist to start playing from that item to the end of the playlist, and click the play button.

To rearrange the list of items in the playlist, see the section "Rearranging and managing playlists," later in this chapter.

To open a playlist in a new window, double-click the icon next to the playlist name in the source pane. You can then browse your music library and drag items from your music library to the separate playlist window.

Making a playlist of an album is simple. Select the Music option in the Library section of the source pane, and select an album — either in Grid or Cover Flow view, or in List or Album List view using the column browser (choose View⇨Column Browser⇨Show Column Browser). Then drag the selected album to an area between playlists in the Playlists section of the source pane (or on top of the heading PLAYLISTS). Or, select the album and then choose File⇨New Playlist from Selection. iTunes automatically creates a new playlist named after the album.

You can create a playlist with all of a podcast's episodes the same way: choose Podcasts in the source pane and select the podcast that you want to make into a playlist, and then choose File⇨New Playlist from Selection.

You might want to play several albums back to back without having to select each album to play it. For example, you might want to use an iPod on that long drive from London to Liverpool to play Beatles albums in the order they were released (or perhaps in the reverse order, following the Fab Four's career from London back to Liverpool). To create a playlist of entire albums in a particular order, drag each album to the same playlist in the order you want to play them. Each time you drag an album, iTunes automatically lists the songs in the proper track sequence for each album. The albums are listed in the playlist in the order that you dragged them.

You can mix videos with songs and other items in a playlist. For example, you can mix songs and music videos, songs and a video documentary, or just a selection of TV shows, music, podcasts, movies, and audio books for an entire day's worth of entertainment. However, if you sync or copy the playlist to an iPod that doesn't play video, the video doesn't copy over to the iPod.

Rearranging and managing playlists

To rearrange the items in a playlist, follow these steps:

1. **Select the playlist in the Playlists section of the source pane.**

   After you select a playlist, the items in the playlist appear in the list pane.

2. **Drag items in the list pane to rearrange the list.**

   - *To move an item (such as a song) up the list and scroll at the same time,* drag it over the up arrow in the first column.

   - *To move an item down the list and scroll,* drag it to the bottom of the list.

- *To move a group of items at once,* press Shift and select a range of items (or press ⌘ on a Mac or Ctrl in Windows while clicking to select specific songs) and then drag them into a new position.

Besides dragging items, you can also rearrange a playlist by sorting it: Just click one of the column headings, such as Name, Time, or Artist.

You can organize playlists into folders in the source pane. Choose File⇨ New Playlist Folder to create a folder in the Playlists section. Then drag playlist names and drop them over the new folder — just like how you treat files and folders in your operating system. Folders are useful for grouping playlists that are similar in content or function. For example, I created a different folder that corresponds to each of my iPod models to organize the playlists I use to sync with those models. (See Chapter 8 to read about synchronization.) You can include smart playlists in folders as well as regular playlists.

Deleting items from a playlist

You can delete items from playlists as you wish. When you delete an item from a playlist, the item is simply deleted from the list — not from the library. You can also delete entire playlists without harming the content in the library. *Note:* You need to switch to the Library section of the source pane (Music, Movies, TV Shows, and so on) if you want to delete items permanently from your library.

To delete an item from a playlist, select the playlist in the Playlists section of the source pane and then select the item. Press Delete/Backspace or choose Edit⇨Delete. In the warning dialog that appears, click the Remove button to remove the selected item from the list.

The one way you can completely delete an item from your library from within a playlist is by selecting the item and pressing ⌘-Option-Delete (Mac) or Ctrl-Alt-Backspace (Windows).

To delete a whole playlist, select the playlist in the Playlists section of the source pane and then press Delete/Backspace or choose Edit⇨Delete.

Using Smart Playlists

Under iTunes DJ (near the top of the Playlists section of the source pane), you can find *smart playlists,* which are indicated by a gear-in-a-document icon. iTunes comes with a few sample smart playlists, such as My Top Rated and Recently Added, and you can create your own. Smart playlists add items to themselves based on prearranged criteria, or *rules.* For example, when you rate your content items, My Top Rated changes to reflect your new ratings.

You don't have to set up anything because My Top Rated and Recently Added are already defined for you.

Of course, smart playlists are ignorant of your taste in music or video. You have to program them with rules by using the song information in iTunes (see Chapter 11 about adding or editing song information, including ratings). For example, you can create a smart playlist that uses the Year field to grab all the songs from 1966. This list, in no particular order, might include The Beatles ("Eleanor Rigby"), Frank Sinatra ("Strangers in the Night"), The Yardbirds ("Over Under Sideways Down"), and Ike and Tina Turner ("River Deep, Mountain High") — a far-out playlist, no doubt, but not necessarily what you want. You can use other fields of information that you entered (such as ratings, artist name, or composer) to fine-tune your criteria. You can also use view options such as *Plays* (the number of times the item was played) or *Date Added* (the date the item was added to the library).

Creating a smart playlist

To create a new smart playlist, choose File⇨New Smart Playlist. The Smart Playlist dialog appears (as shown in Figure 13-1), offering the following choices for setting criteria:

- ✔ **Match the Following Rule:** From the first pop-up menu (refer to Figure 13-1), you can choose any of the categories used for information, such as Artist, Composer, or Last Played. From the second pop-up menu, you can choose an operator, such as the greater-than or less-than operator. The selections that you make in these two pop-up menus combine to create a rule, such as Year is greater than 1966 or, as in Figure 13-1, Composer contains (the words) Woody Guthrie.

  You can also add multiple conditions by clicking the + button (on the right) as shown in Figure 13-2. You then decide whether to match all or any of these conditions. The Match *xx* of the Following Rules option is enabled by default when you set one or more rules.

- ✔ **Limit To:** You can limit the smart playlist to a specific *duration,* measured by the number of songs (items), time, or size in megabytes or gigabytes, as shown in Figure 13-2. You can have items selected by various methods, such as random, most recently played, and so on.

- ✔ **Match Only Checked Items:** This option selects only those songs or other items in the library that have a check mark beside them, along with the rest of the criteria. Selecting and deselecting items is an easy way to fine-tune your selection for a smart playlist.

- ✔ **Live Updating:** This allows iTunes to continually update the playlist while you play items, add or remove items from the library, change their ratings, and so on.

After setting up the rules, click the OK button. iTunes creates the playlist, noted by a gear-in-a-document icon and the name *untitled playlist* (or whatever phrase you used for the first condition, such as the album or artist name). You can click in the playlist field and then type a new name for it.

Figure 13-1: Set the first match rule for a smart playlist.

Figure 13-2: Use multiple conditions and a time limit for a smart playlist.

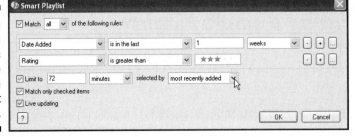

A smart playlist for recent additions

Setting up rules gives you the opportunity to create playlists that are smarter than the ones supplied with iTunes. For example, I created a smart playlist with criteria (as shown in Figure 13-2) that does the following:

✔ Includes any item added to the library in the past week that also has a rating greater than three stars.

✔ Limits the playlist to 72 minutes to be sure that it fits on a 74-minute audio CD, even with gaps between the songs. It also refines the selection to the most recently added if the entire selection becomes greater than 72 minutes.

✔ Matches only selected items.

✔ Performs live updating.

Editing a smart playlist

To edit a smart playlist, select it from the Playlists section of the source pane and choose File⇨Edit Smart Playlist. Or, you can Ctrl-click or right-click (Mac) or right-click (Windows) the playlist to show the contextual menu, and then choose Edit Smart Playlist from the contextual menu. Either way, the Smart Playlist window appears with the criteria for the smart playlist.

For example, to modify the smart playlist so that items with a higher rating are picked, simply add another star or two to the My Rating criteria.

Adding a Touch of Genius

The Genius feature works with Apple's iTunes Store content to match your tastes to other iTunes users using a technique called *collaborative filtering*. The Genius feature analyzes the music in other people's iTunes libraries — people who also have the same song you selected (if they also turn on the Genius feature in iTunes). All this information is shared anonymously. The only music Genius knows, however, is the music available in the iTunes Store.

For the Genius feature to work, you need an iTunes Store account (see Chapter 6), and you must turn on Genius to enable iTunes to scan your music library and catalog your iTunes collection. The scanning process may take a few minutes or (for very large collections) a few hours, but you can continue using iTunes while it scans your music.

To turn on Genius, choose Store⇨Turn On Genius, enter your Apple ID and password for your iTunes Store account, and click the Continue button. You can turn it off by choosing Store⇨Turn Off Genius. If you add new music, you can tell iTunes to immediately update the Genius feature with new information by choosing Store⇨Update Genius.

Creating a Genius playlist

To create a Genius playlist, select a song in the list pane and click the Genius button (the button with the atom icon) at the lower-right corner of the iTunes window. iTunes displays the Genius playlist in the list pane based on the selected song. You can limit the number of songs for the Genius playlist by clicking the Limit To pop-up menu in the top row of buttons on the right side of the list pane, as shown in Figure 13-3.

You can refresh the Genius playlist with a new batch of songs based on the selected song by clicking the Refresh button in the top row of buttons (see Figure 13-3). When you refresh a Genius playlist, you lose the previous version of that playlist.

Figure 13-3:
Limit the
number of
songs for
the Genius
playlist.

To save a Genius playlist, click the Save Playlist button in the right corner of
the top row of buttons. The playlist is saved with the Genius icon using the
name of the selected song and listed in the Genius section of the source pane
(above the Playlists section). You can revisit this Genius playlist and refresh
it, or change its song limit. You can also rearrange the songs in the Genius
playlist by dragging them. To sort the songs, click the column headers in the
list pane — just like other playlists.

You can sync your saved Genius playlists with your iPad, iPod, or iPhone
(see Chapter 8 for details). Synchronized Genius playlists on the iPad, iPod,
or iPhone contain the same songs that appeared in the iTunes version of the
playlist. See Chapter 15 for details on using Genius playlists with your iPad,
iPod, or iPhone.

Playing Genius mixes

The Genius of iTunes is that it can take into consideration everything in your
library and, comparing your library to other libraries, come up with an inter-
esting mix of songs. To give you a taste of what's possible with the Genius
feature, check out Genius Mixes.

Start by selecting Genius Mixes in the Genius section of the source pane (Genius must already be turned on as described earlier in this section). iTunes compiles a set of Genius mixes based on your library, as shown in Figure 13-4. Each square represents a separate mix. As you hover over a square, a play button appears; click the play button to play the mix.

Figure 13-4: Generate Genius mixes from your entire library.

Chapter 14

Gimme Shelter for My Media

*Y*ou might think that your digital content is safe, stored as-is, on your iPad, iPod, iPhone, Apple TV, and hard drive. However, demons in the night are working overtime to render your hard drive useless — and at the same time, someone left your iPad out in the rain, your iPhone can't phone home, your iPod is lost in the supermarket, and your Apple TV is on the fritz.

Copyright law and common sense prohibit you from using copyrighted content and then selling it to someone else. However, with iTunes, you're allowed to make copies of the content and apps that you own for personal use, including copies for backup purposes.

This chapter boils down everything you need to know about keeping your library backed up, and burning discs to make copies of some of your content. For example, I burn audio CDs or MP3 CDs to make safety copies of songs I buy from the iTunes Store. I also like to custom-mix songs from different artists and albums onto an audio or MP3 CD.

I burn data DVDs to back up my video files — and I also copy my entire iTunes library to another hard drive as a backup, as I describe in this chapter. This operation is very important, especially if you've purchased items that don't exist anywhere else in your collection but on your computer. That way, even if your hard drive fails, you still have your iTunes library.

 To find out how to consolidate media files into one library, how to manage multiple iTunes libraries for easier synchronization with multiple devices, and how to move a library from one computer to another (such as a PC to a Mac or vice versa), visit this book's companion Web site.

You should not rely on your iPad, iPod, iPhone, or Apple TV as your sole music storage device or as a backup for your iTunes library. Although purchases you make with your iPad, iPod touch, or iPhone *are* copied back to your iTunes library, you can't copy any other content from your iPad, iPod, iPhone, or Apple TV to your computer via iTunes. It's a one-way trip from iTunes *to* your iPad, iPod, iPhone, or Apple TV because record labels and video distributors don't want indiscriminate copying, and Apple has complied with these requests. You can, however, use *third-party utility programs* (not supported by Apple) to copy content both ways.

To find out more about third-party utility programs for managing your iPod or iPhone, visit the Tips section of my Web site (www.tonybove.com).

The iTunes Store uses Apple FairPlay technology for some content (such as commercial movies and TV Shows), which protects the rights of copyright holders while also giving you some leeway in using the copyrighted content. But you can still copy the media files freely so that backup is easy and straightforward on either a Mac or a PC.

Do not violate copyright law. You're allowed to copy content for your own use, but you cannot legally copy content for any other purpose. Consult a lawyer if you're in doubt.

Burning Your Own Discs

Once upon a time, when vinyl records were popular, rock radio disk jockeys (who didn't like disco) held disco-meltdown parties. People were encouraged to throw their disco records onto a pile to be burned or steamrolled into a vinyl glob. I admit that I shamelessly participated in one such meltdown. However, this section isn't about that. Rather, *burning* a disc is the process in which the CD drive recorder's laser heats up points on an interior layer of the disc to record information.

Using recordable CDs and DVDs

If you have a CD-R, CD-RW, or DVD-R drive (such as the Apple SuperDrive for a Mac) and a blank CD-R (*R* stands for *recordable*), you can burn music, audio books, and audio podcast episodes on audio CDs that play in most CD and DVD players. You can fit up to 74 minutes of music on a high-quality audio-format CD-R; most can go as high as 80 minutes. Blank audio CD-Rs (I'm talking discs now and not drives) are available in stores that carry consumer electronics.

You can also burn an audio CD-R of song files in the MP3 format, which is useful for backing up a music library or making discs for use in MP3 CD players. You can play MP3 files burned on a CD-R in MP3 format on any MP3 disc player, on combination CD/MP3 players, on many DVD players, and (of course) on computers that recognize MP3-formatted CDs (including computers with iTunes). An MP3-formatted CD-R can hold more than 12 hours of music. You read that right — *12 hours on one disc.* This is why *MP3 discs* are popular: They are essentially CD-Rs with MP3 files stored on them.

If you have a DVD burner, such as an Apple SuperDrive, you can burn *data discs* in the DVD-R or DVD-RW format to use with other computers. This approach is suitable for making backup copies of media files (or any data files). A DVD-R can hold about 4,700,000,000 bytes (more than 4GB).

Creating a disc burn playlist

To burn a CD (actually a CD-R, but most people refer to recordable CD-R discs as *CDs*), you must first define a playlist for the CD. (See Chapter 13 for a play-by-play on how to create a playlist.) You can use songs encoded in any format that iTunes supports; however, you get higher-quality music with the uncompressed AIFF and WAV formats or with the Apple Lossless format. (You can back up your library to DVD without creating a playlist, as I describe in the section "Backing up to DVD-Rs or CD-Rs," later in this chapter.)

If your playlist includes music purchased from the iTunes Store in the older protected AAC-encoding format (before 2009), some rules might apply. You can burn seven copies of the same playlist containing protected songs to an audio CD, but no more. As of this writing, all music you purchase in the store is in the newer unprotected iTunes Plus format, with no limit on burning discs.

You can get around this limitation by creating or using a new playlist, copying the protected songs to the new playlist, and then burning more CDs with the new playlist.

Calculating how much music to use

When you create an audio CD playlist, you can calculate how many songs can fit on the CD by totaling the durations of the songs. You can see the size of a playlist by selecting it; the bottom of the iTunes window shows the number of songs, the duration of the songs, and the amount in megabytes for the selected playlist. Click the duration to see a more precise total time for the playlist, as shown in Figure 14-1.

Figure 14-1:
Click the
duration of
the playlist
below the
List pane
to see the
total time.

In Figure 14-1, the selected playlist takes about 1.1 hours (1:08:54, to be precise) to play, so it fits on a standard audio CD. (The 15 songs take up only
94.5MB of hard drive space; they were purchased from the iTunes Store.)

A one-hour playlist of AIFF-formatted music, which occupies over 600MB of
hard drive space, also fits on a standard audio CD. You calculate the amount
you can fit on a standard audio CD using the duration, not the hard drive
space occupied by the music files. Although a CD holds between 650MB and
700MB (depending on the disc), the music is encoded in a special format
known as CD-DA (Compact Disc-Digital Audio or Red Book) that fills byte sec-
tors without error-correction and checksum information. Thus, you can fit
about 90MB more — 740MB total — of AIFF-formatted music on a 650MB disc.
I typically put 1.1 hours (about 66 minutes) of music on a 74-minute or an
80-minute CD-R, leaving minutes to spare.

Always use the actual duration in hours, minutes, and seconds to calculate
how much music you can fit on an audio CD — either 74 or 80 minutes for
blank CD-Rs. I recommend leaving at least one extra minute to account for the
gaps between songs.

You do the *opposite* for an MP3 CD or a data DVD. Use the actual megabytes
to calculate how many song files can fit on a disc — up to 700MB for a blank
CD-R. You can fit lots more music on an MP3 CD-R because you use MP3-
formatted songs rather than uncompressed AIFF songs.

If you have too many songs in the playlist to fit on a CD, iTunes gives you the
option to cancel the burn operation, or to burn as many songs in the playlist
as will fit on the CD (either audio or MP3). Then it asks you to insert another
CD to continue burning the remaining songs in the playlist.

Importing music for an audio CD-R

Before you rip an audio CD of songs that you want to burn to an audio CD-R,
you might want to change the import settings (as I describe in Chapter 7).
Use the AIFF, WAV, or Apple Lossless formats for songs from audio CDs if you

want to burn your own audio CDs with music at its highest quality. You can also burn MP3-formatted songs to an audio CD, but the quality is not as good as with AIFF, WAV, or Apple Lossless.

AIFF is the standard digital format for uncompressed sound on a Mac, and you can't go wrong with it. *WAV* is basically the same thing for Windows. Apple Lossless provides CD-quality sound in a file size that's about 55 to 60 percent of the size of an AIFF or WAV file. Both AIFF and WAV offer the same custom settings for sample rate, sample size, and channels (to see how to customize your settings before ripping audio CDs, see Chapter 7). You can choose the automatic settings, and iTunes detects the proper sample rate, size, and channels from the source. Apple Lossless is always set to automatic.

The songs you purchase from the iTunes Store are supplied in an unprotected AAC format that carries no restrictions. (The format is also known as iTunes Plus.) However, you may still have songs in the older protected AAC format in use up until 2009. You can't convert the protected format to anything else, but you can still burn the songs onto CDs, and the quality of the result on CD is acceptable. Audio books also come in a protected format that can't be converted by iTunes, but you can burn them onto CDs with acceptable quality.

The AAC format is similar in audio quality to the MP3 format but takes up less space; both are acceptable to most CD listeners. I think AAC offers a decent trade-off of space and quality and is suitable (although not as good as AIFF or Apple Lossless) for burning to an audio CD.

For a complete description of these formats, visit this book's companion Web site.

Switching import formats for MP3 CD-Rs

MP3 discs are essentially CD-Rs with MP3 files stored on them. Consumer MP3 CD players are readily available in consumer electronics stores, including hybrid models that play both audio CDs and MP3 CDs.

You can fit 8–12 hours of stereo music on an MP3 CD with the MP3 format — the amount varies depending on the encoding options and settings you choose. For example, you might be able to fit up to 20 hours of mono (monaural) recordings because they use only one channel and carry less information. On the other hand, if you choose the setting to encode stereo recordings at a high bit rate (above 192 bits per second), you may fit only nine hours.

Only MP3-formatted songs can be burned on an MP3 CD-R. Any songs not formatted in MP3 are skipped and not burned. Audible books and commercial spoken-word titles are typically provided in an audio format that uses security technologies, including encryption, to protect purchased content; however, you can include anything that is formatted in MP3, including audio books from other sources. But you can't burn an MP3 CD-R with Audible files; any Audible files in a burn playlist are skipped when you burn an MP3 CD-R.

Burning a disc

Burning a CD is a simple process, and getting it right the first time is a good idea because when you burn a CD-R, it's done — right or wrong. You can't erase content and reuse a CD-R. Fortunately, CD-Rs are inexpensive, so you won't be out more than a few cents if you burn a bad one. (Besides, they're good as coasters for coffee tables.)

Follow these steps to burn a disc:

1. **Select the playlist and then click the Burn Disc button.**

   The Burn Disc button appears in the lower-right corner of the iTunes window whenever you select a playlist (refer to Figure 14-1). After clicking Burn Disc, the Burn Settings dialog appears, as shown in Figure 14-2.

2. **Select options in the Burn Settings dialog and click the Burn button.**

   See the following section for instructions on selecting these important options.

Figure 14-2:
Choose burn settings before burning the disc.

3. **Insert a blank disc.**

   iTunes immediately checks the media and begins the burn process, displaying a progress bar and the names of the songs burning to the disc.

   If you chose the MP3 CD format, iTunes skips over any songs in the playlist that aren't in this format.

   When iTunes finishes burning the disc, iTunes chimes, and the disc is mounted on the Desktop.

4. **Eject the newly burned disc from your drive and then test it.**

5. **Don't delete your burn playlist yet.**

You can cancel the burn operation at any time by clicking the X next to the progress bar, but canceling the operation isn't like undoing the burn. If the burn has already started, you can't use that CD-R or DVD-R again.

If the playlist has more music than can fit on the disc using the chosen format, iTunes asks whether you want to create multiple audio CDs with the playlist. If you choose to create multiple audio CDs, iTunes burns as many full songs as possible from the beginning of the playlist and then asks you to insert another disc to burn the rest. To calculate the amount of music in a playlist, see the earlier section "Calculating how much music to use."

Spoken-word fans: Audible audio books with chapter markers are burned onto a CD with each chapter as a separate track.

Choosing your burn settings

Set the following options in the Burn Settings dialog to ensure that you burn your CD right the first time (refer to Figure 14-2):

- ✔ **Preferred Speed:** Choose a specific recording speed or the Maximum Possible option from the Preferred Speed pop-up menu. iTunes typically detects the rating of a blank CD-R and adjusts the recording speed to fit. However, if your blank CD-Rs are rated for a slower speed than your burner or if you have problems creating CD-Rs, you can change the recording speed setting to match the CD's rating.

- ✔ **Disc Format:** The disc format is perhaps the most important choice you have to make. Decide whether you're burning an audio CD (CD-R), an MP3 CD (CD-R), or a Data CD (CD-R) or DVD (DVD-R or DVD-RW). Your choice depends on what type of player you're using or whether you're making a data backup of files rather than a disc that plays in a player. Choose one of the following:

  - *Audio CD:* Burn a normal audio CD of up to 74 or 80 minutes (depending on the type of blank CD-R) using any iTunes-supported music files, including songs bought from the iTunes Store. Although connoisseurs of music might use AIFF or WAV for songs to be burned on an audio CD, you can also use the AAC and MP3 formats.

  - *MP3 CD:* Burn an MP3 CD with MP3-formatted songs. No other formats are supported for MP3 CDs.

  - *Data CD or DVD:* Burn a data CD-R, CD-RW, DVD-R, or DVD-RW with audio files. You can use any encoding formats for the songs. ***Important:*** Data discs won't play on most consumer CD players: They're meant for use with computers. However, data discs are good choices for storing backup copies of songs bought from the iTunes Store.

✔ **Gap between Songs:** You can add an appropriate gap between songs, just like commercial CDs. With this option enabled, you can set the gap time as well. You can choose from a gap of 0 to 5 seconds, or None. I recommend leaving the menu set to the default setting of 2 seconds for playlists of studio-recorded songs, and None for concerts and songs recorded live. Albums and song selections that you set to be gapless (see Chapter 7) are likewise gapless if you set the Gap between Songs option to None.

✔ **Use Sound Check:** Musicians do a sound check before every performance to check the volume of microphones and instruments and their effect on the listening environment. The aptly named Use Sound Check option in the Burning preferences dialog turns on the Sound Check feature to balance your tunes, volume-wise.

Note: This option, for audio CDs only, works regardless of whether you're already using the Sound Check option in the Playback preferences for iTunes playback as described in Chapter 12. You can select this option for burning without ever changing the preferences for iTunes playback.

✔ **Include CD Text:** Selecting this option adds the artist and track name text to the CD for certain CD players (often, in-car players) that can display the artist and track name while playing a CD.

Studying Files in an iTunes Library

If you like to keep your records properly filed, you'll love iTunes and its nice, neat file-storage methods. For all content items, iTunes creates a folder named for the artist and subfolders within the artist folder named for each album. These folders are stored in the iTunes Media folder unless you change your storage preferences. Note, however, that if you updated a previous version of iTunes that used the iTunes *Music* folder, iTunes continues to use the self-same iTunes Music folder.

Finding the iTunes library

The default method of storing content in the iTunes library is to store all media files — including music, videos, podcasts, and audio books — in the `iTunes Media` folder (or iTunes Music folder if you updated from a previous version of iTunes), which is inside the `iTunes` folder. With this method, media files that you drag to the iTunes window are copied into the `iTunes Media` folder (without deleting the original files). The `iTunes` folder also has folders for mobile applications and album artwork. So that's easy — everything is inside the `iTunes` folder.

On a Mac, iTunes stores your content library in your home folder's `Music` folder. The path to this folder's default location is

```
your home folder/Music/iTunes/iTunes Media
```

On a Windows PC, iTunes stores your content library in your user folder. The path to this folder's default location is

```
your user folder/My Documents/My Music/iTunes/iTunes Media
```

 iTunes maintains a separate `iTunes` folder (with a separate `iTunes Media` folder) in each home folder (Mac) or user folder (PC). If you share your computer with other users who have home folders, each user can have a separate iTunes library on the same computer (and, of course, a separate iPad, iPod, or iPhone that syncs with it). You need only one copy of the iTunes program.

 If you want to add content to the iTunes library without copying the files to the iTunes Media folder, you can copy a link to the original files without copying the files by doing the following:

1. **Choose iTunes⇨Preferences (Mac) or Edit⇨Preferences (Windows).**

2. **Click the Advanced tab in the iTunes Preferences dialog.**

3. **Turn off the Copy Files to iTunes Media Folder When Adding to Library setting.**

However, if a content file is only linked to the iTunes Media folder and not copied to it, you can't change the file's name or move it to another folder (or rename the folder, either).

Locating a media file

You can find the location of any media file by selecting the item (such as a song or video), choosing File⇨Get Info, and then clicking the Summary tab of the information dialog that appears. You can see the file type next to the Kind heading of the Summary pane. The Where section tells you where the song is, as shown in Figure 14-3.

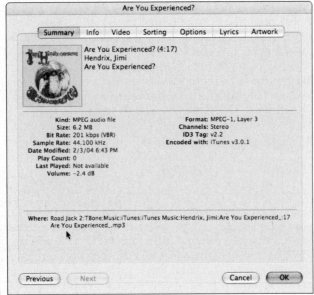

Figure 14-3:
Locate a
media file
from its
information
dialog.

You can also open the folder that contains the media file for any item. Select the item in List, Grid, or Cover Flow view. Then, on a Mac, choose File⇨Show in Finder (or press ⌘-R); in Windows, choose File⇨Show in Windows Explorer (or press Ctrl-R). iTunes gives control to the operating system, which displays the folder that contains the media file. You can show the file if it's on your hard drive but not if it's in a shared library on another computer.

Copying media files

You can easily store the music that you rip from your CDs in other locations: After the music becomes digital, you can copy it endlessly with no subsequent loss in quality. You can copy media files to other hard drives and computers without any restrictions on copying — just keep in mind that protected items, such as movies and TV shows you purchased from the iTunes Store, have some playback restrictions (see Chapter 6 for iTunes Store details).

To copy the media file for an item to another hard drive or folder (such as a song or video), you can drag the item directly from the iTunes window to the other hard drive or folder.

You can also copy the files and folders from the iTunes Media folder to other hard drives or other computers using the operating system's copying function.

For example, on a Mac, you can use the Finder to copy content files. Windows PCs offer several methods, including using Windows Explorer, to copy files. For example, copying an entire album, or every song by a specific artist, is easy — just drag the folder to its new home folder on another hard drive.

Backing Up an iTunes Library

Backups? You don't need no stinkin' backups!

Yes, you do, so think twice about not making them! I know: Backing up your files can be inconvenient and can eat up the capacity of all your external hard drives. Still, it must be done. And fortunately, it's easy to do, either manually as described in this section, or automatically with a system backup utility such as Apple's Time Machine.

With iTunes, you can copy your library to another hard drive on your computer or to another computer. You can burn as many data DVDs as needed to store all the files.

Backing up to DVD-Rs or CD-Rs

Apple provides a handy assistant that walks you through backing up your iTunes library, playlists, and iTunes Store purchases to CD-Rs or DVD-Rs. You can choose to back up the entire library, perform *incremental backups* (only items added or changed since the last backup), or save only store purchases. Choose File⇨Library⇨Back Up to Disc and then choose one of the following:

- ✔ **Back Up Entire iTunes Library and Playlist:** This might take a stack of DVD-Rs (or a truckload of CD-Rs), but it's worth doing if you have no other way to back up your library.

- ✔ **Back Up Only iTunes Store Purchases:** This is an essential procedure because if you lose these files, you have to repurchase them. You can use CD-Rs or DVD-Rs.

- ✔ **Only Back Up Items Added or Changed Since Last Backup:** Use this method to copy only items that were added or changed since your last backup.

To restore your iTunes library from a stack of backup DVD-Rs or CD-Rs, open iTunes and insert the first disc. Then follow the instructions that appear automatically after inserting the disc.

Backing up to another hard drive

To copy your entire library to another hard drive, locate the iTunes folder on your computer (see the section "Finding the iTunes library," earlier in this chapter). Drag this folder to another hard drive or backup device, and you're all set. This action copies everything, including the playlists in your library.

The copy operation might take some time if your library is huge. Although you can interrupt the operation anytime, the newly copied library might not be complete. Finishing the copy operation is always best.

If you restore the backup copy to the same computer with the same name for the hard drive that holds the iTunes library, the backup copy's playlists work fine. Playlists are essentially lists of songs with pathnames to the song files. If the hard drive name is different, the pathnames won't work. However, if you export individual playlists, or all of your playlists, in the XML (eXtensible Markup Language) format beforehand, you can then import them back into iTunes when you restore your backup to realign the playlist pathnames to the new hard drive.

To export a playlist, select the playlist in the Playlists section of the iTunes source pane, choose File➪Library➪Export Playlist, and then choose a location on your hard drive. To export all of your playlists at once, choose File➪Library➪Export Library.

To import a playlist into iTunes, choose File➪Library➪Import Playlist, and then browse for and select the playlist's.XML file on your hard drive. To import all the playlists at once, choose File➪Library➪ Import Playlist and choose the iTunes Media Library.xml file (or iTunes Music Library.xml file for previous versions of iTunes).

Part IV
Playing it Back on Your iPad, iPod, or iPhone

The 5th Wave

By Rich Tennant

"What I'm doing should clear your sinuses, take away your headache, and charge your iPod."

In this part . . .

Part IV is all about playing content with your iPad, iPod, or iPhone, including music, videos, podcasts, audio books, and photos (for apps and online use, see Part V).

✓ Chapter 15 shows you how to locate and play songs. You learn how to find songs, shuffle and repeat songs and albums, and create playlists right on your iPad, iPod, or iPhone. I also describe how to set the volume and tweak the sound.

✓ Chapter 16 describes how to locate and play videos, including movies, TV shows, and YouTube videos. You can skip forward or backward, scale the picture to fit the display, and bookmark your favorite sections. I also show you how to play podcasts and audio books.

✓ Chapter 17 is all about synchronizing photo albums with your iPad, iPod, or iPhone, viewing and shooting photos and videos, sharing them with friends, and putting on a slide show.

Chapter 15

The Songs Remain the Same

*E*ven though the iPod and iTunes have irrevocably changed the entertainment industry and how you enjoy music, one thing remains the same: You still play songs. You just play them with more *panache* on your iPad, iPod, or iPhone.

You can pick any song that you want to hear at any time. You can also shuffle through songs to get an idea of how wide your music choices are or to surprise yourself or others. Browse by artist and album, select a playlist, and even create playlists on the fly — this chapter explains it all, for any iPad, iPod, or iPhone.

Locating Songs on Your iPad, iPod, or iPhone

With thousands of songs on your iPad, iPod, or iPhone, finding a particular song by its title may turn your finger into a scrolling stone. It may be faster to locate albums by cover art or to find songs by searching for artist (or composer), genre, album, or playlist. You can browse your music any number of ways without interrupting the music you're playing.

Going with the Cover Flow

Cover Flow (also called the *cover browser*) lets you flip through your cover art to select music alphabetically by artist. The iPod classic, iPod nano, iPod touch, and iPhone (as well as some earlier sixth-generation models) can display the cover art for albums. (Oddly for a device with a large display, the iPad doesn't yet offer Cover Flow as of this writing.)

To browse music by cover art with an iPod touch, choose Music from the Home screen; on an iPhone, choose iPod from the Home screen. Then turn the iPod touch or iPhone quickly to view it horizontally. This movement changes the display to landscape mode and displays the cover browser.

Slide your finger across the album covers to scroll swiftly through the music library, or tap to the right or left of the cover art in the foreground to move forward or backward an album cover at a time.

Tap the Play button in the lower-left corner to start playing the first song in the foreground album; the play button turns to a pause button so that you can tap it again to stop playback. Tap the *i* button in the lower-right corner (or tap the foreground cover art) to list the songs in that album. Then you can tap a song to start playing it.

The Cover Flow browser is also available on the iPod classic. Choose Music from the main menu and then choose Cover Flow from the Music menu.

To browse by cover art on an iPod classic, scroll the click wheel clockwise to move forward or counterclockwise to move backward through album covers. You can also press the fast forward or rewind buttons to step forward or backward in your library one cover at a time. Press the select button in the middle of the click wheel to select the album in the foreground; a list of songs appears. Use the click wheel to scroll the list of songs and then press the select button to select a highlighted song.

Browsing artists, albums, and songs

You can quickly and easily locate a song by looking up the song's artist, album, or song title. Like iTunes, the iPad, iPod, and iPhone organize music by artist and then within each artist by album. To browse music on an iPod touch, choose Music from the Home screen; on an iPad or iPhone, choose iPod from the Home screen.

To browse by artist, tap the Artists icon in the bottom row on an iPod touch or iPhone, or the Artist button on an iPad, which appears in the bottom row of the display. A scrollable list of artists appears, with an alphabet listed vertically along the right side.

To browse music by albums on an iPad or iPod touch, tap Albums along the bottom of the display; on an iPhone, tap the More icon, which displays a list of options including Albums, and then tap Albums. The album titles appear in a scrollable list with the album cover on the left side and an alphabet listed vertically along the right side.

If you choose Genius Mixes to sync along with other music to your iPad, iPod touch, or iPhone (as I show in Chapter 8), or if you sync your entire music library, the Genius button appears in the lower-left corner of the Music screen on an iPod touch, or the lower-left corner of the iPod screen on an iPhone, shifting the other buttons to the right (Albums on the iPod touch and Videos on the iPhone move to the More menu). In that case, to browse by albums on an iPod touch, tap More and then tap Albums. (For more about Genius Mixes, see "Selecting Genius Mixes" in this chapter.)

To locate songs by title on an iPad, iPod touch, or iPhone, tap Music on the iPod touch Home screen or iPod on the iPad or iPhone Home screen, and tap the Songs icon along the bottom row of the Music or iPod screen, or the Songs button in the bottom row of the iPad display. A scrollable list of songs appears with an alphabet listed vertically along the right side.

On the Artists, Albums, or Songs screen, tap any letter in the alphabet on the right to scroll the list directly to that letter. Slide your finger up and down the alphabet to scroll quickly, or tap any letter in the alphabet to scroll the list directly to that letter. Tap an album title or its cover art to see a list of songs in the album. Tap a song title to start playing the song.

On an iPod touch or iPhone, you can flick your finger down to see the very top of the Artists, Albums, or Songs screen, which shows the search field. (On an iPad you can always see the search field in the top-right corner of the iPod music display.) To search, tap inside the search field in the top, and start typing in the onscreen keyboard that appears. Suggestions appear below matching what you type — you can tap a suggestion to go right to it.

The iPod nano offers icons you can tap on its Home screens to browse songs organized by Playlists or Artists (on Home screen 1), or Songs, Albums, Genres, or Composers (on Home screen 3). Tap an icon to see a list — you can flick to browse song and album lists, and tap the menu bar at the top of any list to return to the top. Long lists include an alphabetical index on the right side of the screen — drag your finger down the index to show a large index letter superimposed over the list, and when you reach the letter you want, lift your finger. Swipe right to return to the previous menu (and continue swiping right to return to the Home screen).Follow these steps with an iPod classic to locate a song by artist and then by album:

1. **Choose Music from the iPod main menu.**
2. **From the Music menu that appears, choose Artists.**

3. **Select an artist from the Artists menu.**

   The artist names are listed in alphabetical order by last name or the first word of a group. Scroll the Artists menu until the artist name is highlighted and then press the select button. The artist's menu of albums appears. (You can also select All Albums at the top of the Artists menu to go directly to the Albums menu.)

4. **Choose All Songs or the name of an album from the artist's menu.**

   You can find All Songs at the top of the artist's menu. Press the select button to choose it, or scroll until an album name is highlighted; then press the select button. A song list appears after you choose either an album or All Songs.

5. **Select a song from the list.**

   The songs in the album list are in *album order* (the order that they appear on the album); in the All Songs list, songs are listed in album order for each album.

To choose an album directly on an iPod classic, choose Albums from the Music menu. The Albums menu appears, displaying albums in alphabetical order. Choose an album from the Albums menu. Then select a song from the list.

Follow these steps with an iPod classic to locate a song by its title:

1. **Choose Music from the iPod main menu.**

2. **From the Music menu that appears, choose Songs.**

3. **Select a song from the Songs menu.**

   The songs are listed in alphabetical order by title. Scroll the Songs menu until the song title is highlighted and then press the select button.

Choosing playlists

When you synchronize your iPad, iPod, or iPhone with your entire iTunes library, your iTunes playlists are included. Well, that makes sense, doesn't it? You can choose to synchronize your iPad, iPod, or iPhone with only specified playlists, as I describe in Chapter 8.

To browse music by playlist on your iPod touch or iPhone, tap Music on the iPod touch Home screen or iPod on the iPhone Home screen, and tap the Playlists icon along the bottom row of the Music or iPod screen. A scrollable list of playlists appears. To browse music by playlist on your iPad, tap iPod on the iPad Home screen, and the playlists appear in the left column under the Library heading.

Tap a playlist title on an iPad, iPod touch, or iPhone to see a list of songs in the playlist and tap a song title to start playing the song.

On an iPod nano, tap Playlists in the first Home screen, and then tap a playlist title in the list of playlists to see a list of songs in the playlist. Tap a song title to start playing the song.

Follow these steps to locate a playlist on your iPod classic (or earlier models):

1. **Choose Music from the iPod main menu.**

2. **From the Music menu, choose Playlists.**

3. **From the Playlists menu that appears, choose a playlist.**

   Playlists are listed in alphabetical order. Scroll the Playlists menu to highlight the playlist name and then press the Select button. A list of songs in the playlist appears.

4. **Select a song from the list.**

   The songs in the playlist are in *playlist order* (the order defined for the playlist in iTunes). Scroll up or down the list to highlight the song you want.

Controlling Song Playback

To play a song on an iPad, iPod nano, iPod touch, or iPhone, tap the song title (or the play button in Cover Flow on an iPod touch or iPhone). On an iPod classic, scroll the list as previously described to highlight the song title and then press either the select button or the play/pause button to play the selected song.

When the song finishes, the iPad, iPod, or iPhone plays the next song in the sequence that appeared in the list you chose it from. See the section "Repeating songs," later in this chapter, to find out how to repeat albums and playlists.

Controlling playback on an iPad, iPod touch, or iPhone

Whenever you play a song on an iPad, iPod touch, or iPhone, you see the album cover associated with the song on the Now Playing screen. You also see the buttons for playback control — previous/rewind, play/pause, and next/fast forward. (See Figure 15-1 for the iPod touch or iPhone, and Figure 15-2 for the iPad.) Slide your finger along the volume slider to change the volume.

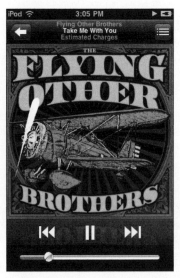

Figure 15-1:
Tap the
iPod touch
Now Playing
screen
under the
album title
(left) to
show more
buttons, the
scrubber
bar, and lyr-
ics (right).

Figure 15-2:
Tap the iPad
Now Playing
screen to
show more
buttons, the
scrubber
bar, and
even lyrics.

Tap the next/fast forward button once to play the next song in sequence, and tap the previous/rewind button once at the beginning of a song, or twice during the song, to play the previous song. You can fast-forward through a song by touching and holding down the next/fast forward button, and you can rewind a song by touching and holding down the previous/rewind button.

You can tap the bullet-list button in the upper-right corner of the iPod touch or iPhone screen or the lower-right corner of the iPad screen if you want to display a list of the album's contents. You can then tap the title of another song on the album to start playing that song.

To return to menus and make other selections when playing a song on an iPod touch or iPhone, tap the left-arrow button in the upper-left corner of the display. On an iPad, tap the album cover thumbnail image in the lower-right corner of the display to return to the Now Playing screen, and tap the left-arrow button in the lower-left corner of the display to return to the main iPod menu screen.

While a song is playing, tap the iPad display, or tap underneath the left-arrow button or the album title on an iPod touch or iPhone, to show more buttons and the scrubber bar for navigating through the song (for the iPod touch or iPhone refer to Figure 15-1, right side; for an iPad, refer to Figure 15-2).

If lyrics are available in the iTunes information, they also appear (to find out how to paste or type lyrics into the lyrics field, see Chapter 11). To turn on or off the display of lyrics, choose Settings⇨iPod from the iPad or iPhone Home screen, or Settings⇨Music from the iPod touch Home screen, and tap the On button next to the Lyrics & Podcast Info option to turn it off. Tap Off to turn it back on.

To skip to any point in a song, use your finger to drag the playhead along the scrubber bar. To finely scrub through a song on an iPod touch or iPhone, after dragging the playhead, slide your finger down the screen (toward the physical Home button) to slow the scrubbing.

To start a song over from the beginning, drag the playhead on the scrubber bar all the way to the left or tap the previous/rewind button once.

If you're viewing another content menu on the iPod touch or iPhone, tap Now Playing at the upper-right corner of the display to go directly to the Now Playing display. On an iPad, tap the Now Playing cover art in the lower-left corner of the display.

You can control music playback while using another app, or while the iPod touch or iPhone is locked. Double-click the physical Home button, and then flick left to right along the bottom row to see the music controls. Tap the Music icon on an iPod touch to go back to the Music app, or the iPod icon on an iPhone to go back to the iPhone app. See Chapter 3 to learn more about using the Home button double-click to multitask your apps and lock the display orientation to portrait.

Controlling playback on an iPod nano

Playback on the iPod nano is slick and easy. If the Now Playing screen is not showing, tap the Now Playing icon on the Home screen. The album artwork for the current song appears — tap the artwork to show the play/pause, previous/rewind, and next/fast-forward song controls, as shown in Figure 15-3 (left side). Swipe left again to show the next screen with more controls — the repeat, genius, and shuffle icons, and the scrubber bar, as shown in Figure 15-3 (right side). Swipe left yet again to see a third screen showing lyrics (if you added them in iTunes). The dots at the bottom of the screen show the number of screens available.

Figure 15-3:
Tap the Now Playing artwork to see controls (left) and swipe left to see the scrubber bar and more controls (right).

To pause playback, tap the pause icon (or disconnect your earphones). To start playing again, tap the play icon. Tap the next/fast forward button once to play the next song in sequence, and tap the previous/rewind button once at the beginning of a song, or twice during the song, to play the previous song. You can fast-forward through a song by touching and holding down the next/fast forward button, and you can rewind a song by touching and holding down the previous/rewind button.

You can tap the "i" icon in the lower-right corner of the first Now Playing screen (refer to Figure 15-3, left side) to display a list of the album's contents. You can then tap the title of another song on the album to start playing that song. To return to menus and make other selections when playing a song, swipe right.

To skip to any point in a song, swipe left to the second Now Playing screen, and use your finger to drag the playhead along the scrubber bar. See

"Repeating songs" and "Shuffling song order" in this section to learn more abou the repeat and shuffle icons, and see "Consulting the iTunes Genius" to learn more about using the genius icon.

You can cross-fade songs on an iPod nano, just like in iTunes (as I describe in Chapter 12). A *cross-fade* creates a smooth transition from the ending of one song to the beginning of the next one. To set your iPod nano to cross-fade songs, tap Settings⇨Music from the second Home screen, and tap the Off button next to Audio Crossfade in the list to turn it on. (Tap On to turn it off.)

Controlling playback on an iPod classic

While a song is playing, the artist name and song name appear on the Now Playing screen along with the album cover and a progress bar. To pause playback, press the play/pause button while a song is playing. To stop playing a song, press the play/pause button again (the same button).

To skip to any point in a song, press the select button to reveal the scrubber bar. Scroll the click wheel to move the playhead across the scrubber bar forward (to the right) or backward (to the left) in the song.

Press the select button multiple times to cycle through the options: scrubber bar, Genius Start button, rating bullets, shuffle settings, and lyrics (if you typed them in for the song, as I explain in Chapter 11, or if they were included with a downloaded song). After the rating bullets appear, scroll the click wheel to add a rating to the song. For details on the Genius feature, see the section "Consulting the iTunes Genius," and to find out how to shuffle, see the section "Shuffling song order," both later in this chapter.

Press the next/fast forward button once to play the next song in sequence, and press the previous/rewind button once at the beginning of a song, or twice during the song, to play the previous song. You can fast-forward through a song by pressing and holding down the next/fast forward button, and rewind a song by pressing and holding down the previous/rewind button.

To start a song over from the beginning, move the playhead on the scrubber bar all the way to the left or press the previous/rewind button once.

While playing a song, you can browse the album or its artist as well as assign the song to an On-The-Go playlist or Genius playlist. Press and hold the select button, and a menu appears with the following choices: Start Genius, Add to On-The-Go, Browse Album, Browse Artist, and Cancel. Scroll the click wheel to choose an option.

To return to the menus and make other selections when playing a song, press the Menu button or press and hold the select button until a menu appears on top of the cover art.

You can cross-fade songs on an iPod classic, just like in iTunes (as I describe in Chapter 12). A *cross-fade* creates a smooth transition from the ending of one song to the beginning of the next one. To set your iPod classic to cross-fade songs, choose Settings⇨Playback⇨Audio Crossfade from the main menu and press Select to turn it on. (Press Select again to turn it off.)

Repeating songs

If you want to drive yourself crazy repeating the same song over and over, your iPad, iPod, or iPhone is happy to oblige. (You might want to try repeating "They're Coming to Take Me Away, Ha-Haaa" by Napoleon XIV, a favorite from the old *The Dr. Demento Show* radio broadcasts — and perhaps they will come to take you away.) More than likely, you want to repeat a playlist or album, which you can easily do.

While a song is playing, tap the iPad screen; on an iPod touch or iPhone, tap underneath the left-arrow button or the album title; on an iPod nano, tap the Now Playing screen and swipe left. The repeat and shuffle buttons appear, along with the scrubber bar. (Refer to Figure 15-1 for an iPod or iPhone, Figure 15-2 for an iPad, and Figure 15-3, right side, for an iPod nano.)

Ordinarily, when a song finishes, the iPad, iPod, or iPhone plays the next song in the sequence that appeared on the screen (Playlists, Artists, Songs, Albums, and so on) you chose it from. When it reaches the end of that list, it stops — if you chose the last song in an album on the Albums screen, the iPad, iPod, or iPhone stops after playing it. But if you tap the repeat button once while the songs are playing, the entire sequence repeats. If you chose an album, the album repeats; if you chose a playlist, the playlist repeats.

After you tap the repeat button once to repeat the sequence of songs, the repeat button shows blue highlighting. Tap the repeat button again to repeat only the current song — the button changes to include a blue-highlighted numeral 1. Tap it once more to return to normal playback.

You can set your iPod classic (or older models) to repeat a single song, or to repeat all the songs in the selected album or playlist, by following these steps:

1. **Locate and play a song.**

2. **While the song plays, press the Menu button repeatedly to return to the main menu and then choose the Settings menu.**

3. **Scroll the Settings menu until Repeat is highlighted.**

   The Repeat setting displays Off, One, or All next to it.

4. **Press the select button until the setting changes to** One **to repeat one song or** All **to repeat all the songs in the album or playlist (or** Off **to turn Repeat off).**

   If you press the button more than you need to, keep pressing until the setting you want reappears. The button cycles among the Off, One, and All settings.

You can also press the previous/rewind button to repeat a song.

Shuffling song order

Maybe you want your song selections to be surprising and unpredictable, and you want your iPad, iPod, or iPhone to mess with your mind. You can *shuffle* song playback to play in random order, just like an automated radio station without a disk jockey or program guide. The shuffle algorithm is as random as it gets (not taking into account a fundamental tenet of chaos theory that says a pattern will emerge). When an iPad, iPod, or iPhone creates a shuffle, it reorders the songs (like shuffling a deck of cards) and then plays them in the new order.

On an iPad, iPod nano, iPod touch, or iPhone

When you are playing a song or a song is paused, you can just shake your iPod nano, iPod touch, or iPhone, and it shuffles the songs in the album you are playing. By default, your iPod nano, iPod touch, or iPhone is set to shuffle when shaken (not stirred). To turn this feature off, choose Settings⇨Music from the iPod nano or iPod touch Home screen or Settings⇨iPod from the iPhone Home screen, and tap On for the Shake to Shuffle option to turn it off. (Tap Off to turn it on.)

You can also set your iPad, iPod touch, or iPhone to shuffle songs across its library. To turn your iPad, iPod nano, iPod touch, or iPhone into a random song player, browse songs as I show in "Browsing artists, albums, and songs" in this chapter. . The Shuffle option appears at the top of a song list (you may have to flick downward to see it). Tap Shuffle to turn on Shuffle for that list of songs. For example, if you chose an album, or a playlist, tapping Shuffle at the top of the song list for that album or playlist shuffles only the album or playlist songs.

You can also set the iPad, iPod nano, iPod touch, or iPhone to shuffle songs within an album or playlist after starting the album or playlist. Start playing a song in the album or playlist, and then tap the iPad Now Playing screen, or tap underneath the left-arrow button or the album title on the Now Playing screen of an iPod touch or iPhone, or tap the iPod nano Now Playing screen and swipe left. The repeat and shuffle buttons appear, along with the scrubber bar (refer to Figure 15-1 for an iPod touch or iPhone, Figure 15-2 for an iPad, and Figure 15-3, right side, for an iPod nano). Tap the shuffle button to shuffle songs within the currently playing album or playlist.

Want to repeat an entire album or playlist but still shuffle the playing order each time you hear it? Start playing a song in the album or playlist and then set your iPad, iPod nano, iPod touch, or iPhone to repeat all the songs in the album or playlist as described in the section "Repeating songs," earlier in this chapter. Then set the iPad, iPod nano, iPod touch, or iPhone to shuffle the songs as described in this section.

On an iPod classic

To turn your iPod classic into a random song player, choose Shuffle Songs from the main menu.

To shuffle songs in an album or a playlist, or to shuffle albums, follow these steps:

1. **Choose Settings from the main menu and scroll to Shuffle.**

   The Shuffle setting displays Off next to it.

2. **Press the select button once (Off changes to Songs) to shuffle the songs in the next album or playlist you play. Press select again (Songs changes to Albums) to shuffle the albums without shuffling the songs within each album.**

   When you set Shuffle to Songs, the iPod classic shuffles songs within the currently playing playlist or album, or if nothing is playing, the next album or playlist you choose to play. When you set Shuffle to Albums, it plays all the songs on the currently playing album (or the next album you play) in order and then randomly selects another album in the list and plays through it in order.

   If you press the select button more than you need to, keep pressing until the setting you want reappears. The button cycles among the Off, Songs, or Albums settings.

Playing an iPod shuffle

Speaking of shuffling, the *iPod shuffle* is a special iPod designed with song shuffling foremost in mind — it offers no display or menus for selecting specific songs or albums by title. The idea is to use iTunes to put songs, audio books, and podcasts — as well as playlists of these elements — on the iPod shuffle (as I describe in Chapter 8), clip it to your clothes or something, put the Apple-supplied earbuds in your ears, and listen.

You can use the front-panel controls on a fourth-generation iPod shuffleto control playback, or use the earbud's remote controller with third-genera-tion models (see Chapter 1 for details on remote-controller earbuds). The VoiceOver button on the top of the fourth-generation iPod shuffle tells you the name of the song you're playing (as well as your battery status), and lets you choose from a spoken menu of playlists — VoiceOver also works with the earbud's remote controller for third-generation models.

Starting playback

The iPod shuffle has a three-position switch on the top for playing songs in playlist order, for shuffling songs randomly, and for turning it off. To start playing songs, plug in the earbuds into the iPod shuffle and place them in your ears, and slide the three-position switch from Off to Play in Order (the icon with arrows chasing each other in a closed loop) or Shuffle (the icon showing arrows crossed).

Playback starts as soon as you turn the three-way switch away from Off — to indicate this, the iPod shuffle status light blinks green once. However, if the iPod shuffle is already playing before you plug in your earbuds, playback may stop. To start playback, press the play button (the center button) on the iPod shuffle, or the play button on the remote controller (or toggle the three-way switch to Off and back to Play in Order or Shuffle).

Controlling playback

To pause playback, press the play/pause button in the center (or the earbud remote controller's center button) once. The iPod shuffle status light blinks green for 30 seconds.

To go forward to the next track, press the next/fast-forward button, which is to the right of the play button, once — the status light blinks green once. (With an earbud remote controller, press the center button twice quickly.) To fast-forward through the current track to the next track, press and hold the next/fast-forward button.

To go back to the previous track, press the previous/rewind button on the left of the play button once (or press the center button of the earbud remote controller three times) — the status light blinks green once. To rewind through the current track to its beginning and then to the previous track, press and hold the previous/rewind button.

If you set the three-position switch to Play in Order, going backward or forward navigates in the order the songs were copied to the iPod shuffle or the order within each playlist. However, if you set the position switch to Shuffle, the playing order is randomized first. Then going backward skips backward within the shuffle order, and going forward skips forward within the shuffle order. For example, suppose your iPod shuffle plays the 14th song, then the 5th song, and then the 20th song. In that case, pressing the previous/rewind button within the first six seconds of the 20th song takes you back to the 5th song, and pressing it again takes you back to the 14th song. From there, pressing the next/fast-forward button skips through the songs in the same order again: the 14th song, the 5th song, and then the 20th song.

Using VoiceOver to Choose Playlists

If you enabled VoiceOver for your iPod shuffle in iTunes when you set it up (as I describe in Chapter 2), or enable it now as you synchronize your iPod shuffle (as I describe below), you can hear the iPod shuffle speak song titles and artist names, a menu of playlists for you to choose from, and the status of your battery charge. (With a third-generation iPod shuffle, you need the Apple Earphones with Remote and Mic or the In-Ear Headphones with Remote and Mic to use VoiceOver to navigate playlists.)

The iPad models, and the iPhone 3GS and iPhone 4, offer VoiceOver as part of the accessibility features to make it easier to use for people with visual, auditory, or other physical disabilities. (You can turn the accessibility features on or off by choosing Settings⇨General⇨Accessibility from the Home screen.) It works by telling you about each element on the screen as you select it. However, on an iPad or iPhone, VoiceOver changes the gestures you use to control the device — once VoiceOver is turned on, you have to use VoiceOver gestures to operate the iPad or iPhone — even to turn it off.

To find out all about VoiceOver and the gestures you need to know how to operate the feature on your iPad or iPhone, see the free tips section of my Web site at www.tonybove.com.

To enable VoiceOver, sync your iPod shuffle to iTunes. The Summary page of sync options appears — you may have to scroll it to see all the options. Under Voice Feedback, select the Enable VoiceOver check box to turn it on (or deselect it to turn it off). With an iPod shuffle, you also have the option to choose the language you want from the Language pop-up menu. This sets the language for spoken messages and playlist names, as well as many of the song titles and artist names. Finally, click the Apply button to apply these settings.

To hear the title and artist of the song, press the VoiceOver button on the top of the fourth-generation iPod shuffle (or press and hold the center button of the earbud's remote controller for a third-generation iPod shuffle – and if you press the center button twice quickly to go to the next track, the next message plays as well).

On a fourth-generation iPod shuffle you can navigate after pressing the VoiceOver button to hear the info about the next or previous track. While a track is playing, press next/fast-forward to skip to the next track and hear its info; press previous/rewind to move to the previous track and hear its info. If the iPod shuffle is paused when you do this, you can immediately press the VoiceOver button or play/pause button to play the track you navigated to.

To hear the playlist menu, press and hold the VoiceOver button (or the center button of the earbud's remote controller for a third-generation iPod shuffle) until you hear the names of playlists. The playlist menu announces the current playlist (if one is playing), "All Songs," other playlists in alphabetical order, Genius Mixes, podcasts, iTunes U collections, and finally audio book titles. As you listen to the playlist menu, you can press the next/fast-forward or previous/rewind button to move forward or backward in the playlist menu. After hearing the item you want, press the VoiceOver or play/pause button (or the center button of the earbud's remote controller once) to select it. If you don't want to choose anything from the playlist menu, you can exit by pressing and holding the VoiceOver button (or center button of the earbud controller).

 If you've synced an iPod shuffle with the VoiceOver option turned on, iTunes adds a new option to the Options tab of the Get Info dialog: VoiceOver Language. You can use it to pick a different language for specific songs. After selecting the songs in iTunes, choose File⇨Get Info, click the Options tab, and then choose a language from the VoiceOver Language pop-up menu. Click the OK button to finish.

Ordering Playlists On-The-Go

You can create new playlists and edit playlists directly on your iPad, iPod nano, iPod touch, or iPhone, queuing the songs in the order you want. This option is particularly useful for picking songs to play right before making a long drive. (Hel-*lo!* You shouldn't be messing with your iPad, iPod, or iPhone while driving.) You can give these new playlists names, and sync them back to your iTunes library.

You can also create a single temporary, "On-The-Go" playlist on your iPod classic. The selections appear automatically in a playlist appropriately called *On-The-Go*, on the Playlists menu.

Making playlists on an iPad, iPod touch, or iPhone

Follow these steps with an iPad, iPod touch, or iPhone to add a playlist and select songs for it:

1. **Choose Music from the iPod touch Home screen or iPod from the iPad or iPhone Home screen.**

   The Music or iPod screen appears.

2. **On an iPod touch or iPhone, tap Playlists, and then choose Add Playlist from the Playlists menu; on an iPad, tap the plus (+) sign in the bottom-left corner under the list of playlists.**

   The New Playlist dialog appears and the keyboard pops up, as shown in Figure 15-4 (left side).

3. **Type a name for the playlist and tap Save.**

   The Songs list appears with a plus (+) sign next to each song and next to an Add All Songs option at the top, as shown in Figure 15-4 (right side). If you have only several dozen albums, this list isn't too long, and you can skip to Step 5. If you have a lot more music, narrow your search with Step 4.

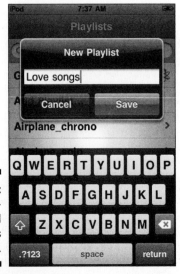
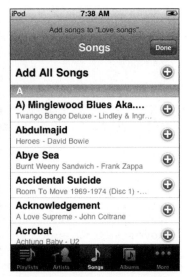

Figure 15-4: Add a playlist (left), and select songs for it (right).

4. (Optional) Narrow your search for songs to add to the playlist.

Tap the browsing buttons along the bottom row (refer to Figure 15-4, right side) to narrow your search as you select music for your new playlist.

5. Tap the plus (+) sign next to a song you want to add to the playlist.

As you tap the plus sign for a song, the song is included in the new playlist, and it turns gray in the list so that you know it has already been selected.

6. Repeat Steps 4 and 5, adding songs in the order you want them to be played.

You can continue to add songs to the list.

7. Tap the Done button when you're finished adding songs.

The Done button appears at the top (refer to Figure 15-4, right side) while you select songs, just waiting for you to finish. After touching Done to finish selecting songs, your iPad, iPod touch, or iPhone saves the playlist and displays it with Edit, Clear, and Delete buttons, as shown in Figure 15-5 (left side).

Figure 15-5:
Playing the playlist (left); editing the playlist (right).

8. (Optional) Edit the playlist.

The songs in the playlist are in *playlist order* (the order you added them). You can change that order by tapping the Edit button, which displays the playlist with a plus (+) sign and Done button at the top, and a move icon (three horizontal bars, like half of an I-Ching symbol) on the far right side of each song, as shown in Figure 15-5 (right side). Drag the move icon for a song to move it up or down the list. Tap the plus (+) sign if you want to continue adding songs, or tap Done to finish. Your iPad, iPod touch, or iPhone saves the edited playlist and presents it again with Edit, Clear, and Delete buttons.

9. **To start playing the playlist, tap any song.**

   Scroll up or down the list to choose a song, and tap the song title to play the playlist starting from that song. You can tap Shuffle to shuffle the songs in the playlist.

Although playlists don't take up too much space (they're just lists, not the content itself, which is already on your device), you may want to delete some of them if you have too many to select from. To delete an entire playlist, tap Delete (refer to Figure 15-5, left side). To clear the contents of a playlist but save the its name (so that you can add more songs without naming it again), tap Clear.

To delete an item from a playlist, choose the playlist, and tap Edit as described in Step 8 in the previous list. In addition to the move icon on the far-right side of each song, a circled minus sign (–) appears on the far-left side of each song, as shown in Figure 15-5 (right side). Tap the circled minus sign (–) to show the Delete button, and then tap the Delete button to delete the song from the playlist.

When you delete listed items, they disappear from the playlist, but they are still in your iPad, iPod, or iPhone; only the playlist is changed.

Making playlists on an iPod nano

Follow these steps with an iPod nano to add a playlist and select songs for it:

1. **Tap Playlists on the Home screen.**

   A list of playlists appears.

2. **Flick down and tap the Add button.**

   The name New Playlist 1 appears at the top (each new playlist is numbered; New Playlist 2 would be next), and the categories appear in a list for selecting songs: Artists, Albums, Genres, Songs, Composers, Audiobooks, and Podcasts.

3. **Tap a category (such as Artists or Albums) and an item (such as an artist or album), and then tap individual songs or Add All Songs.**

   Each list of songs appears with an Add All Songs option at the top.

4. **(Optional) Swipe right to continue adding songs or other items.**

   Swipe right from a song list to tap another artist or album, and swipe right again to tap another category.

5. **Repeat Steps 3 and 4, adding songs in the order you want them to be played.**

   You can continue to add songs to the list.

6. **Tap the Done button when you're finished adding songs.**

   The Done button appears at the top while you select songs, just waiting for you to finish. After touching Done to finish selecting songs, your iPod nano saves the playlist at the end of the list of playlists.

To select the playlist, swipe right to go back to the list of playlists, or to the Home screen and tap Playlists, flick to the end, and tap the playlist.

You can add more songs to the playlist you just created, or to any playlist in your iPod nano; you can even delete items from playlists or delete playlists entirely. To add more songs to a playlist, flick down to show the Edit and Clear buttons. Tap Edit, and then tap the Add button. To delete items from the playlist, tap Edit, and then tap the circled minus sign (–) next to the item to show the Delete button; tap Delete to delete the item. Tap Done to finish. To clear the playlist, select the playlist, flick down to show the Edit and Clear buttons, and tap Clear. To delete a playlist (any playlist, even ones you synchronized to the iPod nano), tap Playlists from the Home screen, flick down, and tap the Edit button. You can then tap the circled minus sign (–) next to the playlist to show the Delete button; tap Delete to delete the playlist.

When you delete listed items, they disappear from the playlist, but they are still in your iPod nano; only the playlist is changed.

Making an On-The-Go playlist on an iPod classic

To create, select, and then play items in your On-The-Go playlist for an iPod classic, follow these steps:

1. **Locate and highlight a song, album title, or audio book.**

2. **Press and hold the select button until the menu appears, and then choose Add to On-The-Go.**

3. **Repeat Steps 1 and 2, adding items in the order you want them to be played.**

   You can continue to add items to the list of queued items in the On-The-Go playlist at any time. Your iPod keeps track of the On-The-Go playlist until you clear it, save it, or synchronize your iPod.

4. **To play the On-The-Go playlist, scroll the Music menu until Playlists is highlighted and then press the select button.**

5. **On the Playlists menu that appears, scroll to highlight On-The-Go at the bottom of the menu, and press the select button.**

   A list of songs in the On-The-Go playlist appears.

6. **Select a song from the list and press the select button.**

   The songs in the playlist are in *playlist order* (the order you added them). Scroll up or down the list to highlight the song you want, and press the select button to play the playlist starting from that song.

To delete an item from an On-The-Go playlist in your iPod classic, follow these steps:

1. **Select the On-The-Go playlist.**

   Choose Music from the main menu, scroll the Music menu until Playlists is highlighted, and then press the select button. The Playlists menu appears. Scroll to On-The-Go and press the select button, and the list of items in the playlist appears.

2. **Locate and highlight the item you want to delete.**

3. **Press and hold the select button until the menu appears, and choose Remove from On-The-Go.**

4. **Repeat Steps 2 and 3 for each item you want to delete from the playlist.**

After creating the On-The-Go playlist, it remains defined in your iPod until you clear it.

It turns out that when you synchronize your iPod with your iTunes library, the On-The-Go playlist is automatically copied to your iTunes library and then cleared. (You can rename the playlist there, just like any other playlist — see Chapter 13.)

To clear the On-The-Go playlist in an iPod classic, follow these steps:

1. **Choose Music⇨Playlists⇨On-The-Go from the main menu.**

2. **Select Clear Playlist in the list of items in the playlist.**

   The Clear menu appears, showing the Clear Playlist and Cancel options.

3. **Select the Clear Playlist option.**

   All the items disappear from the On-The-Go playlist. If you don't want to clear the playlist, select the Cancel option.

Consulting the iTunes Genius

The Genius button for creating Genius playlists in iTunes (wisely laid out for all to see in Chapter 13) has also been incorporated into the iPad, iPod nano, iPod classic, iPod touch, and iPhone to create Genius playlists. You can also listen to your Genius Mixes in your iTunes library on your iPad, iPod, or iPhone.

For Genius to work, it has to recognize the song you select — and you also need enough songs on your iPad, iPod, or iPhone that are (basically) similar. As for the mechanics of it all, you do need to set up an account in the iTunes Store if you don't already have one (see Chapter 6) and then enable the Genius feature in iTunes as I describe in Chapter 13. Finally, you have to synchronize your iPad, iPod, or iPhone as described in Chapter 8 so that the Genius is activated. (You can also add Genius playlists and Genius Mixes along with other playlists in iTunes to your iPad, iPod, or iPhone while syncing.)

Creating a Genius playlist on an iPad, iPod touch, or iPhone

To create a Genius playlist on an iPad, iPod touch, or iPhone, choose Music from the iPod touch Home screen or iPod from the iPad or iPhone Home screen and follow these steps:

1. **Locate and start playing a song to base the Genius playlist on.**

   The Now Playing screen appears when the song is playing.

2. **Tap the Now Playing screen to see the control buttons.**

   Tap underneath the left-arrow button or the album title while a song is playing. The repeat, Genius, and shuffle buttons appear (refer to Figure 15-1 for the iPod touch or iPhone, and Figure 15-2 for the iPad). The Genius button is the one in the center sporting the atom icon.

3. Tap the Genius button.

The Genius playlist appears based on the song you were playing, with New, Refresh, and Save buttons at the top. You can flick your finger to scroll the list. Tap any song to start playing the playlist from that song. If you navigate to other screens, you can return to the Genius playlist by tapping Genius Playlist in the Playlists menu.

4. (Optional) Refresh the Genius playlist by tapping Refresh.

Refreshing a playlist changes it to include different songs based on the same song you played (depending on how many similar songs you have in your iPad, iPod touch, or iPhone).

5. Save the Genius playlist by tapping Save.

The playlist is saved in the Playlists section of your iPad, iPod touch, or iPhone using the title of the song it is based on. The playlist is copied back to your iTunes library when you sync your iPad, iPod touch, or iPhone. That's all you need to do — the next steps are optional.

If you subsequently refresh a saved Genius playlist before syncing, the saved playlist is refreshed and you lose the previous version of it.

6. (Optional) Create a new Genius playlist by tapping New and then selecting a new song to base it on.

After touching New, the song list appears for selecting a song. Choose a song, and your iPad, iPod touch, or iPhone creates a new Genius playlist and starts playing the song, displaying the Now Playing screen.

7. (Optional) After Step 6, return to the Genius playlist by tapping the left-arrow button on the Now Playing screen.

To delete an existing Genius playlist already saved by name, select the playlist, and then tap Delete at the top of the list.

You can refresh any Genius playlist by selecting the playlist and tapping Refresh at the top of the list.

You can set an iPad, iPod touch, or iPhone to create a Genius playlist based on a song *before* you actually start playing the song itself. Just choose Music from the iPod touch Home screen or iPod from the iPhone Home screen, tap Playlists, and then tap Genius Playlist at the top of the list of playlists, and a list of songs appears. On an iPad, just tap iPod from the Home screen, and then tap Genius at the top of the playlists in the left column, and a list of songs appears. Select a song, and your iPad, iPod touch, or iPhone creates a Genius playlist based on it and then starts playing the song you selected. To return to the Genius playlist, tap the left-arrow button on the Now Playing screen.

Creating a Genius playlist on an iPod nano

To create a Genius playlist on an iPod nano, follow these steps:

1. **Locate and start playing a song to base the Genius playlist on.**

   The Now Playing screen appears when the song is playing.

2. **Tap the Now Playing screen to see the control buttons, and swipe left to see the second set of controls (refer to Figure 15-3, right side).**

   The repeat, Genius, and shuffle buttons appear. The Genius button is the one in the center sporting the atom icon.

3. **Tap the Genius button.**

   The Genius playlist appears based on the song you were playing, with Refresh and Save buttons at the top. You can flick your finger to scroll the list. Tap any song to start playing the playlist from that song.

4. **(Optional) Refresh the Genius playlist by tapping Refresh.**

   Refreshing a playlist changes it to include different songs based on the same song you played (depending on how many similar songs you have in your iPod nano).

5. **Save the Genius playlist by tapping Save.**

   The playlist is saved in the Playlists list using the title of the song it is based on. The playlist is copied back to your iTunes library when you sync your iPod nano.

If you subsequently refresh a saved Genius playlist before syncing, the saved playlist is refreshed and you lose the previous version of it.

To delete an existing Genius playlist already saved by name, select the playlist, flick down, and then tap Delete at the top of the list.

Creating a Genius playlist on an iPod classic

To create a Genius playlist on an iPod classic, follow these steps:

1. **Locate and start playing a song to base the Genius playlist on.**

   The Now Playing screen appears when the song is playing.

2. **Press and hold the select button until a menu appears on top of the Now Playing screen.**

3. **Choose Start Genius and press the select button.**

   The new Genius playlist appears, with Refresh and Save Playlist at the top of the list. Scroll the list to see all the songs, and select any song to start playing the playlist associated with that song.

4. **(Optional) Refresh the Genius playlist by selecting Refresh at the top of the Genius playlist.**

   Refreshing a playlist changes it to include different songs based on the same song you played (depending on how many similar songs you have in your iPod).

5. **(Optional) Save the Genius playlist by selecting Save Playlist (under Refresh at the top of the Genius playlist).**

   The playlist is saved in the playlists section of your iPod using the title of the song it is based on. The playlist syncs automatically with your iTunes library the next time you connect your iPod and sync it (as I describe in Chapter 8).

If you subsequently refresh a saved Genius playlist, the saved playlist is refreshed and you lose the previous version of it.

Selecting Genius Mixes

Genius Mixes are generated by iTunes from songs in your library that go great together (see Chapter 13 to learn how to apply the touch of Genius). Genius Mixes are synced automatically if you sync everything to your iPad, iPod touch, iPhone, or iPod nano, or you can sync specific Genius Mixes as playlists — see Chapter 8 to learn how to sync by playlist.

If you choose Genius Mixes to sync along with other music to your iPad, iPod touch, or iPhone (as I show in Chapter 8), or if you sync your entire music library, the Genius button appears in the lower-left corner of the Music screen on an iPod touch, or the lower-left corner of the iPod screen on an iPhone, shifting the other buttons to the right (Albums on the iPod touch and Videos on the iPhone move to the More menu). On an iPad, Genius Mixes appears near the top of the playlists column on the left (above Genius).

To play your Genius Mixes on your iPod touch, choose Music from the Home screen and tap the Genius icon in the lower-left corner. On an iPhone, choose iPod from the Home screen and tap the Genius icon in the lower left corner. On an iPad, choose iPod from the Home screen and tap Genius Mixes in the list of playlists in the left column. On an iPod nano, tap Genius Mixes on the first Home screen.

The iPad shows the cover art collages for the Genius Mixes in a grid on the right side of the screen. On an iPod touch, iPod nano, or iPhone, you can flick with your finger left or right to browse the Genius Mixes — the dots at the bottom of the Genius Mixes screen indicate how many Genius Mixes are synced to your iPod touch, iPod nano, or iPhone. To start playing a Genius Mix, tap the Play arrow in the middle of the screen for a Genius Mix.

Adjusting and Limiting the Volume

Because an iPad, iPod, or iPhone can be quite loud when set to its highest volume, I recommend turning down the volume before using headphones.

To adjust the volume on an iPad, iPod touch, or iPhone, play something (like music). While the content is playing, press the volume button on the left side of the iPod touch or iPhone, or the right side of the iPad, at the top (to increase the volume) or bottom (to lower the volume). On an iPod nano, press the volume buttons on top — Volume Up (+) or Volume Down (–).

You can also use the volume slider on the iPod touch or iPhone screen at the bottom of the Now Playing display (refer to Figure 15-1). Slide the volume slider to the right (to increase the volume) or left (to decrease the volume). Tap the Now Playing display on an iPad (refer to Figure 15-2) to show the volume slider, and then you can adjust the volume by sliding the volume slider.

To adjust volume for an iPod classic, start playing something. While the content is playing, change the volume by scrolling the click wheel. A volume bar appears in the iPod display to guide you. Scroll with your thumb or finger clockwise to increase the volume or counterclockwise to decrease the volume.

To adjust the volume for an iPod shuffle, press the Volume Up (+) or Volume Down (–) buttons on the front panel, or on the earbud remote controller.

You can also limit the highest volume for your iPad, iPod, or iPhone to be lower than the actual maximum. This limit can help protect your hearing while you're listening to content from sources with different volume levels.

To limit the volume to be lower than the actual maximum volume on an iPad, iPod touch, or iPhone, follow these steps:

1. **Choose Settings from the Home screen.**

2. **Choose iPod from the Settings screen of an iPad or iPhone, or Music from the Settings screen of an iPod touch.**

3. **Choose Volume Limit from the iPod Settings (iPad or iPhone) or Music Settings (iPod touch) screen.**

   A volume slider appears with a silver knob.

4. **Slide your finger on the volume slider to limit the volume.**

   Slide the knob with your finger to the right to increase the volume or to the left to decrease the volume.

5. **Tap the iPod button (iPad or iPhone) or the Music button (iPod touch) in the upper-left corner of the display to set the limit and return to the previous menu, or if you want, tap the Lock Volume Limit button to lock the volume limit.**

   If you accept the new limit without locking it, you get to skip the next step; you're done. The lock is useful for locking the volume limit so that others (such as your children) can't change it. However, it also means that you have to enter the volume limit code to unlock the iPad, iPod touch, or iPhone to change the volume limit.

6. **Set the volume limit code for locking the volume limit.**

   If you tapped the Lock Volume Limit button to lock the volume limit, your iPad, iPod touch, or iPhone displays four squares for entering a code number. Tap the calculator-style number pad to type numbers for your code and be sure to make up a code that you can remember! (If you don't want to enter a code, tap the Cancel button.)

To limit the volume to be lower than the actual maximum volume on an iPod nano, tap Settings on the second Home screen, tap Music, and then tap Volume Limit. Slide the volume slider with your finger to the right to increase the volume or to the left to decrease the volume. To remove the volume limit, slide the volume slider all the way to the right. You can also tap Lock Volume Limit button to lock the volume limit — on the keypad screen that appears, tap digits to make a four-digit passcode. Reenter the passcode to set it. To remove the lock, tap Music, tap Volume Limit, and then tap Unlock Volume Limit and enter the passcode. (If you forget the passcode, you need to restore your iPod nano — see Chapter 21).

To limit the volume to be lower than the actual maximum volume on an iPod shuffle, connect it to your computer for syncing, as I describe in Chapter 8. The Summary page of the iPod shuffle sync options appears. Select the Limit Maximum Volume check box and drag the volume slider underneath this option to set the maximum volume. Finally, click the Apply button to apply the new setting.

Tweaking the Sound

You can do some tweaking of the sound quality in your iPad, iPod, or iPhone in addition to the usual sound adjustments you make in iTunes (which I describe in amplified detail in Chapter 12). You can use the same Sound

Check option provided in iTunes to standardize the volume level of all the songs. You can also use the iPad, iPod, or iPhone equalizer to choose presets for different musical genres, listening environments, or speakers.

Peaking with the Sound Check

To enable Sound Check to work in your iPad, iPod, or iPhone, first follow the steps in iTunes described in Chapter 12 to sound-check your iTunes library. After syncing your iPad, iPod, or iPhone with the sound-checked library (as I describe in Chapter 8), you can take advantage of the volume leveling in your iPad, iPod, or iPhone.

To turn on Sound Check in an iPad, iPod touch, or iPhone, choose Settings⇨Music from the iPod touch Home screen or Settings⇨iPod from the iPad or iPhone Home screen. Tap the Off button next to the Sound Check option to turn it on. Tap On to turn it back off.

To turn on Sound Check in an iPod nano, tap Settings on the second Home screen, tap Music, and then tap the Off button next to the Sound Check option to turn it on (tap On to turn it back off).

To turn on Sound Check in an iPod classic, choose Settings⇨Playback⇨Sound Check⇨On from the main menu. To disable it, choose Settings⇨Playback⇨Sound Check⇨Off.

To turn on Sound Check in an iPod shuffle, connect it to your computer for syncing, as I describe in Chapter 8. The Summary page of the iPod shuffle sync options appears. Select the Enable Sound Check option, and click the Apply button to apply the new setting. After the iPod shuffle syncs with the iTunes library, the songs in your iPod shuffle are sound-checked.

All things being equal (ized)

You can use the iPad, iPod, or iPhone built-in equalizer presets to improve or enhance the sound coming through a particular stereo system and speakers. With the equalizer presets, you can customize playback for different musical genres, listening environments, or speakers.

The iPad, iPod, or iPhone equalizer uses a bit more battery power when it's on, so you might have less playing time.

To set an equalizer preset on an iPad, iPod nano, iPod touch, or iPhone, choose Settings⇨Music from the iPod nano or iPod touch Home screen or Settings⇨

iPod from the iPad or iPhone Home screen, and tap EQ to display a list of presets. You can scroll the list of presets and tap a preset to select it — a check mark appears next to it after you select it. The equalizer is set to Off until you select one of the presets.

To select an iPod equalizer preset on an iPod classic, choose Settings⇨Playback⇨EQ from the main menu to display a list of presets. You can scroll the list of presets and press the select button to select one. The equalizer is set to Off until you select one of the presets.

Each equalizer preset offers a different balance of frequencies designed to enhance the sound in certain ways. For example, Bass Booster increases the volume of the low (bass) frequencies; Treble Booster does the same to the high (treble) frequencies. To see what a preset actually does to the frequencies, choose Window⇨Equalizer in iTunes to open the iTunes equalizer; then select the same preset by name. The faders in the equalizer show you exactly what the preset does.

Find out how to assign standard iTunes presets or your own custom presets to specific songs, audio books, podcast episodes, and videos — and use those presets when playing these items back on your iPad, iPod, or iPhone — by visiting the free tips section of my Web site (www.tonybove.com).

Chapter 16

Bring Videos, Books, and Podcasts

. . . .

. . . .

*T*he Buggles sang "Video Killed the Radio Star," but both coexist quite nicely on your iPad, iPod touch, or iPhone, which is not only a fantastic music player (and the current iPod nano can even play FM radio), but also a terrific video player, with crisp, clear picture quality. Video appears horizontally on an iPad, iPod touch, or iPhone screen (in what's known as *landscape mode*), and if you rotate it 180 degrees to the opposite horizontal position, the video adjusts accordingly (videos can also play in portrait mode on an iPad). All the controls you expect in a DVD player are right on the screen at the touch of a finger.

You can also play audio books and podcasts on this multimedia machine. The iTunes Store offers an amazing selection of TV shows, movies, audio books, and podcasts. (See Chapter 6.) This chapter shows you how to control video playback, skip forward or backward, and scale the picture to fit your screen. It also shows you how to watch YouTube videos on your iPad, iPod touch, or iPhone.

Everything's Coming Up Videos

Movies, TV shows, and music videos are easy to locate and play. Videos you purchase from the iTunes Store are ready to use, but videos you bring in from other sources may have to be converted first for use on your iPad, iPod, or iPhone. You can use a variety of applications to convert your video, such as Handbrake (`http://handbrake.fr/`) for Mac or Windows, or you can use iTunes.

To convert a video using iTunes, select the video and choose Advanced⇨Create iPod or iPhone Version or Advanced⇨Create iPad or Apple TV Version.

To find out more about why videos need to be converted and how to prepare your own videos and convert imported videos for use with an iPad, iPod, or iPhone, visit the free tips section of my Web site (www.tonybove.com).

To locate and play a video on your iPad, iPod touch, or iPhone, follow these steps:

1. **Tap Videos on the iPad or iPod touch Home screen, or tap iPod on the iPhone Home screen and then tap the Videos icon at the bottom of the screen.**

   Note: If you choose Genius Mixes to sync along with other music to your iPhone (as I show in Chapter 8), or if you sync your entire music library, the Genius button appears in the lower-left corner of the iPod screen, shifting the other buttons to the right (the Videos button moves to the More menu). In that case, in order to select videos, tap More on an iPhone, and then tap Videos. (For more about Genius Mixes on your iPhone, see Chapter 15.)

2. **Scroll the Videos screen on an iPod touch or iPhone to see the sections for Movies, TV Shows, Music Videos, and Podcasts (video podcasts only). On an iPad, tap the Movies, TV Shows, or Music Videos buttons along the top.**

   The video titles are listed in alphabetical order within these sections.

3. **Tap the title of an item to play it.**

To play a video on an iPod classic or iPod nano, follow these steps:

1. **Choose Videos from the main menu to select a movie, TV show, or imported video. Choose Music from the main menu to select a music video.**

2. **Scroll the menu until the title is highlighted and then press the Select button to play your selection.**

   Hold the iPod nano horizontally to view the picture. If you rotate the iPod nano to the opposite horizontal position, the video adjusts accordingly.

Videos are automatically set to remember the playback position when you pause them. (See how to pause in the next section.) This feature lets you pause a video or TV episode in iTunes while you synchronize your iPad, iPod, or iPhone. After syncing, you can continue playing the video or episode on your iPad, iPod, or iPhone from where you paused. This feature also works in reverse: If you start playing a video on your iPad, iPod, or iPhone and then pause, and then you sync it with iTunes, the video retains the playback position so that you can continue playing it in iTunes from where you paused.

Playback at your fingertips on an iPad, iPod touch, or iPhone

To control playback on an iPad, iPod touch, or iPhone, tap the screen to show the video controls (as shown in Figure 16-1 for an iPod touch or iPhone; the iPad looks basically the same). You can tap again to hide them.

Scrubber bar with playhead   Scale

Figure 16-1: Tap the screen to use playback controls (iPod touch).

Play/Pause Volume

Previous/rewind   Next/fast forward

Tap the play/pause button while a video is playing to pause the playback. To raise or lower the volume, drag the volume slider along the bottom of the screen. (See Figure 16-1.) To stop watching a video before it finishes playing, tap the Done button in the upper-left corner of the display or press the physical Home button.

You can fast-forward through a video by touching and holding down the next/fast forward button, and you can rewind a video by touching and holding down the previous/rewind button.

To skip to any point in a video, drag the playhead along the scrubber bar along the top of the screen. To start a video over from the beginning, drag the playhead on the scrubber bar all the way to the left or tap the previous/rewind button (if the video doesn't contain chapters).

If the video contains chapters, you can skip to the previous or next chapter by tapping the previous/rewind or next/fast forward button. To start playing at a specific chapter, tap the bullet-list button that appears in the upper-right corner if a video contains chapters.

If a video offers an alternative audio language or subtitles, a Subtitles button appears. Tap the Subtitles button and then choose a language from the Audio list or a language from the Subtitles list, or tap On to turn off subtitles.

You can delete a video directly from your iPod touch or iPhone by flicking left or right across the video selection in the Videos menu and then tapping the Delete button that appears. To delete a video directly from your iPad, touch and hold the video's thumbnail image until an X appears in the thumbnail's upper-left corner; tap the X to delete the video. If your video is still in your iTunes library, you can sync the video back to your iPad, iPod touch, or iPhone again or manually copy it back to the device (as I explain in Chapter 8). However, if you delete a *rented* movie from the iPad, iPod touch, or iPhone, it's deleted permanently.

Scaling the picture on an iPad, iPod touch, or iPhone

Videos are displayed in landscape mode on an iPad, iPod touch, or iPhone. You can also scale the video picture to fill the screen or to fit entirely within the screen. Tap the scale button in the upper right corner of the display, or just double-tap the video picture itself to switch from one to the other. The scale button on an iPod touch or iPhone shows two arrows facing away from each other — refer to Figure 16-1 — when the picture fits entirely, or facing toward each other when the picture fills the screen. The scale button on an iPad shows a display icon with a solid bar when the picture fits entirely, or two arrows pointing up and down if the picture fills the screen. The scale button on an iPad only appears if the video is in widescreen format.

Filling the screen may crop the sides or top and bottom to give you a larger view of the center of the picture. Fitting to the screen assures that the entire picture is shown, but you may see black bars on the sides or top and bottom.

Playback under your thumb on an iPod nano or classic

The video playback controls on an iPod classic or iPod nano work the same way as with songs — you use precisely the same buttons, in other words. Scroll the click wheel to adjust the volume as you would for a song (as I describe in Chapter 15).

To pause playback, press the play/pause button while a video is playing. To start again, press play/pause again.

To skip to any point in a video, press the select button to reveal the scrubber bar. Scroll the click wheel to move the playhead across the scrubber bar forward (to the right) or backward (to the left) in the video.

Press the next/fast forward button once to play the next video in sequence (such as the next episode of a TV show), and press the previous/rewind button once at the beginning of a video, or twice during the video, to play the previous video in sequence. You can fast-forward through a video by pressing and holding down the next/fast forward button, and rewind a video by pressing and holding down the previous/rewind button.

If the video contains chapters, you can skip to the previous or next chapter by pressing the previous/rewind or next/fast forward button — but remember, this trick works only if the original video was set up to contain chapters.

To start a video over from the beginning, move the playhead on the scrubber bar all the way to the left, as previously described, or press the previous/rewind button once. To return to menus and make other selections on an iPod classic or iPod nano, press the Menu button.

YouTube on Your iPad, iPod touch, or iPhone

With the iPad, iPod touch, or iPhone, the newest and most popular videos in YouTube are right in your hand. All you need to do is connect online to the Internet (see Chapter 4 for details). You can search for and play videos, bookmark favorites for later playback, and share videos with others by e-mail.

Tap YouTube on the Home screen to run the YouTube app. If this is your first visit to the YouTube app, the Featured screen appears, with thumbnails of video clips and their titles. Otherwise, the screen you were viewing when you last used the app appears.

You can tap the Most Viewed icon at the bottom of the YouTube app display (refer to Figure 16-2, right side) to see today's most-viewed videos, the faves for this week, and the most popular of all time. After you've saved your favorites as bookmarks (see the section "Bookmarking and sharing," later in this chapter), you can go right to your favorite videos by tapping the Favorites icon at the bottom of the YouTube app display.

Tap the More icon at the bottom of the YouTube app display on an iPod touch or iPhone to see even more screens, including Top Rated (the best of the best), Most Recent (the most recent videos added), and History (all the videos you've played so far). You can also tap the Sign In button in the upper left corner of the Favorites screen to sign in to your YouTube account and access the My Videos section of your account.

The History screen offers a Clear button so that you can clear your history at any time.

Running down a stream: Playback control

Tap a selection to play the video. YouTube *streams* the video to your iPad, iPod touch, or iPhone — sending it bit by bit — so that you can start playing it immediately.

Tap the video picture to see the controls (see Figure 16-2, left side), which are exactly like the video controls described in the previous section. The progress of the downloaded video stream appears in the scrubber bar. Even though you can play the video as it streams, you might want to pause it for a few seconds so that more of the stream is downloaded. You can then play the video without any hiccups (depending, of course, on the speed and stability of your connection).

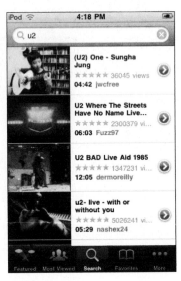

Figure 16-2:
Video
playback
(left) and
searching
(right) with
the YouTube
app.

Bookmarking and sharing

The YouTube app offers a couple of handy buttons on its videos (see Figure 16-2, left side):

✔ **Bookmark button (a book icon):** This button appears to the left of the previous/rewind button, and you can use it to bookmark the video so that you can easily find it on the Favorites screen.

✔ **Share button (an envelope icon) on an iPod touch or iPhone:** This button is located to the right of the next/fast forward button. Tap it to share the video by e-mail.

✔ **Info/share button (icon with two arrows) on an iPad:** This button takes you to the information screen with comments and related videos, as shown in Figure 16-3.

Tap the bookmark button to save a bookmark for the video — the video selection appears in the Favorites screen (tap the Favorites icon in the bottom row to see the Favorites screen). (The Bookmark button is gray rather than white if the video is already bookmarked.)

Tap the share button on an iPod touch or iPhone to bring up the e-mail sending screen to share the video with others via e-mail — see Chapter 18 for details on how to fill out the e-mail message

On an iPad, tap the info/share button to go to the video's information screen, shown in Figure 16-3. Tap the video picture in the information screen to bring up the Add, Share, Rate, and Flag buttons. These buttons work just like the Web version of YouTube — click Add to add the video to your playlist, Share to share it by e-mail, Rate to rate the video with stars, and Flag to flag it for viewing later. If you haven't signed into your YouTube account, a login screen appears for typing your user name and password.

You can also view information about a video on an iPod touch and iPhone as well as related video selections. Tap the right-arrow button on the right side of each selection (refer to Figure 16-2, right side) to see information about the video and to use the Bookmark or Share buttons.

To delete entries from your Favorites screen (especially those news stories that have gone stale), tap the Favorites icon at the bottom of the display to show your bookmarked favorites; then tap the Edit button (in the upper-right corner of the iPod touch or iPhone screen, or the upper-left corner of the iPad screen). The Favorites screen changes to include circled minus (–) signs next to each video on an iPod touch or iPhone, or circled X buttons in the upper-left corner of each video on an iPad.

To delete a bookmarked video on an iPod touch or iPhone, tap the circled minus sign, which rotates and displays a Delete button over the selection; tap the Delete button. To cancel deletion, tap the rotated circled minus sign again. To delete a bookmarked video on an iPad, tap the circled X button. Tap the Done button in the upper-right corner of the Favorites screen on an iPod touch or iPhone, or in the upper-left corner of the iPad screen to finish editing.

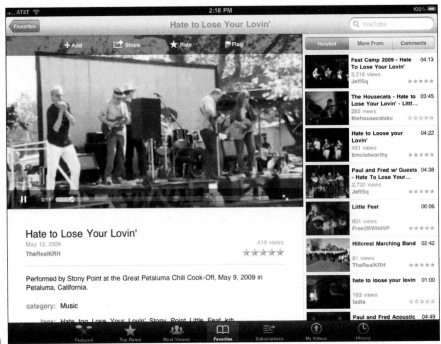

Figure 16-3:
YouTube on
an iPad: Tap
the picture
to show
Add, Share,
Rate, and
Flag.

Searching for videos

To search for the videos on YouTube that everyone's talking about, tap the Search icon in the bottom row of icons on an iPod touch or iPhone, and then tap the search entry field that appears at the top of the screen. On an iPad, tap the search entry field in the top-right corner of the screen. The on-screen keyboard pops up, ready for your search term. (For instructions on using the on-screen keyboard, see Chapter 3.)

If the entry field already has a search term, tap the circled X in the right corner of the field to clear its contents. Then tap out the letters of the search term using the on-screen keyboard and tap the Search key on the keyboard. Immediately after tapping Search, video selections from YouTube appear below, as shown in Figure 16-2, right side (in which I type just **u2** to get the latest U2 music videos).

You can scroll this list by dragging up and down. If a video selection appears that satisfies your search, tap it to play it without further ado.

One Chapter at a Time: Audio Books and Podcasts

Audio books are, naturally, organized into chapters or parts. Podcasts are also organized into parts, called *episodes,* and both play the same way. The audio book title or podcast name and episode appear on your iPad, iPod, or iPhone display along with its cover — similar to a book or album cover.

After syncing your audio books and podcast episodes (as I describe in glorious detail in Chapter 8), you can play them on your iPad, iPod, or iPhone. Audio books and podcasts are automatically set to remember the playback position when you pause. If you pause playback on your iPad, iPod, or iPhone and then sync with iTunes, you can resume playback at that position on the iPad, iPod, or iPhone, or in iTunes.

Finding and playing on an iPad, iPod nano, iPod touch, or iPhone

For the literary-minded, you can find audio books by tapping Music on the iPod touch Home screen or iPod on the iPhone Home screen, and then tapping the More icon at the lower-right corner of the Music or iPod screen to see the More screen. You can then select Audiobooks on the More screen. To find audio books on the iPad, tap iPod on the Home screen, and choose Audiobooks in the Library column on the left side of the screen. To find audio books on the iPad nano, tap Audiobooks on fourth Home screen.

Scroll the Audiobooks screen to select and play an audio book. Tap an audio book on the Audiobooks screen that appears and then tap a chapter or part to play it, starting from that point. The audio book chapters or parts are listed in proper order for each book.

You can find podcasts by tapping Music on the iPod touch Home screen or iPod on the iPhone Home screen, and then tapping the More icon at the lower-right corner of the Music or iPod screen to see the More screen. You can then select Podcasts on the More screen. To find podcasts on the iPad, tap iPod on the Home screen, and choose Podcasts in the Library column on the left side of the screen. (Video podcasts can also be found in the Movies section of Videos.) To find podcasts on the iPad nano, tap Podcasts on second Home screen.

Scroll the Podcasts screen to select and play a podcast episode. Podcasts are organized by podcast name (which is like an album name), and episodes are listed within each podcast in the order that they were released (by date). A blue dot appears next to any podcast that has unplayed episodes.

You control the playback of an audio book or podcast episode exactly the same way as a song (see Chapter 15) — you can pause playback by tapping the play/pause button and so on. You can control video podcasts the same way you control videos. (See the section "Everything's Coming Up Videos," earlier in this chapter.)

Finding and playing on an iPod classic

Podcasts, naturally, have their own menu on an iPod nano or iPod classic. They're organized by podcast name (which is like an album name), and podcast episodes are listed within each podcast in the order that they were released (by date).

To play a podcast episode, choose Podcasts from the iPod classic or iPod nano main menu. Scroll the Podcasts menu until the podcast name is highlighted and press the select button; then scroll and select an episode. A blue dot appears next to any podcast that has unplayed episodes.

To play an audio book, choose Music from the iPod classic or iPod nano main menu, and then Audiobooks from the Music menu. The audio book episodes (collections of chapters) are listed in the proper order for each book. Scroll the list of audio book episodes until the one you want is highlighted and then press the select button to play it.

Playing the FM Radio in an iPod nano

The third- and fourth-generation iPod nano models include an FM radio that displays station and song information for radio stations that support RDS (*Radio Data System*). If the station supports iTunes Tagging, you can tag any songs you hear for later purchase from the iTunes Store. You can also pause a radio broadcast and resume playing it from the same point up to 15 minutes later.

Connect your earbuds or headphones to your iPod nano first because the iPod nano uses the earbud or headphone cord as the FM radio antenna.

To hear the radio, tap Radio on the fourth-generation iPod nano's second Home screen. The radio screen appears with a station already selected and a radio dial underneath the station's number, as shown in Figure 16-4 (center); as the radio plays, the screen changes to its normal state showing just the station number, as shown in Figure 16-4, left side. Tap the Now Playing screen to go back to the radio tuning controls shown in Figure 16-4, center.

To tune the radio, you can scroll the dial by flicking your finger left or right while you listen for a signal, or tap the right or left arrow buttons to jump from station to station (refer to Figure 16-4, center). Tap and hold these buttons to scan stations and hear a five-second preview of each station. To stop scanning and listen to the current station, tap either right or left arrow.

Figure 16-4:
The iPod
nano FM
radio (left);
tuning
a station
(center);
using Live
Pause (right).

To fast-tune to local stations, tap the "i" button in the lower right corner to show the Radio menu, and then tap Local Stations. Your iPod nano scans the available frequencies and lists the local stations. You can then tap the tiny play button next to a station to listen to the station without leaving the menu, or tap the station to tune to that station and return to the radio controls.

If you hear something you like, save a station as a favorite — tap the star icon in the lower left corner (refer to Figure 16-4, center). After saving one or more favorite stations, tapping the arrow buttons while tuning takes you to the next or previous favorite station. You can also tap the "i" button in the lower right corner to see the Radio menu, and then tap Favorites.

After you tune to a station, swipe left to see the Live Pause controls, as shown in Figure 16-4 (right side). A progress bar appears, filling up as you continue to listen to the station. To pause the broadcast while the radio is playing, tap the play/pause button in the center. The actual time you paused appears above the progress bar. As Live Pause continues, a yellow triangle appears for your pause point in the progress bar, and the progress bar continues to fill up — showing the time that's passed since you paused. Tap play/pause again to resume the broadcast from the point you paused.

This radio is different than normal radios — with the Live Pause feature, it lets you navigate back and forth along the progress bar so that you can hear up to 15 minutes into the past. To skip forward or back in one-minute intervals, tap the next/fast forward or previous/rewind icons. To fast-forward or rewind, tap and hold the next/fast forward or previous/rewind icons. The progress bar displays as completely filled when Live Pause reaches the 15-minute limit. You can still navigate back and forth through the 15 most recent minutes, as long as your pause isn't cleared. Anything older than 15 minutes is cleared to make room for the continuing broadcast. If you pause without resuming for 15 minutes, your iPod nano goes to sleep and clears your paused radio.

To disable Live Pause, tap Settings on the iPod nano's second Home screen, tap General, and then tap the On button next to Live Pause to turn it off. To enable Live Pause again, tap Off to turn it back on.

Tagging a song that strikes your fancy for later purchase from the iTunes Store works great with stations that support iTunes Tagging. To tag a song you hear, tap the tag icon (refer to Figure 16-4, left side) that appears in the lower left corner for stations that support iTunes Tagging. Tagged songs are marked with a tag icon next to the song title, and they appear in the Radio menu under Tagged Songs (tap the "i" button while the radio is playing to see the Radio menu).

The next time you sync your iPod nano to iTunes, your tagged songs are synced to iTunes and removed from the iPod nano. You can preview and purchase these tagged songs by clicking Tagged in the Store section of the iTunes source pane, and then click the View button for the song you want. To preview the song, double-click it or click the preview button. To buy the song, click the Buy button.

To turn the FM Radio off and clear paused radio, tap the square button in the center (which appears only if the radio is on). You can also display the most recently played songs on a station that supports RDS by tapping the "i" icon and then choosing Recent Songs from the Radio menu.

Chapter 17

Your Pocket Picture Player

*T*he world is awash in pictures, from photos and video clips to cartoon images, graphics, and famous paintings. In this chapter, I refer to everything you can *see* as a picture — whether it be a photo, graphic image, or a recorded video clip (a moving picture).

If you like to carry pictures around with you, you're going to love the iPad, iPod, or iPhone as a player for viewing pictures. And if you like to send and receive pictures by e-mail, you're going to love the fact that you can use your iPad, iPod touch, or iPhone to share them with others. This chapter shows you how.

Syncing with Photo Albums and Folders

After importing photos from cameras into your computer, and importing image files from other sources, you can organize them into albums or collections that sync through iTunes. On a Mac, you can use iPhoto (version 4.0.3 or newer) or Aperture. On a Windows PC, you can use Adobe Photoshop Album (version 2.0 or newer) or Adobe Photoshop Elements (version 3.0 or newer).

You can then set up your iPad, iPod, or iPhone to sync with your entire photo library or with specific albums in your library so that any changes you make to the library or to those albums are copied to the iPad, iPod, or iPhone. In addition, any pictures you collect from e-mails on your iPad, iPod touch, or iPhone are synced back to the photo library on your computer.

You don't have to use iPhoto or one of the Adobe products — you can store your pictures in their own folder on your hard drive (such as the Pictures folder in your home folder on a Mac or the My Pictures folder in your My

Documents folder in Windows). You can then use iTunes to sync pictures from this folder, treating the folder as a single photo album. If you have sub-folders in this folder iTunes syncs the subfolder assignments as if they were album assignments.

To find out more about organizing pictures into albums, visit the free tips section of my Web site (www.tonybove.com).

Transferring pictures to your iPad, iPod, or iPhone

To copy pictures from your computer to your iPad, iPod, or iPhone using iTunes, follow these steps:

1. **Connect your iPad, iPod, or iPhone to your computer and then select its name in the Devices section of the iTunes source pane.**

   iTunes displays the Summary page (under the Summary tab of the synchronization pages) to the right of the source pane. (See Chapter 8 for details.)

2. **Click the Photos tab of the sync pages.**

   The Photos sync options appear, as shown in Figure 17-1 (on a Mac, you see iPhoto selected to sync photos from).

3. **Select the Sync Photos From check box and then pick the source of your pictures from the pop-up menu: a photo application, the Pictures (Mac) or My Pictures (PC) folder, or the Choose Folder option.**

   Pick your application (such as iPhoto on a Mac or Adobe Photoshop Elements in Windows) from the pop-up menu to synchronize with its library. If you don't use these applications, pick the Pictures folder on a Mac or the My Pictures folder on a PC, or pick Choose Folder to browse your hard drive or other storage media and select the folder containing pictures.

4. **If you chose a photo application that organizes pictures by album, collection, events, or faces (such as iPhoto), or if you stored pictures in subfolders in your Pictures or My Pictures folder, select one of the following options below the Sync Photos From check box:**

   • *All Photos, Albums, Events, and Faces:* Copies all pictures from the library or folder selected in Step 3, and retains album (or collection) and face assignments set in applications (such as iPhoto) that offer these assignments (for example, iPhoto lets you browse by assigned faces).

   • *Selected Albums, Events, and Faces, and Automatically Include:* Select this option to be more specific about which albums, events, or faces to sync, and to include recent events automatically — you can choose how many recent events or events from the last month or several months from the pop-up menu, or choose All Events or No Events. (In Figure 17-1, I choose No Events.) After selecting this option, you can then make selections in the Albums, Events, and Faces columns.

- *Events column*: If you chose a photo application that organizes pictures by events (such as iPhoto), you can select the check box next to each name (or date, if no name) of an event to synchronize.

- *Albums column:* Lets you choose which photo albums from the library (or subfolders from the folder) selected in Step 3 you want to copy. The idea here is to scroll the list box to see all the albums or collections in your library (or subfolders in your folder) and then select the check box next to each one you want to copy.

- *Faces column:* If you chose a photo application that assigns faces to pictures (such as iPhoto), you can select the check box next to each face's name.

5. **Click the Apply button to apply changes, and click the Sync button if synchronization hasn't already started automatically.**

   iTunes copies the photo library or albums you selected to your iPad, iPod, or iPhone (and deletes all other pictures from the iPad, iPod, or iPhone except those saved in Saved Images or in Camera Roll).

Figure 17-1: Sync photos (iPhoto shown).

Syncing saved pictures with iTunes

Pictures that you receive via e-mail on your iPad, iPod touch, or iPhone, photos you record with your iPhone, and videos you shoot with your iPod touch, iPhone 3GS, or iPhone 4 are stored in a special photo album — Saved Images (on an iPad) or Camera Roll (on an iPod touch or iPhone).

To synchronize these saved pictures back to your computer, connect your iPad, iPod touch, or iPhone to your computer as you normally would to sync it (as described in Step 1 of the previous section).

On a Mac, iPhoto pops up automatically (unless you changed syncing preferences in the Image Capture application) — click the Import All button, or select the pictures you want and click the Import Selected button. After importing the pictures into the iPhoto library, iPhoto asks whether you want to delete the originals from the iPad, iPod touch, or iPhone. Click Delete Originals to delete them from your device (they're safe in your photo library on your computer now) or click Keep Originals to save them on the device — in case you want to sync them with another computer, e-mail them, or upload them to social networks from your iPad, iPod touch, or iPhone.

On a Windows PC, iTunes can be set up to sync with Adobe Photoshop Album or Photoshop Elements (as I describe in the previous section) and automatically transfers the pictures (including video clips). If you don't use those applications, follow the instructions that came with your photo application to import the pictures, or use the Microsoft Scanner and Camera Wizard to save the pictures to a folder of your choice.

Viewing Pictures and Slideshows

You might remember the old days when you carried fading, wallet-sized photo prints, or worse, a deck of slides that required a light box or projector to show them to others. You can now dispense with all that because all you need is your iPad, iPod, or iPhone.

Slide shows are an especially entertaining way of showing pictures because you can include music as well as transitions between them. You can display your slide show on the iPad, iPod, or iPhone, or on a television by connecting your iPad, iPod, or iPhone to the TV using the Universal Dock, Component AV Cable, or Composite AV Cable from Apple (available in the Apple Store).

To find out how to connect your iPad, iPod, or iPhone to televisions, stereos, video monitors, and video equipment, visit this book's companion Web site.

Viewing pictures on an iPad, iPod touch, or iPhone

To view pictures on your iPad, iPod touch, or iPhone, tap Photos on the Home screen. The Photos app displays the last screen you viewed when you used the app before. If this is the first time, the Albums screen appears, as shown in Figure 17-2 (left side) for an iPod touch or iPhone.

You can tap the Albums, Events, Faces, or Places buttons at the bottom of the iPod touch or iPhone screen, or Photos, Albums, Faces, or Places at the top of the iPad screen, to switch screens:

✔ **Photos** (iPad only): Shows thumbnails of all synced pictures (except the Saved Photos pictures). Scroll the thumbnails up or down and tap one to select it and view it. You can also unpinch a thumbnail to see the picture.

✔ **Albums**: On an iPad or iPod touch, the albums include Camera Roll for saved pictures from e-mails and for new photos and video clips shot with the Camera app.

  • On an iPad, open an album by tapping it, or unpinch the album to spread out a preview of the pictures it contains, and then let go to open it.

  • On an iPod touch or iPhone, tap a photo album's name (or the arrow to the right of the name), or tap Photo Library to see all pictures. Thumbnail images appear, as shown in Figure 17-2 (right side). The Photo Library choice displays thumbnails of all the pictures in your iPod touch or iPhone (except the Camera Roll or Saved Images albums). Selecting an album displays thumbnails of only the pictures assigned to that album — scroll the thumbnails up or down to see more of them. Tap one to view its picture.

✔ **Events**: Shows a list of event titles or dates with thumbnails of the first picture of each event (based on the date of pictures in iPhoto). Tap a thumbnail or the event title or date to display thumbnails of pictures from that event.

✔ **Faces**: Shows thumbnails of faces if you've assigned faces to pictures in iPhoto. Tap a face to display thumbnails of pictures with that face, and then tap a thumbnail to view its picture.

✔ **Places:** Shows a world map with pins of locations associated with pictures. Tap a map pin to see a label showing how many pictures were taken at that location, and tap the label to see thumbnails of those pictures. Tap a thumbnail to view its picture.

Options

Figure 17-2:
Tap a photo album, Photo Library, or Camera Roll (left) and then tap a thumbnail (right).

To zoom into the picture to see more detail, double-tap the area you want to zoom into. Double-tap again to zoom out. You can also zoom into an area by unpinching with two fingers, and zoom out by pinching. To pan around a picture, drag it with your finger.

To move to the next picture in the album or collection, flick horizontally across the picture with your finger. You can flick across to go backward or forward through the album or collection of pictures.

Tap the full-screen picture to show or hide the navigation controls and buttons, as shown in Figure 17-3 for an iPod touch or iPhone, and Figure 17-4 for an iPad. On an iPod touch or iPhone, you can jump to the next or previous pictures in the album or collection by tapping the next or previous buttons that appear when you tap the picture. On an iPad, you can jump to any picture in the collection by tapping its thumbnail along the bottom row of thumbnails.

Figure 17-3:
iPod touch
or iPhone:
Tap the
picture for
controls.

Previous   Next

Options   Playslideshow

To set up a slide show, follow these steps:

1. **Choose Settings⬦Photos from the Home screen on an iPad, iPod touch, or iPhone.**

   The Photos Slideshow settings screen appears.

2. **Tap the Play Each Slide For option to set the duration of each slide.**

   You can select ranges from 2 to 20 seconds.

3. **On an iPod touch or iPhone, tap the Transition option to pick a transition to use between photos in the slide show. (See Step 3 below for picking transitions on an iPad.)**

   The Wipe Across transition is my favorite, but you can select Cube, Dissolve, Ripple, or Wipe Down. Tap the Photos button to return to the Photos Slideshow settings screen.

4. **Select the other options as appropriate for your slide show:**

   • *Repeat:* Repeats the slide show.

   • *Shuffle:* Shuffles photos in the slide show in a random order.

Figure 17-4: iPad: Tap the picture for thumbnails and tap Slideshow to play a slideshow.

5. **Tap the Settings button to return to the Settings screen or press the physical Home button to return to the Home screen.**

To play a slide show, follow these steps:

1. **Tap Photos on the Home screen of an iPad, iPod touch, or iPhone.**

2. **Choose a collection type (such as Albums, Events. Faces, or Places) as described previously, and select a collection, choose a picture, and tap it to show the navigation controls and buttons.**

3. **To start the show, tap the play/pause button at the bottom of the picture of an iPod touch or iPhone (refer to Figure 17-4), or tap the**

Slideshow button in the upper right corner on an iPad (refer to Figure 17-4) and then tap Start Slideshow.

On an iPad, you can pick a transition and choose and start playing music before tapping the Start Slideshow button. (On an iPod touch or iPhone, you can start playing a song using the iPod app, and then choose Photos from the Home screen and start a slideshow.)

4. **Flick left or right, or tap the navigation buttons, to move backward or forward in your slide show.**

   Tap any picture to see the navigation controls (refer to Figure 17-3 for an iPod touch or iPhone, and Figure 17-4 for an iPad) to move to the next or previous picture.

5. **Tap the screen to stop the slide show.**

To hear music along with the slideshow on an iPod touch or iPhone, tap the Music icon on the iPod touch Home screen or the iPod icon on the iPhone Home screen, and select a song (see Chapter 7 for details). Then double-tap the Home button to show the four most recently used apps in the bottom row of the screen, and tap Photos again to go back to your slideshow (assuming that it was recently set up in the steps above — you may have to flick left-to-right to see more recently used apps, or repeat Step 1). For more details on multitasking your apps, see Chapter 3.

Viewing pictures on an iPod nano or iPod classic

To view pictures (photos and images, but not video clips) on your iPod nano or iPod classic, follow these steps:

1. **Choose Photos from the iPod nano's second Home screen or the iPod classic main menu.**

   The Photo Albums menu appears on an iPod nano with All Photos at the top, and the Photos menu appears on an iPod classic with All Photos and Settings choices at the top. Both menus offer a list of photo albums in alphabetical order. The iPod nano includes Events, Faces, and Places if you synced collections of those types from iPhoto.

2. **Choose All Photos or an album or event name.**

   The All Photos choice displays thumbnail images of all the pictures in your iPod. Selecting an album or event displays thumbnail images of only the pictures assigned to that album or event.

3. **Flick the iPod nano thumbnails to see more thumbnails, or scroll the click wheel of the iPod classic to highlight the thumbnail you want.**

   You can flick the iPod nano thumbnail screen up or down to see more thumbnails. On an iPod classic, you may have several screens of thumbnails — scroll the click wheel to scroll through them. As you scroll, each thumbnail is highlighted.

4. **Tap a thumbnail on the iPod nano screen, or press the select button on the iPod classic (after highlighting a thumbnail) to open the picture.**

   When you select a thumbnail, your iPod displays the picture.

On an iPod nano, you can swipe left or right to scroll through all the photos. Tap a photo to see controls, and tap the thumbnails icon in upper left corner to return to the thumbnail view. To view a picture sideways on an iPod nano, place two fingers on the screen and rotate in the direction you want the screen to move, until the screen faces the way you want..

You can also double-tap to quickly zoom in on a photo to see more detail, and then drag the image to see different parts in the center of the screen. If you sync a collection of Faces from iPhoto, double-tapping zooms in on the subject's face. Double-tap again to zoom back out to full size.

When viewing a photo on an iPod nano, tap it to see controls; you can then tap the previous/rewind button to see the previous picture in the album or library, or the next/fast forward button to see the next picture. Tap the play/pause button to start a slide show.

On an iPod classic, you can use the previous/rewind and next/fast forward buttons to move backward for forward through photos, and press the play/pause button to start a slideshow. Press Menu to return to the thumbnails, and press Menu again to return to the Photos menu.

To set up a slide show on an iPod nano or iPod classic, follow these steps:

1. **Tap Settings⇨Photos from the iPod nano's second Home screen, or choose Photos⇨Settings from the iPod classic main menu.**

2. **Choose Times per Slide to set the duration of each slide.**

   You can select ranges from 2 to 20 seconds. On an iPod classic, you can also select Manual to set the slide show to advance to the next slide when you press the next/fast forward button.

3. **Choose Transitions to select a transition to use between photos in the slide show.**

   Ken Burns is my favorite on the iPod nano, but Dissolve, Page Flip, and Push look nice, and Origami adds a touch of fun. You can select Cross Fade, Fade to Black, Zoom Out, Wipe Across, or Wipe Center on an iPod classic, or choose Off for no transition.

4. **iPod classic only: Pick your music by choosing Music from the Settings menu and then choose a playlist.**

   You can choose any playlist in your iPod classic for your slide show, including On-The-Go and Now Playing. (On an iPod nano it is easy to quickly start a song in an album or playlist, and then switch to Photos to start a slideshow.)

5. **iPod classic only: Set the iPod to display the slide show by choosing TV Out from the Settings menu.**

   You have three choices for TV Out:

   - *On* displays the slide show on a television. While the slide show plays on your TV, you can also see the slides as large thumbnails on your iPod, along with the photo number within the album or library, and the Next and Previous icons.

   - *Ask* displays a screen requesting that you select TV Off or TV On; you make the choice each time you play a slide show.

   - *Off* displays the slide show with full-size images on the iPod.

6. **(Optional) Select other preferences for the iPod nano or iPod classic slideshow:**

   - *Repeat:* Repeats the slide show. Tap Off next to Repeat on an iPod nano to turn it on; on an iPod classic, scroll the menu to highlight Repeat, and press the select button.

   - *Shuffle Photos:* Shuffles photos in the slide show in a random order. Tap Off next to Shuffle Photos on an iPod nano to turn it on; on an iPod classic, scroll the menu to highlight Shuffle Photos, and press the select button.

   - *TV Signal:* Changes your television signal to PAL for other countries that use PAL as their video standard. Choose NTSC (also referred to humorously as "never the same color") for the U.S. or PAL for countries that use it.

To play a slide show on an iPod nano or iPod classic, follow these steps:

1. **Choose Photos from the second home screen of the iPod nano or the iPod classic the main menu.**

2. **Choose an album or other collection, or All Photos.**

3. **iPod nano only: Tap the thumbnail of the first photo, and then tap the picture to see the controls.**

4. **To start the show on an iPod nano, tap the play/pause icon; on an iPod classic, press the play/pause button.**

   You can also start a slide show when viewing a single picture on an iPod classic by pressing the select button.

5. **iPod classic only: If you previously set TV Out to Ask (as described in the previous section), choose TV On or TV Off for your slide show.**

   - *TV On* displays the slide show on a television (through the video-out connection). You can also see the slides as large thumbnails on the iPod.

   - *TV Off* displays the slide show with full-size images on the iPod.

6. **On an iPod nano, swipe left or right or tap the previous or next icons to navigate the slideshow; on an iPod classic, press the playback buttons.**

   If you set Time per Slide to Manual on an iPod classic, press next/fast forward to move to the next picture and press previous/rewind to return to the previous picture. If you set Time per Slide to a specific duration, use play/pause to pause and play the slide show.

7. **To stop the slideshow, tap any picture to see the controls, and then tap the thumbnails icon in the upper left corner; on an iPod classic, press the Menu button.**

Shooting Photos and Videos with an iPod touch or iPhone

You can shoot photos and videos with a fourth-generation iPod touch, an iPhone 3GS, or an iPhone 4, and you can shoot photos with older iPhone models. You can even edit your videos with the iMovie app (available separately in the App Store) on an iPhone 4. You can shoot photos and video clips in portrait or landscape orientation, and the results are suitable for sharing by e-mail or YouTube.

On the back of the iPhone 4 is a 5-megapixel camera, and on the back of the iPhone 3GS is a 3-megapixel camera. The lens is on the back so that you can see the picture you are about to take on the display. The iPhone 4 back camera can record HD (720p) video with audio, and the iPhone 3GS camera can record video in VGA resolution (640x480) with audio; both record at 30 frames per second. Both offer auto focus, auto exposure, auto white balance, 5x digital zoom, and the ability to just tap the picture to focus; the iPhone 4 also offers a LED flash for still images. The iPhone 4 also has a front camera for shooting VGA-quality photos and video at up to 30 frames per second. Both cameras can be used with FaceTime calls (see Chapter 20 for details).

The iPod touch also has photo and video camera on the back that can record HD (720p) video at 30 frames per second with audio, and shoot photos at 960x720 pixel resolution. The back camera offers 5x digital zoom and the ability to tap the picture to adjust the exposure for lighting conditions. The iPod touch also has a front camera that can record VGA-quality photos and video at up to 30 frames per second as well as show FaceTime video calls.

The original iPhone and iPhone 3G includes a 2-megapixel camera on the back for taking photos.

To take a picture, start by choosing Camera from the Home screen. If you've turned Location Services Off (see Chapter 4 for details), the Camera app first asks if you want to turn Location Services On. Although you don't have to turn it on to take pictures, if you turn it on Camera can tag photos and videos with location information, which is useful for posting photos and videos on Web sites, or just for tracking the locations of your shots and clips.

After choosing Camera, the view through the lens appears in the iPod touch or iPhone display, as shown in Figure 17-5 (left side). On an iPod touch, iPhone 3GS, or iPhone 4, the Photo/Video switch appears in the bottom-right corner. On an iPod touch or iPhone 4, the switch cameras button (circular arrow) in the top-right corner switches from the back camera to the front camera. When you tap the picture on the back camera, the view through the lens includes the exposure area for automatic adjustments, and the 5x digital zoom slider.

Figure 17-5:
Take a photo (left) or record a video (right) with an iPod touch.

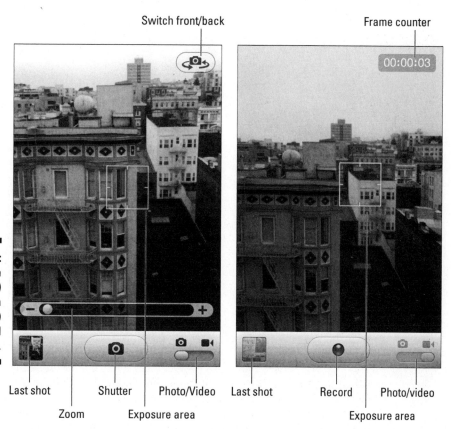

Switch front/back

Frame counter

00:00:03

Last shot   Shutter   Photo/Video   Last shot   Record   Photo/video

Zoom   Exposure area   Exposure area

You can tap an area of the photo if you want to change the exposure adjustment on an iPod touch, or the autofocus adjustment on an iPhone 4 or iPhone
3GS. The blue rectangle (refer to Figure 17-5, left side) shows the area where
Camera is sensing the lighting conditions and focusing the shot. On an iPod
touch, Camera automatically adjusts the exposure of the shot based on the
lighting conditions for the area within the rectangle. On an iPhone 3GS and
iPhone 4, Camera automatically adjusts the focus, exposure, and white balance for the area within the rectangle. Change the area by tapping the photo
in the spot where you want to focus.

Tapping the picture also displays the zoom slider at the bottom of the screen
(camera mode only). You can zoom in or out by dragging the slider (this is a
digital zoom, which magnifies pixels, not an optical zoom, which changes the
focal length of the camera by adjusting the lens).

You can hold the iPod touch or iPhone vertically (for portrait mode) or horizontally (for landscape mode) to snap a photo. On an iPod touch, iPhone
3GS, or iPhone 4, make sure the photo/video switch is set to photo, as shown
in Figure 17-5 (left side); if not, tap or slide the switch to set it to photo. Then
tap the shutter button to take the picture. An image of a shutter closing
appears on the display to indicate a picture was taken.

To shoot video, hold the iPod touch or iPhone vertically (for portrait mode)
or horizontally (for landscape mode), and tap or slide the photo/video switch
to set it to video, as shown in Figure 17-5 (right side). The shutter button
turns into a red record button. Tap the record button to start recording —
it blinks while recording. Tap the blinking record button again to stop
recording.

To see the pictures you've taken, touch the last shot button in the lower-left
corner (refer to Figure 17-5) to see the last picture taken. You can then delete
that picture if you don't want to include it with the pictures to be synced to
your computer. To delete the photo or video clip, tap the trashcan icon in
the lower-right corner, and then touch the Delete Photo button (or Cancel to
cancel).

To learn more about shooting and managing photos and video clips with an
iPhone or iPod touch, visit the free tips section of my Web site (www.tony
bove.com).

You can get better results when shooting pictures if you learn more about
photography and video recording, and a great place to start is *iPhone Digital
Photography & Video For Dummies.*

Sharing Pictures with an iPad, iPod touch, or iPhone

What good is it to collect pictures without sharing them with other people? You can share pictures in your iPad, iPod touch, or iPhone by sending one or more in an e-mail, uploading as many as you want to social networks, and sharing entire photo albums using MobileMe. With an iPhone 3G, iPhone 3GS, or iPhone 4, you can also send pictures using MMS (if supported by your carrier). And with an iPhone 3GS or iPhone 4, you can record video clips and share them the same way, using e-mail or MMS. You can also upload video clips to YouTube or your MobileMe gallery.

Sending a picture by e-mail

To send a picture in an e-mail, tap Photos on the Home screen, and choose a picture for viewing (as I describe previously in "Viewing pictures on an iPad, iPod touch, or iPhone"). Then tap the picture to see the navigation controls (refer to Figure 17-3 for an iPod touch or iPhone and Figure 17-4 for an iPad).

Tap the options button to see the pop-up menu of sharing options, and then tap Email Photo to e-mail a photo or Email Video to e-mail a video clip. If you have MMS support for texting with your iPhone carrier, you also see the MMS option.

The New Message screen appears in the Mail app for e-mail or in the Messages app for MMS messages on an iPhone. The photo or video clip is embedded in the message. You can tap in the message field to enter text. Then fill in the To and Subject fields, as described in Chapter 19.

Sharing pictures by MobileMe

If you've set up a photo gallery on MobileMe to share with others, you can include any picture or video clip in this published gallery so that others can immediately see it. Tap the options button, choose Send to MobileMe in the pop-up menu and select the gallery to include the picture or video clip.

Got friends on social networks? You can share photos using services such as Facebook and MySpace — both offer iPhone apps that let you select photo albums on your iPhone and upload images, as I show in Chapter 20.

You can also tap the options button and choose Assign to Contact in the pop-up menu to assign the photo to a contact in your Contacts list (see Chapter 20 for details), or choose Use as Wallpaper to use the picture as the iPad, iPod touch, or iPhone wallpaper (see Chapter 4).

Selecting and copying multiple pictures

To select more than one picture (photo, image, or video clip) to copy and paste into another app or to share by e-mail, tap Photos on the Home screen, and tap a photo album or entire library to show thumbnails of the album or library (refer to Figure 17-2). Then tap the options button.

The Select Photos screen appears, showing the same thumbnails. Tap each thumbnail on the Select Photos screen, as shown in Figure 17-6 (left side), to select each image. As you tap each thumbnail, a check mark appears in the thumbnail to indicate that it is part of the selection.

The Share and Copy buttons appear at the bottom of the iPod touch or iPhone screen as you make a selection; on an iPad, the Email and Copy buttons appear in the upper-left corner. To e-mail the selected pictures on an iPod touch or iPhone, tap the Share button and then tap Email; on an iPad, tap Email. The Mail app launches and starts a new e-mail message that includes all the selected images (see Chapter 19 for details on sending e-mails).

To copy the pictures to another app or paste them into an existing message, tap the Copy button. You can paste the pictures into any app that accepts pasted pictures — such as a saved e-mail draft message in Mail. Touch and hold to mark an insertion point in the e-mail message (which brings up the keyboard), and the Select/Select All/Paste bubble appears, as shown in Figure 17-6 (right side). Tap Paste to paste the images into the message.

You can also receive pictures from others by e-mail. (Chapter 19 delivers the details on how to check your e-mail.) A down-arrow button appears within a message that contains an attached picture. Tap the down-arrow button to download the picture to your iPad, iPod touch, or iPhone.

After the download completes, tap the picture in the e-mail message, and the Save Image and Cancel buttons appear. Tap the Save Image button to save the picture in your iPod touch or iPhone photo library (in the Saved Images album) or tap Cancel to cancel. If the message has more than one picture (such as three), you can tap a button to save them all.

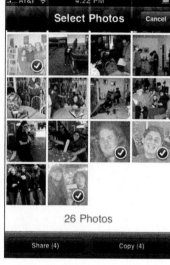

Figure 17-6:
Select
pictures
for copy-
ing (left)
and paste
them into
an e-mail
(right).

Part V
Touching the Online World

The 5th Wave By Rich Tennant

"The sensor in my running shoe is transmitting information and encouragements to my iPod. Right now, Lance Armstrong is encouraging me to stop running like a girl."

In this part . . .

This part takes the concept of playing media to an entirely new level by providing access to the world of online content. Now you can use your iPad, iPod touch, or iPhone to touch Web sites around the world, check your e-mail, engage in social networking, and even monitor your stock portfolio.

✓ Chapter 18 spins the Web and shows you how to surf Web pages with Safari on your iPad, iPod touch, or iPhone. You find out how to search with Google, Yahoo!, or Bing, and interact with Web services to do everything from checking live news feeds to making travel reservations.

✓ Chapter 19 shows you how to turn your iPad, iPod touch, or iPhone into a lean, clean e-mail machine. You can check e-mails from multiple e-mail accounts, send messages, and manage your e-mail settings.

✓ Chapter 20 puts you in contact with your Contacts, helps you manage your Calendar, and connects you not only to your friends with FaceTime video calls, but also with the most popular social networks on the planet @@md Facebook, MySpace, and Twitter. The weather becomes more predictable, your stocks proudly show their charts, and the Earth itself reveals its secrets in satellite and map views.

Chapter 18

Surfin' Safari

. . . .

In This Chapter

▶ Browsing the Web with your iPad, iPod touch, or iPhone

▶ Navigating, scrolling, and zooming into Web pages

▶ Saving and using Web page bookmarks

▶ Saving Web site icons to your Home screen

. . . .

The World Wide Web makes the world go 'round a whole lot faster than ever before. I browse the Web for many different kinds of content and services. It's gotten to the point where I now use the Web to make travel, restaurant, and entertainment reservations, and I purchase everything online, from music, videos, books, and clothing to electronics equipment, garden supplies, groceries, and furniture. I get to track my shipments and purchases, review the latest news, check up on the blogs of my friends and associates, read novels, view slide shows and movies posted on the Internet, and even scan text messages from cell phones — all thanks to the Internet.

I can do all this using the Safari browser on an iPad, iPod touch, or iPhone with an Internet connection, so I rarely need a laptop when I travel. I can also search using Google or Yahoo! — both services are built into Safari, and I can always browse any other search site. All you need to do is connect to the Internet, as I describe in Chapter 4.

Take a Walk on the Web Side with Safari

Safari on the iPad, iPod touch, or iPhone not only lets you browse through Web sites, but also lets you add bookmarks and icons to your Home screen for convenient access. (You can also synchronize those bookmarks with your computer's Web browser, as I describe in Chapter 9.)

 Safari offers privacy settings for secure browsing, including a fraud warning, the ability to block pop-ups and control cookies, and to clear your browsing history, cookies, and cache. To change them, tap Settings⇨Safari. To find out about these settings (such as why you don't need cache for cookies!), see Chapter 22.

Go URL own way

It's a snap to browse any Web site. Just tap out the site's address on the on-screen keyboard. (For instructions on using the on-screen keyboard, see Chapter 3.)

The Web site address is known as a URL (*Uniform Resource Locator*) and usually begins with `http://www.` followed by the name of the Web site or other characters (such as `http://www.apple.com` or `http://www.tony bove.com`). However, you can leave off the `http://www.` part and just go with the rest of the characters of the URL (`apple.com` or `tonybove.com/tonytips`).

For the blow-by-blow account, check out the following steps:

1. **Tap Safari on the Home screen.**

   The iPad, iPod touch, or iPhone displays the last Web page you visited or a blank page, with the rectangular URL entry field at the top, next to an oval search-entry field, as shown in Figure 18-1, left side for an iPod touch or iPhone (for a sneak preview of the iPad on Safari, see Figure 18-2). (If you don't see these two entry fields side by side, tap the status bar at the top of the screen to jump to the top of the Web page.)

2. **Tap the URL field.**

   The on-screen keyboard appears. Above that is an entry field for typing the URL.

3. **If the entry field already has a URL, tap the circled X in the right corner of the field to clear its contents.**

4. **Tap out the URL for the Web page using the on-screen keyboard.**

   Immediately as you start typing the characters of the URL, you see a list of suggested Web sites that match the characters you typed so far (as shown in Figure 18-1, right side). You can scroll the suggested list by dragging up and down. If the Web site you want appears, tap it to go directly to the site without further ado. Otherwise, keep typing the URL, including the extension — the keyboard includes a .com button, next to the Go button, for your convenience.

5. **Tap the Go button on the keyboard (or tap Cancel to cancel).**

   When you tap the Go button, the keyboard closes and the message `Loading` appears in the status bar. Then the Web page loads from the Internet, if the page exists. If you mistyped the URL or the page doesn't exist, you get the message `Safari can't open the page because it can't find the server.` Tap OK and start again from Step 2.

   To cancel entering a URL, tap the Cancel button in the upper-right corner of the screen (refer to Figure 18-1, right side).

Figure 18-1:
A Web page
in Safari
(left); enter-
ing a Web
address
(right).

Navigation bar   Add   Pages

Bookmarks

To stop a Web page from loading if you change your mind, tap the X on the right side of the URL entry field. This X turns into a circular arrow after the page is loaded. To reload an already-loaded Web page to refresh its contents, tap the circular arrow.

Bookmarking as You Go

The best way to keep track of Web pages you've visited and want to visit again is to create bookmarks for the pages. You can then quickly go back to that page by selecting the bookmark. The bookmarks you create in your iPad, iPod touch, or iPhone synchronize with your Safari bookmarks on your Mac, or with your Safari or Internet Explorer bookmarks on your PC, as I describe in Chapter 9.

Follow these steps to save a bookmark:

1. **Browse to the Web page you want.**
2. **Tap the add (+) button.**

Navigation

Pages

Bookmarks

Add

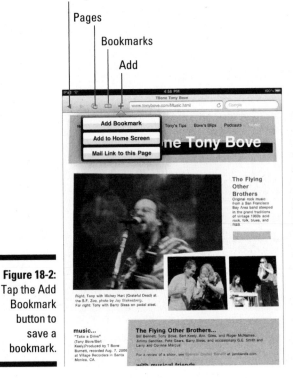 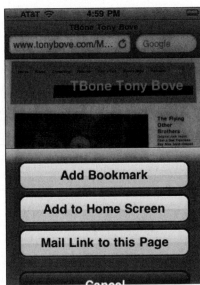

Figure 18-2:
Tap the Add
Bookmark
button to
save a
bookmark.

On an iPod touch or iPhone, the add button — a plus (+) sign — is in the
middle of the navigation bar along the bottom (you can see it in Figure
18-1, on the left side). On an iPad, the button appears in the navigation bar at the top (see Figure 18-2). Tap the button to see the special
options menu, which offers the Add Bookmark, Add to Home Screen,
and Mail Link to This Page buttons (the iPod touch and iPhone include a
Cancel button).

3. **Tap Add Bookmark in the menu to add a bookmark.**

The Add Bookmark menu appears with the name of the Web site in the
title field, ready for editing, along with the on-screen keyboard. Below
that is the actual URL for the Web page, and below that, the Bookmarks
folder.

4. **(Optional) Edit the bookmark's title.**

Before saving a bookmark, you can edit its title with the on-screen keyboard. Tap the circled X on the right side of the title field to clear its
contents, or use the Backspace key on the keyboard to erase backward
from the end of the title, and type the new title.

5. **(Optional) Choose a bookmark folder.**

Before saving a bookmark, you can choose a bookmark folder for saving it; otherwise, Safari saves the bookmark in the topmost level of bookmarks. Tap Bookmarks on an iPod touch or iPhone, or New on an iPad, to see the list of bookmark folders — you can flick to scroll the list quickly or drag it slowly. Select a bookmark folder by touching it.

6. **Tap the Save button to save the bookmark or tap Cancel to cancel.**

The Save button appears in the upper-right corner of the Add Bookmark menu, and the Cancel button appears in the upper-left corner.

You can also add bookmarks to your iPad, iPod touch, or iPhone by syncing bookmarks from your computer's Web browser, as described in Chapter 9.

After saving or adding bookmarks, you can go directly to a bookmarked page on the Web by selecting the bookmark. Follow these steps:

1. **Tap Safari on the Home screen if it is not already running.**

Your iPad, iPod touch, or iPhone displays the last Web page you visited or a blank page. A navigation bar appears that includes the Bookmarks button (see Figure 18-1, left side, for an iPod touch or iPhone, or Figure 18-2 for an iPad).

2. **Tap the Bookmarks button — the one that looks like an open book.**

The Bookmarks menu appears with a scrollable list of folders including the History folder that records your page visits, and other Bookmark-related folders (such as Bookmarks Bar and Bookmarks Menu, provided with the Safari application on Macs and PCs). You can scroll this list by dragging up and down.

3. **Tap a bookmark folder to access its bookmarks.**

For example, tapping Bookmarks Menu opens the folders and bookmarks from the Bookmarks Menu section of Safari on your Mac or PC. Tapping Bookmarks Bar opens the folders and bookmarks in the Bookmarks Bar section. Tapping History opens the history of the Web pages you've visited.

4. **Tap a bookmark to load the Web page.**

Folders have a folder icon to the left of their names, and actual bookmarks have an open-page icon next to their Web page names. Tap a folder to reveal its contents, and tap a bookmark to load a Web page.

You can rotate an iPad, iPod touch, or iPhone sideways to view Web pages in landscape (horizontal) orientation and then double-tap to zoom in or out — Safari automatically fits sections of Web pages (such as columns of text) to fill the screen for easy reading. You can also spread with two fingers to control the amount of zooming.

You can edit your bookmarks and bookmark folders. Tap the Bookmarks button on the navigation bar as I describe previously, and choose the folder to edit or the folder that has the bookmark you want to edit. Then tap the Edit button in the Bookmarks menu. The bookmark folders and bookmarks appear again with circled minus signs (–) next to them. You can then do any of the following:

- ✔ To make a new folder within the selected folder, tap the New Folder button. If you want to create a new folder at the topmost level, first tap the Bookmarks button to go back to the topmost Bookmarks list, tap the Edit button, and then tap New Folder.

- ✔ To delete a bookmark or folder, tap the circled minus (–) sign next to the bookmark or folder and then tap Delete.

- ✔ To reposition a bookmark or folder, drag the move icon on the right side of each bookmark or folder to a new position in the list.

- ✔ To edit the name of a bookmark or folder, tap the bookmark or folder and use the on-screen keyboard to type the new title. (Tap the circled X in the title field to clear its contents first, if you want.)

- ✔ To change where a bookmark or folder is stored, tap the Bookmark Folder field for the selected bookmark or folder and then tap a new folder to hold the folder chosen for editing.

Tap the Done button to finish editing.

Sending a Web link by e-mail

As I describe in Chapter 19, your iPad, iPod touch, or iPhone can send e-mail as well as receive it, as long as it's connected to the Internet. And if you want to share a Web page you just found with your friend, the steps are simple:

1. **Browse to the Web page and then tap the add (+) button.**

   A special options menu magically pops up with the Add Bookmark, Add to Home Screen, and Mail Link to This Page buttons (the iPod touch and iPhone include a Cancel button).

2. **Tap the Mail Link to This Page button.**

   Keep in mind that you must have already set up an e-mail account on your iPad, iPod touch, or iPhone, as I describe in Chapter 9.

   An e-mail message appears, ready for you to finish composing. The Subject field is already filled in with the Web page name, and the link itself is already inserted in the body of the message. The To and Cc fields are left blank — ready for you to fill in.

3. **Tap the circled plus (+) sign on the right side of the To field to select a name from your Contacts list, or use the on-screen keyboard to enter the e-mail address.**

   See Chapter 19 for details on sending an e-mail.

4. **Tap Send at the upper-right corner of the display to send the message.**

Pearl diving with Google, Yahoo!, or Bing

If you've done any Web surfing at all, you already know all there is to know about search engines. They're simply *the* tool for finding Web sites. The three most popular search engines out there — Google, Yahoo!, and Bing — are built into Safari on your iPod touch or iPhone.

 Google is set up to be your default Web search engine, but you can quickly change that. To choose Yahoo! or Bing (or to go back to Google), tap Settings⇨ Safari⇨Search Engine and tap Yahoo!, Google, or Bing. Turning on one search engine turns off the other one.

Follow these steps to search with from within Safari:

1. **Tap Safari on the Home screen.**

   The last Web page you visited or a blank page appears. You can find the URL entry field in the upper-left corner and the oval search-entry field, with `Google`, `Yahoo!`, or `Bing` in gray, in the upper-right corner (you can see `Google` in Figure 18-1, left side, on an iPod touch or iPhone, and in Figure 18-2 on an iPad). (If you don't see these two entry fields side by side, tap the status bar at the top of the screen to jump to the top of the Web page.)

2. **Tap the oval search-entry field.**

   The keyboard appears. Above that is the search-entry field (with a magnifying glass icon).

3. **Tap inside the search-entry field.**

4. **Tap out the letters of the search term using the keyboard.**

   Immediately as you start typing characters, you see a list of suggested bookmarks in your bookmarks folder or history list. You can scroll this list by dragging up and down.

5. **If a bookmark appears that satisfies your search, tap it to go directly to the Web page without further ado. Otherwise, keep typing the search term.**

6. **Tap the Search button on the keyboard.**

   Doing so closes the keyboard and displays the search results. (*Note:* The Search button replaces the Go button on the keyboard when searching.)

Let Your Fingers Do the Surfing

After you've found the Web page you want, you can use your fingers to navigate its links and play any media it has to offer. You can also bounce around from previous to next pages in your browsing session, open multiple pages, zoom into pages to see them clearly, and scroll around the page to see all its sections while zooming.

Scrolling and zooming

To zoom into a Web page in Safari, spread two fingers apart on the screen (unpinch). To zoom back out, bring your fingers together (pinch).

Double-tap the display to zoom into any part of the page. You can also double-tap a column to automatically zoom in so that the column fills the display. Double-tap again to zoom back out.

To scroll around the page, touch and drag the page. (If you happen to touch a link, drag the link so that you don't follow it.) You can drag up, down, or sideways to see the entire Web page, or you can flick your finger up or down to quickly scroll the page. Use two fingers to scroll within the frame on a Web page or one finger to scroll the entire page. All of these gestures work the same way in either portrait or landscape orientation.

To jump to the top of a Web page, tap the status bar at the top of the screen.

It's all touch and go

To follow a link on a Web page, tap the link. Text links are usually underlined (sometimes in blue). Many images are also links that you can tap to navigate to another page or use to play media content.

If a link leads to a sound or movie file supported by the iPad, iPod touch, or iPhone, Safari launches the player for the sound or movie; if the link points to YouTube, the YouTube app launches to play the video. (See Chapter 15 for sounds and Chapter 16 for videos.) Tap an e-mail link to automatically launch Mail with that e-mail as the send-to address.

You can see the link's destination — without following it — by touching and holding down on the link until the destination address appears (next to your finger). You can touch and hold an image to see whether it has a link.

To move to the previous page in your browsing sequence, tap the left-arrow button in the left side of the navigation bar. (Refer to Figure 18-1, left side, for the navigation bar on an iPod touch or iPhone, and Figure 18-2 for an iPad.) Safari replaces the current page with the previous one. If you've just started browsing and this is the first page you've opened, the left-arrow button is grayed out.

To move to the next page, tap the right-arrow button (to the right of the left-arrow button) in the navigation bar. Safari replaces the current page with the next one in the browsing sequence. This button is grayed out unless you've navigated backward to some previous page.

You can always go back to any of the pages you visited by tapping the Bookmarks button on the navigation bar and then tapping History. To clear your History list on your iPad, iPod touch, or iPhone, tap Clear.

Surfing multiple pages

Although you can open Web pages one at a time and switch back and forth between them, you can also open several pages and start a new browsing sequence with each page, just like opening separate browser windows or tabs. Some links automatically open a new page instead of replacing the current one, leaving you with multiple pages open.

On an iPod touch or iPhone, Safari displays the number of open pages inside the pages button in the right corner of the navigation bar at the bottom of the screen (Figure 18-1, left side, shows "2" in the button). The pages button without a number means that only the currently viewd page is open (as in Figure 18-2 on an iPad).

To open a separate page, tap the pages button. Then tap the New Page button in the bottom-left corner of the screen on an iPod touch or iPhone, or the New Page blank thumbnail on an iPad. Safari brushes aside the existing page to display a new one. You can then use your bookmarks, enter a Web page URL, or search for a Web page. (If you change your mind and don't want to open a new page, tap the Done button to cancel.)

To close a separate page, tap the pages button in the navigation bar to display the page thumbnail images and then tap the red circled X in the upper-left corner of the Web page thumbnail for the page you want to close. The page disappears.

To switch among open pages, tap the pages button to display the page thumbnail images, and flick left or right on an iPod touch or iPhone, or up and down on an iPad to scroll the images. When you get to the thumbnail image of the page you want, touch it!

Interacting with pages

Many Web pages have pop-up menus for making choices. For example, Craigslist (www.craigslist.org) offers a pop-up menu for searching through its classified listings. To make choices for a pop-up menu, tap the menu. Safari displays a list of possible choices for that pop-up menu (for example, Craigslist offers the "search craigslist" pop-up with choices for Housing, Jobs, Personals, Services, For Sale, and so on). Choose one by tapping it; you can also flick to scroll the list of choices, or start typing to scroll directly to the first match.

After choosing an option, tap the Done button to finish with that pop-up menu. You can also tap the Previous or Next button to move to the previous or next pop-up menu.

Entering text into a Web site — such as reservation information, passwords, credit card numbers, search terms, and so on — is as easy as tapping inside the text field. Safari brings up the keyboard for typing the text. You may want to rotate the iPad, iPod touch, or iPhone sideways to view Web pages in landscape (horizontal) orientation so that the keyboard is wider and easier to use.

You can move to the next or previous text field by tapping the Next or Previous button at the top of the keyboard, or by tapping inside another text field. To finish typing with the keyboard, tap the Done button. If you don't like what you typed, use the delete key to delete it before tapping Done.

After you finish filling out all the required text fields on the page, tap Go on the keyboard (or tap Search, which some pages use rather than Go). If the Web page is a form, tapping Go automatically submits the form. Some Web pages offer a link for submitting the form, which you must tap to finish entering information.

Copying text

You may want to copy one or more paragraphs of text from a Web page to paste into another app (such as Notes) or into an e-mail message. Although you can e-mail a link to a Web page (as I show in the section "Sending a Web link by e-mail" earlier in this chapter), you may want to copy a section of text and then paste the section into the message itself.

To copy a section of text from a Web page, touch and hold somewhere within the section (also known as a "long tap"). Safari automatically highlights the section with selection handles on either end and displays the Copy bubble. (See Figure 18-3.) Tap Copy to copy the selection.

Figure 18-3:
Copy a
selected
section of
text on a
Web page.

If you zoomed into the Web page and the "long tap" selects only a single word, try zooming out first (pinching) and then trying the "long tap" (touch and hold) again. You can also make a more precise selection by dragging each of the handles. A rectangular magnifier appears for dragging the handle precisely. When you remove your finger to stop dragging, the Copy bubble appears.

For details on pasting the selected text into apps such as Notes or into an e-mail message, see Chapter 3.

Bringing It All Back Home

Got some favorite Web site pages? You can add Web thumbnail icons for them to the Home screen so that you can access each page with one touch. Web icons appear on the Home screen along with the icons of other apps. (Discover how to rearrange the icons and add multiple screens to the Home screen in Chapter 3.)

Follow these steps to add a Web page to your Home screen:

1. **Browse to the Web page you want.**

2. **Tap the add (+) button in the navigation bar.**

   (Refer to Figure 18-1, left side, for the navigation bar on an iPod touch or iPhone, and to Figure 18-2 for an iPad.) The special options menu appears, with Add Bookmark, Add to Home Screen, Mail Link to This Page, and Cancel buttons.

3. **Tap the Add to Home Screen button.**

   The name of the Web site appears in the title field, ready for editing, along with the keyboard. The icon to be added to the Home screen — a thumbnail image of the site or a graphic image defined by the site for this purpose (usually a logo) — appears to the left of the title field.

4. **(Optional) Edit the Web icon's title.**

   Before saving a Web icon to the Home screen, you can edit its title with the keyboard. Tap the circled X on the right side of the title field to clear its contents, or use the delete key on the keyboard to erase backward from the end of the title and then type the new title.

5. **Tap the Add button to add the Web site icon, or tap Cancel to cancel.**

   The Add button appears in the upper-right corner of the display, and the Cancel button appears in the upper-left corner.

Chapter 19

The Postman Always Beeps Once

*Y*our e-mail is just a touch away. The Mail app on your iPad, iPod touch, or iPhone can display richly formatted messages, and you can send as well as receive photos and graphics, which are displayed in your message along with the text. You can even receive Portable Document Format (PDF) files, Microsoft Word documents, and Microsoft Excel spreadsheets as attachments and view them on your iPad, iPod touch, or iPhone.

The Mail app can work in the background to retrieve your e-mail when your iPad, iPod touch, or iPhone is connected to the Internet (see Chapter 4 for details on connecting). If you signed up for Apple's MobileMe service (formerly the .Mac service, now www.me.com), as I describe in illustrious detail in Chapter 9, your iPad, iPod touch, or iPhone can receive e-mail the instant it arrives in the mailbox on the MobileMe service. Services such as MobileMe, Microsoft Exchange, and Yahoo! Mail *push* e-mail messages to your iPad, iPod touch, or iPhone so that they arrive immediately, automatically. You get a single beep when your mail has arrived (unless you turned off the New Mail sound effect, as I describe in Chapter 4).

Other types of e-mail services let you *fetch* e-mail from the server — when you select the account in Mail on your iPad, iPod touch, or iPhone, Mail automatically starts fetching the e-mail, and you can browse your e-mail accounts or even use other apps while Mail fetches messages. You can also tell Mail to fetch more messages by tapping the Fetch (circular arrow) icon in the lower-left corner of the Mail, Mailboxes, or message screens. You can also balance pushing and fetching to save battery power, as I describe in "If Not Push, Then Fetch" in this chapter.

You need to set up your e-mail accounts on your iPad, iPod touch, or iPhone, before using Mail. See Chapter 9 for details on synchronizing, setting up, deleting, and changing settings for e-mail accounts.

Checking E-Mail

You know that you have unread e-mail if the Mail icon on the Home screen shows a number — this is the number of unread messages in your inboxes. As e-mail is pushed (or fetched), this number increases until you read the messages. Tap the Mail icon to start the Mail app.

On an iPod touch or iPhone, Mail starts out by displaying the Mailboxes screen, which gives you quick access to all your inboxes and access to your account mailboxes, as shown in Figure 19-1 (left side). Tap an inbox for an e-mail account to see its message headers, as shown in Figure 19-1 (right side). To see incoming message headers for all your accounts, tap All Inboxes. (You see only one inbox on the Mailboxes screen if you've set up and turned on only one e-mail account.)

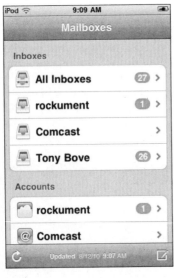

Figure 19-1: iPod touch or iPhone: Tap an inbox (left) to see its message headers (right).

On an iPad in portrait view, Mail shows the selected message; tap Inbox in the top-left corner (see Figure 19-2, left side) to see your accounts, and tap an account to view the mailboxes for that account. In landscape view, the accounts list is always visible in the left column; tap an account to see its mailboxes. Tap a mailbox (such as Inbox), and a list of incoming message headers appears.

Figure 19-2:
Mail accounts on an iPad (left); an e-mail on an iPod touch or iPhone (right).

The message headers include the sender's name, subject, and the first sentence or two of each message, along with a blue dot if the message hasn't been read yet.

The message is the medium

Tap a message header to read the message. You can scroll the message by flicking or dragging your finger, and zoom into and out of the message by unpinching and pinching with your fingers. You can also zoom directly into a column in the message by double-tapping the message, and zoom out by double-tapping it again.

If the e-mail includes an attachment that can't be displayed easily, a button appears within the message showing the icon of an attached file and a right arrow, as shown in Figure 19-2, right side — to view the attachment, just tap the right arrow. If the format of the attached file is one of the supported formats (which include files that have the extensions `.doc`, `.docx`, `.htm`, `.html`, `.pdf`, `.txt`, `.xls`, and `.xlsx`), Mail downloads and opens the attachment. If not, Mail displays a document icon with the name of the file — but you can't open it.

You can see all the recipients of a message (except Bcc, or *blind carbon copy*, recipients) by opening the message and tapping the blue word Details in the upper-right corner of the message. Tap a name or e-mail address that appears to see the recipient's contact information. Tap Hide to hide the recipients.

You can add the sender or recipient to your Contacts list on your iPad, iPod touch, or iPhone by tapping the name or e-mail address. A menu appears with the contact's e-mail address and the Create New Contact and Add to Existing Contact buttons. Tap Create New Contact to create a new contact (or tap Add to Existing Contact if you want to add the information to an existing contact). Tap the e-mail address to send an e-mail to that recipient's address. (See the "Sending E-Mail" section later in this chapter.)

Links appear in a message underlined in blue, and pictures embedded in the message may also have links. Tapping a link can take you to a Web page in Safari, open a map in Maps, or open a new preaddressed e-mail message in Mail. To return to your e-mail, press the physical Home button and tap Mail on the Home screen.

You can mark a message as unread so that it stays in your Inbox: Open the message, tap the blue word Details in the upper-right corner, and tap the blue Mark as Unread text next to the blue dot inside the message. The message is marked as unread — a blue dot appears next to the message header in the mailbox list until you open it again.

On an iPod touch or iPhone, messages are organized by thread (I show you how to change that setting in "What you see is what you got" later in this chapter), so that related messages appear as a single entry in the mailbox. Message threads have a number next to the right arrow, showing the number of messages in the thread — as in the "2" next to the message header Cherry Moon Farms in Figure 19-3. The message header displayed is for the oldest unread message, or the most recent message if all the messages are read. A blue dot appears for any message in the thread you haven't read yet.

To see the messages in a thread, tap the thread in the mailbox. The messages in the thread appear. (On the left side of Figure 19-3, I tapped the Cherry

Moon Farms message header to see the thread's message headers, which appear on the right side of the figure.)

Figure 19-3: Tap a message header thread (left) to see its message headers (right).

To read a message in a thread, tap the message. Within a message, tap the up or down arrows to see the next or previous message in the thread.

Deleting a message

To delete an open message, tap the Trash icon (at the bottom center of the message display on an iPod touch or iPhone, and in the top-right corner of the menu bar on an iPad — refer to Figure 19-2). Mail deletes the message from your iPad, iPod touch, or iPhone, but *not* from your computer or mail server unless it's set up that way — see Chapter 9 for details on setting up e-mail accounts.

You can also delete a message without opening it. In the list of message headers, drag your finger across a message header and tap the Delete button that appears.

To delete a list of messages quickly, choose the mailbox (such as Inbox) and tap the Edit button in the upper-right corner of the screen (or iPad menu). The messages appear with empty circles next to them. Tap each message so that a check mark appears in the empty circle. After checking off the messages to delete, tap the Delete button in the lower-left corner.

Sending E-Mail

You can use the Mail app to reply to any message instantly and send e-mail to any e-mail address in the world. You can even send a message to a group of people without having to select each person's e-mail address.

To send an e-mail, follow these steps:

1. **Tap Mail on the Home screen and scroll to see your accounts.**

   On an iPod touch or iPhone, Mail starts out by displaying the Mailboxes screen, and you can scroll it down to the Accounts section, which lists all of the e-mail accounts that have been synced. On an iPad in portrait view, tap Inbox in the top-left corner (refer to Figure 19-2, left side) to see your accounts; in landscape view, the accounts list is in the left column.

2. **(Optional) Choose an e-mail account from the Accounts screen for sending the e-mail.**

   You can skip this step if you've synced only one e-mail account. If you synced several e-mail accounts with your iPad, iPod touch, or iPhone, you can select one of them or you can use the default account for sending e-mail. (See the next section in this chapter to set the default account.) You can also defer this decision until Step 6.

3. **Tap the pencil-document icon in the lower-right corner of the iPod touch or iPhone Mail screen, or the upper-right corner of the iPad Mail screen (refer to Figure 19-2).**

   The New Message screen appears, as shown in Figure 19-4, along with the keyboard. If you have multiple accounts set up on your iPad, iPod touch, or iPhone, the default account for sending e-mail appears in the From field.

4. **Enter the recipient's e-mail address in the To field.**

   If your recipient is listed in your Contacts, tap the circled plus (+) sign on the right side of the To field (see Figure 19-4) and choose a contact to add the contact's e-mail address to the To field. You can repeat this process to add multiple e-mail addresses to the To field from your contacts.

   If your recipient isn't listed in your Contacts or if you don't know whether the recipient is listed, tap the To field entry and use the keyboard to type one or more e-mail addresses (and use a comma to separate each address). As you type an e-mail address, addresses that match from your Contacts list appear below. Tap one to add it to the To field.

Figure 19-4:
The New
Message
screen.

5. **(Optional) Add more addresses to the Cc or Bcc field.**

You can add e-mail addresses to the Cc (carbon copy) and Bcc (blind carbon copy) fields to copy others. Whereas Cc addresses appear on messages received by recipients, indicating that they were copied on the message, Bcc addresses don't appear on messages received by recipients — they're like stealth readers. Tap the Cc/Bcc letters to expand the message to include the Cc and Bcc fields; enter addresses the same way you do in Step 4.

6. **(Optional) Change the From address.**

You can change the e-mail address for the sender to one of your e-mail accounts. The default e-mail account for sending e-mail is already selected; tap the From field (refer to Figure 19-4) to display a pop-up menu of e-mail accounts and then tap an e-mail account to use as the sender's account.

7. **Enter the e-mail subject.**

Tap the Subject entry field (refer to Figure 19-4) to type a subject with the keyboard; then tap underneath the Subject field to type a message. Press Return on the keyboard when you're finished.

8. **Tap Send in the upper-right corner of the display (refer to Figure 19-4) to send the message.**

You can also forward and reply to any message you receive. Open the message and tap the reply options button — the curled left-arrow that appears in the lower-left side of the message display on an iPod touch or iPhone, or in the upper-left corner on an iPad (refer to Figure 19-2). Then tap Reply to reply to the sender of the message, Reply All to reply to all the recipients as well as the sender (but not the Bcc recipients), or Forward to forward the message to someone else (or Cancel to go back to the message). The New Message screen appears with the keyboard so that you can type your reply or add a message to the one you're forwarding. Tap Send to send the reply or forwarded message.

When you reply to a message, files or images attached to the initial message aren't sent with the reply. When you tap Forward to forward a message, a pop-up menu with the Include and Don't Include buttons appears for a message with an attachment. Tap Include to include the attachment in the forwarded message, or tap Don't Include to forward the message without the attachment.

To save a message as a draft so that you can work on it later, start typing the message as described in the preceding steps, but before tapping Send, tap Cancel in the upper-left corner of the display (refer to Figure 19-4). Then, from the menu that appears, tap Save to save the message in your Drafts mailbox or tap Don't Save to discard the message (or Cancel to go back to typing the message). You can find the saved message in the Drafts mailbox of the same e-mail account. Tap the message to add to it or change it and then send it.

To send one or more photos in a message, tap Photos on the Home screen and select them as described in Chapter 17.

Message Settings and Sending Options

To change your e-mail message settings and sending options, choose Settings⇨Mail, Contacts, Calendars from the Home screen. In the Mail, Contacts, Calendars settings screen that appears, use your finger to scroll down to the Mail section to change your e-mail message settings and sending options, as shown in Figure 19-5.

In the Mail section, you can change global settings for messages in all accounts. To set the number of messages you can see at once in a mailbox, tap Show and then choose a setting. You can choose to see the most recent 25, 50, 75, 100, or 200 messages. (To download additional messages when you're in Mail, scroll to the bottom of your Inbox and tap Download More.)

Figure 19-5:
The Mail
section
of Mail,
Contacts,
and
Calendars
settings.

If you think you have shaky fingers and might delete a message by mistake, you can set Mail to confirm that you want to delete a message first before deleting. Tap the Off button to turn on the Ask before Deleting option. (Tap it again to turn it off.) If Ask before Deleting is on, Mail warns you first when you delete a message, and you have to tap Delete to confirm the deletion.

What you see is what you got

You can also set how many lines of each message are previewed in the message list headers. Choose Preview (refer to Figure 19-5) and then choose to see any amount from zero to five lines of each message. To set a minimum font size for messages, tap Minimum Font Size and then choose Small, Medium, Large, Extra Large, or Giant.

If you want to see the Internet images linked to your e-mails, turn on the Load Remote Images option. However, images downloaded from the Internet can also be used by spammers to collect information, or even harbor malicious code. If you leave it off, your messages appear faster, but you have to touch each image icon to download and see it.

If you care about whether a message was sent directly to you or whether you were sent it as a Cc copy (which still might make it important, but at least you know), you can set whether Mail shows the To and Cc labels in message lists. Tap the Off button for the Show To/Cc Label option to turn it on. (Tap it again to turn it off.) If the Show To/Cc Label option is on, you see To or Cc in the list next to each message.

If you don't want messages to be organized into threads, turn off the Organize By Thread option (tap On to turn it Off). All messages appear as single messages without threads.

Return to sender, address unknown

For those who are obsessive about making sure that e-mails are sent — and you know who you are — Mail can send you a copy of every message you send. Tap the Off button to turn on the Always Bcc Myself option. (Tap it again to turn it off.) The Bcc refers to *blind carbon copy,* and it means that your message is sent and copied back to you without your e-mail address appearing in the recipient's list.

You can add a *signature* to your messages that can include any text — not your real, handwritten scrawl but rather a listing of your name, title, phone number, favorite quote, or all of these — to personalize your e-mails. Tap Signature (refer to Figure 19-5) and then type a signature with the on-screen keyboard. The signature remains in effect for all future e-mails sent from your iPad, iPod touch, or iPhone.

To set the default e-mail account for sending messages, tap Default Account (refer to Figure 19-5) and then choose an e-mail account. Your iPad, iPod touch, or iPhone will use this account whenever you start the process of sending a message from another application, such as sending a photo from Photos or tapping the e-mail address of a business in Maps.

For details on synchronizing e-mail accounts automatically from iTunes or MobileMe, as well as for setting up an account, changing account settings, and deleting accounts manually on your iPad, iPod touch, or iPhone, see Chapter 9.

If Not Push, Then Fetch

The Push and Fetch options control how your iPad, iPod touch, or iPhone receives e-mail. You can set these options for all accounts and specifically for each account.

MobileMe, Microsoft Exchange, and Yahoo! Mail e-mail accounts can *push* messages *to* your iPad, iPod touch, or iPhone so that they arrive immediately after arriving at the account's e-mail server (so can apps from services such as Comcast). With other types of accounts, the Mail app *fetches* messages *from* the account's e-mail server — either on a time schedule or manually. (If manually, you select the account before the Mail app retrieves the e-mail.) Push accounts (such as MobileMe e-mail) can be set to either push or fetch.

You can turn the Push feature on or off as you please. Keeping it on uses more battery power because the iPad, iPod touch, or iPhone receives messages immediately when it's connected to the Internet. When you turn the Push feature off, Mail fetches the e-mail from the accounts instead, and you can set the timetable for fetching, or set fetching to manual.

For optimal battery life, turn Push off and set Fetch to Manually so that Mail fetches only when you tap the e-mail account to read or send e-mail. Pushing e-mail as it arrives, or fetching e-mail often, uses up a considerable amount of battery power; doing both drains the battery even more quickly.

To turn Push on or off, choose Settings⇨Mail, Contacts, Calendars from the Home screen and tap Fetch New Data. The Fetch New Data screen appears. Tap the On button for Push to turn it off (and vice versa).

If you like, set a timetable for fetching e-mail automatically so that you don't have to think about it. Choose a time interval on the Fetch New Data screen — pick Every 15 Minutes, Every 30 Minutes, or Hourly. You can also pick Manually so that Mail fetches only when you tap the e-mail account to read or send e-mail.

You can also set Push or Fetch settings for individual accounts. Scroll the Fetch New Data screen to the bottom and touch Advanced. The Advanced screen appears.

Chapter 20

Using Applications on Your iPad, iPod, or iPhone

A s John Lennon once sang, "Life is what happens to you when you're busy making other plans." And while life happens to you in real time, you can consult your iPad, iPod, or iPhone calendar to view your appointments and look up friends in your list of contacts. You can go further with an iPad, iPod touch, or iPhone and change those appointments in the calendar and contact those contacts, as I describe in this chapter.

Your iPad, iPod touch, or iPhone can also find almost anything on Earth, even itself, and show the location on a map or satellite picture. And although you can't harness the forces of nature, or even the influences that drive Wall Street, you can use Apple-supplied apps for your iPod touch or iPhone, or third-party apps for your iPad, to make better guesses about the weather and the stock market — find out how in this chapter.

To socialize and stay in contact with friends, relatives, and associates, you can use social networks such as Facebook and MySpace to share photos, thoughts, links, and profile information. The App Store offers social networking apps that link you directly to these networks and to messaging sites such as Twitter. With an iPhone 4 or fourth-generation iPod touch, you can make FaceTime video calls with people you know who are also using an iPhone 4 or fourth-generation iPod touch.

The iPod classic offers extras (in the Extras menu) such as Calendars, Contacts, and Voice Memos, as well as click wheel games. The iPad, iPod touch, and iPhone, on the other hand, can run many hundreds of thousands of apps available in the App Store. (See Chapter 6 for details on downloading from the iTunes Store and App Store.) This chapter shows you how to use the Calendars and Contacts extras on an iPod classic, as well as how to use the apps supplied with your iPad, iPod touch, or iPhone.

To find out how to sync and play click wheel games on an iPod classic, or record Voice Memos on an iPod classic, iPod nano, iPod touch, or iPhone, visit this book's companion Web site.

Checking Your Calendar

The calendar in your iPad, iPod, or iPhone isn't just for looking up dates (though it's quite good at that). If you see a blank calendar, it means that you need to synchronize your iPad, iPod, or iPhone with your calendar files from iCal (Mac) or Outlook (Windows), or from MobileMe, as I describe in Chapter 9.

On an iPad, iPod touch, or iPhone, tap Calendar on the Home screen. A monthly calendar appears with events synced from your computer or MobileMe (see Figure 20-1 for an iPod touch or iPhone).

If you've synced multiple calendars to your iPad, iPod touch, or iPhone, they are merged into one calendar. You can select individual calendars by tapping the Calendars button in the upper-left corner to see the list of calendars. Tap All at the top of the Calendars list to view all calendars merged into one or tap a specific calendar to see only that calendar. On an iPod touch or iPhone, you can also tap the Hide All Calendars button to hide all events, or tap the e-mail for your MobileMe account to show the calendar synced with MobileMe.

On an iPod touch or iPhone, tap any day to see the events on that day, which are displayed below the calendar view in a list; tap the event to see the event's information. Tap the List, Day, or Month button to change the calendar view to a list of events, a full day of scheduled events, or a month view, respectively. In Day or Month view, tap the left or right arrows at the top of the calendar to switch days or months.

On an iPad, tap any event to see a pop-up label with the event information. (See the next section about editing the event information.) The iPad also offers a Week button to show a week of events, and a row of days, weeks, or months along the bottom to navigate the calendar quickly.

If you roam around from day to day or month to month, tap the Today button in the lower-left corner of the display to see the calendar for today.

On an iPod classic, choose Extras➪Calendars. If you've synchronized multiple calendars, a list of calendars appears with All Calendars at the top. Press the select button to select All Calendars for a merged view of all your calendars, or scroll the click wheel and press the select button to select a specific calendar. You can then scroll the click wheel to go through the days of the calendar. Select an event to see its details. Press the Next and Previous buttons to skip to the next or previous month. To see your To-Do list, choose Extras➪Calendars➪To Do's.

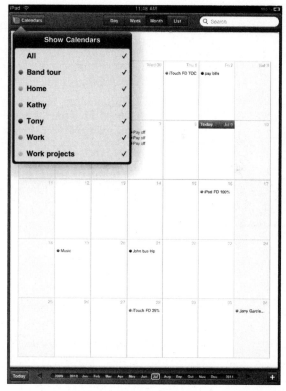

Figure 20-1:
View the
Calendar
(left) and
add an
event (right).

A change is gonna come (to your iPad, iPod touch, or iPhone)

Change happens, and you want to change your schedule or even add new events as you learn about them. Although you can enter appointments and events on your computer and sync them with your iPad, iPod touch, or iPhone, as I point out in Chapter 9, you can also enter and change appointments and events directly in your iPad, iPod touch, or iPhone, and keep changes and additions synced with your computer and with other devices using MobileMe.

To add an event, follow these steps:

1. **Open the Calendar app as described earlier.**

2. **Tap the plus (+) sign in the upper-right corner of the Calendar screen on an iPod touch or iPhone, or the lower-right corner on an iPad.**

   The Add Event screen appears, as shown in Figure 20-1 (center) on an iPod touch or iPhone. On an iPad, the Add Event screen pops up over the calendar view.

3. **Tap the Title/Location button on an iPod touch or iPhone, or tap the Title and Location separately on an iPad, and enter the event's title and location using the on-screen keyboard.**

   The Title and Location fields appear along with the on-screen keyboard.

4. **On an iPod touch or iPhone, tap Done in the upper-right corner to save the entry (or Cancel in the upper-left corner to cancel the entry).**

   The Add Event screen appears again for selecting more options.

5. **Tap the Starts/Ends button to enter the starting and ending times and dates.**

   The Start & End screen appears with a slot-machine-style number wheel to select the date and time.

6. **Tap the Starts button and select the date and time, or tap the Off button for All-Day to turn on the All-Day option.**

   Slide your finger up and down the slot-machine-style number wheel to select the date and time. If you turn on the All-Day option, the number wheel changes to show only dates; select a date for the all-day event and skip the next step.

7. **Tap the Ends button and select the date and time as you did in Step 6.**

8. **On an iPod touch or iPhone, tap Done in the upper-right corner to save the entry (or Cancel in the upper-left corner to cancel the entry).**

   The Add Event screen appears again for selecting more options.

9. **(Optional) Set the event to repeat by tapping Repeat and selecting a repeat time (and then tap Done on an iPod touch or iPhone).**

   You can set the event to repeat every day, every week, every two weeks, every month, or every year (or Never, to not repeat).

10. **(Optional) Set an alert for a time before the event by tapping Alert and choosing an alert time (and then tap Done on an iPod touch or iPhone).**

    You can set the alert to occur from five minutes to two days before the event. You can also set a second alert time in case you miss the first one.

11. **(Optional) If you have multiple calendars synced with your iPad, iPod touch, or iPhone, you can change the calendar for the event by tapping Calendar and choosing a calendar.**

    The Calendars screen appears with a list of your calendars. Tap a calendar's name to choose it. (Tap Done or Cancel to return to the Add Event screen on an iPod touch or iPhone.)

12. **(Optional) Enter notes about the event by tapping Notes and using the on-screen keyboard to type notes.**

    The Notes field appears along with the keyboard so that you can type your notes. (Tap Done or Cancel to return to the Add Event screen on an iPod touch or iPhone.)

13. **Tap Done in the upper-right corner of the Add Event screen to save the event (or Cancel in the upper-left corner to cancel the event).**

    The new event now appears in your calendar.

On an iPod touch or iPhone, tap any day to see the events on that day, which are displayed below the calendar view in a list; tap the event to see the event's information screen. On an iPad, tap any event to see a pop-up label with the event information.

To edit the information, tap the Edit button in the upper-left corner of the information screen on an iPod touch or iPhone, or in the event's label on an iPad. Then follow Steps 3–13 in this section.

The Delete Event button appears at the bottom of the event information only when you're editing an event. After tapping Delete Event, a warning appears to confirm the deletion — tap Delete Event again or tap Cancel.

Yesterday's settings (and today's)

If the calendar events you synced from your computer include alarms, you can turn on your iPod classic or iPod nano calendar alarm so that it beeps for those events. Choose Extras⇨Calendars⇨Alarms. Select Alarms once to set the alarm to Beep, select Alarms twice to set it to None (so that only the message for the alarm appears), or select it a third time to set it to Off. (The Alarms choices cycle from Beep to None to Off and then back to Beep.) For details on setting alarms, see Chapter 4.

On an iPad, iPod touch, or iPhone, you can set alerts for meeting invitations and choose how many weeks of events to sync back to (to clear out old events). Choose Settings⇨Mail, Contacts, Calendars from the Home screen and then scroll the Mail, Contacts, Calendars settings screen to the Calendars section, as shown in Figure 20-2 (left side).

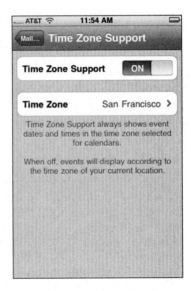

Figure 20-2: The Contacts and Calendars sections for settings (left) and the Time Zone setting (right).

To set the option for how far back in time to sync your calendar events, tap Sync and choose a period of time (such as Events 2 Weeks Back).

If you have a MobileMe or Microsoft Exchange account set up with Calendars enabled, you can receive and respond to meeting invitations from others in your organization that also use MobileMe or Exchange. To set a sound as an alert for receiving a meeting invitation, tap the Off button for New Invitation Alerts to turn it on.

You can also turn time zone support on or off. When time zone support is on, event dates and times are displayed in the time zone of the city you selected. When time zone support is off, events are displayed in the time zone of your current location as determined by the network time. You might want to turn it on and select your home city so that dates and times are displayed as if you were in your home city, rather than where you actually are. For example, if you live in San Francisco and you're visiting New York, turning on time zone support and selecting San Francisco keeps the dates and times in your calendars on San Francisco time. Otherwise, they would switch to New York time.

To turn on time zone support, tap Time Zone Support, and on the Time Zone Support screen (refer to Figure 20-2, right side), tap Off to turn on time zone support (or tap On to turn it off). Then tap Time Zone and enter the name of a major city. As you type, city names are suggested based on what you've typed. Select the city to return to the Time Zone Support screen and then tap the Mail, Contacts, Calendars button in the upper-left corner to return to the settings screen — or, if you're finished making changes, press the physical Home button to leave settings altogether and return to the Home screen.

You can set your iPad, iPod touch, or iPhone to play a beeping sound for your calendar alert. Choose Settings⇨General⇨Sounds and tap the Off button for Calendar Alerts to turn it on. (Tap it again to turn it off.)

Using Your Contacts

The bits of information that you're most likely to need on the road are people's names, addresses, and phone numbers. An iPad, iPod, or iPhone can store that stuff (in the Contacts format) right alongside your content. To see how to sync your personal contacts info on your computer with the info on your iPad, iPod, or iPhone, check out Chapter 9.

To view contacts on an iPad, iPod touch, or iPhone, tap the Contacts icon on the Home screen. The All Contacts screen appears. If you've organized contacts into groups, you can tap the Groups button in the upper-left corner of the screen to show the Groups screen, and then tap a group to see just that group, or tap All Contacts to return to the All Contacts screen.

The contact list is sorted in alphabetical order by last name (in bold) but displayed so that the first name comes first (in the next section, I show how you can change the way it's sorted). Scroll the list of contacts with your finger or tap a letter of the alphabet along the right side to go directly to names that begin with that letter. Then tap a contact to see that person's info screen.

The contact's info screen shows all the information about reaching that contact. Tap an e-mail address to bring up the Mail app and send an e-mail to that contact. Tap a Web site address to load that page into Safari. Tap a physical address (with a street address) to bring up the Maps app and locate the contact on the map.

To view a contact on an iPod classic choose Extras⇨Contacts from the main menu. If you've organized contacts into groups, a list of groups appears, with All Contacts at the top. Press the select button to select All Contacts, or scroll the click wheel and press the select button to select a group. You can then scroll the list of contacts and select a contact. The contact list is sorted automatically in alphabetical order by first name and then last name, or by last name followed by first name.

Orders to sort and display

You can change which way the contacts sort so that you can look up people by their first names (which can be time-consuming with so many friends named Elvis).

On an iPad, iPod touch, or iPhone, choose Settings⇨Mail, Contacts, Calendars from the Home screen and then scroll the Mail, Contacts, Calendars settings screen to the Contacts section (refer to Figure 20-2, left side). Tap Sort Order and then tap one of these options:

  ✔ **First, Last:** Sorts the contact list by first name, followed by the last name, so that *Brian Jones* sorts under the letter *B* for *Brian* (after *Brian Auger* but before *Brian Wilson*).

  ✔ **Last, First:** Sorts the contacts by last name, followed by the first name, so that *Brian Jones* sorts under the letter *J* for *Jones*. (*Jones, Brian* appears after *Jones, Alice* but before *Jones, Norah*.)

On an iPod classic, choose Settings⇨General⇨Sort Contacts and then press the Select button in the scrolling pad for each option:

  ✔ **First:** Sorts the contact list by first name, followed by the last name.

  ✔ **Last:** Sorts the contacts by last name, followed by the first name.

You can also change the way contacts are listed on an iPad, iPod touch, or iPhone — with either their first names followed by their last names or their last names followed by their first names — regardless of how you sort them. Choose Settings⇨Mail, Contacts, Calendars and then scroll the Mail, Contacts, Calendars settings screen to the Contacts section (refer to Figure 20-2, left side). Tap Display Order and then tap one of these options:

✔ **First, Last:** Displays the contacts list by first name and then last name, as in *Paul McCartney*.

✔ **Last, First:** Displays the contacts list by last name followed by a comma and the first name, as in *McCartney, Paul*.

Soul searchin' on an iPad, iPod touch, or iPhone

Can't remember the person's full name or last name? You can search for any part of a person's name in Contacts on an iPad, iPod touch, or iPhone by tapping the Search entry field at the very top of the list of contacts. The search-entry field appears with the keyboard, and suggestions appear as you type.

Tap a suggested name to view the Contacts record for that person. You can then edit or delete the contact information.

Adding, editing, and deleting contacts on an iPad, iPod touch or iPhone

You meet people all the time, so why not enter their information immediately? You can enter new contacts, edit existing contacts, and even delete contacts directly on your iPad, iPod touch, or iPhone, and keep your contacts in sync with your computer. (For sync info, see Chapter 9.)

To add a contact, follow these steps:

1. **Tap the Contacts icon on the Home screen.**

2. **Tap the plus (+) sign in the upper-right corner of the Contacts display on an iPod touch or iPhone, or the bottom of the iPad display.**

   The New Contact screen appears with an Add Photo button on the left, and First, Last, and Company buttons on the right, followed by buttons for phone numbers, e-mail and physical addresses, and other contact information.

3. **Tap the First, Last, and Company buttons to enter the information using the keyboard for each field.**

   When you tap the First, Last, or Company buttons, the onscreen keyboard appears for typing into the field.

4. **Scroll the screen and tap the Phone button next to the mobile label to enter a phone number; tap the label to change it from mobile to another label (such as home) for the number.**

   After you tap Phone, the numeric keypad pops up for typing the number. Tap the number's label to select a different label for the type of phone (mobile, home, work, main, home fax, and so on). After typing a number, another Phone button appears below it, so that you can type more numbers.

   To enter a pause in a phone number (sometimes required for extensions or code numbers), tap the +*# button and tap Pause on an iPod touch or iPhone, which inserts a comma representing the pause (on an iPad, type a comma). Each pause lasts two seconds; you can enter as many as you need.

5. **(Optional) Scroll down and tap the next Phone button to add more phone numbers, following the instructions in Step 4 for each phone number.**

   After typing a number, another Phone button appears below it, so that you can type more numbers — scroll the screen to see it.

6. **(Optional, iPod touch and iPhone only) Tap ringtone to set a unique ringtone for this contact.**

   The ringtone you choose plays whenever that contact makes a voice or FaceTime call to your iPhone, or a FaceTime call to your iPod touch. See "Getting Some FaceTime with Your iPhone 4 or iPod touch" in this chapter for details on making and receiving FaceTime video calls.

7. **Tap the Email button to add an e-mail address using the on-screen keyboard, and tap the home label to change the label for the type of e-mail address.**

   After you tap Email, the on-screen keyboard appears screen appears under the field to enter the e-mail address. Tap the label home to change the label describing the e-mail address. After you type an e-mail address, another Email button appears below it, so that you can type more e-mail addresses — scroll the screen to see it.

8. **(Optional) Scroll down and tap the next Email button to add more e-mail addresses, following the instructions in Step 7 for each e-mail address.**

9. **(Optional) Tap the URL button to add a Web page URL for the contact and tap the home page label to change the label for the type of Web page.**

   After typing a Web page URL, another URL button appears below it so that you can type more Web page URLs — scroll the screen to see it.

10. **Tap Add New Address, tap the home label to change the label for the type of address, and then add the address information.**

    The keyboard appears with entry fields for Street, City, State, and ZIP. Tap the country field to set the country and the label button (set to Home) for the type of address. After typing the address, another Add New Address button appears below it, so that you can type more addresses — scroll the screen to see it.

11. **(Optional) Tap Add Field to add more fields to the contact.**

    You can add a prefix, middle name, suffix, phonetic first and last names, nickname, job title, department, birthday, date, or note. As you tap each field, the New Contact screen appears with the keyboard to type in the information.

12. **(Optional) Add a photo.**

    To add a photo, tap Add Photo in the upper-left corner of the New Contact screen. A pop-up menu appears on an iPod touch or iPhone with Take Photo, Choose Photo, or Cancel; on an iPad, the Photo Albums screen pops up so that you can tap a photo album and then tap a photo. The Take Photo option on an iPod touch or iPhone takes you to the Take Picture screen, where you can tap the camera shutter button to take a picture. (See Chapter 17 for details on taking pictures.) The Choose Photo option takes you to the Photos app, where you can tap a photo album and then tap a photo. Finally, tap Set Photo (or Cancel).

13. **Tap Done in the upper-right corner of the New Contact screen to save the contact information (or Cancel in the upper-left corner to cancel the contact information).**

To edit a contact, tap the contact to see the contact's Info screen and then tap Edit in the upper-right corner of the Info screen on an iPod touch or iPhone, or at the bottom of the iPad screen, to show the circled minus (–) sign and plus (+) sign buttons.

You can edit or delete any information for a contact while leaving the rest of the information intact. Tap any field to edit the information in that field. Tap the circled minus sign (–) next to the information to reveal a Delete button. Tap the Delete button to delete the information, or tap the circled minus sign again to leave it alone.

To change a photo, tap the existing photo in the upper-left corner of the Info screen. A pop-up menu appears for you to tap Take Photo (iPod touch or iPhone only), Choose Photo (Choose Existing Photo on an iPad), Edit Photo, Delete Photo, or Cancel (iPod touch or iPhone only). Tap Choose Photo (or Choose Existing Photo on an iPad) to choose a photo from the Photo app library.

Tap Done in the upper-right corner of the Info screen to finish editing and return to the contact information.

To delete a contact entirely, tap Edit, scroll down to the bottom, and then tap Delete Contact. Remember, if you do this, the contact is also deleted from your contact list on your computer when you sync your iPad, iPod touch, or iPhone.

Earth, Wind, and Finance on Your iPad, iPod touch or iPhone

You can use the Maps app to find almost any location on Earth and obtain driving directions — without having to ask someone out on the street. Your iPad, iPod touch, or iPhone offers Location Services to nail down the unit's physical location, and it offers that information to the Maps app and any other app that needs it, so you can instantly find out where you are in the world.

Your iPad, iPod touch, or iPhone also runs apps that can connect to the Internet to display the most recent information — such as the Apple-supplied Weather and Stocks apps on an iPod touch or iPhone, or third-party apps such as The Weather Channel or Weather HD, and QFolio HD — NASDAQ OMX Portfolio Manager. You can personalize the Stocks app or QFolio HD to reflect your exact portfolio, and you can add cities to the Weather or Weather HD apps to check conditions before you travel to them.

Consulting Maps

The Maps app provides street maps, satellite photos, and hybrid street-satellite views of locations all over the world. It also offers detailed driving directions from any location to just about any other location — unless you can't get there from here.

Tap Maps on the Home screen and a map appears, ready for zooming, scrolling, or searching specific locations. To find out where you are, tap the location button in the lower-left corner of the map screen on an iPod touch or iPhone (refer to Figure 20-3, left side), or the compass icon at the top of the iPad map screen (for a sneak preview, see Figure 20-6). The first time you use Maps, a dialog appears asking whether Maps can use your current location; tap OK to use it. The map then changes to show your general location with a pulsating circle emanating from a blue dot representing your approximate physical location, as shown in Figure 20-3 (right side). This circle continues to shrink as Maps retrieves more-accurate information.

You can zoom in to the map by double-tapping the map with one finger or unpinching with your fingers. To zoom out, pinch with your fingers or double-tap with two fingers. You can also drag the map to pan around it and see more areas.

Figure 20-3:
Maps initial screen (left); my current location (right).

To find a location and see a map, tap the search-entry field at the top of the Maps screen (refer to Figure 20-3, left side). The keyboard appears so that you can enter information. You can find any location by its address or closest landmark, or you can find the physical address of a friend: Type the name of someone in your contacts list or an address, an intersection, the name of a landmark or of a general area, or a ZIP code.

For example, to search for a friend, start typing the person's name. If the letters you type match any names with street addresses in your Contacts list, Maps offers them up as suggestions. Tap a suggested name to look up that person's home or business address.

To search for a landmark, an intersection, a ZIP code, or a type of business, type as much as you know into the search field — such as **94111 pizza** for a pizza shop in the 94111 ZIP code. If the landmark is well known, type its name, as shown in Figure 20-4 (left side). Then tap the Search key on the keyboard. A red pin appears to mark the location you've searched for on the map (see Figure 20-4, right side), with a label showing the address.

To clear the entry from the search field quickly, tap the X on the right side of the field. You can then type a new search term.

Figure 20-4:
Type a
search
term and
tap a sug-
gestion or
the Search
button (left)
to see the
location
(right).

If you search for the name of a business or type of business *after* searching for your own location, Maps is smart enough to locate the closest ones. Multiple pins appear on the map, showing the location of each business.

To bookmark a location after searching for it, tap the circled right arrow on the right side of the pin's label (refer to Figure 20-4, right side) to open the Info screen, as shown in Figure 20-5 (left side). You can then mark the spot with a bookmark that includes a name and description or do other things such as get directions. Scroll the Info screen to find and tap the Add to Bookmarks button at the bottom, which brings up the keyboard so that you can type a name for the location. Tap Save in the upper-right corner of the

Add Bookmark screen to save the bookmark (or Cancel to cancel the bookmark). Tap Map in the upper-left corner of the Info screen on an iPod touch or iPhone to go back to the map.

To go directly to a bookmarked location, tap the Bookmarks icon to the right of the search-entry field on an iPod touch or iPhone (refer to Figure 20-3, left side), or the left of the search-entry field on an iPad, and then tap a location.

Want to see what the location looks like? You can change the view of the location to show a satellite image (if available), a hybrid of street view and satellite, or a list of bookmarked locations. Tap the options button — the curled-page icon in the lower-right corner on an iPod touch or iPhone (refer to Figure 20-3, left side) or the page curl in the lower-right corner on an iPad — to see a menu of options underneath the map. Then tap Satellite to view a satellite image of the site. You can zoom in to the image the same way you zoom in to the map. You can also view a hybrid of satellite image and street map — tap the options button and then tap Hybrid in the menu underneath the map.

Figure 20-5:
The Info screen (left) and the start and end locations for directions (right).

To get driving directions from one location to another, you first need to search for or pinpoint a location and then tap Directions at the bottom of the map screen. For example, if you want to get directions from your current location to a bookmarked location, first find your physical location on the map by tapping the location button as I describe previously, and then tap Directions. In the Directions screen that appears, your current location already occupies the Start field. Tap the Bookmarks icon in the End field and select a bookmarked location for the End field.

You can tap a pin on a map to see the Info screen for that location (shown in Figure 20-5, left side), and then tap Directions to Here or Directions from Here to get directions. The Directions screen appears, with the first location selected as either the Start or End, as shown in Figure 20-5 (right side) on an iPod touch or iPhone, and Figure 20-6 on an iPad. You can also type entries for both the Start and End fields by tapping those fields and using the keyboard.

After setting your Start and End locations, tap Route in the lower-right corner of the keyboard on an iPod touch or iPhone (refer to Figure 20-5, right side), or Start in the lower-right corner of the iPad screen shown in Figure 20-6, to see the route on the map.

You can switch the entry for Start to End (or vice versa) by tapping the looped arrow button to the left of the Start and End fields on an iPod touch or iPhone (as shown in Figure 20-5, right side), or between the fields on an iPad (as shown in Figure 20-6). Using this button, you can get directions one way; then tap the button to reverse the Start and End fields to get directions for the way back.

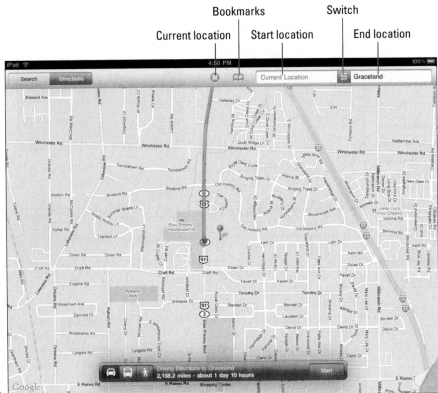

Figure 20-6:
The start
and end
locations for
directions
on an iPad.

As shown in Figure 20-7 (left side) — though you can't see its color in this book — the route on the map is purple on an iPod touch or iPhone and blue on an iPad, with pins marking the start and end locations.

TIP

You can tap the car icon at the top of the screen to see driving directions and the approximate driving time. If traffic data is available, the driving time is adjusted accordingly, but don't expect miracles — the information depends on data collected and services provided by third parties, not by Apple, and traffic patterns change. You can also touch the bus icon to see public transit directions, or the walking-man icon to see walking directions.

To view directions one step at a time on the map, tap Start in the upper-right corner of the iPod touch or iPhone screen (see Figure 20-7, left side) or the lower-right corner of the iPad screen (shown in Figure 20-6) to see the first leg of the journey. Then tap the right-arrow button to see the next stretch. You can also tap the left-arrow button in any of the step-by-step directions to go back a step, as shown in Figure 20-7 (right side). The Maps app patiently walks you through your entire journey.

Figure 20-7:
View the route and tap Start (left) for step-by-step directions (right).

To view all the legs of your journey in a list on an iPod touch or iPhone, tap the options button in the lower-right corner of the display and tap List; on an iPad, tap the list button on the left side of the driving instructions along the bottom of the screen. Then tap any location in the list to see a map showing that leg of the trip.

Riding the storms with Weather

The Weather app that Apple provides with your iPod touch or iPhone looks up the current temperature and weather conditions, and it provides a six-day forecast for any cities of your choice. (On an iPad, you can use free or paid third-party apps such as The Weather Channel, WeatherBug, or Weather HD.)

To use Weather, tap Weather on the Home screen. In daytime, the weather screen is light blue, and at night, it's dark purple. What makes Weather useful is your ability to add your own cities — as many as you need — so that you can look up the weather in multiple locations instantly.

To add a city, follow these steps:

1. **Tap the *i* button in the lower-right corner of the weather display for your city, as shown in Figure 20-8 (left side).**

2. **Tap the plus (+) sign in the upper-left corner of the Weather screen (Figure 20-8, center).**

   A location field appears with the on-screen keyboard (Figure 20-8, right side).

3. **Enter the city's name or ZIP code — as you type, suggestions appear below in a list.**

4. **Choose one of the suggestions or continue typing the city name or ZIP code and then tap Search.**

Figure 20-8:
Tap the *i*
button in
Weather
(left) to view
the list of
cities (cen-
ter) and to
add another
city (right).

The city you chose appears in the list of cities on the Weather screen, with a circled minus (–) sign next to it on the left and three horizontal gray bars on the right.

At this point, you can add more cities by tapping the plus (+) sign in the upper-left corner again. You can also reorder the list of cities by dragging the three gray bars next to a city to a new place in the list.

To delete a city, tap the circled minus sign next to the city name (see Figure 20-8, center) to show the Delete button. Then tap the Delete button to delete it (or tap the circled minus sign again to leave it alone).

Tap the Done button in the upper-right corner of the Weather screen to finish adding cities and see the weather display for your city.

To switch from one city to the next, flick the city weather screen right or left or tap the tiny white buttons at the bottom of the city weather display (refer to Figure 20-8, left side).

Tapping your money maker with Stocks

You can check your financial stocks, funds, and indexes with the Apple-supplied Stocks app on your iPod touch or iPhone. (On an iPad, you can use free or paid third-party apps such as QFolio HD — NASDAQ OMX Portfolio Manager or Bloomberg for iPad.) And whether the news is good or bad, you can quickly e-mail your broker — see Chapter 19.

Tap Stocks on your iPod touch or iPhone Home screen. The Stocks app displays a few stocks and indexes you may be interested in (such as Apple and Google), and it shows updated quotes (although quotes may be delayed by up to 20 minutes). Scroll the Stocks list by dragging or flicking it with your finger.

Swipe the lower section of the Stocks screen for a summary, a graph (as shown in Figure 20-9, left side), or the latest news. To see a current graph of the stock, swipe the lower section to the center and tap the 1d (one day), 1w (one week), 1m (one month), 3m (three months), 6m (six months), 1y (one year), or 2y (two years) button above the graph in the stock reader. Tap the change number next to each stock to switch to show the percentage change, the market capitalization, or the change in price.

Of course, you want to add your portfolio to Stocks. To add a stock, index, or fund to watch, here's what you do:

1. **Tap the *i* button in the lower-right corner of the stock reader, as shown in Figure 20-9 (left side).**

2. **Tap the plus (+) sign in the upper-left corner of the Stocks screen (Figure 20-9, center).**

   The Add Stock field appears with the keyboard (Figure 20-9, right side).

3. **Enter the stock symbol or company name (or index or fund name).**

   As you type, suggestions appear below in a list.

4. **Choose one of the suggestions or continue typing the symbol or name and then touch Search.**

   The stock, fund, or index you chose appears in the list on the Stocks screen, with a circled minus sign (–) next to it on the left and three horizontal gray bars on the right.

Figure 20-9:
Touch the
i button in
Stocks (left)
to view the
list (center)
and to add
another
stock, fund,
or index
(right).

At this point, if you want to add more stocks, funds, or indexes, tap the plus (+) sign in the upper-left corner again. To reorder a list of stocks, drag the three gray bars next to a stock to a new place in the list.

To delete a stock, tap the circled minus sign next to the stock name (refer to Figure 20-9, center) to show the Delete button. Then tap the Delete button to delete it (or tap the circled minus sign again to leave it alone).

Tap the Done button in the upper-right corner of the Stocks screen to finish adding stocks and see the stock reader.

A Day in the Social Life on an iPad, iPod touch, or iPhone

Connecting socially by computer isn't new, but connecting on a digital network anytime and from anywhere makes social networking more instant and gratifying. You can use your iPad, iPod touch, or iPhone to stay in touch with your connections on the leading social networks, including Facebook, MySpace, and Twitter — viewing and typing messages, chatting, uploading and sharing photos, joining groups, and so on.

Ain't it good to know you've got a Facebook friend

Facebook is the fastest-growing free-access social networking site as of this writing, with more than 400 million active users worldwide. If you're one of them (as I am), you already know that you can add friends, send them messages, and update your personal profile with photos, videos, links, and all sorts of Facebook widgets that extend the service's functions.

Although you can do all this using a browser on your computer and using Safari on your iPad, iPod touch, or iPhone, the site itself is far too cumbersome for easy access that way on an iPod touch or iPhone. You can instead use the Facebook app, which lets you check your friends' status updates and photos, start a conversation in Facebook Chat, and upload images from your iPod touch or iPhone. (On an iPad with its large display, you can use Safari to access Facebook as well as apps such as Alive Albums to access FaceBook photos, or Friendly Browser to browse FaceBook.)

After downloading the Facebook app (see Chapter 6 for details on downloading apps from the App Store), tap Facebook on the Home screen. If this is your first time using the app, a dialog appears asking if you would like Facebook to push notifications, such as alerts, sounds, and numeric icon badges, whenever your Facebook account receives messages and notifications. (See Chapter 4 for details on setting app notifications.) Tap OK to allow notifications, or tap Don't Allow to stop them from happening. (You may want to disallow them to save battery power.)

You can then log in to your Facebook account. Tap the E-Mail field and the keyboard appears; type your e-mail address for signing in, and then tap the Password field and type your password. Your Facebook home screen appears showing your live feed. Tap the grid button in the upper left corner to see the Facebook icons for all of the app's features. If you have any messages in your Inbox, a number appears on top of the Inbox icon.

After logging in, the Facebook app remembers your username and password so that you don't have to type them to log in again. (Of course, that means if anyone grabs your iPod touch or iPhone, they have access to your Facebook account — use a passcode to lock up your iPod touch or iPhone, as I describe in Chapter 4, so that no one can use it without the passcode.) If you don't want the Facebook app to remember your login info, tap the Logout button in the upper-right corner of Facebook's icons screen.

The Facebook icons screen includes the Profile icon for showing your profile, the Friends icon to access a list of your Facebook friends, and the Inbox icon to check your messages. You can also tap Chat to chat directly with any of your friends who are online.

The Facebook app even lets you upload and share photos: Tap the Photos icon and then tap the add (+) button to add a new album (type its name and description). You can then tap the camera icon and choose Take Photo to snap a photo or Choose from Library to pick a photo from your iPod touch or iPhone photo albums.

A MySpace odyssey

So you want to be a MySpace cowboy or cowgirl? MySpace, owned by Fox Interactive Media, was the most popular mainstream social networking site until Facebook came along. Today, it's the number-two service, and it's still an awesomely huge network. MySpace focuses on music, movies, and TV shows — just about every band in the universe has a MySpace page, and it's easy to add music to your profile.

You can use Safari on your iPad, iPod touch, or iPhone to access MySpace, but like most social networks, the home page you see is far too cumbersome for easy access that way on an iPod touch or iPhone. The MySpace Mobile for iPhone app is much easier to use for the iPod touch or iPhone. It lets you send and receive messages, check status updates and photos, stay up to date on bulletins, and upload images from your iPod touch or iPhone. (On an iPad with its large display, you are better off using Safari to access MySpace.)

After downloading the MySpace app (see Chapter 6 for app downloading details), tap MySpace on the Home screen. To sign into your MySpace account, tap the blank field under E-Mail and the keyboard appears; type your e-mail address for signing in, and then tap the field under Password and type your password. As you sign in, you can turn on the Remember Me option so that the MySpace app remembers your username and password so that you don't have to log in again.

After you log in, your MySpace Home screen appears with menu selections for viewing and editing your profile, checking the status and mood messages from your friends, checking friend updates, adding comments, reading bulletins, reading blogs, and changing your settings.

Along the bottom of the MySpace screen are the Home button for returning to the Home screen, and buttons for Mail (to check messages), Requests (to view and respond to requests), Friends (for a list of your MySpace friends), and Photos (to upload photos to your MySpace page). To add photos, tap Photos to see the photos already on your MySpace page and then tap the Add Photos button. You can then snap a photo or pick a photo from your iPod touch or iPhone photo albums.

Dedicated follower of Twitter

The most talked-about newcomer to the social network scene is Twitter, a free social messaging utility for staying connected with people in real time. With Twitter, you can post and receive messages that are 140 characters or less — called *tweets*. All public tweets are available to read on the public timeline, or you can read just the ones posted by the Twitter members you follow. You can post a tweet that can be read by all your followers and by anyone reading the public tweets.

Members use Twitter to organize impromptu gatherings, carry on a group conversation, or just send a quick update to let people know what's going on. Companies use Twitter to announce products and carry on conversations with their customers. You can use Safari on your iPad, iPod touch, or iPhone to access Twitter, but there are alternatives that offer a better Twitter experience on your iPad, iPod touch, or iPhone.

For example, you can use the Twitter app with your iPod touch or iPhone to easily flip through all your messages with the flick of a finger. Tap the Twitter app icon on your Home screen, and tap Sign In to sign into your Twitter account. After signing in, you can see recent tweets, search the Twitter timeline, post a new tweet, send direct messages and replies to others on Twitter, and add new friends (called *followers*).

The App Store has several apps for accessing Twitter, but my favorites as of this writing are Twitterific and TweetDeck (both free), which are offered as iPhone and iPad apps. They do all the basic stuff you'd expect a Twitter client for an iPod touch or iPhone to do: You can read messages from people you follow, post messages of your own, and get alerted to private direct messages and public replies.

And wherever you go, "tweetness follows." Twitterific, TweetDeck, and other apps can tap into the location services of your iPad, iPod touch, or iPhone so that with your permission, it can let your followers know where you are and let you know when your followers are posting from a nearby location. You can set options for viewing messages, optimize the interface for left-handed operation, and use its own mini-browser to view linked Web pages without having to quit the app and run Safari. Tweet dreams!

Getting Some FaceTime with Your iPhone 4 or iPod touch

No matter how we communicate, it helps sometimes to have a little face time. Apple has engineered a solution that lets your iPhone 4 or fourth-generation iPod touch make video calls over Wi-Fi to another iPhone 4 or fourth-generation iPod touch. You can use either the front or back camera with FaceTime — the front camera has just the right field of view and focal length to focus on your face at arm's length, but you can switch to the back camera to show what's happening around you. And FaceTime can the use the cameras in either portrait or landscape orientation.

FaceTime calls are not any more intrusive than phone calls — your iPod touch or iPhone rings (you can sync ringtones, as I show in Chapter 8), and an invitation pops up on your screen asking if you want to accept the call. Tap Accept, and the video call begins.

To use FaceTime, you need a fourth-generation iPod touch or iPhone, and be connected to the Internet over Wi-Fi, as I describe in Chapter 4. The person you're calling also needs to be connected to the Internet over Wi-Fi and using a fourth-generation iPod touch or iPhone 4.

With an iPhone 4, you can call any other iPhone 4 user by phone number, and switch to FaceTime. You can also call an iPod touch user by selecting the person in your contacts list — FaceTime uses the person's e-mail address. No setup is required to receive FaceTime calls on an iPhone 4; people can call your iPhone 4 phone number.

Setting up your calling address (iPod touch only)

On an iPod touch, you also need to sign into FaceTime using the FaceTime app and an Apple ID (you don't need to use an app or sign into an account on an iPhone 4, because it uses your carrier account). If you already have an iTunes Store account, MobileMe account, or other Apple account, you can use that Apple ID with FaceTime on your iPod touch (see Chapter 4 about getting an iTunes Store account). After you've signed in, you don't need to do it again for every call.

To sign in, tap the FaceTime icon on theHome screen, tap the Get Started button, enter your Apple ID and password, and then tap Sign In. If you don't already have an Apple account, tap Create New Account to set one up. You can then enter your account information on the New Account screen (see Chapter 4 for details on setting up an account).

On the Location screen, choose your current region and tap Next. You can then enter your e-mail address, which is the address that others will use to call your iPod touch in FaceTime, and then tap Next. If this is the first time for using this address for FaceTime, you will need to check for new e-mail in that account and reply to the confirmation message from Apple — click Verify Now in the confirmation message, and sign into your account to verify it. (If you've already added the account to Mail on your iPod touch, verification is automatic.) The e-mail address doesn't need to be the same as the address you entered for your account ID, but it must be a working e-mail address.

If you use more than one e-mail address, you can add the others to FaceTime on your iPod touch so that people can use them to call you. Choose Settings⇨ FaceTime, then tap Add Another Email. FaceTime verifies the e-mail address as I described above. Now others can call you using any of the email addresses you provided.

Making a video call

You can make a FaceTime video call by selecting a contact in the Contacts app and tapping the FaceTime button in the contact information screen to start the call.

On an iPhone 4, you can select a contact in either Contacts or Phone, and then tap the FaceTime button to start the call. If you are already on a voice call with a person and you want to switch to a video call, tap the FaceTime button in the call options screen.

On the iPod touch, you can select a contact in the Contacts app, or tap the FaceTime app, and then tap the Favorites, Recents, or Contacts icons along the bottom of the FaceTime screen. You can then select a contact and tap the FaceTime button.

A menu pops up with the contact's phone numbers and e-mail addresses. Choose an e-mail address or phone number to establish the video call.

FaceTime places the call, and sends an invitation to the contact. If your contact taps the Accept button in the invitation, you then see the other person on your screen, as shown in Figure 20-10.

Figure 20-10:
A FaceTime
call in
progress.

What you can do while calling

While communicating with your contact in FaceTime (refer to Figure 20-10), A picture-in-picture window shows the image from your iPod touch or iPhone 4 that the other person sees. You can drag the picture-in-picture window to any corner. You can use FaceTime in portrait or landscape orientation — when you rotate the iPod touch or iPhone, the image your contact sees changes to match.

To avoid unwanted orientation changes as you move the camera around, lock the iPod touch or iPhone in portrait orientation as I describe in Chapter 3.

To switch from the front camera to the back camera, tap the switch camera button once; tap it again to switch back to the front camera. You can also tap the mute button to mute your iPod touch or iPhone microphone so that your contact can't hear you, although your contact can still see you, and you can still see and hear your contact. To end the video call, tap the End button.

Don't be shy about using another app during a FaceTime call, if you want to. Just press the Home button, and choose any app. You can still talk with your contact over FaceTime, but you can't see each other. To return to the video portion of the call from another app, tap the green bar that appears at the top of the app's screen.

You can turn FaceTime off if you don't want to receive any calls — on an iPhone 4, choose Settings⇨Phone (on an iPod touch, choose Settings⇨ FaceTime), and tap On for the FaceTime option to turn it off. On an iPod touch, you can also sign into your FaceTime account, or create a new account, from the settings screen by tapping Account or Create New Account.

Part VI
The Part of Tens

The 5th Wave   By Rich Tennant

"In fact it does come with a compass."

In this part . . .

In this part, you find two chapters chock-full of information.

✓ Chapter 21 offers ten common iPad, iPod, and iPhone recovery steps that everyone must take at one time or another, including powering on and off, resetting settings, resetting the system, updating the software, and restoring the iPad, iPod, or iPhone to its original factory condition.

✓ Chapter 22 offers the top ten tips not found elsewhere in the book, including tips on keeping your battery juiced, your screen clean, and your songs rated.

Chapter 21

Ten Steps to Recovery

. . . .

. . . .

*T*his no-nonsense chapter may not be fun, but it's necessary. Humans aren't perfect, and neither are the machines they make. If your iPad, iPod, or iPhone stops working as it should, or an iPad, iPod touch, or iPhone app causes it to freeze up, you can turn to this chapter.

This chapter also covers updating the firmware and software on your iPad, iPod, or iPhone. (*Firmware* is software encoded in hardware.) All software devices need to be updated now and then — it's a good thing because new versions fix known bugs and add improvements.

Finally, I describe how to restore your iPad, iPod, or iPhone to its factory default condition. Restoring to factory condition is a drastic measure that erases any music or information, but it usually solves a software glitch when nothing else does.

Powering Up and Unlocking

To turn on an iPod classic, press any part of the click wheel. If an iPod classic refuses to turn on, check the position of the hold switch on the top. The hold switch locks the iPod buttons so that you don't accidentally activate them. Slide the hold switch to the left, hiding the orange layer, to unlock the buttons. (If you see the orange layer underneath one end of the hold switch, the switch is still in the locked position.)

The "hold" switch for an iPod shuffle is actually the three-position switch (or the on-off switch on older models). Slide the three-way switch to expose the green layer underneath to turn on your iPod shuffle.

To turn on an iPad, iPod nano, iPod touch, or iPhone, press the sleep/wake button. The iPad, iPod touch, or iPhone displays the message Slide to unlock — slide your finger across this message to unlock it.

If you previously set a passcode for the iPad, iPod, or iPhone (see Chapter 4), you must enter the passcode; otherwise, you need to completely restore the iPad, iPod, or iPhone to its original factory condition, as I describe later in this chapter.

Keep in mind that starting up an iPad, iPod touch, or iPhone that was completely turned off takes quite a bit of power — more than if it woke from sleep. If you do turn it off, plug it into AC power or your computer before turning it back on.

Powering Down

The iPad nano goes to sleep after a few minutes of inactivity. An iPad, iPod, or iPhone should be set to go to sleep automatically, unless you change the settings.

The iPod classic lets you set its backlight to turn off automatically by choosing Settings⇨General⇨Backlight and picking the amount of time to remain on (or choosing Always On). This is similar to putting it to sleep.

You can set your iPad, iPod touch, or iPhone to automatically go to sleep by choosing Settings⇨General⇨Auto-Lock and choosing the amount of time before sleeping (or choosing Never, to prevent automatic sleep).

You can force an iPod classic to power off by pressing the play/pause button.

To force your iPad, iPod nano, iPod touch, or iPhone to go to sleep, press the sleep/wake button on the top. To turn it off completely so that it has to start its system again from scratch, press and hold the sleep/wake button on top for a few seconds until a red slider appears on the screen that says Slide to power off and then slide your finger across the slider to turn it off.

Stopping a Frozen App

Apple is not perfect, and neither are the many thousands of developers who create the apps that run on an iPad, iPod touch, or iPhone, and the "extra" or click-wheel games on an iPod nano or iPod classic.

If your iPad, iPod touch, or iPhone freezes while running an app, press and hold the sleep/wake button on top for a few seconds until a red slider appears on the screen that says `Slide to power off` — then press and hold the physical Home button until the application quits. If that doesn't work, see the previous section in this chapter.

If your iPod nano or iPod classic itself freezes, you need to reset its system — see the next section.

Resetting Your iPad, iPod, or iPhone System

Sometimes problems arise with electronics and software that cause your iPad, iPod, or iPhone to stop working properly. You can usually fix the problem by resetting it and restarting the iPad, iPod, or iPhone system from scratch — just like resetting a computer. Resetting the system does *not* restore the iPad, iPod, or iPhone to its original factory condition, nor does it erase anything — your content, apps, and settings remain intact.

Before resetting the system, you may want to connect the iPad, iPod, or iPhone to a power outlet by using the AC power adapter. You can reset your iPad, iPod, or iPhone without connecting it to power if it has enough juice in its battery. However, if you have access to power, it makes sense to use it because the reset operation uses power, and starting up your iPad, iPod, or iPhone from scratch again also uses power.

To reset the iPad, iPod touch, or iPhone, press and hold the sleep/wake button and the physical Home button at the same time for about fifteen seconds, ignoring the red slider that says `Slide to power off`, until the screen goes blank and the Apple logo appears.

To reset the iPod nano, press the sleep/wake button and the volume down button for six seconds, until the Apple logo appears.

To reset the iPod classic, follow these steps:

1. **Toggle the hold switch.**

   Slide the hold switch to the right, exposing the orange layer, to lock the buttons, and then slide it back to unlock.

2. **Press the Menu and select buttons simultaneously and hold for at least six seconds or until the Apple logo appears; then release the buttons when you see the Apple logo.**

   The appearance of the Apple logo signals that your iPod is resetting itself, so you no longer have to hold down the buttons.

Release the Menu and select buttons as soon as you see the Apple logo. If you continue to press the buttons after the logo appears, the iPod displays the low battery icon, and you must connect it to a power source before using it again.

To reset the iPod shuffle, first disconnect it from your computer (if you haven't already done so) and then slide the three-position switch to the Off position. The green stripe under the switch should not be visible. Wait five seconds and then switch the slider back to the Shuffle Songs or Play in Order position.

After resetting, everything should be back to normal, including your music and data files.

Resetting iPad, iPod, or iPhone Settings

Perhaps someone played a practical joke on you and set your iPod language to German (and you don't understand German). Or maybe a fee-based Wi-Fi network has captured your iPad, iPod touch, or iPhone and won't let go. Sometimes you need to reset your settings and preferences.

You can reset all your iPod nano or iPod classic settings, or all or part of your iPad, iPod touch, or iPhone settings, while leaving your content and personal information intact. On an iPad, iPod touch, or iPhone, you can also erase all content and reset network settings.

To reset iPod nano or iPod classic settings, choose Settings⇨Reset Settings from the iPod nano Home screen or iPod classic main menu, and then select Reset (or Cancel to cancel). This resets all the items on the Settings menu to their default settings.

To see your resetting options on an iPad, iPod touch, or iPhone, choose Settings⇨General⇨Reset from the Home screen. The Reset screen appears with the following options:

✔ **Reset All Settings:** To return your iPad, iPod touch, or iPhone to its original condition with no preferences or settings while still keeping your content and your personal information (including contacts, calendars, e-mail accounts, and apps with their data) intact, tap Reset All Settings.

✔ **Erase All Content and Settings:** To erase *everything*, first connect the iPad, iPod touch, or iPhone to your computer or a power adapter and then tap Erase All Content and Settings. This operation can take hours! You can't use the iPad, iPod touch, or iPhone until it finishes. It may be easier and faster to do a full restore from iTunes, as I describe in the section "Restoring to Factory Condition," later in this chapter.

✔ **Reset Network Settings:** You can reset your network settings so that your previously used networks are removed from the Wi-Fi list. This type of reset is useful if you can't find any other way to stop a Wi-Fi network from connecting automatically to your iPad, iPod touch, or iPhone — just tap Reset Network Settings, and you're automatically disconnected. For more details about choosing Wi-Fi networks, see Chapter 4.

✔ **Reset Keyboard Dictionary:** To reset the keyboard dictionary, tap this button. This erases all words that have been added to the dictionary. (Words are added when you reject words suggested by the keyboard and type the word — see Chapter 3 for details.)

✔ **Reset Home Screen Layout:** To reset your Home screen to the default arrangement, tap this button.

✔ **Reset Location Warnings:** Location warnings are requests by apps to use the Location Services. The iPad, iPod touch, or iPhone stops displaying these warnings the second time you tap OK. If you want to start displaying the warnings again, tap Reset Location Warnings.

Checking the Software Version

Make sure that you use the newest version of iTunes. To check for the availability of an updated version for Windows, run iTunes and choose Help⇨Check for iTunes Updates.

If you use a Mac and you enabled the Software Update option in your System Preferences, Apple automatically informs you of updates to your Apple software for the Mac, including iTunes, Safari, iCal, and Address Book. All you need to do is select which updates to download and then click the Install button to download them.

To determine which version of the iOS system software is installed on your iPad, iPod touch, or iPhone, choose Settings⇨General⇨About from the Home screen. To see which version of the iPod system software is installed on an iPod nano or iPod classic, choose Settings⇨About from iPod nano Home screen or the iPod classic the main menu. Next to the word *Version* is information that describes the software version installed.

Updating the Software

Always keep your iPad, iPod, or iPhone updated with new versions of the system software that controls it. iTunes automatically checks for updates of this software and lets you update your iPad, iPod, or iPhone without affecting the music or data stored on it.

iTunes tells you whether your iPad, iPod, or iPhone has the newest software installed. Connect the iPad, iPod, or iPhone to your computer, select it in the iTunes source pane (in the Devices section), and you'll see the Summary page appear to the right of the source pane. The Version section of the page tells you whether your iPad, iPod, or iPhone software is up to date and when iTunes will check for new software.

If an update is available, a dialog appears to ask permission to download it. Go ahead and click the OK button to update the software; you'll be glad you did because Apple often includes new features and battery-saving upgrades. After updating the software, iTunes continues syncing the iPad, iPod, or iPhone until it is finished.

Restoring to Factory Condition

You can restore your iPad, iPod, or iPhone to its original factory condition. This operation erases its storage and returns the iPad, iPod, or iPhone to its original settings. It's the last resort for fixing problems, and it's the only choice if you intend to change the computer you're using for syncing your iPad, iPod, or iPhone.

To restore an iPad, iPod, or iPhone, follow these steps for both the Mac and Windows versions of iTunes:

1. **Connect the iPad, iPod, or iPhone to your computer.**

   iTunes opens automatically.

2. **Select the iPad, iPod, or iPhone in the Devices section of the source pane, and click the Summary tab if it isn't already selected.**

   The Summary pane appears to the right of the source pane.

3. **Click the Restore button.**

   An alert dialog appears to confirm that you want to restore the iPad, iPod, or iPhone.

4. **Click the Restore button again to confirm the restore operation.**

   A progress bar appears, indicating the progress of the restore operation. iTunes notifies you when the restore is finished.

Setting Up and Syncing

After the restore operation finishes (as previously described), iTunes displays the setup screen for a newly minted iPad, iPod, or iPhone — the restore operation makes it like new again.

In the setup screen, as described in Chapter 2, you can give your iPod nano or iPod classic a new name.

For an iPad, iPod touch, or iPhone, iTunes provides the options to restore the settings from a previously backed-up iPad, iPod touch, or iPhone, or to set it up as new. If you choose to set it up as new, you can give your iPad, iPod touch, or iPhone a new name and set the automatic options, as I describe in Chapter 2. See the next section in this chapter if you want to restore from a backup.

The restore operation wipes out your content and apps. If you don't restore from a backup (see the next section), you need to replace them by syncing your iPad, iPod, or iPhone with your computer's iTunes library, as I describe in Chapter 8, and with personal information (contacts, calendars, notes, e-mail accounts, and bookmarks), as I describe in Chapter 9. You also need to resync your pictures, as I describe in Chapter 17.

Restoring Settings from a Backup (iPad, iPod touch, and iPhone)

iTunes provides protection and backs up your iPad, iPod touch, or iPhone settings when you sync the device, so that you can restore the settings you use to customize the device and its apps, including Wi-Fi network settings, the keyboard dictionary, and settings for contacts, calendars, and e-mail accounts. This backup comes in handy if you want to apply the settings to a new iPad, iPod touch, or iPhone, or to one that you had to restore to its factory condition.

To restore your settings, connect your new or restored iPad, iPod touch, or iPhone to the same computer and copy of iTunes you used before. iTunes should open automatically. (If it doesn't, open iTunes manually.) As you start the setup process, iTunes gives you the choice of restoring the settings from a previously backed-up iPad, iPod touch, or iPhone, or setting up the iPad, iPod touch, or iPhone as new. Choose the option to restore the settings and then click the Continue button to finish setting up your iPad, iPod touch, or iPhone. If you choose to set it up as new, follow the step-by-step instructions in Chapter 2 for setting it up.

To delete the backed-up settings for an iPad, iPod touch, or iPhone, open iTunes and choose iTunes⇨Preferences (on a Mac) or Edit⇨Preferences (on a Windows PC). Click the Devices tab, select the iPad, iPod touch, or iPhone in the Device backups list, and then click Remove Backup. You don't need to connect the iPad, iPod touch, or iPhone to do this.

Chapter 22

Ten Tangible Tips

*T*his book is filled with tips, but I've put ten truly handy ones in this chapter that just didn't fit in elsewhere but that can help make your iPad, iPod, or iPhone experience a completely satisfying one.

Saving the Life of Your Battery

Follow these simple rules to extend your battery life:

  ✔ Don't keep an iPad, iPod, or iPhone in a snug carrying case when charging — that snug case can cause overheating.

  ✔ Top it off with power whenever it's convenient.

  ✔ Set your iPad, iPod touch, or iPhone to automatically go to sleep by choosing Settings⇨General⇨Auto-Lock from the Home screen.

  ✔ Set the iPod classic backlight to turn off automatically by choosing Settings⇨General⇨Backlight and picking the amount of time to remain on (or choosing Always On).

Everything else you need to know about your battery is in Chapter 1.

Keeping Your Screen Clean

If the iPad, iPod, or iPhone display has excessive moisture on it from humidity or wet fingers, wipe it with a soft, dry cloth. If it's dirty, use a soft, slightly damp, lint-free cloth — an inexpensive eyeglass cleaning cloth sold in vision-care stores or pharmacies is a good choice. By no means should you use window cleaners, household cleaners, aerosol sprays, solvents, alcohol, ammonia, or abrasives — they can scratch or otherwise damage the display. Also, try not to get any moisture in any of the openings as it could short out the device.

Getting Healthy with Nike

Use your iPod touch, iPhone, or iPod nano as a workout companion with Nike+ running shoes and a Nike + iPod Sport Kit. The kit's sensor fits inside your Nike+ shoe under the insole. A receiver is provided for the iPod nano and first-generation iPod touch (current-generation iPod touch and iPhone models include a receiver).

When you have the kit and the shoes, activate the app on your iPod touch or iPhone — choose Settings⇨Nike + iPod and tap Off for the Nike + iPod option to turn it on. To activate the kit on your iPod nano after connecting the receiver, tap Settings on the second Home screen, and then tap Nike + iPod.

You can track your pace, time, and distance from one workout to the next, and you can pick songs and playlists to match. You can even sync your workout data with Nikeplus.com, see all your runs, and share motivation with runners across the world.

Rating Your Songs

Ratings are useful — the iTunes DJ and Genius features are influenced by ratings, and you can define smart playlists with ratings to select only rated songs so that you can avoid the clunkers and spinal tappers. In fact, when you try to put a music library on your iPad, iPod, or iPhone that's larger than the device's capacity, iTunes decides which songs to synchronize based on — you guessed it — *ratings*.

iTunes lets you rate your songs, but so does your iPad, iPod, or iPhone. You can rate any song on your iPad, iPod, or iPhone as you listen to it. Ratings you assign on your iPad, iPod, or iPhone are automatically resynchronized to your iTunes library when you connect it again.

To assign a rating to a song, start playing the song on your iPad, iPod, or iPhone (see Chapter 15 for details). The Now Playing screen should appear. On an iPod classic, press the select button three times, cycling through the scrubber bar and Genius Start button to reach the rating bullets; then scroll the click wheel to give the song zero to five stars.

On an iPad, iPod touch, or iPhone, follow these steps to rate your songs:

1. **On the Now Playing screen, tap the list button to display a list of the album or playlist contents.**

   The list button is in the upper-right corner on an iPod touch or iPhone, and the lower-right corner on an iPad or iPod nano.

2. **Tap the title of any song in the track listing or leave selected the song that's playing.**

3. **Drag across the ratings bar at the top of the screen to give the song zero to five stars.**

The upper limit is five stars (for the best).

Deleting Apps from Your iPad, iPod touch, or iPhone

You can turn off the synchronization of certain apps in your iTunes library before syncing your iPad, iPod touch, or iPhone to iTunes, as I describe in Chapter 8, so that the apps disappear from your iPad, iPod touch, or iPhone. But you can also delete apps directly from your iPad, iPod touch, or iPhone — except, of course, the bundled apps from Apple.

Touch and hold any icon on the Home screen until all the icons begin to wiggle (as if you're about to rearrange them or add Home screens). To delete an app, tap the circled X that appears inside the app's icon as it wiggles. The iPad, iPod touch, or iPhone displays a warning that deleting the app also deletes all its data; tap Delete to go ahead and delete the app and its data, or tap Cancel to cancel.

To stop the icons from wiggling the Watusi, press the physical Home button on the device, which saves any changes you made to your Home screens.

Deleting Videos and Podcasts from Your iPad, iPod touch, or iPhone

Need more room on your iPad, iPod touch, or iPhone? You can delete any video or podcast episode directly from your iPod touch or iPhone, and delete TV shows or podcast episodes directly from your iPad.

To delete a video on an iPod touch or iPhone, locate the Videos screen, as I describe in Chapter 16. Scroll the Videos screen on an iPod touch or iPhone to see the sections for Movies, TV Shows, and Music Videos. Flick left or right across the video selection and then tap the Delete button that appears. To delete a podcast episode on an iPod touch or iPhone, locate the Podcasts screen as I describe in Chapter 16, and flick left or right across the podcast episode title (episodes are listed within each podcast). Then tap the Delete button that appears.

To delete a TV Show episode on an iPad, locate the Videos screen as I describe in Chapter 16, tap the TV Shows button along the top, and then tap a TV show thumbnail to see its episodes. Flick left or right across the video selection and then tap the Delete button that appears. To delete a podcast episode, locate the podcast episode as I describe in Chapter 16, and flick left or right across the podcast episode title. Then tap the Delete button that appears.

Your video or podcast episode is deleted from your iPad, iPod touch, or iPhone only. When you sync your iPad, iPod touch, or iPhone with iTunes, the video or podcast episode is copied back to your iPad, iPod touch, or iPhone unless you change your sync settings or switch to manually managing music and videos, as I describe in Chapter 8. *Note:* If you delete a rented movie, it's gone forever (or until you rent it again).

Measuring Traffic in Maps

The Maps app supplied with the iPad, iPhone, and iPod touch not only shows you the route to take, but in some areas, it can also show you traffic patterns so that you can avoid the jams. The traffic data is constantly updated and aggregated from a variety of Internet sources by Google. It is available for more than 30 major U.S. cities, including New York, Los Angeles, San Francisco, and Washington.

To use Maps, tap Maps on the Home screen. The Maps app appears (refer to Chapter 20). You can obtain directions first, as I describe in Chapter 20, or just display any location on the map that has highways. To show traffic information, tap the options button (the curled-page in the lower-right corner) to see a menu underneath the map. On an iPod touch or iPhone, tap Show Traffic; on an iPad, tap the Off button next to the Traffic option to turn it on.

When the map shows traffic, highways are color-coded according to the flow of traffic:

- ✔ Green for highways moving faster than 50 miles per hour (mph)
- ✔ Yellow for 25–50 mph
- ✔ Red for less than 25 mph

If you don't see color-coded highways, you may need to zoom out to see highways and major roads.

To stop showing the traffic, tap the option button and then tap Hide Traffic on an iPod touch or iPhone; on an iPad, tap the On button next to the Traffic option to turn it off.

Adding Keyboards and Changing Layouts on Your iPad, iPod touch or iPhone

You can change the layout and language settings for the on-screen keyboard on your iPad, iPod touch, or iPhone by choosing Settings⇨General⇨Keyboard and tapping International Keyboards. The Keyboards screen appears with a language button for the currently selected keyboard language. Tap the language button to see layout options for the keyboard.

The Software Keyboard Layout section offers options for the on-screen (Software) keyboard. These include the AZERTY key arrangement rather than the typical QWERTY arrangement for English. The Hardware Keyboard Layout section offers the virtual layout options for an Apple Wireless Keyboard connected to the iPad, iPod touch, or iPhone. Tap the Keyboards button in the upper-left corner to return to the Keyboards screen.

You can add keyboards for different languages and use them simultaneously. To add an international keyboard, choose Settings⇨General⇨Keyboard and tap International Keyboards to see the Keyboards screen. Tap Add New Keyboard to add another keyboard. A list of languages appears — scroll the list to find the language you want, and tap the language. After tapping a language, the Keyboards screen appears with buttons for the languages you've chosen. You can add as many keyboards as you need, or tap a language button to change its keyboard layout.

You can then switch keyboards while typing information by tapping the globe icon that appears to the right of the 123 key when more than one international keyboard is turned on. The language of the newly active keyboard appears briefly on the spacebar.

Each time you tap the globe icon, the keyboard layout switches to the next language you've turned on, in the order that they appear in the international keyboards list. For example, if you turned on English, French, German, and Japanese Romaji (for a total of four keyboards), tapping the globe icon switches from English to French. Tapping it again switches to German, and tapping it again switches to Japanese Romaji. Tapping the globe icon one more time switches back to English.

Changing Safari Privacy and Browser Settings

You can change Safari's privacy and browser settings on your iPad, iPod touch, or iPhone by choosing Settings⇨Safari from the Home screen.

To speed up text entry into Web pages, turn on AutoFill to automatically fill out Web forms using your contact information and automatically fill in the names and passwords you previously entered. Choose Settings⇨Safari⇨AutoFill, and then turn on the Use Contact Info option. You can then tap My Info and select the contact you want to use for auto-filling. To autofill your names and passwords, turn Names & Passwords on, so that Safari automatically fills them in when you revisit the Web site. To remove all AutoFill information, tap Clear All.

Fraud Warning is usually turned on. It warns you of potentially fraudulent site and doesn't load the page. You can turn it off if you are sure that the site you are visiting is not fraudulent, but be careful!

To browse faster, you can sacrifice JavaScript: choose Settings⇨Safari and turn off JavaScript. Although you need JavaScript for most Web apps and services, you can browse pages faster by limiting the browser to HTML and CSS. You can also turn off the Plug-Ins option to speed up browsing. Plug-ins enable Safari to play some types of audio and video files and to display Microsoft Word files and Microsoft Excel documents.

To block or allow pop-ups, turn Block Pop-ups on or off. Blocking pop-ups stops only those pop-ups that appear when you close a Web page or open one by typing its address. Sorry, the option doesn't block pop-ups that can appear when you tap a link.

You usually leave a "cookie" trail when you visit Web sites. Web sites use those cookies to personalize your experience with the site (such as remembering your user name and password). Some pages won't load correctly unless you turn on the Accept Cookies option. You have a choice of accepting cookies from sites you visited (tap From visited, which is what I do), or from all sites (tap Always), or Never. To clear cookies from Safari, tap Clear Cookies.

If you need to clear the history of pages you visited, tap Clear History. If a Web page you open doesn't show updated content, tap Clear Cache (the cache stores a copy of the page from the last time you visited).

Stopping a Wi-Fi Network from Joining

Your iPad, iPod touch, or iPhone remembers your Wi-Fi connections and automatically uses one when it detects it within your range. If you've used multiple Wi-Fi networks in the same location, it picks the last one you used. (For details on choosing a Wi-Fi network, see Chapter 4.)

But if your iPad, iPod touch, or iPhone keeps picking up a Wi-Fi network that you can't properly join, such as a private network that requires a password you don't know or a commercial network that charges for access, you can tell your iPad, iPod touch, or iPhone to *forget* this particular network, rather than turning off Wi-Fi itself. This is very useful if a paid service has somehow gotten hold of your iPad, iPod touch, or iPhone and won't let you move on to other Web pages without typing a password.

Choose Settings⇨Wi-Fi from the Home screen and tap the circled right-arrow (>) button next to the selected network's name. The network's information screen appears. Tap the Forget This Network button at the top of the screen so that your iPad, iPod touch, or iPhone doesn't join it automatically. Then tap the Wi-Fi Networks button in the upper-left corner to return to the Wi-Fi Networks screen. You can always select this network manually, and you can still continue to use other Wi-Fi networks.

Index